TRAGICALLY SPEAKING

SYMPLOKĒ STUDIES IN CONTEMPORARY THEORY
Series editor: *Jeffrey R. Di Leo*

Tragically Speaking

On the USE *and* ABUSE
of THEORY *for* LIFE

KALLIOPI NIKOLOPOULOU

University of Nebraska Press / Lincoln and London

© 2012 by the Board of Regents of the University of Nebraska

Portions of chapter 2 appeared as "Plato and Hegel on an Old Quarrel" in *Epoché* 13.2 (Spring 2009): 249–66 and "Between Art and the Polis: Between Agamben and Plato" in *Epoché* 16.1 (Fall 2011): 17–36. Portions of chapter 5 appeared as "Parrhesia as Tragic Structure in Euripides' *Bacchae*." *Epoché* 15.2 (Spring 2011): 249–61. Portions of chapter 6 appeared as "Rhiza Aimatoessa: On *Antigone*" in *Intertexts* 11.1 (Spring 2007): 1–23 (Published by Texas Tech University Press).

Poems in the appendix are reprinted with permission from the following: "Stimme des Volks" from *Friedrich Hölderlin: Sämtliche Werke: Kleine Stuttgarter Ausgabe. Bd. 2. Gedichte nach 1800*. hrsg. von Friedrich Beißner (Stuttgart, 1953). "Voice of the People" (first and second versions) from *Odes and Elegies by Friedrich Hölderlin* (Wesleyan University Press, 2008). © 2008 by Nick Hoff and reprinted by permission of Wesleyan University Press. "Voice of the People" is taken from *Friedrich Hölderlin: Poems and Fragments*, translated by Michael Hamburger (Anvil Press Poetry, 2004).

All rights reserved Manufactured in the United States of America

Indexing of this book was paid for by a grant from the Julian Park Publication Fund, University at Buffalo.

Library of Congress Cataloging-in-Publication Data
Nikolopoulou, Kalliopi.
Tragically speaking : on the use and abuse of theory for life / Kalliopi Nikolopoulou.
p. cm.—(Symploke studies in contemporary theory)
Includes bibliographical references and index.
ISBN 978-0-8032-4091-9 (pbk. : alk. paper)
1. Tragedy—History and criticism—Theory, etc.
2. Tragic, The. I. Title.
PN1892.N54 2012
809'.9162—dc23   2012026188

Set in Arno by Laura Wellington. Designed by Nathan Putens.

Στη μνήμη της Μαρίας Ζαχαριάδου-Κοσμίδου. Η ζωή της με δίδαξε για την αγάπη και την αλήθεια πολύ περισσότερο από ό,τι με δίδαξε η φιλοσοφία στα θρανία.

To the memory of Maria Zachariadou-Kosmidou. Her life has taught me more about love and truth than philosophy ever could.

For when misfortune's fraudful hand
Prepares to pour the vengeance of the sky,
What mortal shall her force withstand?
    AESCHYLUS, *Persians*

Yet there is a grace on mortals who so nobly die.
    AESCHYLUS, *Agamemnon*

Contents

Acknowledgments
xi

Introduction
xv

PART 1: OLD QUARRELS

1. Orient/Occident, Ancients/
Moderns: The Tyranny of
Theory over Greece
3

2. An Old Quarrel:
Poetry and Philosophy
52

PART 2: FOR THE LOVE OF TRUTH

3. Habeas Corpus:
Foucault's Fearless Speech
93

4. Plato's Courts:
Phaedrus and *Apology*
119

5. Euripides's Verdict: *The Bacchae*
157

PART 3: PASSIONS

6. Ῥίζα Αἱματόεσσα:
On *Antigone*
171

7. Antigone's Children
209

Appendix
247

Notes
257

Works Cited
305

Index
317

Acknowledgments

I would like to thank the Humanities Institute, University at Buffalo, and the Stanley Seeger Fellowship at Princeton's Hellenic Studies, for offering me time and a rich intellectual environment to pursue my research. At Princeton I profited a great deal from access to modern Greek materials and from my stimulating encounters with Brooke Holmes, Christian Wildberg, and Froma Zeitlin, all of whom made time out of their busy schedules to share their insights with me. My gratitude to all the other fellows, whose daily conversations were sustaining at critical moments of the project. In particular, I would like to mention Anastasia Panagiotopoulou for her friendship and wise input over coffee in her lovely Sparta balcony; Mogens Pelt generously forwarded to me any sources he found relevant; and Gerassimos Moschonas spent many an evening devoted to intellectual exchange. Above all, the graciousness and guidance of Dimitris Gondicas made my stay at Princeton as fruitful as it could be.

The Julian Park Publication Fund, University at Buffalo, has generously supported the indexing fees for this publication. The final version of the book has profited tremendously from the comments of anonymous reviewers. Vassilis Lambropoulos, whose work on tragedy and modern culture remains pivotal for me, expressed his support for the book despite his theoretical disagreements.

My colleagues at University at Buffalo's comparative literature department have supported me in various ways. Indeed, the very scope of this project could not be pursued but in a comparative and interdisciplinary environment. Ewa Ziarek has read and commented on an early version of chapter 1, and found time to teach me how to garden. Rodolphe Gasché's erudition is behind several bibliographical sources, and I remember fondly our carpooling with Plato. Jorge Gracia's support of junior faculty is exemplary. The Tuesdays with Joan Copjec modeled for me what it means to be a firmly convinced yet always open thinker.

Many others have opened venues for my thought as well as provided actual opportunities for its expression. The journal *Epoché* provided me with a forum to present portions of chapter 2 and a slightly modified version of chapter 5. *Intertexts* has published a shorter version of chapter 6. More personally, I would like to acknowledge Claudia Baracchi, whose philosophical subtlety and quiet but powerful eloquence remain an inspiration. Sara Brill, Sean Kirkland, Danielle Layne, and a host of other colleagues in the Ancient Philosophy Society have contributed in explicit and implicit ways to my thinking. Tim Dean, Margarita Vargas, and Alejandro Vallega believed in my work; their friendship and support proved critical at the darkest hours. Dennis Schmidt and Andrew Kenyon have done more for my own belief in this manuscript than they will ever know. I have not enough words to thank them. Christine Irizarry offered her translation skills for a tricky Hölderlin passage. Jeff Di Leo saw the potential of the project immediately, and my editor at Nebraska, Kristen Elias Rowley, has been a paragon of responsiveness and patience. Though this book has led me to take unexpected turns away from my earlier graduate training, the rigorous thinking of my mentor, Eva Geulen, remains paradigmatic for me — her seminars on the end of art still ring fresh in my ear, and this topic constitutes a major concern of the present study.

None of this would have been possible without my students: whether in graduate seminars or in supervising individual projects, it was their curiosity and questioning that has held me to the strictest possible standards. Their remarks, enthusiasm, and involvement have been demanding and rewarding at once.

This book has been in many ways an academic exercise of detouring from what is strictly academic in scholarship — namely, a neutral reporting, a dispassionate theoretical synthesis that disavows the author's convictions. It has had to struggle with its own overstatements and understatements. In this struggle — at times encouraging me and other times checking me — two people have led me out of the labyrinth: Jason Winfree, who reminded me of the importance of the moderns, and Scott Hubbard, who, most of anyone I know, understands the indispensability of the ancients. Their courage has never compromised their brilliance. In their different ways, they both showed me that a philosophy that only interprets the world is a poor excuse for that name.

Finally, Edward Batchelder deserves infinite thanks for everything he has done and infinite apologies for all that I have not done while devoting my time to this project. His insights, his questions, his expertise in German, and his loving patience were guiding lights throughout my writing. He has seen this book in all its stages, edited it meticulously, and commented on it tirelessly. No moment of our life together has he not given all of himself to what I do and what I believe. Fate smiles on me in his presence.

Introduction

Cassandra told them what would happen, but they did not listen. The Trojans perished forever, and so did she. But from the cave of her madness, amid the ravage of her city and a handful of helpless women—in a state of complete obliteration that we moderns would rush to say renders any sense of resistance and of meaning impossible—this is what the virgin spoke:

> The Achaeans came beside Scamander's banks, and died
> day after day, though none sought to wrench their land from them
> nor their own towering cities. Those the War God caught
> never saw their sons again, nor were they laid to rest
> decently in winding sheets by their wives' hands, but lie
> buried in alien ground; while all went wrong at home
> as the widows perished, and barren couples raised and nursed
> the children of others, no survivor left to tend
> the tombs, and what is left there, with blood sacrificed.
> For such success as this congratulate the Greeks.
> No, but the shame is better left in silence, for fear
> my singing voice become the voice of wretchedness.
> The Trojans have that glory which is loveliest:
> they died for their own country. So the bodies of all
> who took the spears were carried home in loving hands,
> brought, in the land of their fathers, to the embrace of earth
> and buried becomingly as the rite fell due. The rest,
> those Phrygians who escaped death in battle, day by day

came home to happiness the Achaeans could not know;
their wives, their children. Then was Hector's fate so sad?
You think so. Listen to the truth. He is dead and gone
surely, but with reputation, as a valiant man.
How could this be, except for the Achaeans' coming?
Had they held back, none might have known how great he was.
The bride of Paris was the daughter of Zeus. Had he
not married her, fame in our house would sleep in silence still.
Though surely the wise man will forever shrink from war,
yet if war come, the hero's death will lay a wreath
not lustreless on the city. The coward alone brings shame.
(*Trojan Women* lines 374–402)[1]

Though it is wise to avoid war, human nature seems incapable of heeding this wisdom. War comes to us, as it came to the Trojans, whether we invite it or not, expect it or not: this catastrophic inclination that governs human action is tragedy of the first order. It is a universal disposition that quickly makes of the perpetrator victim, and vice versa. To admit this is not cynicism, but to deny it ignores categorically the thousands of years of history that have not proved otherwise. Thus, even though in this play the Greeks were the conquerors and the Trojans the conquered, their fates could have easily been reversed. If the women of Euripides's play choose lamentation over castigating speeches against the enemy, it is because they somehow grasp that their situation is as much a general matter of human circumstance as it is the specific result of the Greek invasion and that had they themselves happened upon the fortune of the Greeks, they may have also behaved no better.[2]

It is well-known that Euripides wrote this tragedy with the Peloponnesian War in mind. Its first performance in 415 BC marked hardly a year after the Melian massacre, while a short two years later the war follies of the Sicilian Expedition contributed to Athens's ultimate defeat in 404 BC. There is no question that the line "the wise man will forever shrink from war" expresses what was for Euripides the ideal state of affairs. But tragedy depicts reality as it does ideality, and thus, the second half of Cassandra's line is as legitimate as the first and deserves equal attention: when war comes and cannot be averted, the virtuous ones prefer the way of courage. Inspired by Dionysian frenzy (ἐκβακχεύουσα[3]), the Apollonian priestess who had to shed her priestly regalia for the rags of a slave gives an impassioned defense of the "beautiful death," the tragic death.

How hubristic or naïve her statement sounds to the modern ear! A denial of finitude, a pointless idealization, a patriotic delirium, a false transcendence, an act of violence that aestheticizes death: all these are possible theoretical responses to this passage[4]—responses that hastily flatten the poignancy of this speech, which Euripides deliberately reserved for the lips of the defeated enemy. In conflating the affirmation of fate with violent triumphalism and in reducing the cry for human dignity to a declaration of false mastery, such theorizations overlook how they themselves violate the one whom fate has already violated. But most of all, in deconstructing the infinitude that tragedy allegedly advocates, they forget that suffering, shared mortality, and loss are equally tragedy's essence—albeit not without their other halves also present: perseverance, self-accountability, courage, and even elevation.

Cassandra's speech does not deny catastrophe, for the simple reason that such a speech could not even take place outside the scene of loss. Her words affirm the calamities of war but in a way that refuses the politics of self-pity and resentment with which the modern age has invested the predicament of the victim. It is because she sees the ruin all too vividly that she generously grants to her enemies their losses first, giving them the lion's share of grief. Though driven by their own insolence, the Greeks suffered more, she says, since their dead will always remain apart from their families and their ancestral lands. Their corpses will never be tended lovingly by their wives but will remain buried in a distant country. This is not simply a rhetorical ploy to console her audience of captive women or provide them with some cheap dose of schadenfreude at the casualties suffered by the enemy. It is a fact of war: not to see the body, not to identify the corpse, is never to be able to do the work of mourning. The Greek widows and orphans will have to suffer interminably this fate because of this exported war. Symmetrically, to expire knowing they will never be seen again by their kin and will lay anonymous and unmourned in the land they came to conquer—this is the loveless fate of the Greek soldiers.

But as she mournfully acknowledges the losses of the other side, Cassandra balances her words by singing of a peculiar heroism—that of the defeated. It is thanks to this Greek invasion that Hector was able to show his noble stature and become an illustrious hero. Even Hecuba's old age and measured demeanor do not stop her later from expressing a similarly strange gratitude for this divine destruction, which will allow Troy's grandeur to be remembered in the world of song and legend:

> The gods meant nothing except to make life hard for me,
> and of all cities they chose Troy to hate. In vain
> we sacrificed. And yet had not the very hand
> of God gripped and crushed this city deep in the ground,
> we should have disappeared in darkness, and not given
> a theme for music, and the songs of men to come.
> (*Trojan Women* lines 1240–45)

There is nothing insidious in Hecuba's haunting words or in Cassandra's song of glory. It is another fact of life; it describes the larger, often-inexplicable economy of forces that play around and against human acts. As victory comes at high cost, so too defeat does not preclude the human prerogative to dignity, the capacity to rise to one's circumstance despite all appearances and expectations to the contrary. What a feat for the Athenian playwright to put these words of peculiar sympathy for the conqueror, and at the same time of glorification for the defeated, into the mouth of the foreign enemy—a dispossessed, delirious, adolescent woman!

If, as Nicole Loraux has argued, the tragic voice (*phonē*) spoke what the political speech (*logos*) would not admit,[5] then Euripides's Cassandra has usurped the confident male voice that filled the rational assembly, and made it resound in the opposite landscape—in the ruins of the polis, in the song of a maddened, enslaved girl. In doing so, she transformed it: while the polis declares eternal victories in order to suppress its real losses, Cassandra's praise emerges *out of* loss. An Apollonian priestess and a Dionysian maenad at once, the mad prophetess has combined paean with threnody. At the end of the play, after her many efforts to raise her battered body from the dust and her many doubts regarding the value of perseverance in the face of futility, Hecuba again echoes Cassandra's strength in a different register, one more appropriate to her advanced age and its lessons of suffering. As the voice of the coryphaeus, leading the women hostages into slavery, she concludes:

> O
> shaking, tremulous limbs,
> this is the way. Forward:

into the slave's life.
(*Trojan Women* lines 1327–30)

An acceptance of what lies ahead, a sober yet unyielding determination to rise up, to move forward into the bleakest of futures. Not because of some hope, not because of a hidden plan of escape, not because of a delusion of triumph, but because of the impossibility of lying on the ground in self-pity any further,[6] because it is the human prerogative to assume the worst of fates in a quiet splendor. To accept that her slavery was an inevitable external circumstance without *being* herself a slave: this is an ontological modulation of the subtlest order, a distinction that sounds as theoretically risky as it is actually necessary. Hecuba's last words open to a state of acceptance that is never acquiescence. Her minimal last utterance, her improbable decision to stand up beyond all exhaustion and futility: this physical and moral uprightness marks the great, if invisible to us, distance that separates noble resignation to one's fate from surrender to humiliation.

T. R. Henn used similar terms to describe tragic exuberance: tragedy refuses to reduce the human being to an agent of rationalization who merely copes with life's vicissitudes and nothing more. In tragedy, Henn writes, there is "implicit, not only the possibility of redemption, but the spiritual assertion that man is splendid in his ashes, and can transcend his nature" (288). Terry Eagleton quotes this passage as well but takes issue with its idealism: the grandeur of literature belies the horror of actual war, and "it is hard to see that the victims of Bosnia or Cambodia are particularly splendid in their ashes" (28). Interested in a materialist recuperation of tragedy, Eagleton, who otherwise disagrees with a host of other contemporary critics of tragedy, seems to agree with many of them on this cardinal point, which constitutes by now the staple of any ethical critique of tragedy: namely, that tragic art risks being a false aestheticization of real violence, just as tragic idealism may legitimize and excuse human suffering (28). Can we think the politics of tragedy beyond this elevation of suffering, which has never driven the conservatives away from endorsing tragic art but which has always pushed the progressives to shun it?[7] The core of Eagleton's project is to get around this scandalous definition of tragedy as the idealization of terrible faults that makes the genre sublime and shameless at once.

Of course, this very worry of tragedy's legitimization of human suffering bespeaks Eagleton's own idealism—an idealism attendant to any genuine

Marxism—that implies that if only the philosophical (read, "idealist") conception of tragic art stopped justifying human suffering, the latter's occurrence could perhaps diminish or even vanish.[8] However, what is *tragic* in tragedy has nothing to do with justification or with reason's capacity for correction: the tragic flaw is ontological in its nature—not sociological or psychological—and it remains thus, regardless of our theoretical views of it. Nietzsche's antirealist, antipolitical approach to tragedy captures this element better. Tragedy does not equate the spectator with the protagonist any more than it equates the chorus with average citizens (Nietzsche, *The Birth of Tragedy* 57–59). But in its hieratic remove from particular circumstances, the tragic ethos assumes its universal form, a form that can potentially apply to everyone by not submitting to anyone's specific realities. Not every victim of Cambodia can be like Hecuba, but if there is one—and tragedy grants us this certainty that there is *always at least one*—then in this fact lies tragedy's profoundest realism and ethical importance.

We may question the idealizations involved in Cassandra's and Hecuba's gestures. We may even suspect these women, since they make for unwieldy victims. Still, something in their example and their voice remains unshakable. What invests their voices with the dignity they lay claim to despite any objections to the contrary? What makes them into exceptions? Can we sustain again, afford again, hear again, the truth of that holy madness, despite all the claims that our modern condition is irreducibly different from the ancients? Or is Cassandra's speech simply that—madness, a madness we should shrink from, as does Hecuba herself initially?[9] But even if this is all it is, can we live at all without this madness?

In his famous remark on the nature of historical change, Karl Marx observed that history appears the first time as tragedy, the second as farce.[10] The history of modern philosophy is itself a good illustration of this: Kant wrote a tragedy of antinomies; Hegel, Dante's great heir, wrote the comedy by solving them. However, comedy quickly begat a larger tragedy—the modern tragedy (some may also call it tragicomedy) of being blind to the farcical nature of one's own existence and viewing it, instead, as progress. Though commonly read as a statement on the decline of history, this Marxian phrase may also be read as a pronouncement on the inaccessibility of tragedy as an explicator for our time.

In fact, since at least the famous eighteenth-century quarrel of ancients and moderns, the West's self-definition in relation to the Greeks has been articulated into two opposing camps: we either repeat the Greeks by imitating them (classicism, or neoclassicism, as it is also called), or we depart from them because our modern reality is radically different (German idealism and romanticism to poststructuralism).[11] Though this latter camp would claim a more nuanced position than simply that of renouncing the Greeks, it is in fact structured as an inversion of its opposite: where classicism emphasized continuity without difference, German idealism and its legatees emphasize difference stripped of any essential continuities of human nature. Since the crowning achievement of the Greeks was considered to be their art, the dispute over continuity or discontinuity was largely waged around the question of how modernity should receive the Greek art forms. Most importantly, given the scope of the present project, the debates that originated in German idealism (and its artistic counterpart in romanticism), which have continued to occupy continental philosophy and poststructuralist theory regarding the West's relation to the Greeks, hinge not just on any art form but specifically on tragedy and its ethical vision.

Friedrich Hölderlin, with whom this study begins and ends, invoked this epochal turn from the ancients to the moderns through the poetic figure of the caesura, a term he used to describe the balancing mechanisms of the Sophoclean tragic form as it distributed dramatic action over the course of time. He was also the one who, debunking the revivalist dreams of Johann Joachim Winckelmann, heralded the idea of radical discontinuity between ancients and moderns. His argument, brilliant in many respects, was later recast in one of Nietzsche's *Untimely Meditations* as a critique of a type of historical memory that so indebts the present to its past that it paralyzes the present from creating anything in its own right and from engendering itself.[12] To be like the Greeks, Hölderlin said (and Nietzsche repeated)—namely, to be original in our own right—we have to forget about the Greeks. This epochal cut is the caesura that would balance out modernity's excessive historical debt, much as the early or belated entrance of Teiresias, according to Hölderlin, evened out the weight of the tragic action either at the beginning or the end of a Sophocles play, as was needed. Yet just as the entrance of the blind seer never happened at the same predetermined point, but according to the demands of the action's distribution in each play—as the middle always moved toward either end—the caesura too, as a historically balancing figure, should never be hypostatized in one temporal direction or another. What is ancient and what is modern—historical weight, that is—itself shifts with the passage of time; and in a simply arithmetical sense at least, modernity has already aged by now in calendar years, weighing the balance down on its side more than it cares to admit. Like Teiresias, then, the historical caesura must also be ready to reposition itself and to be renewed, particularly when it begins to settle comfortably in the guarantee of a recent renewal.

Following Hölderlin's lead, Friedrich Nietzsche also declared that tragedy was impossible in the modern world, having died with the appearance of Socrates in ancient Athens.[13] By relying on theoretical reason, Socrates, according to Nietzsche, introduces for the first time thought's delusion of mastery: "the unshakable faith that thought, using the thread of causality, can penetrate the deepest abysses of being, and that thought is capable not only of knowing being but even of *correcting* it. This sublime metaphysical illusion [delusion] accompanies science as an instinct and leads science again and again to its limits at which it must turn into *art*" (*The Birth of Tragedy* 95–96).[14] As Hölderlin did, Nietzsche sees that reflection has become our mode of action, our instinct, and even our art. Unlike Hölderlin, however, for Nietzsche there is no "tragic" without tragedy, which as a genre already translated what was tragic in the Greek's life. The worldview is thus inseparable from the artistic medium that expressed it. Tragedy's eclipse was, for Nietzsche, a decline, the mark of a falsely optimistic culture that, lacking in mental strength to deal with life's blows, relied erroneously on reason's ability to parry them.[15] In other words, we continue to live tragedies but without the means to understand them as such. This is the tragedy of what Nietzsche calls "Socratism," or the age of theory—which, most tragically, does not see any flaws with its own certainties.

Nietzsche's proclamation of the death of tragedy has been echoed by a wide range of contemporary thinkers, many of whom lay a justifiable claim to his legacy. At the same time, however, they are strangely quick to bracket the melancholy with which Nietzsche describes the end of the tragic world, for melancholy is disturbingly close to nostalgia, and nostalgia is a disease that contemporary theory would not want to see afflict one of its forefathers.[16] In fact, the dominant theoretical position since World War II has been almost diametrically opposed to Nietzsche on this point, finding that tragedy serves only to evoke Dionysian ghosts, ones whose mythic embrace too often justifies violence against the Other, and that catharsis itself risks becoming a fascist principle that aestheticizes pain. Tragedy, one senses, should have disappeared down the dark path of myth from where it took its source material to begin with; myth—another word that is supposed to make everyone shudder nowadays, summoning, as it is said to do, the worst specters of Europe's recent past, offering a primitive and violent way of understanding that has no place in any serious epistemology.[17] Consequently, tragedy's death has been viewed as a necessary—even positive—stage in its translation from an ancient theatrical genre to a modern philosophical idea: "the tragic."[18]

This has been particularly true of thinkers allied with poststructuralism, a term that functions here as a specific shorthand for the postwar textualist turn of French thought. Emanating out of the historicist understanding of truth that culminated in Hegel's philosophy, and was further radicalized by Nietzsche and Heidegger (the latter two having been somewhat canonized as poststructuralism's father figures), poststructuralism has impacted not only continental philosophy's but also literary criticism's receptions of antiquity and its ethicopolitical values. Although readers of continental philosophy have a more systematic understanding of this poststructuralism than that which is applied within literary theory, I contend that, despite this fundamental difference, the translation of Greek tragedy into the idea of the tragic has resulted in the elision of the tragic spirit in *both* the philosophical and theoretical versions of poststructuralism (the latter often being colloquially referred to as high theory).[19] Having first served to usher in the climax of Western metaphysics in German idealism, this idea of the tragic also marks the very rift of that discourse—the caesura, or turn—that has led to "the beyond-the-tragic" of contemporary thought's attempts to revise metaphysics and move beyond it.

Because poststructuralism denotes a rather large and diverse field of inquiry that encompasses both philosophically based discourses like postmodernism and deconstruction and socioculturally based ones like critical theory and social construction theory, I should state that my concern for it in this project is necessarily limited to its contested relation to tragedy: in regards, that is, to its explicit—and more often, implicit—dismissal of tragedy as a viable mode of being in and understanding our world.

On the former, philosophical side of the spectrum, two assessments of the end of tragedy will be most operative in this study: (1) Nietzsche's alignment of tragedy's end with modernity's optimistic belief in the omnipotence of rationality, coupled with his clear preference for the lost tragic world; and (2) the post-Nietzschean belief that the end of tragedy is a moral and ontological necessity and that even any recourse to the tragic might be ethically complicit with metaphysical violence. Born in the shadow of the disasters of twentieth-century Europe, deconstruction and its theological offshoots locate an ethical danger in investing faith in the notions of subjective autonomy, presence, "full speech," resistance, and so forth—all vital to the tragic experience, *along with* their opposites (fate and the gods, mortality and the acceptance of loss). Ever since, the thrust of the theoretical enterprise in the humanities has been to a large extent the discovery and overturning of binaries, or even the neutralization of the tension whenever polarity is acknowledged—a neutralization that can take on various forms, of which deferral and undecidability are some of the most privileged.[20] Even philosophers who affirm the importance of the tragic do so only in its German idealist and poststructuralist guise—namely, not as tragedy but as the *philosophy* of tragedy. This translation has so modified the core principles of the tragic world that it has rendered them virtually unrecognizable, attenuating all the *political* force with which tragedy once addressed the *actual* nature of conflict and the importance of human responsibility.

On the latter, cultural side, social construction theories (more prominent in the United States than Europe) and critical-theoretical models (whether dealing with race, gender, sexuality, colonialism, and even artistic production and reception) often maintain the category of the subject, but only as a culturally constructed entity, void of any effective sense of individualized decision and action. In other words, social construction and cultural theory cannot provide adequate explanations for individual acts that transcend their environmental determinations and become exceptional.

Thus, the various strains of both deconstruction and cultural criticism—often thought to represent opposing ends of contemporary theory—share a determinist view of the human being: we are either thoroughly passive at the hands of necessity ("necessity" now having been renamed "alterity") or entirely defined by preexisting cultural codes. Some of the questions that arise out of this revaluation of tragedy are: How much, in the name of originality, have we hypostatized the "truth" that our human condition is and *will remain* exclusively different from that of the ancients? How much, in our quest for originality, which is itself a Greek ideal, have we moved to the other extreme of the spectrum, and when would it be the proper time to reapply the caesura as a redirection? In other words, what if classicism and romanticism/German idealism are but the same Teiresias entering through two different doors at two different times—a cyclical repetition in history of imitation versus originality and vice versa? Are but a full turn like that of Euripides, whose avowed modernity even in the ancient world did not stop him from bringing tragedy back to its most ancient cultic beginnings in *The Bacchae*? Furthermore, how original really is this strategy of the "unhistorical" beginning for modernity, when in fact it is a lesson already offered in the Greek example, as both Hölderlin and Nietzsche concur? Although Hölderlin and Nietzsche's understanding of the original is not limited to what is chronologically new, but describes a leap in historical time, it is also important to remember that the nature of this modern leap is the same as that of its ancient occurrence; and this sameness should matter. Thus, of all else, it is perhaps this paradox of original sameness that sets modernity into a tragic temporality—a race whose course has already been run, yet inevitably will be run again. If this is the predicament of the present, then it continues to be essentially a tragic one, which is the reason why both these thinkers grappled with the question of tragedy even as they pronounced its end.

Hence, for both classicism and romanticism, tragedy has been the site where certain ethical debates have been waged from the Enlightenment on. Questions of whether the human being is determined by outside forces (the divine, necessity) or by individual will (self-consciousness); of whether ethics proceeds from the other rather than from the self; of whether our relation to our historical and cultural origins is continuous or discontinuous; or of whether the very question of origin is itself ethically and epistemologically viable—all are central to Greek tragedy.

Tragically Speaking examines this translation that began in German idealism and culminates in poststructuralism, with its attendant shift from modernity's claim that tragedy is no longer possible to the more current conclusion that even the tragic cannot be placed beyond ethical suspicion. Though this translation of tragedy into the tragic and the ethical has helped continental philosophy articulate a nonmetaphysical type of thinking, this has not been without its costs. This book not only focuses on these costs but argues that they are themselves tragic—the site of a loss that remains unaccounted for by the current theoretical insistence exclusively on the gains and the originality of the translation.

For instance: What happened to the political dimension of tragedy in its German idealist (and more recently, continental- or French-driven) translation? Does the corresponding ontologization of politics into the ethical and then the political not entail a certain attenuation of the real, a bracketing of the actual world for the idea of the world (an idealization that, ironically, nonmetaphysical philosophy ascribes heavily to Plato)? How did tragedy's language of contestation, which assumed agents and their actions, recede seamlessly into the language of singularity and alterity, which replaces the political subject with a theological personal impersonality?

Indeed, of the various losses, it is the elision of politics that might prove the most costly, as becomes apparent in the disparagement of any notion of heroism in contemporary thought. Tragedy, based as it is on the necessity of heroic agency, offers models of resistance. To declare that tragedy is no longer accessible to us also marks off a certain understanding of courage, self-presence, and will, without which any real politics is impossible. Hölderlin's conclusion that tragedy-as-act (the tragic performance) is no longer possible produces exactly this effect: tragedy's public, outward staging of conflict (the actual, the performative, the collectively experienced) becomes interiorized into the private, purely ethical provenance of the tragic (the speculative, the introspective, the singular relation to a singular Other). The resultant era of modern antiheroism, I believe, has led gradually to the current and profound distrust of resistance in most contemporary continental and cultural-theoretical discourses.

Nicole Loraux's exclusive emphasis on tragedy as a mourning song—namely, as a lyrical, antipolitical cry that bespeaks our universal passivity before fate without the attendant epic elements of human decision, responsibility, and agency—is a good example of this strictly antiheroic tendency. Her denial of any sort of agency might be the very reason why she has been so often cited and well received in the work of deconstructive readers of Greek thought such as Michael Naas. Despite my own profound indebtedness to her antipolitical interpretation of tragedy at crucial junctures of this project, I also need to qualify her insights by insisting that tragedy remains irreducible to either a simply epic (rational, deliberative, political) or a simply lyrical (mournful, irrational, antipolitical) interpretation. As a culmination of all hitherto practiced Greek art forms, Attic drama was both formally and thematically speaking a balanced synthesis of epic and lyric, Homer and Pindar, action and contemplation. And as if to drive further the inextricability of these opposites—to stress the coexistence of activity and passivity, will and fate—tragedy realigned chiasmatically the traditionally communal character of epic narration to an individual's dramatic acts and the traditionally subjective character of lyric poetry to the communal movement of choral songs. Emphasizing one pole while sidelining the other—as happens in much of poststructuralist theory, which consistently favors passivity and irrationality over activity and reason—is itself a politically symptomatic gesture, even as it carefully tries to distance itself from actual politics. In downplaying tragedy's contestatory character, which continually involved Athens's actual political scene no matter how allegorically, this modern reinterpretation severely delimits rather than enriches the political horizon once opened by the tragedians.

Additionally, in pursuing how tragedy was reinscribed into the tragic, I focus on the tragic dimension of philosophical thinking itself, particularly as it insists on distancing itself from the immediacy of the tragic world, trying to demythologize what it perceives to be the demonic traces of action, blood, contingency, and passion. While tragedy has provided indispensable examples for philosophy's ethical inquiries, philosophy regards the indeterminable world of tragedy with suspicion—and yet keeps returning to it. Such returns, however, belong themselves to the tragic register: just as in tragedy we learn nothing from repetition but are led to repeat by necessity, so philosophy cannot help revisiting this space that it wishes to avoid and ultimately to invalidate. Accordingly, philosophy's preoccupation with tragedy becomes all the more tragic when it explicitly calls for the end of tragedy, as has happened since German idealism, at least, and possibly even since Plato, though his end was configured as a banishment of an all-too-vital art form rather than the declaration of its demise.

In short, despite its negative treatment by the philosophical tradition and the death knell sounded by even its most ardent philosophical advocates, tragedy has managed to maintain posthumously its privileged status in ethicopolitical thought. This is a rather commonly known fact. What is not discussed, however, is the too obvious paradox of this posthumous existence, this afterlife of tragedy—where the term "afterlife" should resonate in its field-specific sense of *Das Nachleben der Antike* (the afterlife of antiquity), the branch of classical studies in Germany that explored the continuing impact of ancient culture on modernity. What is the status of such a life outside any possibility of revival? Memory, quotation, and even fruitful misquotation of the dead are possible answers to this question. In this sense, there is certainly nothing jarring or paradoxical about the notion of an afterlife. In fact, nothing past is simply dead, though this truism too might prove a tenuous admission of infinitude for contemporary theory, which has staked so much of its ethics and politics on the notion of finitude, critiquing any hints of idealization, transcendence, and infinity as variant delusions of Hegelian sublation, Christian resurrection, and the fascist myth of invincibility.[21]

But even if we can all accept that the past still animates and is animated by the present, modernity's clear and insistent verdict on tragedy's obsoleteness should have removed tragedy from that list of things past that might concern us. How can something so ancient be of ethical importance—whether our ethics is theoretical or practical—after we have decided that there is an irrecuperable ontological rift between ancients and moderns? Such a rift may well entail that tragedy is a theoretically obfuscated, even nonviable, field of knowledge for us, since we can hardly understand its categories. Even more than its theoretical impenetrability, it seems that tragedy should have no practical pertinence in a world that claims to be no more subject to tragic forces and principles. Yet the critical interest in tragedy has not in the least subsided.[22]

Given tragedy's continuing importance alongside its repeated death sentences, an almost perverse question arises: How dead is it really after all these blows? Or rather, to put the question more pointedly and hopefully in a more revealing manner, what does our modern obsession with tragedy's death say about *ourselves* rather than about tragedy? What does it say about our modern wish to be spared of it? In trying to answer these latter questions, I bring Nietzsche's critique of "theoretical optimism" to bear on the discursive practices of contemporary theory.

I would locate some of contemporary theory's optimism and antipathy to tragedy in its "democratic" worldview, which now pervades all aspects of existence and desires to be the overarching legislating principle behind all relations. This view is shared by both aforementioned branches of contemporary theory, no matter how differently each articulates its concept of democracy: a democracy-to-come, a liberal parliamentary democracy, a radical communitarian democracy, a pluralist multiculturalist one, and so forth.[23] While fully appreciating the ethical merits of democratic vision in the history of political philosophy, as well as the improvements it brought about in civic life, it is important to note that tragedy expresses that which exceeds civic relation.[24] It expresses the world of personal intimacy on the one hand and the clash of cosmic forces on the other, which admit as much suffering and injustice as they do joy and dreaming—events and mental states that occur within but point beyond the civic sphere. Thus, the community forged by tragedy is not so much a theoretical cipher at the verge of a messianic futurity, an abstraction deferred to the end of time (which, of course, never ends!), but a community of perpetual consummation, destruction, and regeneration: it is made of the stuff of generational atonement; of intimacy and exclusion; of decisions between the horrible and the more horrible, which choice makes all the difference for understanding what remains always at stake for all of us in different guises. The problem, however, is that not *all of us* have the resources to rise to that understanding, and tragedy admits unapologetically to its incapacity to teach anyone, let alone *everyone*—a deeply undemocratic and inegalitarian admission, for which tragic literature has been consistently shunned by theoretical logic.

This "democratic" impetus underlies theoretical optimism and its concomitant heightened rhetoric about the end of tragedy in poststructuralist circles. Strangely, though, this same contemporary theoretical appeal to democracy is articulated in a prohibitively exclusive academic discourse, which alienates nonspecialist audiences, even if they are otherwise humanistically educated. The counterargument—that linguistic convolution is necessitated by the difficulty of the concepts treated—can be valid, but the abstract formulae of much theoretical language risks forming a bulwark against the very problems it claims to be addressing. Behind it the thinker retreats into an ever-greater self-referentiality. The dissonance between the terrible immediacy of world events and the safely self-referential language of the theoretical humanities that claims to explain them is but one of the tragicomic marks that follow the unproblematic reliance on the powers of theoretical reason.

Thus, Marx and Nietzsche meet at a point where the Greeks had already stood: comedy is the other face of tragedy. Socrates knew this when he said in the *Symposium* (223d) that a good tragedian should also be able to write good comedies. Yet comedy should complement, not replace, tragedy. Hence, when modern thought from Hegel onward proclaims this downward spiral of nihilism to be yet another glorious supersession in the history of philosophical progress, we have already entered a farce, one designed to distract from the age's inability to deal with—let alone affirm—the tragic nature of the human. Nietzsche's epochal diagnosis of theoretical optimism certainly does not exempt post-Nietzschean philosophy from its own untragic nihilism, nor does the latter's critique of rationality, nor even its insistence on its own antisystematicity. Rather, poststructuralism's ultrarhetorical turn may be the very mark of a rationalistic prejudice that wishes to correct tragedy and ultimately dispense with it as well as of an optimism that seeks to subordinate the world to the complexity of theoretical reason. Indeed, it should be noted parenthetically that the difference between reason and rationalism has been dangerously underestimated in modern thought, which collapses them into each other, critiquing all reason as if it were *always* rationalistic and as if the cult of the irrational would remedy rationalism's excesses. Thus, the Greeks of reason and serenity were too easily revised to become a primarily Dionysian people (the "fiery" people of Hölderlin and Nietzsche) and were then disavowed in view of the excesses of Germany's nationalist fire. However, since this nationalist fire has been also theorized as both apex and symptom of modern rationalism, reason (and with it, Apollonian balance) had to be disclaimed as well, most likely to our ethicopolitical detriment. That both these sides persist perennially in their interplay, despite our "nonmetaphysical" theorizations of them, remains tragedy's challenge to us today. On the other hand, theory's attempt to exorcise reason's and passion's demons at once often results in a rationalistic, but not necessarily reasonable or spirited, endeavor.

Let me anticipate the likely objection that contemporary theory is far too self-reflexive about the metaphysical penchants for certainty and rational adequation, and these are exactly what it is trying to combat. Yet the resort to self-reflexivity as panacea does not necessarily heal, but often worsens, the wound: among other problems, self-reflexivity too often serves less a process of fruitful meditation than it provides a cover for self-referentiality and self-indulgence. That uncertainty and antisystematicity are the favored new theoretical positions and that much contemporary theoretical prose assumes a creative or performative use of language (without for the most part risking the terrible possibility of failure that genuine creation always has in store) do not automatically absolve theory from the charge of weak optimism that inheres in discursive thought.

This situation is not so surprising but shows the dulling effect of reflection and hyperdiscursivity; language, and theoretical language in particular, seems to explain away everything, particularly through the self-referential declarations of its own instability, incompletion, open-endedness, and so forth—terms that have become so well-worn as to become illegible. On the contrary, tragic drama demanded not to be simply read as text. Rather, it engaged in a thoroughgoing manner—both aporetically *and* cathartically—not only the cognitive faculties but everything else in the human body and mind. That theory may not see tragedy's persistence in the modern world, however, does not mean that tragedy has lost its relevance. As for us moderns, it turns out that our unquestionably self-confident reliance on theory shares much of the hubris and hamartia of the tragic genre, but regrettably not much of its ennobling nature. Modernity's irreducible difference from the ancients lies not in the fact that tragedy is obsolete or that we inhabit a radically different ontological position but in the ever-more-tragic fact that we are not able to recognize *our tragedy* and call it by its name.

Despite whatever parameters, disclaimers, and qualifications one can try to set when defining a large field of knowledge, as I have tried to do here with poststructuralism, it is impossible not to meet with the charge of generalization. This charge will be all the more readily launched given the critical nature of my overview. Thus, I am thoroughly aware of the potential objections to my generalized use of the term poststructuralism, as I also understand that there are fine points of difference between various theorists and strands of contemporary theory. I would not draw from the later thought of Michel Foucault in the second part of this book had I not respected such differences within the theoretical field and, even more importantly, the radical intellectual changes that take place within the work of a single thinker. Foucault, courageous and honest in admitting to the unexpected turns and outright inversions of thought's journeys, composed his own palinode from poststructuralist denouncer of the subject in all its forms to ascetic thinker of the care of the self, provoking meanwhile all sorts of disputes and disappointments among friends and foes alike. Still, isolated variations—no matter how illustrious—do not in any way undermine the reality of my general claim that poststructuralist theory does not eschew but rather exemplifies the rationalistic optimism of modernity that its own father figure, Nietzsche, had denounced. After all, not all generalities are necessarily untrue, and many a substantive argument would risk never being made out of fear that its generalization will be insensitive to its few exceptions.

Interestingly, this is probably the unspoken assumption that modernity applies to its study of the past, even though it may not always do so sagaciously: "The Greeks," said Hölderlin with a strange certainty, when he really meant the tragedians and more specifically Sophocles and his two plays *Oedipus Tyrannus* and *Antigone*. "The Greeks," said Heidegger again, meaning only the best of their kind, who for him were the pre-Socratics. "The Greeks," said Nietzsche too, who in his famously moody thinking devoted almost as much time to that intellectual nemesis he despised and admired at once,

Socrates, as to his idol, Aeschylus. Of other Greeks—poets, artists, legislators, or philosophers—continental thought and contemporary theory have little, if anything at all, to say. Heraclitus, Sophocles, Plato (or Socrates in his place), and Aristotle seem to do the work of representing the immense variety of philosophical and artistic currents the ancient Greek world produced.

In acknowledging and accounting for my own generalizations, I certainly do not mean to reproduce modernity's tendency to generalize about the past while demanding for itself a more nuanced and complex treatment. Rather, in foregrounding this temporal prejudice, I also wish to note that just as the carefully practiced generalization has its advantages, so the generalized fetishization of carefulness has its pitfalls. Nuance has a great value, but the insistence on nuance often serves intellectual safety, and by risking nothing else, it risks becoming a symptom of the theoretical optimism and the quietude of reason Nietzsche criticized. For all its avowed indebtedness to Nietzsche, contemporary theoretical writing shares very little of Nietzsche's own power of conviction and even less of the offense he feared not mounting against his contemporary academic establishment.[25]

Methodologically, I am not interested in explicating specific writings on tragedy by various philosophers or producing a sequential chronology of tragedy's reception. This kind of commentary is already rich and abundant in the scholarly bibliography on tragedy.[26] Rather, I trace a certain genealogy of tragedy and the tragic, beginning with Hölderlin's translation of tragedy into what became the most enduring German idealist version of the tragic and concluding with the implications of his vision for the contemporary philosophical taboo on the tragic-heroic death. The intervening chapters examine the place of tragedy today by pursuing several key issues and debates that have developed around the contested and now-repressed terms of presence, selfhood, will, and heroism in modern thought, as well as try to restore to the Greeks their own philosophy of the tragic in Plato.

As I have discussed, poststructuralism has radicalized the death of tragedy into an ethical argument in which the very idea of thinking tragedy in relation to our particular historical catastrophes entails a violent aestheticization and a corresponding diminution of the reality of these catastrophes. In contrast, I propose that tragedy is of the utmost ethical *and* political importance, in part because the profundity of tragic thinking lies exactly in its sustenance of opposition as complementarity, not as hierarchical binary in need of correction.

Further, I maintain that the insistence on the radical rift between ancients and moderns is merely another attempt to defend the boundary between philosophy and tragic reality, a boundary that theoretical thinking has tried to keep intact from ancient times onward. Put differently, the fetishization of this rift relies on and bespeaks the rationalist optimism that modernity has "progressed" to overcome tragedy's dark archaism. Thus, despite the fact that many contemporary theoretical discourses view themselves as critiques of rationalism and progress, they share in the long-standing philosophical antipathy to tragedy. They are unwittingly more Platonic than they think when it comes to certain moral dicta and certain attachments to discursive reasoning, while at the same time they share little of Plato's formidable understanding of the divinely inspired, nontheoretical nature of art—an understanding that made of him not only a philosopher of the tragic but a tragic philosopher as well.

Titled "Old Quarrels," part 1 of this book comprises two chapters addressing the quarrels that have defined the modern reception of tragedy historically and philosophically. First comes the quarrel over the Occidental or Oriental nature of Greece in German idealism, which was precipitated by Hölderlin's "Orientalist" interpretations of Sophoclean tragedy as well as by his observations in the "Letters to Böhlendorff" regarding the ontological difference between Greeks and moderns; according to the German poet, Greek nature stemmed from Oriental holy pathos, whereas modern, Occidental nature is self-reflection. This announcement of an epochal turn lies at the source of poststructuralist arguments about the end of tragedy and the absolute discontinuity between ancients (Orientals) and moderns (Occidentals). In addition to arguing against Hölderlin's historicist thesis of an ontological shift, this chapter also offers a critique of the still-overlooked poststructuralist historiographical bias that continues to ignore the issue of modern Greece's virtual absence in this European heritage debate.

The second chapter treats the quarrel between philosophy, on the one hand, and (tragic) poetry and art, on the other. Articulated most succinctly in Plato's *Republic*, this quarrel resurfaced in Hegel's modernity. I opt for a tragic reading of Plato by juxtaposing his expulsion of the poets with Hegel's declaration of the end of art in his *Introductory Lectures on Aesthetics*. Whereas both champion the victory of philosophy over poetry, I argue that Plato's ban issues from a cathartic understanding of tragedy's powers—thus, being itself a *poetic and tragic reaction* that grants art rightfully its universal and diachronic appeal—while Hegel's pronouncement thinks of art purely in terms of a historical logic, which diminishes art to being a function of timely concerns. In reading Plato tragically, I side with Stephen Halliwell's thesis that Plato was also the first philosopher of the tragic, contrary to the German idealist legacy, which maintains that the Greeks had to wait for modernity to be granted a proper understanding of their artistic process. Moreover, by engaging some passing but interesting remarks on Plato by Giorgio Agamben, I contend that Plato's tragic philosophical predilection is inextricably tied to his very suspicion of tragedy and of art in general: it was because art mattered to Plato that he bothered to censor it. In sharp contrast, the infinite freedom and formal autonomy of modern art—celebrated from Hegel to Adorno and beyond—misses the Platonic experience of creativity, which involves an ontological and political unsettling. The modern obsession with art's freedom translates Plato's high tragedy into the weaker register of theoretical reason, where formal autonomy is nothing but a sorry symptom of the diminished impact art has had in modernity. Formal autonomy is, in other words, the artist's last trace of pride in a society that cares little of his or her accomplishments.

Part 2, "For the Love of Truth," contains three chapters that elaborate variously the connection between tragedy and the philosophical desire for truth. My aim in this section is threefold: firstly and most importantly, to show that Platonic philosophy and tragedy share a quest for truth, as Socrates follows the example of tragic heroes who risk everything for the telling of truth; secondly, to suggest that this tragic-heroic stance of truth-telling, whether performed on the dramatic or the Socratic stage, offers a model of political resistance; thirdly, to propose that of all modern and contemporary philosophical practices, it is genealogy—as conceived by Nietzsche and continued by Foucault—that most faithfully bears philosophy's initial tragic marks, thereby also staying true to its most radical ethicopolitical spirit. Since my interest in the truth-seeking function of Platonic thought and tragedy dovetails with Foucault's later work, the first of these chapters is devoted to Foucault's writings on *parrhesia* (truth-telling), which signaled his turn to Socrates and tragedy (Euripides in particular). Opposing deconstruction's language games and departing from many of his own earlier views that enabled social construction theories to submit everything to cultural determination, Foucault's treatment of parrhesia helps me reintroduce the philosophically and culturally contested notions of presence and self-relation—notions that are pivotal both to Plato and to tragic theater.

Concurring with Foucault, who reads Socrates not as a rhetorician but as a truth-seeker and a truth-teller, the next chapter analyzes Plato's *Phaedrus* and *Apology* as dialogues that show the path to truth to be a tragic path. Although philosophy has viewed itself as the sole pursuer of truth, I maintain that tragedy is imminent in truth's pursuit and thus always inextricable from it. Truth's elusive nature along with the blindness and misunderstandings that follow its pursuit constitute the very core of tragedy. Tragedy is, in a strong sense, the search for truth gone awry. Admittedly, the notion that misunderstandings are unavoidable in the search for truth could be read as akin to some rhetorical approaches to philosophy that focus on truth's dependence on language. At the same time, however, to designate these misunderstandings as tragic—as I do here—is obviously to diverge from such approaches that rush to celebrate and capitalize on the inevitable ambiguity of language. Instead of focusing on the axiomatic primacy of language and its rhetorical plays, I side with Plato, who did not consider language to be the "house of Being" but understood it as a human faculty that more likely obfuscates than illumines the ascent to truth.[27]

While the structure of the *Apology* as tragic theater may be immediately apparent to the reader,[28] a brief explanation of the *Phaedrus*'s tragic dimension is due. The *Phaedrus* illustrates the tragic movement of thinking in a twofold manner. Firstly, in contrasting the love of truth to the fetishization of sophistry, this dialogue explains and performs the very drama of philosophy as a search for truth. It thus anticipates the modern philosophical turn that, by historicizing and relativizing truth, not only produced a crisis of legitimation but also effected something counterintuitive to its own ethical objectives: although historical truth may appear less exclusive and more democratic than immutable truth, it is also potentially more violent and restrictive, since what is historical remains bound to humans, their special interests, and their power struggles. Historical truth cannot but also be the truth of power, of unjust law and brutal authority—the truth that Socrates would never grace by that name.

Secondly, in questioning authority without ever assuming to be one, the *Phaedrus* itself has become as much a blind spot in contemporary thought as Plato's philosophy was for many during his own time. In other words, it is through its own history of philosophical reception that the *Phaedrus* illustrates the tragedy of truth's distortion. Plato directs this dialogue on love and inspiration against two targets: first, against the prevailing Sophistic establishment, which subordinated truth to the mechanics of cold rationality and rhetorical manipulation; second, against those who actually mistook him for a rigid rationalist and a Sophist. Ironically, then, Jacques Derrida's reading of this dialogue in "Plato's Pharmacy," which has been celebrated precisely for the freshness of its rhetorical approach vis-à-vis the canonical insistence on the centrality of love in this text, is actually a return to the very establishment that Plato was speaking against. "Plato's Pharmacy" treats this dialogue as an exemplar of the inherent instability and untranslatability of philosophical language, arguing that the multiple and mutually contradictory connotations of some of its terms foreclose the possibility of any stable meaning even at the level of the Greek original. Nonetheless, this realization does not stop Derrida himself from obtaining some surprisingly stable, albeit "hidden," meanings out of this dialogue—namely, that the *Phaedrus* relies on various problematic hierarchies, such as those of presence over absence and speech over writing. Derrida's politics of linguistic suspicion thus uncannily repeats a rationalist, sophistic mode of reading that implies authority, even as it tries to destabilize it in others. Over and against Derrida's line of thinking, I elaborate several other arguments by classicists Giovanni R. F. Ferrari and Seth Benardete, who focus on the speech/writing binary not so much as a hypostatized distinction but as an effect of Plato's critique of the inflexibility of authority, whether such authority be scholarly, legal, or moral in kind. In pitting love against law, the *Phaedrus* ensconces itself in the tragic repertory, which rehearses this strife repeatedly and of which *Antigone*—the last conceptual unit of this book—becomes the supreme example.

Following the readings of these Platonic dialogues, the concluding chapter of this second part turns to *The Bacchae* in light of Foucault's interest in Euripides and parrhesia. Even though Foucault treats this tragedy cursorily, preferring to map the passage of parrhesia from the old inspired truth-seekers to Athens's civic orators (the Sophists) in Euripides's *Ion*, I maintain that *The Bacchae* gives us a more compelling—if also catastrophic—understanding of the ascent to truth. The play sets a fatal confrontation between two irreconcilable modes of truth-telling: human and divine. That the human element is utterly destroyed at the end of this confrontation bespeaks the tragic Socratic insight that human wisdom is worth little or nothing.

Lastly, entitled "Passions," part 3 consists of two chapters that explore the ethical and political importance of tragedy through the figure of Antigone, the tragic heroine who more than any other has inspired continental philosophy from German idealism onward. While the first of these two chapters treats Sophocles's *Antigone* and its critical rereading by Judith Butler, the final chapter, "Antigone's Children," undertakes the tragic question of the intentionality of one's death, while relating it to two acts of collective self-sacrifice as a form of resistance in modern Greek history. Siding against Butler's appropriation of the play for the purposes of social construction theories, and steering clear of the deconstructive ethical formula that "we are simply exposed to the Other," chapter 6 maintains that Sophocles shows in the character of Antigone the perfect harmony between outer destiny and subjective will, between self-knowledge and self-accountability, between words and deeds. Antigone, like Socrates, is a musical character, one whose *logos* harmoniously corresponds with her *bios*. Furthermore, Antigone's adherence to the unwritten law—namely, her desire to ascend to what is eternally true and not obey what is historically dictated and didactically written—offers a vindication of the *Phaedrus*'s truths on the tragic stage.

That one can choose one's death is a fundamental tragic prerogative. Yet the notion of death as an object of human will has been consistently attacked by poststructuralist theory—most notably in the thought of Maurice Blanchot and Emmanuel Levinas. Naturally, in an era that has killed the subject, the idea of death as a subject's intention sounds simply absurd. Indeed, it could well be said that contemporary theory's aversion to tragedy stems precisely from tragedy's exposition of death not only as fate but also as an object of human intention. The book's final chapter approaches this issue through a close reading of Hölderlin's poem "Stimme des Volks," which reflects on mass suicide as a mode of resistance in the ancient city of Xanthos. Subsequently, I forge a link between this tragic notion of the intentionality of one's death and two modern acts of communal resistance in the nineteenth-century Greek struggle for independence: the 1803 collective suicides of the women of Zalongos in Epirus and the 1866 explosion of the Arkadi Monastery in Crete by its besieged inhabitants. Both acts repeat in modernity the Antigonian lineage (and tragic lineage more generally) of self-destruction in the face of the intolerable. The dark circumstances under which these people were called to make a decision in common and to undertake an action so unthinkable to the comfort of theoretical contemplation emphasize the nature of tragedy as *action* and political experience (drama, deriving from *dran*, means "to act"[29]) rather than as text subject to individual ethical reading.

With no Anglo-American disciplinary equivalent to the cumbersome German *Das Nachleben der Antike*, this book has to be situated somewhat awkwardly in a transitional space—something we may call the relation of ancients and moderns. The difficulty of assigning it clear academic borders might well be because my own concerns with tragedy have for a long time exceeded the category of academic interest, forming instead a crucial endpoint in an autobiographical story.

Having studied the classics in the earlier part of my education in Greece, I was compelled already then by the vision of the tragedians, which I later sought to rediscover in the modern European lyric's preoccupations with catastrophe. The step to poststructuralism came naturally, as did the step back to German idealism and romanticism that brought me full circle: tragedy, again. As my excursion into German idealism incited my interests in the Greeks more than in the moderns and as my research into the Greeks intensified, I encountered a fundamental impasse with many of the ethicopolitical inversions, assumptions, and neutralizations that contemporary thought has helped canonize in the humanities over the recent decades: the fetishization of absence over presence, and writing over speech; the insistence on the authority of the text over the authenticity of an act; the concomitant evaporation of the political into the ethical; the false certainty that the theorist's self-reflexive retreat is the only legitimate response to the call of thinking. All these premises can only be possible if one first ends the tragic worldview, which would run counter to and upset all of them.

Tragedy as a "grave act" requires presence, speech, self-relation, and self-accountability; these modes of self-presentation involve a *public* dimension and are all necessary if our acts are to be thought of not only as responses to the singular, theologized Other of contemporary ethics but to the many others of actual political contestation. Furthermore, even my ethical obligation to the Other does not simply proceed from that Other, to whom it nonetheless remains always directed. It proceeds first and foremost from my relation to myself, from my presence to myself. Surely, the Other, Necessity, Fate, and the gods taunt me; they require me to respond. But how I respond—my ethical choice, that is—has very little to do with them and all to do with me. Even to recognize that there is another in front of me and even to grasp that I am obliged to respond to this alterity require me to have a prior ethical relation to myself. This priority holds true even if one assumes the modern notion that the self is itself split and thus always other to itself—namely, if one accepts

Hegelian alienation as the mark of Spirit, as the process of self-objectification through which the human being attains self-consciousness, differentiating itself from the rest of the natural world; for such a division is still generated from *within* the self. It is the self who first divides itself (hence, *self*-division, *self*-split) and, in this capacity, shows itself to be unlike the other creatures who, despite encountering members of their kind, can never effect the same movement of otherness *within themselves*. Hegel's awareness of this ontological priority is shown in the fact that he returned the alienated aspect back to the self—a recuperation poststructuralist critiques have found totalizing and oppressive to the nonidentical.

Can I live with myself if I do such and such? This is the question from where all responsibility begins. This is why even though Antigone and Ismene share very similar sociocultural environments (they are of the same family and social standing and have been raised with the same moral values) and even though they are both confronted by the same Other (the corpse of Polyneices), they act in radically different ways, because each has a different relation to herself and to her own limits. Can I live with myself—that is, can I be *present to myself* in my decision? This is the essential question that the profoundly moral being, however, hardly ever needs to ask; in other words, it hardly needs to other itself before answering it. Recall that Antigone never poses it, as she never divides herself before deciding. Her decision is immediate: she would have always buried that brother, no questions asked. Thus, to extrapolate from this rather heuristic question a process of self-objectification that amounts to an absolute split and an irreducible otherness of the human being from itself is at best a theoretical overstatement. Tragedy, in contrast, understands that self and other, presence and decision, necessity and freedom pose for us real and worldly problems that require philosophical agon and urgent answers, not linguistic games and hyperbolic constructs that make the world appear and disappear with a sleight of hand. Hence, my title, *Tragically Speaking*, emphasizes exactly this importance of speech as self-presence and responsibility (as in tragic theater) for any effective criticism of the rationalizing and solipsistic impulses of the theoretical endeavor.

It goes without saying that such a project of trying to engage what has repetitively been deemed as irrecuperable must face realistically not only its limits but its very "impossibility," as the contemporary theoretical vocabulary would say. It is not hard to see that the impossibility of writing tragedy in the modern world can extend equally to the impossibility of writing *about* tragedy. To begin to write on tragedy may itself now belong to the sphere of farce. Yet like many others, I too have found the call of tragedy so irresistible as to risk this repetition. *Tragically Speaking* is the speaking of this repetition; and in many ways, this is a book about repetition. It is also, however, a book written from a certain theoretical dislocation, a being-out-of-step with one's time, affirming something that has actually been made a moral taboo in the modern world, the more it is given lip service in political speeches and popular opinion alike: freedom. By no means do I refer to this commodity that the West has been exporting violently everywhere in its "free markets"—this ugly economic and supposedly democratic correlative of the philosophical egoism of free will. Rather, I remain captivated by another kind of freedom—invisible, unnameable, and even censored in the present language of perfect submission, but not necessarily inexistent.

Tragedy has been the stage where I have encountered it at its subtlest but most enduring form, for tragedy shows freedom neither as licentious play nor as the sure success of the all-mastering, rational human will. Tragic freedom, always in tension with the overwhelming order of things, comes not as a cheap reward but as a constant responsibility most likely accompanied by loss. It appears never as an optional choice but as an ineluctable necessity: one simply *has to*. The question is what one *does* with this "has to." Though external circumstance may more often than not repeat itself, tragedy illuminates the subtle differences in each individual's response to life's unalterable predicament. William McCollom writes, "Choice is at the heart of tragedy. Any philosophy which denies the reality of the self or of its activity, including its choices, destroys at the same time a necessary basis of tragedy" (4). This book is concerned with such theoretical efforts, both deliberate and unwitting, to efface the necessity of tragedy (and thus of freedom) and to do so ostensibly in the service of an ethical agenda: unfastening ethics from its traditionally individualist and allegedly violent entanglements with the categories of the self and choice. Needless to say, the theoretical imperative behind this revaluation assumes a particular notion of the self as always being selfish and of choice as always meaning control—notions that could not be further from the tragic universe. In so destabilizing subjectivity qua selfhood, this new ethics inadvertently destabilizes the field of responsibility as well: if there is no choice, there is also no consequence. Human meaninglessness is affirmed no more with tragic regret but with a nonchalance that can only be afforded by theoretical distance.

Thus, this book is also a departure from the lessons learned of my own theoretical education, into a territory yet uncharted—one that cannot be mapped within the Occidental (the European or American) theoretical perspective any more than it can be restricted within the Oriental parameters Hölderlin and others rushed to ascribe to it. This ancient terrain beckons us but remains strange as well—something of a historical enigma, the site of a peculiar harmony and a terrible contestation at once: the harmony and contestation between absolute and contingent, infinite and finite, God and mortal, blood and word, fate and freedom, Orient and Occident, philosophy and art. In relation to this balanced strife and the striving toward balance, let us recall H. D. F. Kitto's understanding of the function of the golden mean in Greek culture:

> The doctrine of the Mean is characteristically Greek, but it should not tempt us to think that the Greek was one who was hardly aware of the passions, a safe, anaesthetic, middle-of-the-road man. On the contrary, he valued the Mean so highly because he was prone to the extremes.... He sought control and balance because he needed them; he knew the extremes only too well. When he spoke of the Mean, the thought of the tuned string was never far from his mind. The Mean did not imply the absence of tension and lack of passion, but the correct tension which gives out the true and clear note. (252)

Greek balance is not anodyne any more than the extremes it tries to bridge obey a neat hierarchy: the opposing extremes are *both* equally important, just as the balance and strife that alternately regulate them are themselves equally important. It is from these fragile but miraculously held complementarities—*and not from hierarchical binaries*—that tragedy sprang, and it is to the perpetual recalibration of these opposing forces that tragic experience always points. Tragedy speaks these oppositions despite all philosophical attempts to silence it, and it has spoken them in different languages and different forms, though its exclusive expression remains Attic drama: it speaks them in the decisions of individuals and groups to resist in the face of total annihilation, in acts of love and sacrifice, but also in the fury of revenge, the fit of jealousy, and the plight of any exile to find a land to die. It speaks them despite the fact that official thought may deem these experiences inadmissible for being too "empirically" contingent, too "anthropological," and not sufficiently philosophical, thus calling into question their symbolic efficacy and even their historical legitimacy.

True enough, repetition is not only sameness but difference as well: nothing recurs exactly the same way. Time takes care of that, and we do not step in the same river twice. However, difference does not eliminate the persistence of that something that keeps reappearing, returning, piercing through. The question of the tragic has been one of these around which modernity has critically returned to define itself in its difference from the ancients. Indeed, as I have already outlined, tragedy has offered the locus of more than a linguistic or cultural translation: it has been interpreted as the translation of ontological dispositions, of what it means to be a modern versus a Greek. But if the discourse on tragedy proves itself to be a site of repetition, it is most likely because tragedy's own structure admits first and foremost to repetition. By speaking the unavoidable, tragedy opens to eternal returns, for mortals cannot conquer the unavoidable even as they are always driven to confront it. Tragedy is the inevitability of its own repetition. To say or to think otherwise would be farce.

TRAGICALLY SPEAKING

I

OLD QUARRELS

I

Orient/Occident, Ancients/Moderns

THE TYRANNY OF THEORY OVER GREECE

Τῆς Ἀσίας ἂν ἀγγίζει ἀπὸ τὴ μιὰ · τῆς Εὐρώπης λίγο ἂν ἀκουμπᾶ
στὸν αἰθέρα στέκει νὰ · καὶ στὴ θάλασσα μόνη της!

Though touching Asia on one side · and brushing Europe on the other
it stands there all alone · in aether and in sea!

Odysseus Elytis, *The Axion Esti*

Hölderlin

A specter is haunting Europe: the specter of Greece—the ancient Greece of European desire and the modern Greece of philosophical scorn, the Greece we have yet to complete and the Greece we have always already surpassed. No other topos, geographical or cultural, has been as contested in modern European thought as this one, since in serving as the origin of the West, Greece emerged as Western civilization's own Oedipus: a figure both powerful and beleaguered at once, a giver of blessings and a polluter from whom one needs to be cleansed. Ultimately, however, to ask whether we should continue to be "Greeks" or to break with them—the question that structured the classicism/romanticism debate—is to ask an Oedipal, thus inescapably Greek, question.

Contemplating the nature and task of modern thought in relation to the Greeks, the poet Friedrich Hölderlin (1770–1843) drew a temporal distinction between antiquity and modernity that amounted to an ontological shift: the terms "ancients" and "moderns" now designate not only two distant chronological epochs but also two radically different modalities of being, and thus of thinking and creating. Hölderlin articulated this temporal distinction most concisely in a letter to the German philhellene Casimir Urlich Böhlendorff,[1] by using geographical terms. Indeed, we could call them cosmological terms, since their geography involves the solar trajectory: the Greeks are for Hölderlin Orientals in that they are associated with a beginning, with the dawn of thinking. The Germans (and, ostensibly, some other modern European peoples) are called Hesperians, referring to the time of the sunset, of the vesper.

The poet's unusual gesture of separating the Greeks from the Occident, which they were traditionally thought to have founded, relies on a chiasmatic relationship he draws around the issue of the nature/culture divide between ancients and moderns. To summarize Hölderlin: the Greeks' nature (holy pathos, sacred fire) is our culture, whereas our nature (measure, reflection, and the capacity for clear representation) was their culture. Since for Hölderlin it is harder to "freely use" one's own nature (*das Eigene*) than to excel in the foreign (*das Fremde*) (149), it follows that the Greeks were better masters of representation than of sacred fire. We moderns, on the other hand, must gain mastery of the foreign (sacred fire) before excelling eventually in our native trait (measure), thus learning from the failure of the Greeks, who, having lost touch with their native powers, were ruined as a result of their excessive preoccupation with the acquired—namely, with form. This mirroring schema is also drawn by Peter Szondi in "Überwindung des Klassizismus" ("The Overcoming of Classicism"), his dialectical reading of this letter that turned the Hölderlin reception in postwar Germany, distancing the poet from his recent nationalist appropriations by the Stefan George circle and Martin Heidegger.[2]

However, this orderly schematization is anything but easy to decode once we consider closely each of its related terms. Perhaps the hardest term to be unlocked and, not surprisingly, the one around which all interpretation founders—both Hölderlin's interpretation of the Greeks and the later interpretations of Hölderlin—is that of "nature." On the most primary level, the term "nature" imposes a distinction between outer nature (which, for the sake of concision, I will capitalize as Nature for the next few pages) and human nature. Thus, Nature refers to the external world, and nature to the inner predilection or talent that drives an individual (or a people, as it seems more fit to Hölderlin's epochal vision) to be the way it is in the world. The spontaneity of this latter, inner tendency Hölderlin associates with freedom. The turn toward one's own natural tendency after the pursuit of the foreign he calls the "patriotic turn," also translated as "native reversal" (*die vaterländische Umkehr*). Subsequently, what preoccupies his thought and his poetry is the search for this freedom that results from inhabiting properly our spontaneity (our nature), from existing in a harmonious correspondence with what constitutes our surrounding reality (Nature).

At this juncture, we should emphasize the significance of Hölderlin's preoccupation with the nature and historical destiny of a people as opposed to individual human nature and fate. If human nature is viewed in the historical terms of a people rather than of an individual (who could always turn out to be exceptional, aberrant, and inassimilable by a greater historical necessity—in other words, who could be Nature unto him- or herself), then human nature is easily translated into being a cultural response to Nature: the means by which a particular people at a particular time exists, shares in, and relates to whatever it perceives as its world. This is why, concurring with Szondi, Andrzej Warminski writes that, for Hölderlin, "the Greeks were not nature but rather the response to a nature"[3] (Warminski 30), a realization that was key to the poet's break with classicist claims of Greek naïveté. Hence, far from being immediate or natural, human nature, even in its most spontaneous manifestation, forms already a response, a reaction. It will soon become apparent that this denaturalization of nature is the crucial step through which Szondi corrects Hölderlin's nationalist reception.

Such thinking on Hölderlin's part is traceable to Kant's critical philosophy, which began by establishing the limits of theoretical reason. Writing consciously in response to Kant, Hölderlin understood outer Nature to be another name for the noumenal world of the thing-in-itself, which remains forever unknowable and inaccessible to us outside our subjective categories of cognition: we can only respond to it by constructing it in our own terms, never by knowing it in its own. Accordingly, the nature of the Greeks is for Hölderlin already a kind of culture, insofar as it designates the specific way in which they and they alone could imagine themselves in the world they had constructed for themselves. In fact, we see that the very distinction between Nature and human nature collapses as both are shown to be conceptual categories removed once and twice, respectively, from the external world. Therefore, to think of Nature as an external and eternal force that happens—that recurs with an indeterminable regularity but that somehow in its unpredictable eruptions might be pursued, willed, and even embodied by a particularly gifted being—is inadmissible to Hölderlin's thought. Such a precritical, anti-Kantian understanding of Nature will have to wait for Nietzsche in order to be (re)articulated in modernity. As for Hölderlin, it is this Kantian understanding of Nature as always already a construction that enables him to overcome classicism and renounce its imitation of the Greeks. If, from Plato's and Aristotle's aesthetics onward, Nature had always begged imitation as its pairing concept, it was because Nature was thought to be a stable original, an objective thing "out there" that the human being could emulate through art. The moment Kant subjectivizes Nature, no response to it is more natural than another, and soon imitation goes out the window. If Praxiteles's nudes are no more privileged expressions of Nature than are Picasso's cubes, then there is no need for a normative aesthetics. Thus, via Kant, Szondi can save Hölderlin from nationalist appropriations by unhinging the pair Nature/imitation and by denaturalizing the hitherto normative link between them: once Nature and its truth are unreachable, the imperative to mimic Nature becomes moot, and Szondi can dispel the German nationalist fantasy of imitating Greek fire.

We begin to see the abyssal structure of Hölderlin's seemingly neat, symmetrical chiasmus: the Greeks are not Nature. Their nature (holy pathos) was a quasinatural, quasicultural disposition, their form of creativity, in other words, which corresponded to whatever their own mental image of Nature was—a Nature, however, that ultimately eluded them, even though they did not know this, lacking a Kant to tell them so. Their culture (form) consisted of the specific rules of presentation, the skills with which they expressed outward the contents of their inner disposition—a disposition that, in turn, eludes the Hesperians, though they must somehow learn it. The initial chiasmus is now complicated due to this unknowable factor of Greek nature (their form of creativity). If the Greeks themselves did not know *that* their own nature eluded them, they could never cognize and represent to themselves the assumptions underlying their own creative practice. The question is how this may inflect the chiasmatic symmetry with which we commenced.

It is Warminski who most systematically attempts to answer this question and, on account of it, departs from Szondi's dialectical reading. I will try to summarize some of the most pertinent aspects of his argument, which is rather convoluted, not least because of the multiple intermediaries involved: Warminski is responding to Szondi, who is responding to Hölderlin and to Hölderlin's other, less politically palatable receptions (read, "primarily Heidegger's"). Add to this chain the present author, and we have a fine example of the abyssal structure of modern criticism as well. At any rate, for

Warminski, even though Szondi grasped Hölderlin's denaturalized nature as Hölderlin's break with classicism, he failed to see that the inscrutability of Greek nature upsets the mirroring relation between Greece and Hesperia, creating an asymmetry. Szondi transforms the unknowable nature of the Greeks (unknowable and unrepresentable *for* and *to* the Greeks) into the mirror image of the Hesperians, thus making it an object of representation. Through the mediation of this representation, through the vocabulary of art (*Kunst*), he then resolves the asymmetry: art as reflection of the respective natures of Greeks and Hesperians offers the mediating link shared by both cultures and epochs. Thus, Szondi reinscribes Hölderlin into the mimetic tradition of aesthetics—namely, the narrative of self-representation that the West constructs about itself, positing the Greeks at its origin (Warminski 35). The moment Szondi unfastens Hölderlin from one kind of classicism (the imitation of Greek art), he attaches him to another (the classical narrative of reflection). In Warminski's own words, "this is how Hölderlin overcomes classicism (*Klassizismus*) without turning away from the classical (*Klassik*)" in Szondi's Hegelianization of him (31–32).

Effacing the historical dimension of this letter, which both Szondi's and Heidegger's readings preserve despite their different ideological colorings but which inevitably leads to anthropologization and mimeticism of some sort, Warminski offers a strictly linguistic, rhetorical reading: this is "a letter from the 'workshop' of one poet to another poet," he remarks, that is concerned with the rules of *poetry* and not with the history of *art* or the historical relation between the Hesperian and Greek cultures (34). Thus, the relation between Greece and Hesperia must be read tropologically, through the asymmetry of its chiasmus, and not in terms of a philosophy of history or an aesthetics that juxtaposes consciousness to its object. Aesthetic narratives are reflective; and in concerning themselves with the *image* of Hesperia reflected in the art of Greece and vice versa (Warminski 33), they have nothing to do with a poet's workshop and a poet's concerns. I emphasize image in opposition to reading and poetry because Warminski's argumentative consistency against mimesis and the aestheticization of the Greeks rests on this attack on the image: his text is interspersed with hierarchized binaries of the rhetorical letter versus the mimetic image, of reading versus seeing, and of the poetological versus the aesthetic, all of which align him with a man he likes to steer clear of in other ways—Heidegger. (It must be stressed that only in its visual, that is, mimetic, component should art become a disparagement for Warminski; Hölderlin's letter, after all, actively inquires about poetic *techne*, thus explicitly thinking of the *art* of poetry.)

Back to Warminski's redrawing of the chiasmus, however. To read the relation of Greece/Hesperia rhetorically rather than dialectically is to reconfigure it completely by locating the foreign not *between* the related terms but *within* them: the Greeks are not Hesperia's foreigners, but they are foreign to themselves. They do not help us represent ourselves any more than they could help represent themselves. They simply *allegorize* themselves, pointing to themselves as others of themselves, though ever unable to *symbolize* this internal division for themselves (Warminski 40). Their doubleness is thus not reflexive, and so they remain as opaque to themselves as they do to us. To sum up: in appropriating form, the Greeks lived and created as the other of themselves but did not have the means (not enough skills, not enough "artfulness") to consciously reflect on and represent the meaning of their practice.

The Greeks: life amid unconscious creation. Put in these terms, it is difficult to see how his rhetorical treatment—what Warminski calls the Greek "allegory of unreadability" (40)—would not fold back into the idea of Greek art as naïveté, which his entire theoretical edifice was meant to undo. I suppose he would offer a rhetorical rebuttal of this sort: to read unreadability as naïveté is not to read it (just like a Greek!) but to make it symbolize by giving it a definite signified, thus also failing the only *real*, that is "nonexistent," Greeks (42), who point ceaselessly to their nonexistence—for in a rhetorical mode of existing such as this one, only the capacity to read oneself would usher in existence, and Warminski's Greeks cannot read themselves. Of course, one could pose a similar question to Warminski as the one he poses to art historian E. H. Gombrich[4]: how did we decide that the Greeks are allegorical rather than symbolic, when rhetoric—no less than aesthetics—is a Greek framework as well? How, in other words, is not Warminski reading his allegorical Greeks still with the same Greek eyes he would prefer to shut for good?

But it is not only Szondi who is guilty of this aesthetic mimeticism, according to Warminski. Philippe Lacoue-Labarthe too, in his "Caesura of the Speculative," risks a mimetic account when he reads Hölderlin's poetics of the caesura cathartically and thus ritualistically and anthropologically (Warminski 40–41).[5] While I will be returning to considerations of the caesura below, suffice it to underline once again the antimimetic impetus of Warminski's thought as indicative of a theoretical stronghold in poststructuralist criticism: a fear of affect, a taboo on embodiment, and a distaste for the real world accompanied perhaps by a slight condescension toward anyone who invokes it. Ironically, these attitudes reflect the colors of philosophy rather than rhetoric, which at least in its Greek birth was indubitably political, meant to elicit affects, engage and convince individuals, and produce social change.

Furthermore, such antimimeticism goes hand in hand with a discourse of death, the necessary post-Hegelian ingredient of theory, pervasive in Warminski's text as well. Notably, however, this is not the death of anyone or anything, thus, not a tragic death. Such death would be cathartic and real, worthy of someone's mourning, an experience of some sort. But any such experience is already superseded by the theoretical avant-garde, which has *theoretically*, and always only theoretically, guaranteed the grammatical impossibility of experiencing death as a dying person: the "I" of the "I die" is catachrestic, because it is already dead, Warminski reminds us in a Hegelian manner (41), implying that when language's most universal pronoun is used to indicate the most specific being, nothing of this specificity remains intact. Beyond all the internal duplicities Warminski unearths in the Orient and the Occident, beyond all the rhetorical nuances he evokes against the historical, aesthetic, or mimetic readings, it is this linguistic death that gathers together all the parts of his theoretical exercise: the death of inscription—the letter's "death*ful* spirit," as he calls it (41)—which, unlike tragic death, does not have any content, and thus, it is not supposed to work and exploit its own deathliness.[6] This is an apt example of the poststructuralist suspicion of tragic death, which I have noted in my reading of Cassandra in the introduction: by invoking something more than flat finitude, tragic death is assigned in contemporary theory the unethical role of instrumentalizing mortality, of working to exact a meaning from something as meaningless and arbitrary as death itself. Except that the scriptural, "empty" death works too, perhaps more assiduously than any other kind: it works ceaselessly at the engine of theoretical supersession. Theoretical death as impersonal, linguistic death, literally a grammatical nebulousness dangling from the desk of an academician, sweeps everything and nothing in its passage—a death that makes of death a light matter but that invests contemporary theory with a claim to radicalism, which in fact belongs already to theory's own classical past, to its birth in the late 1960s.

Thus, "Greece"—the origin, referent, object, subject, body, or whatever other content one wishes to give it to free it from the quotation marks—is dead, and the point of theory is to compete to see how much deader it can get it to be. After consciousness "understood" biological death (as if this were *really* possible), symbolized it in the death of consciousness, and thus superseded it, a new stage has been reached in this formal procession of radicalizations: the rhetorical death, the endless death without death. Only in such full, triple death (but should we not surpass the old Western trinity and invent a next kind?) can we make sure that the playing field is level, and that we just might one day become our own originators. How Greek, indeed: Oedipus to the third power. Appropriately, dissatisfied with Szondi's overcoming that spares the moderns from imitating the Greeks but preserves the Greeks aesthetically, and wary of Lacoue-Labarthe's Aristotelian attachments, Warminski's reading competes for the largest and deathliest possible abstraction.

In closing my discussion of Warminski's interpretation, I offer some questions and remarks whose simplicity should not detract from what they might show of the motivation, conscious or not, behind this rhetorical reading: Firstly, if both the Greeks and the Hesperians are doubly different, different from each other and from themselves—regardless of their ability to signify this for themselves or not—are they not also still similar in this double division? In other words, might not their discontinuity be as relative as a certain kind of continuity might be plausible? And if so, shouldn't the propensity for one reading over the other be understood as itself a valuation, a commitment, a stake, rather than an objective, naturalized, inevitable approach—the linguistic one—which alone claims to deserve the designation of high theory?

Secondly, Warminski's entire argument rests on the asymmetry of our not knowing Greek nature. But could such a problematic as the one of nature and creativity, so essential to Hölderlin's concerns, be the exclusive matter of rhetoric? On the contrary, I think that Hölderlin's agonizing attempt to find a content—that is, to find those golden rules and conditions for poets—is not exhausted by rhetoric alone but involves history, the history of philosophy, and, above all, a worldly concern with the crisis of modern life. Necessarily, this project involves politics with all its unpalatable and potentially dangerous misappropriations as well, such as the ones Hölderlin suffered, because this is an inevitable fact of existing in the world and participating in its crises, crises that have effects beyond the confines of purely conceptual and rhetorical abstractions.

Lastly, one more remark concerning the philosophical dimension of this inaccessibility of Greek nature: as I have previously observed, the repudiation of the real, the historical, and the anthropological is symptomatic of Kant's severe delimitation of experience—a delimitation that Kant imposed in an anything but lighthearted manner, since he did so actually to save epistemological certainty from its derailment by radical skepticism. In other words, Kant's limits mark an intellectual sacrifice of sorts, not a neutral undertaking; it is because of this tragic dimension of Kant's philosophy that his German idealist heirs turned to tragedy to rehearse the issues of modernity, as Dennis Schmidt rightly maintains (Schmidt 75). Just as Kant had to forfeit experience to save some claim to it for us, so Hölderlin may have had to sacrifice his Greeks to save them for our future, in the way Szondi intimated, because we may need them more than we think we do. Yet any comparable sense of agony is lacking from the kind of poststructuralist readings that reduce every tension to linguistic exigency and thus safely contain every potentially radical event within the purview of the word.

As we will continue to draw out the complexities of this Oriental/Occidental divide, it is important to recapitulate the principal assumptions underlining this Hölderlinian schema; we must not forget that Hölderlin's ultimate interest in the Greeks is not the Greeks but only the ways in which their response to their world can help him understand how the moderns could pursue the free use of the national (*das Eigene*)—that is, how the moderns can embody their spontaneity and know it as such, as "their" spontaneity. How can *we* come to live in our own skin, so to speak, is Hölderlin's actual concern. In a truly Kantian manner, it is this interest in freedom that guides his exploration, and it is because of this emphasis on freedom that Hölderlin needs to spare the moderns the work of obedience: imitating the ancients. The present cannot simply serve as an instrument for revealing the past's greatness. Yet in unfettering the present from its servitude to the past, Hölderlin commits another act of instrumentalization—one that we take for granted, however, since it works to our benefit: by positing the Greeks as an example to be learned from, this kind of instrumentalization often ends up in self-interested distortions and historical misappropriations in order to offer the present an illusion of progress and the promise of originality. In this reversal, our very own modern patriotic reversal, the dead are condemned to serve the living ad infinitum.

The manipulative character of this historiographical gaze, which makes the (dead) Greeks *work for us*, along with the even-more-pressing question of whether Hölderlin's search for freedom can even be served through an epochal logic such as his, which has little patience for individual exceptions, are some of the issues that will motivate our further analyses. To say the least, it is regrettable how the West, at the moment it imagines itself in decline (the sunset, the vesper) for its inability to live in its own skin, turns the past into its own current image of inadequacy and meaninglessness, making out of its own experience the retrospective transcendental condition of everyone and everything: death was always meaningless, nature was always culture, truth was always historical—all statements whose absoluteness betrays the otherwise relativist spirit of modernity.

Having laid out some of the debates concerning the relation of Orient and Occident, I will now turn to Hölderlin's writings on tragedy, where he posited Greek poetry as a kind of passage between these two worlds, partaking in aspects of both. The reasons why tragedy is of great significance will soon become evident, but suffice it for now to note that in his commentary on the Sophocles translations, particularly the "Remarks on 'Antigone,'" Hölderlin metaphorized the passage of Greek nature from Oriental sacred fire to Occidental intellection through the tragic figures of Antigone and Oedipus. Antigone and Oedipus furnish two different moments of being Greek, one of which serves as the reversal (or translation) of the other: Antigone, on the one hand, is the archaic, Oriental Greek who exists in holy pathos alone, devoured by divine enthusiasm. Françoise Dastur explains this principle of the orientalization of the Greeks as Hölderlin's corrective to moments of excessive self-identity either on the part of nature or of culture. The Orient functions as a differential mark, a kind of caesura that interrupts the onrushing movement toward the self-same: Antigone's Oriental fire, expressed in her limitless desire for death, compensates for Sophocles's excessive mastery of form. As such, she becomes the figure of the patriotic reversal, reminding the Greeks what was innate to them but appeared as foreign: pathos rather than form. Dastur writes:

> It seems, in fact, that the Orient is formed in this double figure (figure of separation and of limitlessness) every time there is the menace of an excess in the one or the other direction—an excess of culture and art, therefore an excess of separation from nature, or an excess of enthusiasm and thus an excessive union with the All. Thus, opposed to the figure of Empedocles which embodies the spirit of impatience and the speculative desire for a premature union with totality, comes the figure of the adversary, Manes, the Egyptian priest, he who endures, and who both questions Empedocles'

right to reconcile oppositions and personifies the capacity to endure the tension between art and nature. But opposed to this figure, as to that of Oedipus who sees himself return to a terrestrial world and a solely spiritual death, a "deathless death," is the figure of Antigone who accomplishes the native reversal of the Greek which takes her back from European sobriety to the Oriental element of celestial fire. (164–65)

As Dastur's explication suggests, it is important to understand the double moment in orientalization as a *balancing* act. In other words, the Oriental should not be simply conflated with the passionate that always opposes itself to Occidental measure in a dialectical way: it is not an issue of one pole depending on the other dialectically as, for instance, Nietzsche's Dionysian/Apollonian opposition is often interpreted to be, with Dionysus needing Apollo in order to appear and Apollo needing Dionysus to lend a content to his form.[7] Instead of mutual tension and interdependence *between* Orient and Occident, Hölderlin's notion of the Oriental articulates this dialectic *within* itself as a mark of internal difference and intimate strife. Hölderlin's Orient is a differential and torn but also balancing and corrective figure: it imposes limits where excessive fusion threatens them (Manes), and it destroys limits where excessive reflection obstructs nature's fusional impulse (Antigone). In the former instance, the Oriental appears in the guise of "art," giving shape to the chaos of "nature," thus performing a kind of Apollonian function; in the latter, performing a Dionysian function, it embraces the chaos of "nature" to prevent the risk "art" runs of becoming an elaborate but empty form. I enclose the notions of art and nature in quotes because the Oriental in either of its guises designates mainly an aesthetic category—a caesura that redirects the works of art as they alternately sway from the rawness of nature to the artificiality of techne.

This is another way of repeating Szondi's claim that the Greeks do not constitute Nature but a response to Nature. The Orient is not the fire of Nature but a poetic response to *a* nature. The Orient, in other words, reorients the disoriented vector of the work back to its center. In this corrective function, the temporality of the Orient proves to be not only one of beginning, but also of retrospect. Except, the retrospective movement is almost imperceptible with the Greeks, as if the correction (the "native reversal") happened virtually simultaneously with the act it was supposed to revise, in the manner of Sophocles who let his heroine correct his literary propensities while he was creating her. Because they were an early people, the distance between original and reversal for the ancient Greeks was infinitely smaller than it is for us moderns. The immediacy of this Sophoclean correction offers a model of a nascent reflexivity to which I return later on in this chapter.

Consequently, the Greeks are, for Hölderlin, Oriental in this double sense: first, as bearers of holy fire, a people of the sunrise; secondly, and by the time of Sophoclean tragedy, in the sense of inclining toward an equilibrium of form and passion, which Hölderlin associates with the reversing function of the caesura, the turn or break through which a poetic composition calibrates form to meaning. In the particular tragedies under discussion, the caesura as a formal expression of measure is identified with the prophet Teiresias and thus also with the moment of fate and fatality around which both Antigone's and Oedipus's plots turn. Because everything has been decided in *Antigone* in the first half of the play (we already know of Creon's edict and Antigone's choice), Teiresias appears later in the second half; conversely, because in *Oedipus Tyrannus* the main events concatenate in the second half (the investigation of Laius's murder and the revelation of Oedipus's parricide and incest), Teiresias appears earlier on in the first half.

In designating Teiresias as a pivot, Hölderlin addresses not only the formal, quantitative demands of balancing the plot's temporality of before and after by distributing the weight of action and the burden of consequence—something like Aristotle's definition of tragedy as a calculable whole with beginning, middle, and end; he also foregrounds the specific thematic significance the prophet has in Sophoclean drama as a figure who offers a balancing solution to tragic excess: Teiresias's entrance marks the last chance given to humans to avert tragedy, but somehow mortal limitations always conspire so that the characters fail to grasp his wisdom. In the blind figure of the seer, double-sexed, punished and rewarded by the gods, we also face this double fact: the human being does, at least theoretically, have the potential to choose wisely but almost never actually takes that choice. Teiresias as the caesura is not only the catastrophic break but also an anchoring hinge, a moment of balance and order in a terribly disorderly human world. This is why in *Antigone*, he warns Creon for having disturbed the natural order by burying a living person while letting a corpse rot above ground, intimating there is still time for the right order of redress, even though Creon misses the crucial sequence of unburying first and burying second:

> you have thrust one that belongs above
> below the earth, . . .
>
> . . .
>
> while one that belonged indeed to the underworld
> gods you have kept on this earth without due share
> of rites of burial.
> (Lines 1136–41)

Nevertheless, the discussion of the caesura as a sign of Greek art's desire for harmony, propriety, and balance has been displaced in the contemporary reception of Hölderlin in favor of construing it solely as a differential figure of discontinuity and interruption.

It seems to be of little consequence that the interruption serves a purpose beyond itself—namely, the prevention of extremity and the desire for equilibrium.[8] If, however, we do consider this other, intentional moment of the caesura, Hölderlin begins to show more affinities with his contemporaries in their reception of the Greeks than the poststructuralist interpretation of him allows. Indeed, even though Hölderlin is an exception among European luminaries of the neoclassical and romantic age in theorizing Greek nature as Oriental fire, we see, upon considering the secondary meaning of Oriental as reversal toward balance, that his concern for measure was in keeping with the spirit of his age, which reflected modernity's discontent with its own lack of measure. And even though balance may remain for Hölderlin's Greeks more of a striving desire than an attained state, this still does not invalidate the more general remark that something of this fragile equilibrium fascinated him as much as it did European classicism at large.

The attention Hölderlin and the other German idealists pay exclusively to Sophocles from among the three great tragedians corroborates this passion for the middle. Sophocles's tragic world stands at the very middle of the Attic aesthetic experiment, between the overpowering divine principles of Aeschylus and the intricate psychological conflicts of Euripides. To Sophocles fell the strange task of harmonizing the mortal with the divine after he himself effected their ruinous separation. Here is Karl Reinhardt on the difference between Sophoclean and Aeschylean drama:

> The Aeschylean hero might fall victim to the clash between gods and men, he might be overthrown, hunted, driven and tortured in the most horrible way, but he could never lose at one stroke his connection with

what surrounded him, his sense of belonging, and so he could never stand alone, excluded, abandoned and betrayed like Sophoclean man. For in Aeschylus there is as yet no purely mortal sphere that is distinct from the divine whole. Aeschylus belongs to the end of the late archaic period, but he evokes much older forces which still loomed dimly over his age in the realm of ritual, law and custom more than in that of poetry and fully-formed concepts; he is more interested in bringing out the contradiction between these forces, their richness, their distribution, overthrow or rebellion, than in the riddle of the boundary between man and god. (3)[9]

Because the separation between mortal and divine spheres is a fact of life in Sophocles, the subsequent need for harmony and resolution is foregrounded in his plays in a way that would have been impossible for Aeschylus, whose overarching divine order takes care of everything in advance. And although the resolution in Sophocles, just as in Aeschylus before, implies the triumph of the divine, the interlude of hubris is no less essential to the ethical ascent. Reinhardt's description of the eventually humbled Sophoclean hero is poignant: "This humility, this 'coming to one's senses', would not receive such high praise if the genuinely great mortal were not so reckless, so arrogant, so averse to moderation, so preoccupied with his own virtue, so endangered and so proud" (3). Finally, in a remark pertinent to our present discussion, Reinhardt ascribes Hölderlin's specific interest in *Antigone* and *Oedipus Tyrannus* to the fact that they constitute themselves "transitional works," belonging to "the poet's middle period" and "display[ing] his strongest powers" (8). "Middle" seems to emerge as the operative word.

It is this fragile middle state of human freedom in the face of divine abandonment (for there can be no human freedom without a certain divine abdication—the human abdication of God and God's abdication of the human) that classical tragedy first thematized but that has continued to occupy Western ethical thought long after the disappearance of Attic theater. In fact, the importance of tragedy for philosophical thinking—whether positively or negatively assessed—centers on the terms "mortal" and "divine": on their "complementarity" or "hierarchy," the balance or strife between them. Assuming various names throughout the history of Western philosophy and theology (contingency versus the absolute, will versus fate, self versus Other, culture versus nature, activity versus passivity), this polarity has delimited the horizon of ethical thought. It is therefore not an overstatement to say that the fate of its balance dictates the direction of ethics. In contemporary theory, yet again, the tipping of the scales has all but defined the vicissitudes of what it means to be human: an absolutely free subject or a subject to absolute necessity? Thus, my insistence on the balancing aspect of Hölderlin's orientalization anticipates my later discussions concerning the reapplication of a similar caesura in the direction of contemporary ethical discourse, which has for some time now radicalized the pole of passivity, while occluding any relationship to freedom and to oneself. In other words, if the orientalization of the Greeks was necessary for Hölderlin as a corrective to self-sameness, we should consider a symmetrical corrective in contemporary thought that balances out the excesses of alterity with a sense of freedom. The question is whether this application can be called "orientalization," or even "occidentalization," anymore, or whether freedom might mean also freedom from such fraught and exhausted historicophilosophical coordinates.

With these general comments on the function of orientalization in place, we can now return to Hölderlin's remarks on what specifically constitutes Antigone's Oriental disposition. In her self-comparison with Niobe shortly before entering her tomb, Hölderlin recognizes the moment in which the human is seized by the god and—transported to a heightened state of consciousness—exceeds consciousness altogether. In short, Hölderlin reads the reference to Niobe as Antigone's hubris, which is paid by her actual death: "It is a great resource of the secretly working soul that at the highest state of consciousness it evades consciousness and that, before the present god actually seizes it, the soul confronts him with bold, frequently even blasphemic word and thus maintains the sacred living potential of the spirit" (*Essays and Letters* 111). Oedipus, on the other hand, dying a "deathless death," as Dastur put it (165), anticipates the more spiritual and self-reflexive Occidental character,[10] for whom death is no more an ordeal of the sensuous body but rather a question of the spirit. "Following the particularly Greek manner," writes Hölderlin, "the word turns *more mediately factual* by taking hold of the sensuous body; following our time and mode of representation, more immediate by taking hold of the more spiritual body" (113).

Despite Hölderlin's emphatic translation of the Niobe comparison as a moment of hubris, the Sophoclean text is much more ambiguous. The German poet speaks of Antigone's blasphemy because he unquestionably espouses the response of the chorus, an assembly of Theban elders that has been frequently noted for its vacillation and occasional hostility to the heroine. But even their words cannot be so easily construed to accuse her of hubris or sacred frenzy. Here is the exchange in Sophocles:

> ANTIGONE:
> But indeed I have heard of the saddest of deaths—
> Of the Phrygian stranger, daughter of Tantalus,
> whom the rocky growth subdued, like clinging ivy.
> The rains never leave her, the snow never fails,
> as she wastes away. That is how men tell the story.
> From streaming eyes her tears wet the crags;
> most like to her the god brings me to rest.
> CHORUS:
> Yes, but she was a god, and god born,
> And you are mortal and mortal born.
> Surely it is great renown
> for a woman that dies, that in life and death
> her lot is a lot shared with demigods.
> (Lines 885–96)

We see Antigone citing the myth of Niobe to express her own sense of abandonment by the gods: just as Niobe became a rock with streaming tears after the gods deprived her of her children, so too Antigone will be immured by Creon into a cave. The chorus's response, in turn, is more inflected than Hölderlin's reading allows: while the elders remind Antigone of her mortal roots as opposed to Niobe's divine descent, they proceed not only to agree with the basic tenet of Antigone's comparison but even to reinforce it. It is they, in fact, who glorify her fate as being equal to the gods', and their earlier praise of Antigone's destiny has even implied that Antigone's predicament surpasses Niobe's in that the former consciously chose the moral high road whereas the latter committed hubris unthinkingly: "Yes, you go to the place where the dead are hidden, / but you go with distinction and praise" (lines 878–79).

Hölderlin can maintain his thesis only insofar as he takes the chorus's initial reaction at face value, considering Niobe to be divine and thus interpreting Antigone's comparison to be an impassioned claim to godlike status. But even beyond these obvious words of the chorus, we should not forget that Niobe's myth involves many other details that would warrant this comparison, details that were too obvious to the ancient audience to even be mentioned.

For instance, while Niobe may indeed have been of divine lineage (at least according to the variant myth that describes her as the daughter of Dione), she was still punished because she compared herself to the gods. Apparently, despite her own half-divine nature, Niobe trespassed when she boasted about her fertility to Leto, who only had two children, albeit divine ones—Apollo and Artemis. By way of avenging their mother's wounded pride, Apollo and Artemis slaughtered all fourteen of Niobe's children, who remained unburied for several days until the gods took pity on her and allowed burial. Antigone's similarity to Niobe, then, might be more legible in the context of lamentation than of hubris alone: Niobe's tears and her inconsolable loneliness were legendary in antiquity as symbols of mourning and formed quite an intertextual motif in the works of various authors. Sophocles, in fact, may be consciously re-citing two such strong citations of this myth before him: Homer's *Iliad*, where Achilles compares Priam's mourning of Hector to Niobe's mourning of her offspring (24.602–27), and that by Aeschylus, whose *Niobe* is no more extant. Indeed, Antigone's comparison to Niobe is on target—her brother was unburied like Niobe's children, and her relation to Polyneices is described as a maternal one: upon seeing the ritual dust removed from his body, Antigone lets out a

> shrill cry
> of an embittered bird
> that sees its nest robbed of its nestlings.
> (Lines 466–68)[11]

To all this, we must add that Niobe is not only a Phrygian stranger but also the wife of Amphion, one of the founders of Thebes, and thus herself a Theban princess, much like Antigone.

My belaboring of the myth serves to suggest that Niobe's mourning is as much, if not more, ground for Antigone's comparison than the unconscious moment of hubris and divine madness Hölderlin assumes it to be. After all, since Niobe behaved hubristically according to the myth—and the myth insists on this much more emphatically than on her divine lineage—it would seem that a comparison to her functions as a simultaneous admission of guilt on Antigone's part: guilt, of course, not for making this comparison, but for another act of hubris. Is Sophocles's Antigone then hinting self-consciously through this similarity that she too has committed hubris by burying her brother and obeying divine law over mortal law? This does not make much sense, and in any case, Hölderlin's own comment suggests that she could not be self-conscious at this moment but that her "blasphemy" constitutes the sacred, unconscious response to divine provocation. Yet to side selectively with the chorus's initial words and stress Niobe's divinity over her mourning in order to enable a hubristic reading of Antigone means also to forego the most obvious and well-known—hence, omitted by Sophocles—resonances of the myth: the fact that Niobe is above all a figure of human mourning rather than a great divinity to whom mortals like Antigone should refrain from comparing themselves. The Niobe of the ancients is human, all too human in this sense, and offers a perfectly legitimate moment of comparison for a woman who laments the family she has lost, the marriage and children she will never have, and even her own impending death toward which she walks just as alone as Niobe once had found herself.

More than this, however, what is elided in Hölderlin's reading of hubris (which Hegel also follows by rendering both Creon and Antigone equally guilty) is the chorus's actual conclusion. In elevating Antigone's death, this conclusion implicitly suggests that, whereas divine Niobe was punished by the gods for her hubris, mortal Antigone will attain glory via her punishment by a mortal king, since her moral decision will be recognized by the gods as divine service. To consider all these details, however, would have attenuated Hölderlin's forceful but historically motivated translation, which aims at producing an epochal divide along the Oriental/Occidental axis. Thus, the poet can construct an irrational, Oriental Antigone who—in contrast to more mediated, self-conscious, Occidental literary figures—suffers the blows of the divine with a sensuous immediacy, dying a factual (tragic) rather than a spiritual (philosophical) death.

Indeed, the Oriental character of Greek art, writes Hölderlin, is "mediately factual" in that its idea, still overwhelmed and mediated by the sensuousness of its material, compensates for this excessive formal materiality by killing the actual sensuous body that appears in its contents, the body of Antigone. In contrast, the Occidentals, by taking on the Oedipal drama as the exemplar of representation, move to a more reflexive mode, where the work's idea—namely, Oedipus's self-reflexive quest for his origin and its repercussions—is masterfully matched by the form of its presentation, which becomes now more ideational. In their immediacy—that is, in their coincidence with each other—form and content in the Oedipal drama now express the very ideality of the spirit that inheres in them equally.[12] Punished not by death but by exile and later dying a death that could not be witnessed even by his immediate kin, Oedipus elides the question of the body by transporting it to the realm of symbolization. In such a scheme, Antigone accomplishes the patriotic reversal of Oedipus inasmuch as she foregrounds the innate Oriental fire of the Greeks that disrupts their masterful appropriation of measure and self-reflection.

Notwithstanding the pluralistic and even conflicting nature of the intellectual and artistic achievements of Greek antiquity itself, Hölderlin's focus on this particular poetological division has drawn more theoretical attention to his ingenuous novelty as a reader than to the enduring richness of the Sophoclean text: our Antigone is now Hölderlin's translation of her. It has indeed been argued that by commenting on these divisions within the Greek world, and more specifically by doing so through *translations* of tragedy, Hölderlin ostensibly translates his own self-reflexive modernity into the ancients. He reads the calculus of Greek poetry, which, though allegedly untheorized by the Greeks themselves, was still at work in their verses—an unconscious kind of calculus that nonetheless could account even for such an incalculable thing as passion. According to this line of argumentation, Greek art carries within it an "other" origin—invisible and inaudible to the Greeks—that waits to be decrypted, translated, and made conscious. Hölderlin, then, assumes the historical destiny of fulfilling the Greeks, of putting into words their own silent foreignness to themselves.[13]

The double gesture of linking Greek nature to sacred madness and of positing the end of such nature within Greece in the emergence of the Oedipal character distinguished Hölderlin from his classicist contemporaries,[14] inaugurating a modernity that has shifted radically away from classicism's revivalist tendencies.[15] This is why poststructuralist thought, in the wake of Nietzsche's reappraisal of the Greeks and Heidegger's interpretation of Hölderlin, has recast Hölderlin as the initiator of a decisive modern turn away from classicism. We have witnessed this recent reception of Hölderlin's anticlassicism in Szondi's and Warminski's analyses; but to assess its significance vis-à-vis the poet's most famous predecessor and theoretical rival, I will provide a cursory comparison to Johann Joachim Winckelmann (1717–68), whose art theory exemplified the aesthetic values of German classicism.

Hölderlin's insistence on the fiery nature of the Greeks now stands in stark contrast to Winckelmann, who proposed reason and measure to be the Greeks' innate characteristics, which they expressed in the serenity of their art: "The last and most eminent characteristic of the Greek works is a noble simplicity and sedate grandeur" (Winckelmann 72). While extremely influential to thinkers such as Lessing and Goethe as well as to the painter Jacques-Louis David, Winckelmann was later critiqued by Nietzsche, among others, for overlooking the Dionysian, irrational elements of Greek art. Winckelmann's work, which was in fact incipient of a historical thinking of art forms,[16] can itself now be historicized in view of its post-Enlightenment reception: his relation to the Greeks reflects Enlightenment's adherence to reason, while Nietzsche's emphasis on the Dionysian belongs to the aftermath of romanticism and its attendant critiques of reason. Subsequently, contemporary intellectual history and philosophical inquiry alike have been skeptical of Winckelmann's Hellenism and of the (neo)classical revivalism that his thought engendered. Notwithstanding his project of historicizing art styles for the first time, his nostalgic attitude toward the past has been charged with a certain ahistorical naïveté that dreams of reproducing the Greeks through imitation: "There is but one way for the moderns to become great and perhaps unequalled; I mean by imitating the ancients" (Winckelmann 61). Despite any merits this critique of nostalgia claims, it should be noted that the concept of imitation is never as simple as it often seems, and this holds true in Winckelmann's case as well.

To clarify at the outset, there are at least two levels of imitation involved in Winckelmann's aesthetic theory: firstly, he describes the Greeks' successful imitation of nature in their representations of the male nude; secondly, he exhorts the moderns to imitate the Greeks on account of his admiration for their natural imitative skills. But imitation is by no means mindless reproduction in either of these two instances. In the case of the Greeks, on the one hand, Winckelmann maintains that their practice of imitation transcends a mere copying of nature by infusing nature with a spiritualized aspect and idealizing it in the work: "It is not only nature which the votaries of the Greeks find in their works but still more, something superior to nature; ideal beauties, brain-born images" (62); or again: "To form a 'just resemblance, and, at the same time, a handsomer one', being always the chief rule they observed, . . . they must, of necessity, be supposed to have had in view a more beauteous and more perfect nature" (65). Even though Hegel excluded any mention of nature from his aesthetics, his own understanding of the spiritualized character that inheres in art's sensuous form echoes Winckelmann's. Thus, imitation of nature involves also excess; it involves going beyond empirical nature to reach an ideal that can only be an effect of the human mind, a "brain-born" effect.

On the other hand, in the case of the moderns too, Winckelmann's notion of imitation calls for nuance. After all, what does he mean when he exclaims that the moderns will become "unequalled" through their imitation of the ancients? Unequaled with respect to whom? Will the moderns be unequaled by the future generations of artists, or is it more likely to assume that they will have exceeded the very people they have imitated—namely, the Greeks? Or, conversely, how can he expect the moderns to succeed at all at such an imitation when he calls Homer and the ancient Greek artists "inimitable" (61, 69)? Should we dismiss these epithets as mere hyperboles by a consummate art connoisseur, or should we read in them the ambiguous and even competitive interaction they envision between two epochs? When he also writes that the lesson of "unity and perfection" of the Greeks will help the modern artist "to ennoble the more scattered and weaker beauties of our nature," thus recognizing the different attitudes toward both nature and beauty held by the Greeks in contrast to the moderns (68), it seems that he grasps, albeit minimally, the essentially historical nature of this endeavor and that he points to a dynamic and productive interrelation between the ages rather than a static imitation.

But it is Hölderlin's essay entitled "The Perspective from Which We Have to Look at Antiquity" that drives this point forward: "We dream of originality and autonomy; we believe to be saying all kinds of new things and, still, all this is reaction, as it were, a mild revenge against the slavery with which we have behaved toward antiquity" (*Essays and Letters* 39). At stake in Hölderlin is the fulfillment of our own nature through the proper mode of its presentation. Since one's relation to one's nature is always subject to time, it follows that because of our place in history, we moderns cannot afford to emulate the ancients, even if such emulation is more of an adaptation than a crude imitation. Antiquity cannot provide the answer to our quest to fulfill our nature, since "antiquity appears altogether opposed to our primordial drive which is bent on forming the unformed" (39), writes Hölderlin regarding our disposition for form, measure, and calculation rather than holy pathos. Nonetheless, the question of imitation does not entirely disappear even in Hölderlin; rather, it takes on a different course that can only be stated somewhat paradoxically. Because the moderns must imitate the Greeks in achieving originality, they should no more imitate the Greeks: "With the exception of what must be the highest for the Greeks and for us—namely, the living relationship and destiny—we must not share anything identical with them" (*Essays and*

Letters 150). Put differently, in Hölderlin, we do not imitate Greek forms as in Winckelmann—that is, we do not imitate *how* and *what* the Greeks actually did—rather, we imitate or learn from *who* they were: a destinal people, a people who attempted to show properly their relation to their world. This is what the moderns also need to fulfill, but with the proviso that our nature and our world are essentially different from theirs and thus confront us with a different set of relations requiring equally different forms of presentation.

Winckelmann's failure, then, does not lie in his conception of imitation, strictly speaking, but in his inability to see how the difference between our two worlds has transformed the very nature of imitation itself. Beyond a formal process of copying, adapting, or even loosely re-creating the past, the question of imitation now involves a peculiar moment of repetition that is at the same time original: it involves the disclosure (again as in the Greeks but also for the first time in our time) of our relationship to our destiny, which means the attainment of a proper relationship to our world and the understanding of our own timeliness. As Hölderlin's orientalized revision of antiquity suggests, Winckelmann's inability to see the difference hinges on his misguided rationalist portrayal of the Greeks, since the rationalism of the moderns is hardly under dispute. In fact, his miscalculation of Greek nature was most likely due to his own modern bias: in imagining the Greeks to have always been rational and serene, he imagined them to be not so different from the Enlightenment Europeans of his own time and, by extension, from all moderns. As such, it follows that imitating the Greeks would have seemed to Winckelmann to be a natural solution. To see an essential difference, to recognize in modern self-reflexivity a formidable ontological shift, Winckelmann would have had to change "his" Greeks and, like Hölderlin, imagine them first in their native religious fervor, before he could turn them into masters of measure and form—namely, masters of the foreign. Winckelmann was mistaken to think he was speaking about the Greeks, when in fact he was speaking about himself and his fantasy of Greek antiquity.

In fact, Winckelmann did recognize the passionate aspects of Greek art but aligned these aspects with earlier forms, while attributing "noble simplicity and sedate grandeur" to the Greeks' mature, more reflexive styles: "Arts have their infancy as well as men; they begin, as well as the artist, with froth and bombast: in such buskins the muse of Aeschylus stalks, and part of the diction in his Agamemnon is more loaded with hyperboles than all Heraclitus's nonsense. . . . In all human actions flutter and rashness precede, sedateness and solidity follow" (73). In this sense, his historiographical construction of the early (passionate)/late (measured) Greeks is similar to Hölderlin's early pathos/late measure divide. What differentiates the two Germans is their assessment regarding which of these two Greek stages is more properly Greek. I suggest that it is because he wishes for a sharp contrast between ancients and moderns, between modern reflexivity as our first nature and ancient sobriety as only the Greeks' second nature, that Hölderlin insists on the primacy of holy pathos in Greek antiquity. Again, though both privilege the Greeks in relation to balance, Winckelmann admired their attainment of it, while Hölderlin accented their strife to achieve it through the caesura.

In Hölderlin's historiographical revision, we confront the most contested of German idealism's effects on the study of classical Greece: the Greeks are merely an excuse to speak about ourselves. In the poet's own words: "This is why the Greeks are indispensable *for us*" (*Essays and Letters* 150, my emphasis). There is obviously a lesson to be extracted here, a lesson Hölderlin attempted to distill in a calculus of the tragic form. It is my contention that Hölderlin's own tragedy of reflection lies in this teleological gesture, this turning of the tragic into a lesson, into a cautionary tale indeed: how not to end up like the Greeks, vanished before fulfilling the free use of the national. As a testimony to his own astuteness, Hölderlin writes explicitly of this tragedy of reflection a few lines down: "For this is the tragic to us: that, packed up in any container, we very quietly move away from the realm of the living, [and] not that—consumed in flames—we expiate the flames which we could not tame" (150). Our tragedy is that we retreated from existence into sheer abstraction. We do not suffer, any more than we enjoy, the exquisite terror of a full life. Hölderlin understands his tragedy, which is that he does not know how to do otherwise but to reflect on tragedy—hence, his most poignant "mistake" of turning to the Greeks (the tragic people) to extract some type of lesson, when in fact tragedy yields none.

It was Nietzsche who expressed this essentially antiutilitarian thrust of tragedy—an antiutilitarianism that serves as the reason why tragedy is inadmissible in the modern world but why also it continues to offer an inspiring instance of living otherwise. In his fragment "What I Owe to the Ancients" from *The Twilight of the Idols*, Nietzsche writes, "One does not *learn* from the Greeks—their manner is too strange, it is also too fluid to produce an imperative, a 'classical' effect" (106). One does not learn how to act; one just acts, lives: the enormous and yet infinitesimal difference between the poet who could not do otherwise than reflect and the philosopher who could not but dream and sing of life's splendor. Hence, the Zarathustra fragment "The Hammer Speaks" reappears as a postscript to *The Twilight of the Idols* (112) to offer a model of this tragic knowledge, which cannot be learned but only lived: to become hard, which means to live with the fact that there is no lesson and no ethics, no command and no justification in this world. This world, of which we are so passionately a part, in joy as well as in suffering, is just this hardness on which only a harder diamond can etch a line. To become hard, to become worthy of one's circumstance: this is Nietzsche's response to the question of how to freely use the national—for this hardness is nothing else but the innate human desire to express its freedom in an act that exceeds its narrow egotistical confines and makes it *truly* rather than *merely* human. This version of the national (*das Eigene*) is no more specific to the Oriental or the Occidental but only to what has always compelled the human being toward its most creative capacity; it is the mark of the exceptional rather than of that which can be mapped in any prearranged, historically determined ontology.

"Greece," Greece: The Oedipal Drama of Discontinuity

Since we have already touched on this notion of mapping, implied in Hölderlin's distinction, I would like to stop parenthetically and acknowledge a set of ethicopolitical concerns deriving from his speculative historiographical model of reading others for the sake of ourselves. Surely, Hölderlin's map does not intend to describe any recognizable territorial entities of the sort that we call countries, or nation-states; rather, it aims at presenting a temporalized ontology, in which the difference between ancient and modern sensibilities becomes articulated in spatial terms. Additionally, anyone familiar with the recent scholarship on Hölderlin, examples of which I have already discussed above, would know that those Greeks should not be anthropologized: they should not be considered as empirical beings belonging to a culture that forms a reliable epistemological object for us or that deserves our attention in itself, since "itself" is really only what we make it to be.

In fact, those Greeks never existed (Warminski 42). Their ancient community too, this "Greece," is nothing but an ideational construct in the German poet's mind, a heuristic device assisting him in reflecting on our present concerns. Even Sophocles, whom Hölderlin obviously cares to translate, does not claim much attention on his own. It seems as if he continues to exist thanks only to his renewal by Hölderlin and, later, by Heidegger. As a representative of this de-anthropologization, I will cite again Warminski's text, which remains a veritable tour de force of a rhetorical reading not only of Hölderlin's Oriental/Occidental divide but of its philosophical reception in Heidegger, Szondi, and Lacoue-Labarthe. As I have already mentioned, Warminski's reading of Hölderlin, interested only in the rhetoricity of allegory (of how it says otherwise) and not at all in the contents of *what* it says otherwise, takes issue with everything in Hölderlin scholarship that points to content, which for him is the sinful mark of mimeticism. In short, Hölderlin, for some legitimate but other not-so-legitimate reasons, has become the darling of these sorts of hyperdiscursive and ultralinguistic forms of criticism; as such, the mere hint of a discussion concerning the *actual* creative capacities and incapacities of *actual* human beings can be easily dismissed as mimetic naïveté — the kind of Bataillean anthropologization in Lacoue-Labarthe that makes Warminski uncomfortable (Warminski 41).

This tacit theoretical prohibition against addressing the actual cultures included in Hölderlin's historiographical discourse, however, by no means renders his project innocent or transparent, and, as usual, one should expect its reception to be even less so. Hence, my remarks here imply a larger critical discussion regarding the inevitably instrumental character of any historiography, which is always written from the vantage point and for the purposes of the present. While some reconstructions are more conscious and sensitive of their embeddedness and teleology and thus attempt to do as much justice and as little violence as possible to the past they seek to understand, history cannot be written *but* from this vantage point. I am of the opinion that Hölderlin's brilliant gesture of orientalizing the Greeks precisely in order to invent our difference from them is no freer of this historiographical problematic than is Winckelmann's nostalgia: between Hölderlin and Winckelmann, classicism and romanticism, and then romanticism and poststructuralism lurks an abyss, over which the moderns exchange their visions of the Greeks in a differential economy that depicts modernity self-applaudingly as the completion of the ancients and, simultaneously, as the radical departure from them. Modernity configures itself around these two conflicting narratives of progress (completion), on the one hand, and of disjuncture (ontological and epistemological shifts), on the other. Such contradiction is not in itself a problem, if it is followed by the modest admission that both these narratives of progress and originality share in an instrumental logic that accrues the most credit for the present by reserving the least attention for the past. With little interest in the dimension of loss that marks any historiographical reflection, much of contemporary theory influenced by Hölderlin's turn revels in the narrative of irrevocable discontinuity between ancients and moderns, while characterizing this discontinuity largely as a gain: as the beacon of our emancipation from tradition and as the condition of possibility for our originality. Poststructuralism, itself historically viewed, functions as the last apex in the history of post-Hegelian supersessions and radicalizations.

Nicole Loraux notices this self-serving gesture in the practice of translation, a practice that actually lies at the heart of historiography as well. As her charge against the instrumental aspects of some modern translators (Jean-Paul Sartre's translation of *The Trojan Women*, in this case) centers on the translation of Greek tragedy, her remarks should resonate in the immediate context of discussing Hölderlin's translations of Sophocles, which presently enjoy critical acclaim for exactly what is presumed to be their distortion (or renewal, depending on perspective) of the Greek text. Loraux writes, "The categorical imperative of every translator—to faithfully bridge the distance between the original and the translation—demands that the translator/interpreter agree to serve the text rather than use it, unless the avowed intent is to distort it" (7). I do not engage Sartre's tragedy here specifically, but his ethicopolitical motivations for turning to tragedy remain essential to this project—namely, the search for the space of freedom and individual resistance that tragedy affords.[17] Consequently, though I concur with Loraux's particular charges against Sartre's textual choices, her exclusive emphasis on the passive element of mourning in tragedy obstructs her from seeing tragedy's other half, the passion for freedom that inspires Sartre's political imagination. This passion Loraux can only read as the resentment of his vanquished—"the hatred of the conquered for the conqueror" (Loraux 5). In this sense, Loraux's privileging of lyric lamentation over epic plot participates in the overall elision of politics that has marked the modern and contemporary study of tragedy. While I am greatly indebted to her insight that tragedy stages the experience of personal suffering and is thus in some sense "antipolitical" (27), it holds equally true that deliberate action is also constitutive to tragedy. To think freedom and action *alongside* suffering and thus to restore to politics its rightful and humane dimension might well be what tragedy urges us to do. Still, I take her larger point that a translator (and a historiographer) ought to sustain a relationship with past texts that avoids instrumentalization.

Returning, however, to the issue of discontinuity in the relation between ancients and moderns, I would like to briefly rehearse its twofold problematic. The first concerns the implications of this term "discontinuity" as it functions explicitly in Hölderlin—namely, to demarcate the rift between ancient Greeks and Hesperians, whereby "Hesperians" designates the Germans and, by extension, possibly the French, who entered the battles of classicism apparently as Germany's sole worthy rivals. The second, latent, thus potentially more sinister, problematic involves the discourse of discontinuity as it is silently applied between the ancient Greeks and another people, who too may have dreamed of themselves at least as partly European and who may have certainly had some reasons to believe they bore a special relation to the ancient Greeks—at least as special as their European neighbors imagined themselves to have had: the modern Greeks.

Concerning the first and explicitly articulated discontinuity between ancient Greeks and modern Europeans: the irony of this supposition lies in the fact that by disclaiming their relation to the Greeks (even as this disclaimer reinscribes the ancients in our present, albeit only negatively, in the form of Oedipal rebellion[18]), the moderns by no means afford themselves an original destiny, at least not in the sense of it being unprecedented and unindebted. Instead, modernity engages in yet another translation, an exchange of its hitherto Greek-based origin for another origin, which is also equally ancient but whose overall philosophical continuity into modernity is not scrutinized, in large part because of the triumph of monotheism: Judaism and its begetting of Christianity.[19] As Hölderlin's Dionysus sometimes borrows the name of Christ (the other coming god[20]), later, in poststructuralist philosophy, the monotheistic shift takes an even more ancient turn. Hebrew theology with its distant and disincarnate god, historically presented as the competing counterpart of Greece's anthropomorphic paganism,[21] can now be found at the end of this Oriental Hölderlinian vector, offering to poststructuralist thought an alternative ethics of absolute passivity to the external command, thus grounding ethical responsibility exclusively in the Other and never in a relation to self. Theocentrism versus anthropocentrism, religion versus reason, difference versus identity, singularity versus universality, ethics versus aesthetics, truth versus myth, withdrawal versus disclosure, the impersonal versus the incarnate, iconoclasm versus mimesis: these are, then, some of the attendant binaries that have been used to describe the legacies of Jews and Greeks, frequently at the expense of other modalities in both Judaism and Hellenism that do not conform to such neat division.[22]

What is original, then, in this return? The appropriation of a different origin appears timely in bringing about new affinities, in recognizing that our present way of being—or more strictly, our image of our present way of being—might be better reflected in another modality than the Greek. But most of all, it comes as an ethical requirement, a necessary gesture of redress for Europe's culminating crime and for its hitherto disavowed debts. Therefore, the continuity between Jews and moderns in this case serves to heal, at least philosophically, the disenfranchisement and discrimination that former absolutizations of difference had produced against Jews. What is implied, then, for the Greeks, in this European relay of schemes of continuity and discontinuity from one people to another, will be my next question. For now, it is important to note that post-Holocaust European history binds modernity to the Jews in a singularly special relationship—one of responsibility but one that also repeats in a different register the special relationship to one's proper or intimate foreigner (*das eigene Fremde*) that Hölderlin had already imagined between Greeks and Germans. In a certain limited sense, modernity's turn toward Judaic ethics is already anticipated in Hölderlin's orientalization of the Greeks. His difference from Winckelmann could be perhaps rearticulated in these terms: Hölderlin's Greeks are at first Semites, people of the holy, who had to learn Occidental forms.[23]

This repetition or relay bears fraught and politically uncanny implications. On the one hand, the special relationship of modernity to Judaism accounts for a marked, if not so frequently commented on, coalescence of Hebrew messianic theology with the advent of postwar thought, particularly under the umbrella of poststructuralism in continental philosophy and literary studies.[24] The most crucial, and I believe limiting, corollary that proceeds from this coalescence is the critique of freedom and the relation to self as anthropocentric delusions. On the other hand, this special relationship—which was once articulated with respect to the Greeks in terms of being the moderns' own other, who could be used and surpassed in the formation of our Hesperian identity—can no more sustain itself in those same terms without carrying overtones of Europe's long-standing historical othering of the Jews. The current relation to the Jew can no more be a relation to one's own other, but to an otherness made proper to *us* (Hesperians), a relation to ourselves as other: the modern experience of uprooting, the new universal continuity.

Thus, the Greek is lost, condemned forever to his ruinous past and to the darkness of myth, the deadest and most foreign of our foreigners, because he forgot his piety for love of form, while the Jew through centuries of ordeals, pain, and persecution managed to survive because he guarded his faith, the faith that reached modernity as its founding monotheism. Lastly come we, the Hesperians, faced with Hölderlin's paradoxical task: though our nature is calculation, we should learn to excel first in what is foreign before undertaking the much harder task of the free use of our native traits. We must learn the holy, what the Greek had and abandoned, what the Jew continues to lay claim to. Europe's unending Oedipal romance: pitting one parent against the other.

A quick glance now to the second problematic, where we confront the virtual erasure of modern Greeks from these all-important discussions regarding the fate of Europe's destiny and of its special foreigners. Apparently, the modern Greeks (an expression that must have first rung as an oxymoron to the West, since these occupied, insurrectionary Mediterranean tribes were scarcely viewed as European, and even less so as Greek) are not welcome even to witness Hellenism's great funeral. It behooves them to learn the news belatedly and by chance, as a philosophical fait accompli. To be fair, Hölderlin's *Hyperion* draws its inspiration from the contemporary events of the Greek struggle for independence, but its irremediably idealistic landscape ends up only showcasing the poet's profound philosophical disenchantment with the fiery disposition that knows no mediation, which for Hölderlin drives awry modern revolutionary consciousness. In turn, this disenchantment reinforces his assumption that the real Greeks have indeed vanished in incompleteness, without having excelled in the free use of the national — the holy fire. For, after all, the holy fire of these contemporaries of his does not count. For one, they are no Greeks at all; and in any case, their fire is not used properly, since its immediate and felt reality offends the age of spiritual abstraction.

It is of little concern that this fire did conjure for those modern Greeks — now one of Europe's new others (though unrecognized as such) — profoundly old legends of autonomy and that it did even help bring about the attainment of some kind of political self-determination. Indeed, one can easily anticipate the immediate theoretical objection that the freedom of the nation-state can never compare to the genuine freedom promised by philosophical inquiry, particularly in the form of its abstract, discursive supersessions. Political freedom and the will to self-determination became all too quickly subjects to be deconstructed: as simply negative processes of emancipation *from* something, they carry in their negativity so many kinds of violence of their own.[25] Whatever merits we may grant to this objection, one thing is clear: such objection runs aground on Hölderlin's own dream of a Swabian community and, even more so, on Hegel's culmination of German idealism into a philosophy of the state. In other words, the German passion for a political community, and especially Hölderlin's search for belonging that haunted him until the very end, could find no timelier thematization than in the everyday reality of the autonomous movements of their neighbors. Yet these neighbors must apparently pay dearly the price of their immaturity, which made them think that they can act toward their freedom and assume their destiny, rather than simply reflect on it.

This erasure, which may be at least excused in the nineteenth-century milieu, given precisely the conflicts and complexities of the revolutionary climate in southeast Europe, is even more peculiar as it subsists in the contemporary philosophical context, where it is taken for granted with no problematization of its own historicity. It is even a misnomer to say that the erasure is taken for granted, since it does not even register as erasure—another way of saying that, for philosophy, the only Greeks are dead Greeks. To even suggest that several expressions of resistance in the modern and contemporary Greek world offer an evocative reeruption of the tragic principle of human freedom in our posttragic landscape is unworthy of philosophical attention.[26] It could, along with some of my present remarks, be reduced to an identitarian position, a nebulous anthropological or folkloric myth, or a cultural complaint among the many others that have come and passed and that have no immediate bearing to the "higher" tasks philosophical thinking has ahead of itself. And yet this is no simple cultural matter, any more than any cultural matter is truly simple. It too involves a strange kind of uprooting of a people,[27] this time while it remained under occupation within that general area the ancient Hellenes called their homeland. Greeks and Jews meet yet again at infinity: two different, two parallel paths of an uprooting.

Mindful of this erasure, Lorenz Gyömörey writes:

> Like all Europeans, I also grew up with the teachings that European civilization was born in Greece, that we, the civilized people of the world, are the offspring of wonderful human beings such as Pericles, Socrates, Plato, Phidias, and many others. We have learnt to pronounce "democracy" and "politics" and "economy" and "theater" and "poetry" and a thousand more Greek words, but never did a single teacher tell us how strange it is that such civilized peoples as the Germans and the French could not find in their rich languages words to express the most basic achievements of the

human mind: we are the offspring of the ancient Greeks—full stop. And no teacher could be found to tell us that even though we are the offspring of the ancient Greeks, there exist also some poor relatives who are called Greeks, and who may also be the offspring of "our" ancient ancestors. (9, my translation)

I should frame this present discussion by stressing that my critical parameters remain partial to a philosophical understanding of the spirit behind German idealism's reception of Hellenism, rather than a programmatic attempt to substantiate a theory of a continuous or discontinuous Greek history. The latter is out of the question, not only because I profess no expertise on this period of Greek history and am no historian; mostly, it is because I do not agree with this hypostatized binary of continuity and discontinuity as a fruitful model for describing the manifold expressions of historical becoming to begin with. The notion of Greek continuity has been advanced eloquently by Constantine Paparrigopoulos in the nineteenth century;[28] and though I remain sympathetic to his panoramic viewpoint of Greek history and recognize its historical necessity, I do also recognize the following fact: that in his need to buttress the ideology of the nascent Greek state, his historical vision of continuity is often overstated. As for the claims of absolute discontinuity, they now abound in contemporary Greek criticism, presenting themselves as scientific facts coming to dispel the romantic rants of the proponents of continuity. But let us recognize that they too obey ideological imperatives, serving to buttress the Europeanization of Greece and the recent introduction of postmodernism and its attendant discourse of political correctness in the Greek academy.[29]

That said, all in all, I have no interest in special interests, and quite frankly, I do not believe that my investment in the ancients' passion for freedom would be well served by arguing for special access to antiquity by the modern Greeks alone. In fact, the latter, particularist claim would be directly opposed to this more universal concern for the possibility of an experience of freedom as responsibility that motivates this study and of which the Greeks (ancient or modern) form but one of many historical examples that for linguistic, cultural, and other reasons remain unavailable to this author. Thus, far from claiming an irredentist history, I am intrigued by something else, by the other side of the coin, so to speak: by the ethicopolitical implications for contemporary theory of Europe's insistence on monopolizing the reception of Hellenism in a strange banquet of ghosts, featuring the dead Greeks on the one hand and the deadened Hesperians on the other.

While this debate of continuity and discontinuity is currently alive in the Greek-speaking context, it remains largely absent from the philosophically inclined circles of discussion of German idealism and its historiography. Furthermore, I find particularly revealing the eagerness with which contemporary discourse in Greece attempts to conform questions of its self-definition to what is perceived as a Western prototype of thinking national identity—regardless of the pointed historical differences of their respective national formations—because it wishes to streamline successfully, if belatedly, modern Greece with the European cultural and political imperatives.

The liminality of this case is thus evidenced from both the European and the Greek sides. On the one hand, in the context of postwar philosophical antihumanism, any consideration of the uncanny resemblance between recent events in Greek history and the ethical conundrums of tragic action—insofar as both involve a passion for the practical expression of human will—would be dismissed as an unreliable anthropologism, or nonphilosophical culturalism. Such historical events, which form visible instantiations of these tragic principles in our times, would be inadequate to the seriousness of philosophy, which, despite its postwar concerns for the singular, cannot really shed its deep-seated suspicion of the exceptional and the untimely.

On the other hand, the current Greek critical environment unwittingly corroborates the continental philosophical position of the end of the subject and its freedom but does so largely not in a philosophically proper method. Rather, it does so through the new ethnography—cultural studies. The recent anthology edited by Stephanos Pesmazoglou (*Myths and Ideologemes in Contemporary Greece*) is exemplary of this type of cultural demythologization, as is the following observation by Pesmazoglou himself that is supposed to awaken the Greeks from the slumber of their ancestral worship: "If, as it was aptly demonstrated during the interwar period, the then-contemporary German resembled much more his contemporary Frenchman, or Englishman than a medieval German and/or Visigoth . . . then this holds equally true with the contemporary Greek: he bears more of a resemblance to contemporary Europeans and contemporary Turks than he does to his ancient predecessors, the Athenians, the Mycenaeans, the Minoans in the absurd claims about absolute diachronic continuity in the self-sameness of the Greeks" (24–25, my translation).[30]

The explicit corollary of this method is to marginalize as nationalist or essentialist—or worse, irrational and incoherent—any philosophical meditations that focus on the *actual* (and not simply imaginary or mythological) tenacity of certain ancient principles in the modern Greek experience. The claim that a persistent disposition toward a tragic sense of freedom and justice is formative of many modern Greek authors, or that Antigonian ethics echo in acts of resistance marking the last two centuries of Greek history, risks being called an essentialist non sequitur.[31] In short, it is more fashionable, and of course less risky, to argue on the side of absolute discontinuity on an immediately available, culturally evidenced level, for any other speculation may well lead to nationalist derailment. Without underestimating the danger of essentialisms and nationalisms and the reasons why current scholarship is reluctant to consider philosophical and poetic evocations of diachrony, I submit that such one-sided treatment has its own share of theoretical and practical pitfalls.

Let us first consider summarily the most obvious objection to diachronic claims. Of all the specific historical and cultural developments that through the late-antique, Byzantine, and Ottoman empires naturally interrupted any kind of continuity and contiguity between ancients and moderns, the most obvious and groundbreaking would be the turn from paganism to monotheism—a turn that shook the foundations of the ancient world. Indeed, that the "great Pan is dead" is not news to modernity but reached Elizabeth Barrett Browning's ears from as far back as Hellenistic, early-Christian antiquity in the story of ancient sailors who first heard of it and cried it back in despair off the shores of Greece (Browning 280). The story, however, does not stop with the espousal of monotheism as the decisive stamp of discontinuity. We must also think of language: the linguistic argument, advanced by both Hölderlin and Heidegger, tells us that language—poetic language, in particular—founds a people.

But here too, this fact is either unknown or ignored: more than its ancient roots are still visible in Greek language's modern usage, along with the various other influences that have crossed its path. Strangely, this mark of the ancient language, which has been the conscious source for much of the poetic and poetological production and reflection of twentieth-century Greek writers,[32] is not enough to ground this linguistic community in its history but only to be a cause of concern. Indeed, the question of the relative continuity of language is sometimes redirected to the total discontinuity of religion, with the argument that Christianization has entirely changed the semantic universe of the language, eclipsing and distorting its original meanings. After all, as Hölderlin seems to suggest in his "Bread and Wine," poetic language involves the way a people communicates (with) its god(s) (*Hyperion and Selected Poems* 178–79); thus, if the Greeks have converted, their language must also be essentially Christian, no matter how it might preserve other modalities—latently, but also in its immanent shaping of a markedly non-Western version of Christianity[33]—that are inaudible still to the Western ear. Moreover, the lived experience of ritual practices and belief systems, which have preserved pagan elements next to Christianity (a juxtaposition that to Western thought would seem a logical conundrum, if not an atavism), is of course readily derided as an unreliable anthropologism that has no place in the ideational horizon of philosophical reflection.

A proper reception of the Greeks by the Greeks has thus been intercepted, disarticulating any relation, even one of mourning—a disarticulation that perhaps helps modern Hesperians to achieve two things. Firstly, by making the ancients a thing of the past without the least trace in the present, any potential dispute to the modern claim of an utterly original destiny is neutralized. The sibling rivalry with the "other moderns"—the modern Greeks, that is—is short-circuited thanks to the implicit assumption that they are not even coeval to this reception and have nothing to bring to the table. Secondly, as a result of this attitude, it is easier to ignore or even justify the political and intellectual disenfranchisement of that entity that came to be modern Greece over the modern period, where, until recently, it has been considered at best the distant backyard of European politics. Interestingly, this cultural atopia, this fundamental ambivalence that Greeks have in relation to their own history and that positions them somewhat askew in the modern European imaginary, might well be the very site from which to reconsider this binary of continuity and discontinuity, of Orient and Occident. Not seamlessly continuous but not really discontinuous by their own first admission, the modern Greeks gradually have felt compelled to interiorize the philosophical fait accompli, the imperative of their thorough disidentification and disaffection. Is this not what Hölderlin said they do best? Excel in the foreign, if a bit too much, and then forget themselves and disappear? A peculiar form of continuity, one dare say, of that which is never itself, of that which has never even been, as Lacoue-Labarthe suggested earlier.[34] Who are they? People with no roots, some inchoate Byzantines banded opportunistically together, with no claim to any recognizable culture that existed before the nineteenth century, into which they were born somewhat ex nihilo. This is at least one of the muted, if not always so silent, narratives of this omission.

As I already hinted, this impossible binary of continuity and discontinuity that structures the consciousness of modern Greece has never been given due attention in the European imaginary, and its philosophical and political implications are too intricate and manifold to be fully delineated in this rather sketchy presentation. However, even if we cannot follow all the contours of this history, it is important to at least introduce the general peculiarities that classical reception inaugurates when it enters the unstable topology of Greece, both ancient and modern: at times the origin of Europe, at times honorable foreigner (a guest of bygone times, as in Hölderlin), and at other times the enslaved neighbor from Europe's periphery. It is therefore my contention that the topic of Oriental versus Occidental cannot be exhausted at the doorstep of German idealism, or of the poststructuralist reception of Hölderlin and Hegel, but has to extend its chronotope to address this uncharted other territory, an extension that may prove surprisingly fruitful in addressing urgent contemporary questions regarding globalization or even the much-debated notion of the clash of civilizations.

To conclude this detour: despite the fact that almost every branch of poststructuralism has advanced some sort of critique of instrumentalization and despite the widely accepted deconstruction of the metaphysics of presence, a systematic critique of the instrumentalization of the past by the present (a specifically geographical and cultural Western European present) in poststructuralist historiography itself is, to my knowledge, still lacking.[35]

Between Hölderlin and Nietzsche

Following in Hölderlin's vein, Nietzsche, Heidegger, and later thinkers who favor Heidegger, especially Heidegger's Nietzsche, have gradually intensified the same historical algorithm: whatever poetic or philosophical event was incipient in ancient Greece met its end there also — an end that Nietzsche himself had still deemed worthy of mourning but that we now have almost entirely recast as a welcome sign of our irreducible alterity. The end of tragedy, in particular, enjoys a greater ethical significance from German idealism onward, because tragedy had hitherto offered the exemplary site of contestation between the two foundational ethical categories of freedom and necessity.

As I have already mentioned, Dennis Schmidt makes this amply clear when he traces the reasons why the German idealist preoccupation with the tragic followed from the impact of Kant's thought. Schmidt argues convincingly that three basic tenets of Kant's philosophy are all reflected in the tragic genre, such that his intellectual heirs found in tragedy a fruitful model to rehearse them: (1) Kant's antinomial mode of thinking, particularly the third antinomy between freedom and nature; (2) the importance of aesthetic form for the cultivation of ethical consciousness; and (3) the reactivation of the sublime (75). Concerning this third aspect, Schmidt focuses on its importance for the discussion of monstrosity and sacrifice in tragedy, but I think that the sublime's relation to tragedy rests more prominently in the antinomial affective states it produces in the subject—negative in its awe, positive in the subsequent feeling of elevation. However, tragedy's reliance on antinomial conflict proves still insufficient to the kind of ambivalence, or undecidability, that is privileged by poststructuralist thought. In fact, that tragic freedom and elevation oppose brutal necessity serves not only to disqualify tragedy as an example of "good" undecidability but also to invalidate tragedy's ethical claim altogether. Eventually, the historical weight in post-Hegelian and, especially, postwar European thought tips the scales of tragic action always on the side of external determination: this is more obvious in the continental philosophical discourses, where the infinitization of alterity is the new name for necessity (God as the absolute Other). However, even when theory espouses the rhetoric of agency (as social construction and identity politics do), its agents are hardly responsible for their choices. Their acts are effects of social structures, and they themselves are products of cultural determination. Whether God or culture, only one side of the tragic polarity is fulfilled.

But does Sophocles's tragedy say so unequivocally that necessity wins in the case of Antigone, just because she died when the king wished her to die?[36] Or that she could have avoided her death had she, Creon, and the kinship structure constructed themselves differently?[37] Either way, a certain sanctimony becomes unavoidable at the moment tragic action is required to conform to an idea. Ideas—even those of ambivalence, multiplicity, and the undecidable, which have gained currency in recent years—remain ideas; and in their search for an ethical imperative, they actually neutralize tragedy's ethical import, which stems precisely from tragedy's refusal to be bound by ideational systems.

Here one can draw a crucial distinction between Nietzsche and his heirs.

For Nietzsche, the tragic worldview is exemplary, even in its evanescence, precisely because it claims a relation both to freedom and necessity. That the conditions for tragedy are nonexistent in the present world, because freedom collapsed into necessity, and that submission is subsequently hypostatized as the only responsible ethical stance—this is the dawn of *our* tragedy. From Schelling onward, what has been called "the tragic"—which, among other things, denoted the freedom of self-overcoming (and not only the self-erasure of absolute fatalism)—is still inscribed both in the ideas and the emotional texture of Nietzsche's writings on tragedy: melancholy for the loss of a beautiful death mixed with upheaval against whatever erects itself as a necessity.[38]

Even though this stance can be easily dismissed as a metaphysical nostalgia for a "full subject," I would like to suggest that it marks the untimely moment of Nietzsche's truth, his openly tragic insight for an unwittingly tragic age. Nietzsche's historiography takes freedom seriously, while our age—to the detriment of modern ethical life, I believe—has rendered freedom ethically suspect through a peculiar revaluation of the revaluator. Now, the one who resists becomes the perpetrator of violence by refusing to endure the necessity of his or her oppression. Antigone's distinction between human oppression (Creon) that can and ought to be resisted and natural necessity (the evils sent by the gods) is rendered inoperative in the post-Hegelian world, where God is resurrected in the state.[39] We are left then with this dangerous slippage where historical contingency stands equivalent to natural necessity, a slippage yielding a darkly pious ethical imperative: infinite abandonment to necessity, the destruction of any kind of will, the moral and ontological validation of unfreedom. Strangely too, as necessity becomes humanized, or at least secularized in the state entity, human resistance, the other pole of the freedom/necessity binary, becomes nullified. Once able to challenge even the gods, the human being now can no longer even recognize the human origins of the state or any other social structure; a new and menacing deity, the structure reigns through the law of abandonment to its necessity.

To endure this terrible new transcendence of domination and determination as our proper necessity is poststructuralism's new ascetic ideal, perhaps even its contribution to European nihilism. Thus, Nietzsche's tragic attachment to the possibility of individual revolt as self-overcoming was critiqued by Heidegger as a thinking still bound by the metaphysics of the subject and of the will—the mortal error that makes Nietzsche a tragic thinker, after all. In turn, this critique is upheld and further belabored by Blanchot, Derrida, Levinas, and a host of other poststructuralist thinkers, for whom abandonment to necessity (the Other) is the minimal trace left of the tragic world.[40] Tragedy's relevance becomes its irrelevance: the insouciant prerogative for freedom and self-determination that is by nature violent becomes a past privilege that does not suit the theoretical piety of our present.

These are some of the discontents of what Simon Goldhill calls "the generalization of 'the tragic'" from German idealism onward, a generalization that risks even in the most inspired analyses to hypostatize and hierarchize particular sufferings as "truly tragic," escalating eventually into the claim of the "beyond-tragic" of absolute suffering. In short, the moment the tragic takes flight from tragedy, from the contradictory demands of action and experience to the theoretical requirements of a nonmetaphysical ontology, the work of instrumentalization sets in. Despite my disagreements with some of Goldhill's examples of the political appropriation of the tragic,[41] I could not agree more with his modest conclusion: "Before we write a sentence that begins 'the tragic is . . . ,' 'the essence of tragedy is . . . ,' we should recall how often ancient tragedies show up the inadequacy of such generalizations as a response to the violent narratives of human conflict" (62).

This parenthesis on the instrumentalization of the tragic is of course closely tied to the questions of self-reflexivity and belatedness germane to modernity: with no tragedies (acts) of our own, we seek the tragic (ideas, essences) through which to reflect on our predicament. However, as I have mentioned earlier, this introspection may not be an exclusively modern European concern but one that appeared in some guise to the ancient Greeks as well. Surveying the ancient intellectual tradition itself, as it progressively relocated truth from poetry to natural philosophy to political thought, from the Homeric bards to the Ionian philosophers to the Athenian Sophists, we can surmise that this early/late split was already operative. The distinction of sunrise and sunset, holy pathos and reflexivity, ancient and modern, which Hölderlin inscribed specifically within the tragic genre in the work of Sophocles, can be in fact further referred to one more set of terms: it is the distinction between poetry and philosophy—and to be even more generically precise, between archaic poetry and philosophy. By archaic poetry, I mean Homeric and Hesiodic poetry, those mythopoetic and theogonic compositions where myth and word collapse into each other. Such collapse was deeply problematic for philosophy's own beginnings, which were intended to be the departure from myth. Thus, Heraclitus, who criticized Homer and Hesiod on account of having no account (no logos),[42] was echoed again in Plato. Yet it would be too hasty to equate Heraclitus's charge against mythopoesis with a wholesale condemnation of poetry qua creation. On the contrary, the oblique and paradoxical style of the obscure philosopher offers an exemplary instance of what Heidegger calls poetizing thinking (*dichtendes Denken*).[43]

This poetizing dimension of pre-Socratic thought was noted by Jean-Pierre Vernant as well, though not in these exact terms. In his structural-anthropological history of the origins of Greek thought, Vernant elaborates on the early/classical split and its implications not only for the sphere of philosophy per se but more generally for the nature of the Greeks that had shifted significantly from the archaic to the classical times. Passing from Heraclitus to Plato—from an early form of rationality concerned with cosmic order to classical philosophy concerned with Being and Knowing (Vernant 130–31)—announced a simultaneous passage from one type of existence to another, an existence crystallized around the political organization and self-understanding of the Greeks. In this schema, despite the tremendous leap they took from a religious toward a secularized cosmogony and from *basileia* to *isonomia* (from kingship to equality before the law), the so-called natural philosophers appear to Vernant to be "closer to mythological construct than to scientific theory" (104). In contrast, the classical philosopher emerges as a full-fledged political theorist, disinterested in the natural world and drawn to practical reason, the kind of reason that seeks not to explore nature but to regulate human relations (132). Vernant's genealogy traces the classical philosopher less to the sage and more to the expert sophist and the rhetorician.

Peculiarly, then, the Greeks afford us two kinds of beginning: the beginning and the beginning of *an* end—not necessarily of *the* end but of an end of that first beginning.[44] Therefore, Hölderlin's very gesture of defining modernity as a radically new epoch is itself an old gesture. Undoubtedly, Hölderlin's world is different from that of the ancients, but what remains essentially the same is the impulse to articulate this difference around an age-old binary: passion versus measure, spontaneity versus self-reflection, or poetry versus philosophy. It goes without saying that, like all binaries, this one too cannot keep its poles firmly distinct from one another. After all, poetry does require measure, and the Ionian philosophers did think in verse. Hölderlin also, whose distinction of ancients and moderns around the binary of pathos versus measure instigated my comments here, was concerned with poetic measure and form. In fact, his preoccupations with the Greeks stem chiefly from this practical urge to find the "lawful calculation" for modern poetry,[45] and it is with this question of proper poetic measure that he opens his "Remarks on 'Oedipus'" (*Essays and Letters* 101). However, for Hölderlin such formal calculations hinge on a more primordial calculus, one that cannot be reduced to simple arithmetic: this is the calculus of destiny, the measure of the immeasurable that shows itself in our relation to the holy.[46] Hence, the terms "measure" and "poetry," momentarily and perhaps counterintuitively constructed as opposites, should resonate in two different but related registers. Measure as metrics refers to the prosodic aspect of poetry; but poetry as *poesis*, and not as simple versification, points beyond metrics, opening to the sacred space of creation, where measure makes sense only as the measure of the immeasurable.

Yet to ask the question of measure even as it pertains to the immeasurable—that is, to the holy—is itself the burden of a self-reflexive era, where the relation to measure is never a given but the result of a conscious search. Thus, while poetry and philosophy both partake in measure as well as spontaneity, Hölderlin's narrative invites for its elucidation the broader distinction that I am making here, which maintains heuristically at least a more definitive gap between the spontaneous principles of poetry and the formalizing impulses of philosophy. From Homer to Heraclitus, then, as well as from Homer to Plato (but also, and significantly so, from Heraclitus to Plato), the difference in the being of the Greeks can be traced along this difference between poetry and philosophy. The Heraclitian and Platonic critique of the poets thus bespeaks a conscious distinction between two modes of discourse, one of which is associated with an earlier and more incomplete way of thinking, while the other marks the beginning of a new and more systematic era for thinking. This quarrel is very old indeed by the time book 10 of the *Republic* was written.

Interestingly, this early/late distinction describes not only the passage from poetry to philosophy but also the passage *within* philosophy from contingent observations to more organized forms of thought. Philosophy too, in this narrative at least, seems to have been born twice: first with the pre-Socratics, then with Socrates, whose own double sailing thematizes such double beginning.[47] Both beginnings, however, share a stark opposition to what preexisted philosophy and thus had to be reckoned with by being displaced: poetry, the sign of the archaic, of the naïve, of what needs to be thought because it cannot think itself. This is why Socrates in the *Apology* counts the poets among the unwise, for they cannot explain the things they say, having no consistent logos as Heraclitus had already charged: "They do not write poetry through wisdom, but by a sort of genius and inspiration; they are like diviners or soothsayers who also say many admirable things, but don't understand a word of what they say" (22c). Suddenly, the significance shifts from what one says to whether one understands or means what one says, implying that the human being is in full mastery of the logos. This is why tragedy gets the hardest of blows in the *Republic*,[48] since tragedy insists that a human being, though free and proud, cannot possess such mastery. The concomitant question, which will be returning in many guises throughout this study, is whether tragedy itself knows, whether it knows that it knows, or whether it just shows.

At any rate, I would suggest that the reason philosophy has pitted itself so relentlessly against tragedy involves what these two accounts of the human share at the core: both philosophy and tragedy point to a certain horizon that goes beyond gnosiological questions to address the practical—that is, ethical or political, if you will—question of how to live. Even the most abstract philosophical discussions today have a vital stake in this concern of how to exist properly in the world. The currently widespread prioritization of ethics over ontology—the passion with questions of community, the neighbor, the Other, and so on—reflect, at the limit, a passion for the question of the good life. Tragedy too, in showing the trials and tribulations of unsuspecting humans, addresses the question of the order of this world, of where the human being properly belongs in time.

By way of recapitulating what is at stake in these disparate splits and double beginnings from the ancients to the moderns and within the ancients themselves, it should be emphasized that the ancient/modern distinction is not a chronological one. It cannot be assigned a simple date either in modernity or in antiquity. These splits are linked with certain figures or with certain discursive shifts and changes in art forms. But their alignment is historical not in a sequential sense; rather, each time they occur, such alignments articulate in their specific way the otherwise ever-existing, transhistorical demand to define one's present in relation to one's past. I suggest that the construction of an ancient/modern split appears as a defining historical distinction at moments when this difference between poetic and philosophic modes of discourse comes to the fore, with the reflexive, philosophical understanding positing itself as the more modern, sophisticated form of discourse than the poetic. The ancients then were also confronted with a modernity, which they identified with the progress of systematic thought as opposed to the archaic indeterminacy of the poetic world.

Jacqueline de Romilly points to an ancient source, unavailable to us in extant form, that confirms this: having already mastered the rhetorical techniques of the Sophists, Euripides wrote the tragedy *Antiope*, a poetic work that consciously addressed this split within the ancient world. Textual citations indicate that the tragedy staged a debate between the sons of Antiope regarding which way of life is good. While one of the sons favored the poetic and creative life, the other sided with the life of action, which in this particular context should be understood to mean the civic life, the life that involves discursive rather than poetic modes of expression. Not surprisingly, adds de Romilly, Plato's *Gorgias* quotes this Euripidean passage where Callicles exhorts civic life, confirming once again that the debate between the poetic and the politicophilosophical modes of life was very much alive among the Greeks themselves (*Pourquoi la Grèce?* 245–46). The flip side of this historical realization shows that the very gesture of distinction Hölderlin and modern thought in general claim as quintessentially modern (not only are we different from the ancients, but we are marking uncharted territory in articulating this difference) is essentially the effect of a repetition: the modern is as ancient as the ancient, but it is not as clear whether the ancient—or rather the archaic—can ever be subsumed by the modern. It may mark and haunt the modern, as it marked and haunted Plato's and Heraclitus's own modernity, but it could never be subsumed by philosophical modernization. It thus had to be thrown out of the polis in a cathartic gesture (catharsis stems from *kathairein*, which means separation and purging) that disavows it because it cannot ultimately regulate it.

If the Greeks were already somewhat reflexive, as both Hölderlin suggests and as the difference of the ancient philosophers from the poets does as well, then the question is, how does our reflexivity differ? Is it a matter of quantity, in that we are *more* reflexive than the Greeks? Or is it a matter of quality, in that the *mode* of reflexivity itself has been transformed through the practice of self-reflection? And regardless of either of these questions, what does it mean that we enter the modern era of reflexivity with Socrates, that is, with—not without—the Greeks? It is with respect to this question of reflexivity, which begs the question of the limit of thinking (for instance, is there thinking beyond conceptual reflection?), that the question of tragedy remains not just as relevant or urgent but absolutely as contemporary as it was for the Greeks.

Tragedy, Nietzsche told us, ended with Euripides, because his work resembled more a Socratic dialogue than a tragic plot. Aristotle's laudatory description of Euripides in book 13 of the *Poetics* as "the most tragic of the poets" (1453a29–30) on account of his technically complex plots turned out to be the very reason Nietzsche disliked this poet: Euripides was too self-reflexive for his own good and, thus, the least tragic of the poets. Let us note again how the ancient/modern split is reproduced in Nietzsche's distinction between the earlier, more poetic Aeschylus and the later, more philosophical Euripides, even though Nietzsche, to the dismay of a traditional philosophical audience, prefers the poetic to the philosophical. At any rate, hoping my playfulness will not be dismissed as a mere game of topsy-turvy, I will venture to say that Euripides was not self-reflexive enough; for if he were, he would have called himself a dialectician instead of a tragedian. But Euripides was no Hegel, and he did not reflect on his writing practice critically, even if his tragedies sounded like a critical practice to Nietzsche. Thus, if tragedy indeed died with Euripides—and this is not even Nietzsche's last word on its fate—it died unreflexively, unaware of its own nascent reflexivity. Therefore, it also died with its birthmark intact—namely, with its everlasting appeal to the unreflexive—and this could be as good an explanation as any for the enigmatic relation Nietzsche's title of birth has to this death narrative. Tragedy ultimately lacked the resources to reflect on the destructive principles that reflexivity imported in its plots. This consideration, which is rather dormant in Nietzsche's text, could add another dimension to his critique of modern reflexivity: after all, how good is a reflexivity that began unreflexively, without the ability to think of its own advent? And is it not this initial blind spot that later transforms itself into another peculiarly unreflexive moment of reflexivity, that of the theoretical false optimism of modern thought, which dismisses everything it cannot normalize and surmount? What if, in its compulsion to deny the insurmountable by rationalizing it, reflexivity returns to the unreflexive aspect of tragedy through the backdoor? However, such furtiveness already points to a distortion—namely, the modern distortion that conflates reflexivity with thought and unreflexivity with its opposite, the lack of thought.

We should then clarify what the terms reflexive and unreflexive mean beyond this immediate antonymic relation. The unreflexive element of tragedy, I want to insist, is not an enemy to thought, insofar as thought involves an engagement with the world that is not limited to speculation, explanation, and understanding, insofar as thought is not just another synonym for rationality. In such a scheme, tragedy's rejection of reflexivity proves essential to the domain of the insurmountable, of which tragedy is an expression, while reflexivity's thoughtless denial of the insurmountable belongs to the sphere of delusion—the farce that is *our* tragedy. I can foresee the immediate objection that this is exactly what contemporary philosophy has been all about: the critique of rationality and the acceptance of the insurmountable—what else could one make of Heidegger's thrownness or Levinas's abandon? This is correct, but I find that its vision of the insurmountable does not address the point I am attempting to make: by linking it exclusively to what supersedes the human from the outside, contemporary theory already delimits the purview of the insurmountable to the inhuman alone. I suggest that we view it as what simply exceeds, and whose provenance cannot be so certainly decided (or perhaps calculated) between the within and the without.

At any rate, all this in retrospect sheds new light on Hölderlin's remarks that reflexivity qua calculation is our modern nature. This is also the point where Hölderlin and Nietzsche radically diverge; for even though Nietzsche is also a kind of cultural historiographer, he does not reduce individual human expression to a cultural predicament. Unlike Hölderlin's categorical diagnosis of modernity as irreducibly reflexive, a diagnosis that disallows any possibility for an untimely consciousness to emerge, Nietzsche commends the improbable, antihistorical emergence of individuals like Socrates or his fictional Zarathustra. That calculation is our nature, then, constitutes the very tragedy of modernity, but one way to deny this inconvenient truth has been to construct modernity as the end of tragedy. Hölderlin himself certainly bemoaned the modern blindness that mistakes the calculus of destiny for a merely technic understanding, thus reducing the immeasurable measure to a mechanical calculation. But this worry is confined to the uses and abuses of reflexivity not to its nature per se.

The problem, I suggest, lies rather deeper with Hölderlin's unshakeable conviction that we are now irremediably reflexive beings, that our ontology is calculation and reflection. This is not at all to say that he is wrong in his description—to the contrary—but rather to register my unease with the critical complacency that arises with such an overvaluation of reflexivity. Indeed, Hölderlin's assertion of our difference from the ancients with respect to reflexivity has assumed the form of a categorical imperative in much of continental thought today, where any talk of return to the ancients—minus of course Hölderlin's own, which is exempted for being a reflexive turn—is disparaged as futile and nostalgic. I suspect that the philosophical aversion that such a backward gaze generates has much to do with its obstinate childlikeness, its naïve, aberrant refusal to accept what is considered obvious and reasonable—in other words, with its adherence to a certain passion that could never translate into a theoretically reflexive stance. Such passion, along with many others that inhabit the world of tragedy, is cast out as ontologically and historically impossible.[49] Like Lot's unfortunate wife, who could not help but look back nostalgically on her ungodly town, the one who turns away from the god of reflexivity and toward that unilluminated ancient time must pay for the indiscretion: the thought will turn to stone, hard and raw like its object of contemplation, unsuitable for the flexible operations of modern discursivity.

There might yet be another way to approach Hölderlin, one that does not simply dwell on the hypostatization of this difference between ancients and moderns, unreflexivity and reflexivity, but that emphasizes the alternative vision of the poet's own dissatisfaction with the current state of affairs. This would require rethinking his conclusions about our relation to the Greeks from within the terms of his own thought. Hölderlin tells us in the letter to Böhlendorff that the hardest thing to master freely is one's own nature. This is why the Greeks, whose inner nature was holy pathos, were better at mastering what was foreign to them, reflexive measure. For us moderns, whose nature is reflexive calculation, the chiasmus dictates that we would be better at mastering holy pathos, thus also fulfilling the nature of the Greeks, who have been our proper foreigners. Only after that can we begin to address the excellence of our proper nature: calculation, measure, reflection.

However, the problem with this modern task lies in a twofold paradox: First, the very task of mastering holy pathos sounds not just impossible but actually impious. It was perhaps the gods' peculiar gift to the Greeks to give them holy pathos as their first nature, so that—as Hölderlin maintains—they could not master it on account of its proximity, mastering instead what is more suited for mastery: measure and form. That they failed at being most pious was the Greeks' piety, so to speak. Yet as I mentioned earlier, no historiography fails to aggrandize the grave and noble tasks of its own present in relation to the past, and Hölderlin's is no exception, despite his otherwise critical stance against the moderns. His response to this modern paradox of an impious mastering of pathos is rather well-known and richly commented on: our impiety constitutes a "pious infidelity," an even more difficult and higher order of piety that we are called to join and during which we turn away from the god(s) who absconded, thus remembering, imitating, and honoring piously their gesture of infidelity.[50] Suddenly, the Greeks' felicitous failure to master holy pathos, which makes them less excellent in piety precisely because it recognizes the human inability to master the sacred, is transformed into an actual lack in need of completion: the completion will come in (the future of) our modernity as another impiety, which must be higher, being performed as it is by a reflexive nature that can recognize and imitate the movement of the god(s). This futural, messianic thrust, however, despite all its various appeals these days, serves, among other things, to confirm the theoretical optimism that often defers confronting present failures to the project of a world to come, as it symmetrically and cheerfully announces this same present to be the past's completion.

The second paradox involves the *unnatural* nature of our own modern nature. If our inner proclivity is already reflexive calculation (something by nature learnable!), then a question arises concerning the meaning of a nature that is already acquisition—namely, the meaning of "second" in "second nature" when there is no first to begin with, or when first is second. Can there be such a nature that is simply acquisition, and can any god save us when nature is thus entirely confined to the reflexive?[51] The Greeks could learn form because form is learnable. But how can one excel in holy pathos when one's path to it is only reflection? These are the harder questions that I believe Hölderlin's text opens, but does not answer—in fact, it cannot answer, because their answer cannot come from within a speculative apparatus. The difficulty, or what I would call the tragedy, of the moderns is that we have to learn what is by nature unlearnable—passion—at a time when our resources are limited to reflection. What would it be nonetheless for us to imagine reaching holy pathos completely outside our native route, that is, completely outside reflection? It would mean learning not only to give up our proclivity for mechanistic calculation but even to give up measure as a conscious question and quest. For what makes measure disclosive rather than mechanistic in the first place is its givenness, its priority over any conscious searching and mastering. In fact, I would suggest that the moment measure was reduced to mechanical calculation most likely coincides with the moment measure became the object of a search.

In this sense, more than ever, the wisdom of tragedy may be most urgent, since tragic works illumine how the mechanism of reflection can be exceeded, all the while using intelligible forms of expression. Tragedy shows measure in its givenness—the givenness of invincible necessity against which we measure ourselves, but also another kind of givenness, whose inherent dynamism makes it harder to determine it as precisely that, a sure given: this is the gift of character, that admixture of chance and cultivation, of nature and desire, that fundamental improbability that makes out of human beings unique, strange, and unrepeatable vehicles of their own fate. As such, tragic measure reveals itself as the unexpected destination of a course of action, not as the most unpleasant of already pondered answers to a contemplative question.

Furthermore, if we are not to reduce tragedy to a didactic diatribe about how to avoid catastrophe by limiting oneself to one's proper niche, we see that tragedy does not pertain to neat limits but to contestation. Tragedy is contestation of limits, entrance into the unknown; and this is why, in blatant disregard to the democratic setting against which they act, its protagonists are still kings and heroes, not everyday folks. Could this very anachronism of tragedy, which proved so relevant for democratic Athens, prove again equally relevant for our allegedly ultrademocratic era? This is indeed the question to which Nietzsche's work responds in the affirmative, pointing out the fact that we now live in the age of the tragedy of science. With Socrates, Nietzsche observes, we stopped being spectators of an aesthetic form and unwittingly brought art into life. Ever since, we have lived the tragedy of reflexivity that—paradoxically, yet in tandem with the tragic law—has rendered us unreflexive and, in fact, blind to our own tragic condition. Far from announcing a categorical end of tragedy, this understanding pushes us to see where tragedy has migrated today, what are its new forms, its new topoi. By recognizing in Socrates the new Satyr, Nietzsche again pointed us in the right direction: tragedy in modernity is not simply a topic of philosophy; it is philosophy. As if by some strange revenge plot, philosophy assumes the shape of its ancient foe.

(Ir)resolutions

When the magnitude of his crime was revealed to Oedipus, he inflicted on himself blindness and exile by way of atonement. This means that in some way the ancient parricide understood the stakes of that fatal accident. But he *understood* by way of suffering—in his aimless peregrinations, in his wrath and curses against his own sons, in *living out* this fallen existence. Nietzsche's agonizing question to us in his madman parable can thus be rearticulated as the question of whether we will be able one day to stand deservingly next to Oedipus: will we ever understand the magnitude of our parricide, of the death of God? Or, better, will we ever be worthy of the suffering that this death has brought us? For Nietzsche, it would hardly be an issue of academic exercise of reflecting on this death through an objective exposition of the logic by which the mono- of monotheism devolved easily into a nothing, as the god who became human became the state and soon disappeared into the meaningless brutality of diffuse power. In contrast to this conceptual mechanics, Nietzsche's understanding involves shudder, the capacity to be riveted by this event so as to react to it in a worthy manner. Has the death of God shaken us to the point of worthy reaction?

It is my modest proposal that contemporary theory's new moral certainty—that the ghost of God, this impersonal nothing, is the powerful new necessity in front of which the annihilated human must obey—presents itself too quickly (and perhaps too dangerously) as the solution. It condenses in too short a time those light years, while it is unusually confident of its radicalizations, of its theoretical capacity to preview the event and, thus, neutralize a priori its impact. How can there be the threat of a real end, a nondiscursive fissure, a felt wound, when all these are theorized and accounted for in advance? How can life dare take place and commit such hubris in front of theory? Beyond the end of tragedy, the death of God, and the end of man, there remains only theory, the endless proclaimer of ends and supersessions. An achievement, indeed! Yet at the end of Nietzsche's history stands not the Hegelian sage but someone like the blind, suffering Oedipus. Light years communicate an event that has already happened but reaches us later. And this does not mean that it eluded its agents but rather the simpler fact that it eludes us and that we are unworthy of it until we are able to relive it—not necessarily with the deliberation of a mimetic reenactment but in the fortitude of happenstance. Perhaps, then, the question is not whether Sophocles understood his character or Oedipus understood himself in his own fiction. And perhaps even more than that, it is not the question of whether we moderns can complete the Greeks through disclaimers and supersessions: to think that is to continue being under the spell of the angry Oedipus. The question is whether we can let him touch us with his blind touch and bless us, like he did Theseus, the just Athenian king, and so cast out his marvelous spell.

Orient versus Occident, continuity versus discontinuity—a quarrel whose resolution seems to have been long decided in our Westernized world of technology, science, and reflection. We live decidedly, Hölderlin announced, in the world of reflexivity, with "our" Greeks a lost people of incompletion, from whom we can only keep the importance of the relation to a creative becoming, but a becoming they and we could never share. We are discrete, different, completely and irrevocably discontinuous. And yet, is not the very cosmological distinction of Orient or Occident that marks the history of modern philosophy the indelible mark of a certain Greece, by which I mean this and only this: a pagan echo; a mimetic anachronism; the solar splendor; the trace of nature; the real and visible worlds that refuse to disappear in the monotheistic—hence, absolutizing—path of modern reflection?

An Old Quarrel

POETRY AND PHILOSOPHY

Plato as First Philosopher of the Tragic

Having sketched the general historical and philosophical context of the quarrel of ancients and moderns, which hinges on the significance of art and nature for the Greeks as opposed to for us, I will now turn to the more specific quarrel between art and philosophy. My focus will be on two versions of the end of art—one ancient, the other modern: Plato's banishment of the poets from his ideal city and Hegel's famous declaration that "art is, and remains for us, on the side of its highest destiny, a thing of the past" (*Lectures on Aesthetics* 13).[1] Before delving into this project, some words of clarification are due concerning potential objections to the interchangeability of the terms "poetry," which my title—following Plato[2]—juxtaposes to philosophy, and "art," which I will often use in lieu of poetry.

Andrzej Warminski, for instance, whose reading of Hölderlin I have engaged in the previous chapter, insists on a sharp distinction between art and poetry. In his argument, art is synonymous with the image and, therefore, with a mimetic, symbolic impulse. It follows that art belongs to the sphere of representation and reflection from which aesthetic narratives such as Hegel's proceed. In contrast, poetry's reliance on words, sounds, rhythms, and tones exemplifies the antimimetic thrust of language that Warminski aligns with rhetoric and allegory as opposed to image and symbol. Poetics as linguistic antimimesis, then, is presented as the other of the dominant reflexive tradition of aesthetics and representation. It is, of course, not my intention here to assess the merits of so firm a distinction between language and image; whatever its merits or pitfalls, it is certainly instrumental to Warminski's general argument and consistent with his privileging of rhetoric over mimesis.[3] I am merely citing it as a likely critical objection against my choice to use poetry and art synonymously—a choice, however, that is not arbitrary on my part. Insofar as poesis means an act of creation in general and is not limited to works of prosody alone, the English term "art" applies comprehensively to this creative domain, while the term "poetry" describes rather exclusively verse. Additionally, my decision conforms with the thinkers I discuss in this chapter: it conforms with Hegel, whom Warminski critiques for reading the Greeks aesthetically (instead of rhetorically) in order to invent them as the origin of his own Western aesthetic narrative; it also conforms with Giorgio Agamben, with whom I conclude this chapter and whose discussion of art encompasses both linguistic and nonlinguistic works.

Above all, however, I follow Plato, who does not confine poesis to verse when he raises the problematic of creative works, even though it is true that tragic verse does preoccupy him the most, as it is also true that his attitude toward tragedy remains of utmost relevance to this study. Nevertheless, Plato also speaks of music, painting, and their interrelation with poetry, since they all play an equally important role in affecting the human soul. In fact, as philosopher and art historian Edgar Wind has observed, Plato's suspicion of art in his time was largely due to a recent development that had rendered the different branches of art independent of one another and thus brought about the fragmentation of the human soul.[4] As the arts grew isolated within their autonomous domains, they targeted different registers of the soul, compartmentalizing the human being and fostering discord rather than harmony among its faculties:

> It is precisely this development of the part in isolation from the whole that, because of its inherently destructive force, and its impulse towards self-sufficient perfection, leads to disruption and discord. Once the arts have become free their balanced hierarchy of relationships with one another also begins to shift. Now a harmonious rhythm which is suited to a noble gesture may invest one that is ignoble, and we may be so enchanted by its magic that we either fail to notice that the gesture is ignoble or feel that it actually heightens the charm of the effect.... During the transition from the fifth to the fourth century, Greek art did, in fact, undergo that refinement of its several branches, and that assertion of the separate identity of each, against which Plato directs all the resources of his logic and eloquence. ... Plato contends that this shift affects not only art in the narrower sense,

but all other spheres of life. It penetrates Greek philosophical and legal thinking in the doctrines of the Sophists, and Greek politics in the persuasions of the demagogues. (Wind 6–7)

Wind is correct to note that this condition of discord did not constitute for Plato (and for the ancients more generally) a salutary moment in human culture, in direct opposition to the moderns who regard discord as the sole mode of progress.[5] But if the fragmentation of art induced psychic discord, a more integrative approach to art practice would not be the automatic solution either. At this juncture, it is crucial to recall that tragedy was for the Greeks not simply text but this type of integrative synthesis of linguistic, visual, and vocalic elements in a bodily mimesis. Yet it was exactly this *holistic* character of tragic mimesis, which so vividly invited further emulation, that contributed to Plato's disapproval of the morality of the tragedians, even though he directed his critique mainly against the mythic plots. In other words, the very excellence of art—its *total* virtuosity and capacity to touch overwhelmingly the human soul—presents also the greatest danger. To quote Wind again:

> The same forces to which Greek art owes its highest point of development are those which broke up and destroyed the Greek state. The same power of language and versatility of form which enables the Greek as artist to attain perfection deprived the Greek as citizen and the Greek as statesman of his mainstay. And this proposition, which Plato, from the context of his own time and place, recognizes as decreeing the fate of his own nation, is generalized in his work into a universal principle destined to claim validity far beyond the confines of the Greek world: the principle that art and the state are by their very nature in conflict, since precisely those tensions between the powers of the soul which the legislator attempts to overcome and resolve are those which the artist maintains and intensifies. The passions the law forbids us are those out of which the dramatist creates his tragedies. (7–8)

Therefore, Plato's decision to subordinate art to the state is inextricably linked to his negative but nonetheless high appraisal of art's power. By way of anticipating the gist of my argument, let me make the following observation: for all our contemporary talk about art and our fetishization of art and the artist's freedom, Plato's estimation of it remains ultimately a foreign experience to us. For him, art had the power to bind and to loose; for us, it is a pleasantly domesticated commodity even when it terribly wishes to shock or disrupt us. In fact, our relation to art is best described by this vicious circle: just as we render ourselves comfortable in art's freedom, it pursues all venues to unsettle us—obscenity, horror, irony, indifference, nihilism. And as such venues become permissible, so art's shock value is reduced to an insignificant gimmick in the space of representation.

In elaborating this age-old tension between philosophy and art and the double end of art in Plato and Hegel, I hope to unravel at least three layers of the tragic at work in this contestation as well as in the relation of ancients to moderns. Firstly, I maintain that Plato's attitude toward art was of a tragic nature, something exemplified in his very critique of the tragedians that relied on an overestimation rather than underestimation of art. When, in book 10 of the *Republic*, Socrates laments the fact that he will have to ban the poet he loves—Homer—in order to keep the city safe, Plato confronts us with the tragic logic of a dilemma whose poles will remain *always* irreconcilable (art versus the polis) and whose resolution demands an inevitable sacrifice of one or the other pole. This "always" of tragic irreconcilability is vastly different from Hegel's optimistic historical narrative of art, in which, once art was sublated into philosophy, we would be spared its dispute with politics. However, to say that Plato's response to tragedy was tragic is to imply that Plato's philosophy as a tragic philosophy is also the first philosophy of the tragic, in contrast to the German idealist and like-minded contemporary philosophical claims that the Greeks had tragedies but no notion of the tragic qua metadramaturgical worldview.

This is also Stephen Halliwell's thesis in *The Aesthetics of Mimesis*: "One commonly drawn corollary of the Germanic cast of interest in the tragic is the claim that while ancient Greece created the first and most concentrated tradition of dramatic tragedy, it lacked anything that can be classified as an explicit notion of the tragic. But I contend . . . that there are important grounds for ascribing to Plato the first conscious delineation of something we can coherently identify as 'the tragic'" (99). Insofar as a theory of tragedy is supposed to draw from theater (or whatever other particular art form) some universal conclusions about the world, Halliwell shows that Plato's reading of the tragedians does exactly that: in the plots of the tragedians, Plato finds the aspects that define human life existentially to be tragic—a flawed, scarred, and unharmonious life. But this is also where Plato radically diverges from the tragedians. Tragic life, in Plato's view, is not worthy of being repeated: this is the cardinal fault of theater, which seduces the spectators into perpetuating a false state of existence. Instead, the tragic life is in dire need of being redirected: this is the promise of transcendence given by philosophy in its contemplation of the true life of the Ideas—a destination toward which the human being should strive with no guarantee it will ever reach it. Yet in insisting exactly on this distance that separates worldly life from the true life—an insistence for which Plato has been sharply criticized in modern thought—Plato's philosophical translation of tragedy into the tragic itself remains faithful to the element of human inadequacy that was at the heart of so many tragedies. Put differently, Plato's philosophy of the tragic is itself tragic. In contrast, the philosophy of the tragic in German idealism and its legatees optimistically elevates reflection to the point of annulling and superseding any such distance between theory and life, to the detriment perhaps both of moral thought and of an understanding of life's tragic actualities.

It thus becomes evident that Plato's entire philosophical edifice could be construed as a reaction to his theory of the tragic (of the flawed life), which he distilled from the poets: "The first (theoretical) formulation of the tragic [belongs] to a thinker whose special motivation was precisely to challenge and contest it at a deep level of philosophical principle" (Halliwell 99). While Halliwell develops this thesis about Plato as the first philosopher of the tragic by tracing Plato's reconfiguration of tragic poetry into an ontology of the tragic life in order to philosophically counteract it,[6] I advance the same thesis from what could be its opposite end: I focus on Plato's own ambivalence toward art as itself enacting a tragic-dilemmatic structure within the philosophical logos. To put it more succinctly: whereas Halliwell's Plato is a thinker of the tragic, mine is a tragic thinker, a thinker who thinks tragically. Both versions, however, point to the fact that with Plato we have entered the precinct of the tragic well before German idealism.

The second tragic layer involves the difference between the ancients and moderns concerning their respective responses to art's truth content and thus to its political possibilities. As I have emphasized above, the modern obsession with art's freedom turns out to be, both tragically and ironically, a misunderstanding of art's most essential task of unsettling and transforming us. If Plato exiled art from the city precisely on the grounds that it could unsettle the civic order, art in modernity has become a state institution, since—even in its most provocative proclamations—it actually threatens very little or nothing at all. If Plato also exiled art for being a lie, thus making it by default the negative yardstick of truth, what dark fate does art's unqualified inclusion in our world signal for truth? Does truth itself not risk becoming as limitless, diffuse, and insignificant as its limitless, evil twin?

Thirdly, I suggest that, in its continuing quarrel with poetry, philosophy unwittingly participates in a prototypically tragic structure: repetition. The more philosophy claims itself as rationality's calm alternative to art's dark and irrational character (to art's tragic predilections, that is), the more it enmeshes itself in the drama of a violent struggle against its purported enemy. With methods, concepts, and categories in hand as its weapons, philosophy manages unfailingly to be always the first to strike and the one to announce itself victorious at the end. Indeed, art's defeat by philosophy is by now an inevitable repetition in the history of the West. How revealing, then, that—even as the modern structures of thinking differ from those of the ancient world and even as the modern marginalization of art obeys a different reasoning from that of its ancient banishment—philosophy's self-definition as the true logos is still bound up with this recurrent conflict with art, staged over and over from Heraclitus to Plato to Hegel.

Plato's Specter in Hegel's Aesthetics and Beyond

It is well-known that in Plato's hierarchy of representation, art occupies the lowest position in relation to truth: while the Ideas or Forms (Εἴδη) are at the top of the pyramid, nature and the empirical world follow as poorer copies of these Forms, and even further below one finds art, which is only an imitation of nature—namely, an imitation of an imitation. For this reason, as well as for its capacity to provoke base emotions, Plato exiled art from his city. Whatever other modifications occurred to this Platonic edifice over centuries, this imitative relationship of art to nature remained essentially intact.

In modern times, particularly at the height of classicism in the eighteenth century, this mimetic aspect took yet another turn: the realism of Greek artworks became itself idealized as nature and the moderns became obsessed with imitating the Greeks, who had already become nature. The aesthetics of Christian Wolff and Johann Joachim Winckelmann are marked by this revivalist impulse, as were many of the eighteenth-century poets and luminaries who were debating how to translate Homer in order to distill the rules of how to write successful epic poems themselves. We can begin to see how the aesthetics of imitation resulted in the preoccupation with very particular—and, at times, empty—rules for how to write good "Greek" poems or sculpt beautiful "Greek" statues, even if the situation at the time did not call for a "Greek" poem or statue in these exact terms. We can also begin to see that such a practice, instead of thinking of art in terms of its universal essence (for which the classicists admired the Greeks in the first place), ended up producing an aesthetics of good taste with its instruction manuals—namely, an individualist, bourgeois aesthetics. Hölderlin's claim of radical discontinuity between Greeks and moderns was, as we saw in the previous chapter, a response precisely to these extremes of classicism, where imitation was often reduced to reproduction and the adherence to dead forms could do very little to accommodate new contents. Kant's *Critique of Judgment* opposed this ideology of taste and argued for more universal criteria of the aesthetic experience. However, even with Kant, nature continued to occupy a privileged position in relation to art, as he compared the harmonious relation of part and whole in an artwork to the purposeful cohesion of a natural organism. Nature had to wait for Hegel to be taken completely out of the equation.

As a culmination of Western aesthetics, Hegel's introductory remarks on art bear the traces of many of his predecessors, of whom Kant is for obvious reasons the most visible. But insofar as Plato stood symmetrically at the beginning of aesthetic theory, he also marks, both explicitly and implicitly, a special site of commentary in Hegel's thinking of the end. Thus, in my analysis, I pursue specifically the points where Hegel most expressly differs from Plato, in order to see how this difference, which Hegel attempts in good faith, may lead to a place not so far from Plato. How much, in other words, is the beginning in the end? How does Hegel's declaration of the end of art echo Plato's ban on poetry insofar as they are both responses to art's inability to express the truth? At the same time, despite these symptomatic convergences between the two, I will argue that Plato's censorship of art does more justice to the strangeness of the creative experience than does the logic of Hegelian aesthetics, for which art is just another of the many stages Spirit overcomes in its progress.

Hegel's most radical intervention in the history of aesthetics was the excision of nature from the realm of art altogether. This excision is the necessary corollary of his antimimetic—hence, also anti-Platonic—understanding of art. Contrary to Plato—who placed art lower than nature, thinking it to be a partial representation of a natural original—Hegel refuses this disparaging logic. Instead, Hegel considers the artwork to be more alive than nature because it is an "offspring of mind," enlivened, therefore, by Spirit (*Lectures on Aesthetics* 33). Because it is born of human deliberation, art belongs to the world of Spirit, unlike inchoate nature. As the product of human activity, art partakes in the freedom germane to all works of negation and transformation. Hegel, however, carefully differentiates artistic activity both from mechanical labor, which is unfree imitation, and from the unrestrained license that proponents of genius theories confuse for true freedom (30–32).

Hegel writes, "We may . . . begin by asserting that artistic beauty stands *higher* than nature. For the beauty of art is the beauty that is born—born again, that is—of the mind; and by as much as the mind and its products are higher than nature and its appearances, by so much the beauty of art is higher than the beauty of nature" (4). The legibility of this passage hinges on the enigmatic expression of art's beauty being born and born again. If the beauty of nature is born in a spontaneous, necessary yet accidental—hence unfree—manner, the beauty of art is higher, for it is twice born: born *out* of the realm of natural contingency and born again *into* the world of the human mind. It is the beauty that, although relying on natural materials, itself proceeds from the human determination to produce works of freedom. Beauty must be thought under the rubric of freedom. Not all that is free may necessarily be beautiful, but the beautiful cannot be thought outside freedom, that is, outside the Spirit's ascent toward self-reflection. Indeed, Hegel's most succinct definition of art says exactly this—namely, that art is the sensuous representation of the Idea (9). The material beauty of the artwork is a means to the revelation of truth. We see that Hegel's definition is expressionist and nonmimetic: higher than nature, artistic beauty is now an expression of Spirit. Uncannily, in considering the beautiful a vehicle on the way to truth, Hegel reaches Plato via the exactly opposite route: by granting appearance a legitimate relation to truth, rather than thinking them antinomially as Plato did.

In a long, inspired passage of the *Phaedrus*, Plato too wrote that beauty among all the other Forms has the unique capacity to attract the human soul and to remind it of these other Forms in the firmament, which the soul had once witnessed before it became incarnate, fell into this world, and forgot them. Of all the earthly copies of these heavenly Forms, it is only beauty that incites us to love and that makes us pursue it, trying to reach the other Forms (wisdom, justice, prudence, the good) along with it:

> But of beauty [κάλλος], I repeat that we saw her there shining in company with the celestial forms; and coming to earth we find her here too, shining

most clearly through the clearest aperture of sense. For sight is the most piercing of our bodily senses, though wisdom [φρόνησις] is not seen by it—for wisdom would cause furious passions of love [δεινούς ἔρωτας] if, coming into view, she offered any such clear image of herself; and so would the rest that are lovable. But as it is, beauty alone has this prerogative, so that it is most visible and that which most excites love. (*Phaedrus* 250d1–e1)

It seems that wisdom, if it showed itself clearly, would provoke so much passion that it would be catastrophic. Thus, it needs an intermediate link to be reached: beauty. Still, the *Phaedrus* locates beauty in the beloved, in the pursuit of philosophical eros, not in a work of art, where appearance for Plato is reduced to mere illusion.

However, appearance in Hegel is not simply illusion or lie (*Schein*); it is also a mode of disclosure, a revealing (*scheinen*). If we accuse art of being deceptive, he maintains, it is only because we conceive of reality in a restricted and incorrect manner, thinking that reality is reducible to empirical matter. Such view of reality as external immediacy, however, consists in mere semblance, or "bad" appearance. It is no genuine reality at all, since the real is the actual, not the empirical. In his reconciliation of the ideational and the empirical worlds through this process of actualization, Hegel departs from, but also strangely re-cites, Plato's own idealism.

Once freed from merely adequating a natural original, art now assumes its own internal formal demands, which are indifferent to external—even moral—requirements (Hegel, *Lectures on Aesthetics* 52). Hegel seems to allow for art's formal autonomy when, unlike Plato, he refrains from subjecting art to didactic and moral ends, at least in his own "first sailing," so to speak. However, soon Hegel admits that art risks becoming incoherent in its expression of diverse feelings that are often self-contradictory and unable to be organized conceptually under a single moral principle: hatred and love, anger and compassion, grief and joy, and so on. But to prevent such derailment by way of imposing moral rules seems to be out of the question. Since "morality involves reflection" (58), to impose morality on the artwork would mean to deprive art of its formal autonomy and assign it an external purpose instead—that of serving thought. Of course, the extreme exponent of aesthetic didacticism is Plato, who, in the early part of the *Republic*, still allowed admittance to the poets with moral and civic-minded tales, the poets who practiced "good" imitation. Such *immediate* moral injunction, however, would be inadmissible for Hegel, whose dialectical edifice relies on the mediation of opposites. He must instead find a way to *mediate* between disinterested form and moral content.

At this exact moment, displacing but also repeating Plato once more, Hegel introduces the state's relation to art by making the former a model for the latter. He observes that the emotional disarray of purely formal art risks making art inchoate, like nature. Thus, formal freedom must be curbed by the introduction of a rational and unifying principle that gathers the manifold, much as the state regulates individual acts:

> Just in the same way the State and the social life of men are, of course, credited with the purpose that in them *all* human capacities and *all* individual powers are to be developed and to find utterance in *all* directions with *all* tendencies. But in opposition to so formal a view there at once arises the question in what *unity* these manifold formations must be comprehended, and what *single end* they must have for their fundamental idea and ultimate purpose. As such an end, reflection soon suggests the notion that art has the capacity and the function of mitigating the fierceness of the desires. (53)

Just as the state manages to direct all its various constituent parts to the service of a single collective purpose, so art must organize the disparate emotions it produces in order to convey an intelligible and coherent content. On one level, the relation of part to whole in the artwork is referred away from the Kantian natural organism to state organization. On another level, if art were the inassimilable other of Plato's state, it now obeys—better, it exemplifies—stately harmony. Art borrows and displays the state's unifying principle.

Furthermore, if Plato expelled art as a threat to the rational purposes of the state on account of its emotional character, Hegel reconstitutes the aesthetic treatment of emotions as being in accordance with civic purposes. Art alienates and appeases the emotions by representing them, thus transporting the human being from natural savagery to civilization: "The mitigation of the violence of passion has for its universal reason that man is released from his immediate sunkenness in a feeling, and becomes conscious of it as something external to him, towards which he must now enter into an ideal relation. Art by means of its representation, while remaining within the sensuous sphere, delivers man at the same time from the power of sensuousness" (54). Notably, this passage concludes Hegel's defense of a specific emotion that art helps attenuate: grief, whose prolonged depiction Plato also disapproved of in the tragedies.[7] "In art, the sensuous is *spiritualized*," writes Hegel again (44); and even though he will pronounce art inadequate to Spirit's ascent for precisely "remaining within the sensuous," he also recognizes its relative supersensuousness, its capacity to point beyond its sensuous form.

In a single gesture, Hegel grants art a direct relation to thought—it is the sensuous expression of the Idea—yet in doing so, he also deprives art of its autonomy for the sake of manifesting Spirit. Unfettered from the external demand of copying nature faithfully and granted with a newfound freedom and inherent worth, art is now charged with serving another external end—admittedly higher than imitating mere natural objects: it serves (again) the Idea. Where Hegel thought he avoided Plato, the latter's specter seems to have crossed him. To not repeat Plato in consigning art to servitude, Hegel must cancel this teleological end; he thus follows up with a second end that terminates art qua sensuous form and preserves it only as an object of the philosophical gaze. As there are two ends for art, there are also two Hegels: One, the modern liberator, raises art from its devalued place in the Platonic hierarchy, sparing it Plato's immediate moral requirements. The other, wearing a strange mask, approaches us with Plato's features—translated but somehow tragic in having faced a certain vision of the impossible in the very existence of art: this is the Hegel torn by an equally ancient conundrum, the conundrum of an art that is both formally autonomous and responsible for its truth content.

Let us briefly recall that Plato too faced a similar limit. On the one hand, as an effect of divine madness, poetry is holy but politically unreliable; its contents are not guaranteed, and they exceed the rational form of any civic institution. On the other hand, as a product of good imitation that broadcasts heroic messages, poetry risks being exactly that—a product, which is appropriate for the education of the average citizen but which can hardly aspire to the truth of divine revelation. Plato was fully aware that imitative poets are at best useful teachers but not necessarily great poets. Pressed against this limit, both Hegel and Plato agreed on their next move: to displace poetry, make it a thing of the past, and offer philosophy as the most proper and invigorating site for thinking.

Plato's theory of mimesis has been thought to yield such a disparaged place to art that we cannot charge Hegel for reading it in exactly this manner. Can it, however, be seen from an askew perspective to reveal something different from what it seems to say? This is the question that I would like to briefly introduce here and to continue rehearsing in the next section as well.[8]

In *The Man without Content*, Giorgio Agamben considers Hegel's end of art from the perspective of the culmination of Western aesthetics, asking what the future of art holds after the closure of aesthetic theory, which Agamben also identifies with the closure of art's "metaphysical destiny" (54).[9] In this project of considering art poetically (creatively) rather than aesthetically (theoretically, logically), Agamben returns several times to Plato, in a favorable manner, I might add. I believe that the reason for such treatment has to do with the fact that, although Plato instigated aesthetics—what became the *science* of judging art—his motives were not of an aesthetic nature. Indeed, the figure of Plato is important for Agamben because Plato's motivation in banning art from the city stemmed from a profound and almost terrifying intimation of the truths that art affords us. Art for Plato belonged to the rank of the extraordinary and, thus also, the potentially dangerous; it was never a matter of taste and thus could not be simply appreciated amid other cultural commodities, as it so often happens in our world.

Agamben mentions repeatedly that, for Plato, art was the site of disclosure of divine fear (θεῖος φόβος), a state of shudder that put everything at stake. Therefore, rather than appraising art as an object of taste, Plato alternately admired it and dreaded it. Tapping into the symptomatic nature of Plato's expulsion of poetry from the city, Agamben reminds us that Plato's relation to art was fundamentally ambivalent: it involved a deep-seated worry about the sensitive and dangerous affects that tragic art mobilized, but this worry implied at the same time an unparalleled respect for the arresting power of art. How else can one reconcile Plato's condemnation of art's passionate character as a threat to reason with his exaltation of poetry's healing power, which, like love and prophecy, saves reason from its deadly coldness? Plato's defense of divine madness against the calculating aspects of uninspired rationality in his *Phaedrus* (244a8–245b2) testifies to this fundamental ambivalence: poetry's irrationality may well be dangerous for the functioning of the city, but what a great risk a rational society would run without its prophets, healers, poets, and lovers, all of whom share in divine madness!

Agamben, of course, is by no means the first to recognize Plato's ambivalence toward art. Plato's readers have long been aware of this issue. Wind is a good example of this, as his above-cited essay treats the same question of θεῖος φόβος, albeit in a more systematic fashion than Agamben does.[10] Summarizing Plato's arguments about art, Wind observes that art's sources in divine madness (θεία μανία) make it prone to excess, and excess in turn provokes the divine to respond punitively (θεῖος φόβος). The artist must heed this divine fear and try to moderate his excesses. When divine inspiration first visits him, the artist should not simply surrender to its ecstatic state but should be forewarned of the return of Dionysus, who will curb the enthusiasm at whatever cost to save us from the very exorbitance divine intoxication has caused.[11] Divine fear is therefore the antidote to divine mania (Wind 7). To be sure, here lies art's double bind, which Wind cannot resolve because it erects a stumbling block for Plato himself—the philosopher's tragic insight into the artist's equally tragic predicament: once the artist is possessed by the god, how can his flawed humanity—ever so weakened by demonization—respond preemptively and logically to the god's imminent threat? It might be to avoid this very conundrum that Agamben, unlike Wind, elides the distinction between fear and madness, focusing on divine fear less as a requirement of measure for the artist and more as the attuned spectator's (Plato's own) powerful reaction to the extraordinary circumstances art presents.

One could say that it was precisely as an answer to this *tragic* question of how to survive divine madness that the practice of philosophy came to Plato. In other words, the philosopher is that unique being capable of turning inspiration into reason, of translating madness through pious fear. The following tripartite structure might help schematize where the philosophical logos stands in relation to the poetic and the Sophistic—the two other logoi that preoccupied Plato in his search for the proper path to truth:

	POET	*PHILOSOPHER*	*SOPHIST*
ORIGIN:	divine madness	divine madness	cold rationality
END:	divine madness	reason	cold rationality
MODE:	faith, fanaticism	truth-seeking	skepticism

This schema shows, on the one hand, that the philosopher and the poet both share their origin in divine inspiration. On the other hand, the philosopher is more distanced from the Sophist, since the latter's cold rationality does not compare to the former's inspired reason. Still, the philosopher differs from both poet and Sophist in this: whereas both poet and Sophist start from and end in the same place, the philosopher is the only creature whose mental process is differentiated. Plato thus *allegorizes* Sophistic coldness and poetic fervor at once, by introducing a movement within thought. In regard to poetry, which concerns us specifically in this chapter, Plato allegorized the poets by making their thought worthy of philosophical investigation, just as he also allegorized his own thinking by writing philosophy in a poetic form. Warminski's claim that modernity makes audible to the Greeks what was inaudible to them in their own works overlooks the fact that Plato—Greece's own modern—had already performed this. This is another way of arriving at Halliwell's conclusion again: with Plato, the Greeks are already reflecting on their artistic tradition.

To return to Agamben's Plato, however: while Agamben is indeed not alone in reading Plato for his ambivalence toward art, his recourse to the ancient thinker proves significant in view of the specific task he sets forth—namely, to think about the fate of art after its Hegelian end. His interest in Plato, then, involves the larger question of the relation between ancients and moderns through their respective attitudes toward art. Rather unique among contemporary continental thinkers in recognizing in Plato's ban on the poets a productive way of thinking about art today, Agamben's citation of Plato implies an even more important—albeit tacit at best—admission: if Plato has still something to say to us about art, it may well be because his understanding of it was not merely historical, as Hegel's was. That Plato was so preoccupied with art's impact on society is, of course, a mark of his times, since for the Greek polis, art and its artists meant a great deal—a reality that is admittedly no longer ours today. But insofar as his understanding of art is also transhistorical, his concerns with the political effects of art remain relevant in our modernity as well. The Platonic prohibition thus acquires special significance for Agamben's reflection on our current and future relation to art: what would our world be like if art could have again such an impact as it did *then*?

Following Agamben further in this direction, I maintain that if Plato's anxiety about art is at all justified, this is also because his understanding of art *does justice* to art's terrible freedom—a freedom that resists systematization and determination and that is not always coincident with the operations of self-consciousness as Hegel would later require. Rather, it is a freedom that, like the spontaneity of inchoate nature, stems from and testifies to the immediate outbreak of passion Plato banned and Hegel rushed to sublate through the mediating role of representation. Nevertheless, in understanding that the origin of creativity lies in divine inspiration rather than self-consciousness, Plato seems also to have understood far better than Hegel the peculiar place art holds for humans, even as he knew that this irrational origin is the very reason he himself held art under suspicion.

Let us then begin with Agamben's most interesting citation of Plato, which will continue to occupy us in the next section as well. Agamben quotes the famously ambivalent passage from the *Republic*, where Plato qualifies his edict of expulsion:

> If a man who was capable by his cunning of assuming every kind of shape and imitating all things should arrive in our city, bringing with himself the poems which he wished to exhibit, we should fall down and worship him as a holy and wondrous and delightful creature, but should say to him that there is no man of that kind among us in our city, nor is it lawful for such a man to arise among us, and we should send him away to another city, after pouring myrrh down over his head and crowning him with fillets of woo[1]. (Plato, *Republic* 3.398a1–8, qtd. in Agamben 3)[12]

This passage begs the question of imitation, which prompted the introduction of Agamben's book into our discussion. As in the *Ion*, these early books of the *Republic* show that Plato's reproach against the poets involves chiefly their lack of requisite technical skill—hence the lack of knowledge and self-reflection behind the contents they produce: poets create out of inspiration, not out of knowledge. In turn, divine inspiration translates into lack of control over their work, a fact that renders the work potentially dangerous in its public reception. This is why the only kind of poetry admitted in the ideal city, at least initially, is a poetry that serves civic purposes: heroic hymns or encomia are such genres.[13] On the one hand, we have what appears to be Plato's unequivocal decision concerning the devalued status of art as imitation, while, on the other, we have the commendation of imitative poetry as the only politically responsible kind.

It is important to note at this juncture that imitation in Plato is a two-way street: art imitates the external world but can also be imitated by the young who are exposed to it through pedagogy. This seemingly straightforward observation, however, points to something crucial: it says that art's function as imitation may hinge less on its previous relation to an original it was supposed to copy and more on its own status as the origin of future imitative acts by the citizens. Art becomes a problem for Plato less in how it imitates nature and more in how it is to be imitated by human nature. Put differently, art becomes a problem when it is viewed as being itself an origin: as an originary creation, art is not *of* human but of divine origins, and Plato suspects that it cannot be *for* humans either (at least not for the uninitiated humans, so to speak). If I may be allowed the somewhat provocative but also suggestive expression, art might be too truthful for Plato, much more truthful than its official place in his own hierarchy allows. This, in fact, could be the reason why he had to expel it, as opposed to Hegel, for whom art's truth was, to the contrary, wanting. Though this issue will be treated more thoroughly in the next section of this chapter, I wish to alert us at this point to the subtle possibilities beneath Plato's simultaneous critique of art as imitation and his commendation of imitative poetry as a means of civic education. As with other of Plato's twists and turns, here too the philosopher demands to be read through his obliqueness and his ambivalence, in a way that engages the internal dynamism of his texts.

To follow Plato through his obliqueness means to entertain the fact that he intuited and feared the essence of art as expression of a far higher nature than mere animal nature; perhaps also of a nature far more inaccessible, if also less determinate and benevolent, than the shimmering sky of his Ideas—the spiritual world, whose bright light, however, dazzles and obstructs the escaped prisoner from reaching its heights. Art's showing of the dazzling divine sun may put at risk the purpose of the journey out of the cave. What if now the escapee sees even less than he did in the cave? While both Hegel and Plato agree that "beauty is truth, truth beauty," to Plato alone belongs that other, more enigmatic, Keatsian insight: "That is all ye know on earth and all ye need to know"; for the rest might well be too terrible for ordinary contemplation.

But to say that art (and specifically tragic poetry) may be "too" truthful for Plato is to endow him with a tragic understanding of truth. Struck, that is, by art's excess, an excess that speaks as much the greatness as the derailment of being in its unpredictability, Plato's only response was cathartic in at least two senses of this term: Firstly, he removed art from the city, as if separating the pure from the impure (*kathairein*), cleansing the body politic from the "sickness" that is art. Note in this context the image of the poet's ritual honoring before his expulsion in the above quote, an image that recalls the treatment of a scapegoat. Secondly, however, Plato responded cathartically also in the specific mimetic sense this term took on later in Aristotle's theory of tragedy: Plato felt the greatness of the poet, sympathized with the poet's plight, but nonetheless resolved to expel him for the greater good. Viewed in this sense, Plato's thoughts on art do not constitute a theory but rather an undergoing, a suffering. This is why I insist on the mimetic aspect of catharsis rather than the by-now-emptied-out term "performing," which has gained much currency in contemporary theoretical circles. A mere rhetorical ploy of putting on identities, subjectivities, and other such things, "performance" is for the most part now secure from the blows that body and mind both received in tragic theater. Plato does not simply perform his affects in order to match rhetorically his ideas; such a gesture would be more germane to the thinking of representation, and Plato does not think in terms of representation. Plato undergoes the poet's plight because he himself knows quite well that he is as strange a creature to the multitude as is the poet—this multitude he wishes to deliver from illusion's danger.

A more metaphorical way of describing this same reaction of Plato to art: struck by art's relentless rays, Plato's only response was of the kind Hölderlin recognized in the moment before the divine seizes a mortal being—blasphemy.[14] Plato's blasphemy becomes the law of art's expulsion. Here, for instance, is the probable tragic motivation behind his charge against the intense lamentation fostered by tragedy: Plato knows that *this* warrior's death remains an irrecoverable loss, even as a culture of honor can elevate his death to mean something larger than his life. He knows also that, confronted with such an inconsolable experience, the fallen man's kin have all the right in the world to mourn. Yet it is this uncontestable experience of mourning that has to be contested by philosophy's demand for universal laws that prescribe country over individual, duty over love, polis over nature, and most of all, in this case, reason above suffering. No matter how implicit this intimation is in Plato's text, it makes of Plato himself a tragic figure, something Agamben seems to point toward and perhaps the reason why Plato's own portrayals of his mentor, Socrates, always point to this tragic form.

It is worth noting that Agamben himself does not explicitly acknowledge the importance of this cathartic mimeticism for his symptomatic reading of Plato. The reason for this omission will become clearer in the next section, where we examine more closely Agamben's philosophical affinities. Yet it is through this mimeticism that Plato manages to communicate the strange mix of pity and fear—the emotions that, according to his brightest pupil, underlie the tragic experience: the fear for the poet who wanders around possessed and vulnerable and the fear for what the poet's words may induce in us; the pity with which the philosopher must undertake the burden of ridding the polis of this miraculous being so that the many can live securely, because the wise one, who understood (like the unlucky sovereign of the tragic plays), committed the terrible act on their behalf.

This would be, then, Plato's greatest difference from Hegel, who—evidently less transparent in his condemnation—nonetheless relegated art to obsolescence on the grounds that it was inadequate to manifesting Spirit in purely spiritual terms. Even though for the most part Plato condemned art for its irrationality, his own attitude toward art was in part affective and not uniformly logical, as his response was—accordingly—poetic, not aesthetic. Hegel, on the other hand, starting less prejudicially and with the intent to give art all its proper dues, succumbed eventually to an aesthetic/scientific logic that led him to expunge art from the necessities of modern life. Hegel's version of the end bears the mark of the detached, disinterested reflexivity of the modern world of post-Enlightenment secularist progress. And though it would be unfair to charge Hegel with a univocal understanding of progress, it would be equally unfair to simply accept the subsumption of art into philosophy as the inevitable corollary of a historical necessity, in which art happens to be inadequate to the current modality of Spirit. Still, while we may understand why art for Hegel is too sensuous, it is rather surprising to find that for Plato, for whom it occupied the lowest place in the hierarchy of representation, art turns out to be too spiritual.

In concluding these remarks on Plato and Hegel, I wish to spell out their difference by contrasting two operative terms in their respective discussions of art: διαφορὰ (difference, dispute) for Plato, *Aufhebung* (sublation, subsumption) for Hegel. In *Republic* 10, before he consolidates the expulsion of the poets, Plato refers to this old tension between poetry and philosophy. He writes, "παλαιὰ μέν τις διαφορὰ φιλοσοφίᾳ τε καὶ ποιητικῇ," which has been often rendered as, "there is from of old a quarrel between philosophy and poetry" (607b5–6). Though the term "quarrel" certainly captures part of the tension Plato wants to describe, διαφορὰ has other pertinent meanings. The Liddell-Scott-Jones dictionary defines διαφορὰ as the movement of carrying something over or across, a movement that can be further designated as variance, disagreement, and difference. Philosophy and poetry are in dispute because they are different, because they are at odds with each other. But difference does not mean that they are completely unrelated, either. Had they had nothing in common over which to dispute, they would probably never be in this dispute to begin with. We may imagine that truth is the apple of their quarrel. Yet what remains fascinating in Plato's version of the quarrel is that it cannot be resolved in a logical, mediated manner. After all, the solution of banning the poet can hardly be described thus, since it shuns the very calmness and civility that reflexive theoretical discourse prides itself in having mastered. But in its overt intolerance, in its raw immediacy, the Platonic solution honors art's legitimacy in this strife as philosophy's valiant other and does not hand over the victory to philosophy with a bloodless sleight of hand.

In contrast to διαφορά, the Hegelian Aufhebung rewrites Plato's end of art as also the end of this difference. Art as sensuous activity is canceled, and what remains of this cancellation is the discursive contemplation of artworks in aesthetic theory. Art is thus renamed in philosophy, which entails a certain diminution of the realm of thinking: there is no more space for thinking outside reflexivity, no chance for a thought to emerge out of sensuous experience. No longer does art think in its creative capacity. Now one thinks in art's place, and this "one" is necessarily a philosopher. Now we think in meta-thoughts; more sadly still, we live a meta-life, a life atrophied from the lack of creative energies and poisoned from the contempt with which we view any desire "to make things," a life numbed in its artificial calmness, where no other alternative, no real difference, threatens the fortress of self-reflexivity. To remind us, then, of such real antagonisms, which bore great fruits even in their most violent manifestations (are the fruits of tragedy, after all, not those of great conflict?), is why Plato's work remains crucial today. In his dark farewell to the ancient poet, Plato strangely beckons us now to feel (again) the shudder of art.

Plato, Agamben, and Modern Art

As I have already suggested but not fully elaborated, Agamben's intellectual affinities underlie his elision of the mimetic and cathartic aspects of Plato's thought. Thus, before pursuing further our discussion of imitation and artistic production, a brief contextualization of Agamben's philosophical loyalties is due, since they inflect his interpretation of concepts in Greek aesthetics. Fruitful as it can sometimes be, the adoption, even partial, of poststructuralist interpretations of the ancients is not without its risks: hasty and self-serving translations that are often mistranslations; a general disregard for the historical and textual specificity of ancient sources that works in the service of our modern historical and political agendas; and the theoretical confidence in speculations that run contrary to fact—a confidence, moreover, that even invests itself with the power of fact. These have been some of the charges contemporary thought has incurred.

Despite his erudition and well-attested influence in current theoretical and sociopolitical circles, Agamben is by no means immune to such charges when it comes to his readings of the Greeks. A good student of Heidegger, Agamben is partial to making epochal declarations and unearthing (inventing would be the sharper term) definitive binaries in Greek thought that are retroactively exposed as the sources of everything that has gone wrong with the West. This penchant for hypostatizing "hidden dichotomies" to account for epochal violence is something that James Gordon Finlayson astutely criticizes in Agamben's biopolitical theory, which anchors its argument on a thinly argued distinction Agamben attributes to Aristotle: *zoe* (bare natural life) versus bios (political life).[15] As Finlayson observes, however, "far from conceiving the relation between mere life and the good life to be one of exclusion or opposition, Aristotle thinks of them as two internally related and continuous, albeit qualitatively distinct, layers of life" (112).

Finlayson's objection bears repeating when considering some further dichotomies Agamben sets up in *The Man without Content*, which—interestingly—are reducible to this same binary of bare life and political life. Though in Agamben's book on art the featured Aristotelian binary is different, that of praxis versus poesis, Agamben still manages to refer this binary to the previous biopolitical terms: Agamben interprets Aristotle as aligning the will-to-act with an animalistic drive, so that the man of action becomes quasisynonymous with the animal.[16] It is then from this animalistic, vital, or sensuous man that Agamben derives his modern "man of taste," whose consumerist attitude toward art entails a diminution of art's importance, as Agamben correctly notes. Of course, it could be argued more forcefully that the man of taste is least of all an effect of animal drive and most of all a symptom of a deadened culture—a symptom of artificiality, we could say, being aware of the unfortunate presence of "art" in this term at the same time. After all, the image of the robust and vital agent is more likely to summon Nietzsche's Dionysian artist rather than the effete connoisseur of the eighteenth-century salon culture. Nevertheless, this seems to be beside the point for Agamben, who, following Heidegger, understands "enlivened" to mean simply bestial and never something ensouled, as did the Greeks.

It becomes immediately evident from this that Agamben's interest in Plato's emphasis on divine terror—which I find salutary insofar as it implies a cathartic Plato—directly contradicts Agamben's stated discomfort with sensuousness: divine terror and catharsis as emotional states involve the senses. It is likely for this reason that Agamben cautiously avoids the term catharsis when speaking of Plato's reaction to art, but his avoidance cannot in itself prevent us from considering the strong affective and cathartic presuppositions on which his understanding of Plato ultimately rests. For this reason, and despite all these objections, I continue to find his symptomatic reading of Plato not just symptomatic of Agamben himself but an intriguing insight into Plato's conflicted thinking of art and, by extension, into the way philosophy has been haunted by art all along. (This haunting continues today, as continental philosophers such as Agamben himself still try to save art as a path to truth after it has been repeatedly condemned by philosophy for deception, immorality, and spiritual inadequacy.)

My understanding of what is at stake in Plato's theory of art is framed from the outset by two interrelated distinctions in his thought: (1) the distinction between art (poetic inspiration) and philosophy or politics (rational account), which Plato brings to the limit in his measure of the ban, and (2) the distinction, which Plato does not make, between the origin of the artwork in divine madness and the actual artwork itself, the materialization of which involves human skill (techne). Since Plato defined techne as exclusive of poetic inspiration, he thought of art qua creative practice exactly not as an *art* in the sense of techne but as a divine gift;[17] his sporadic espousal of civic-minded imitative poets, moreover, does not help us determine clearly whether these poets possess a skill in the strong sense of techne. I think it is the lack of this distinction between the power of inspiration and the mediation of techne that leads him to the extreme measure of the ban. Yet in choosing to align art solely with inspiration, Plato brushed against the essence of the creative spirit in a way that the modern preoccupation with decorum and taste and the contemporary obsession with form above all else do not.

The question of art, at least from the moment art became subject to question, seems to be that of a distinction, a boundary. Asking whether art is good or bad for common morality, Plato set a boundary between good imitation (exemplarity) and bad imitation (artistic deception), thus banning art from the polis. Instead of Plato's morally laden question, the more secular modern spectator asks a seemingly different one, which concludes likewise with yet another boundary: confronted with a work of abstraction, the modern spectator is compelled to ask, is this art or gibberish—thereby putting art in the tribunal of taste, where the lines between good art and bad art, high art and low art, art and non-art are to be drawn.

Upon a second glance, however, this modern boundary between art and non-art turns out to designate our current anxiety about the deceptive character of art, our suspicion that art poses as art when in fact it is not. Consequently, even the modern question, which seems to be concerned exclusively with the artwork itself rather than its moral or political function, can be referred to an ethicopolitical dimension, that of art cheating its public. Thus far we are not so removed from Plato's anxiety. Whether in the sphere of politics or of aesthetics, art appears only as subject to judgment. Art is an impostor that threatens the city either by offering improper contents for public consumption or by remaining illusory even when its contents are commendable or worst of all perhaps—and this is the predicament of the modern spectator—by its perversion of imitation, since art can also imitate itself in addition to imitating nature or the world at large. Hence, the paradox of art being what it is not (non-art) precisely by being exceedingly what it is supposed to be: a masterful imitation of everything, including of itself.

Yet even though the fear of dupery may be a reason shared between the Platonic expulsion of art from the city and the modern preoccupation with art's authenticity, the anxiety about art is experienced differently in these two moments and yields two different responses: this of the censor and that of the connoisseur. As Agamben's argument implies, the modern compulsion to distinguish art from non-art is precipitated by the idiosyncratic vocabulary of modern art and thus bespeaks art's marginalization from modern life. Paradoxically, having torn down the wall Plato erected between art and the city—a wall no more befitting to our modern sensibility for tolerance—we admit art freely into our commodity culture, where it cannot but fall into obscurity and solipsism. Indeed, Agamben maintains that, despite the current proliferation of artists and artworks, art has withdrawn from public consciousness since its political relevance amounts to little more than its own formal self-referentiality. Now that political art is everything but a scandal, art's effect on politics is minute compared to the time of its Platonic contestation. This is why Plato's ban on art, although it has instituted aesthetics, does not itself originate in an aesthetic understanding of art. In other words, though it reads as a verdict, it is not rooted in a thinking of art through a judgment of taste, as is that of the modern critics or spectators. Agamben is well aware of this fact, and it is because of this that he finds Plato's violent response to art more appropriate than he does art criticism's tolerance, a tolerance afforded precisely by the eclipse of art and its diminishing impact on us.

But what about the nature of art and its claims to truth led Plato to such considerations? Let us first attempt to approach this question through some hints Agamben gives us. Agamben describes the poetic principle with a quotation from the *Symposium* and goes on to derive from it one of his dichotomies, which—although not so categorical in the ancient Greek world—show us how modern thought has come to polarize and hierarchize what once were complementary oppositions. The binary in question is that of poesis and praxis as indicative of two mutually exclusive modes of production—creating or making versus doing or operating. Agamben writes, "In the *Symposium* Plato tells us about the full original resonance of the word ποίησις: 'any cause that brings into existence something that was not there before is Ποίησις.' Every time that something is pro-duced, that is, brought from concealment and nonbeing into the light of presence, there is ποίησις, pro-duction, poetry" (59–60). Soon afterward, invoking Aristotle this time, Agamben adds, "The Greeks ... made a clear distinction between *poiesis* (*poiein*, to 'pro-duce' in the sense of bringing into being) and *praxis* (*prattein*, 'to do' in the sense of acting)" (68). Agamben's use of the hyphen in "pro-duction" aims to differentiate between these two modes of producing. But in so polarizing them, Agamben's reading of the Greeks assumes the Heideggerian critique of technology, since it is the technological mode of existence that has brought about the divorce of techne from poesis and reduced techne merely to the technological.

Following the logic of this epochal critique in Agamben, there is, on the one hand, poetic pro-duction, where the prefix "pro-" suggests the creation of something previously nonexistent—a mode of creation common both to nature and to works of art. This mode of creative making allows for a connection with nature (*phusis*) as well as for a differentiation from it. Pro-duction acknowledges the difference of a natural process (for instance, the blossoming of a flower) from a work of art (for instance, the painting of a flower) in that the former originates in itself whereas the latter originates in human skill; all the while, pro-duction refers the human work back to nature in that both nature and artwork obey the same creative principle of giving birth to something hitherto nonexistent. On the other hand, there is the form of production without the hyphen, an activity that relies solely on techne as the hallmark of the work's absolute difference from nature. In other words, the relative difference between the artwork's birth in the human spirit and the flower's birth in nature's self-spontaneity (which the term techne used to designate without denying the common poetic principle behind natural and human works alike) is now radicalized: now techne severs forever any connection between human artifice and nature. Modern technology stands, of course, both for Heidegger and Agamben as the quintessential example of this form of production, which yields products and consumer goods as opposed to artworks and craftworks. The technological mode of production is so pervasive as to define our very mode of being and become our ontology. We live and breathe this technological mode; and as a result, we have forgotten what it means to engage in poetic creation: "We are so accustomed to this unified understanding of all of man's 'doing' as praxis that we do not recognize that it could be, and in other eras has been, conceived differently" (Agamben 68).[18]

In its free admission into the city, modern art is not exempt from this problematic of instrumental production and commodification. Plato's "unreasonable" ban that separated art from politics may have been lifted, but it has been tacitly reissued elsewhere: evacuated of its power to affect us, art slowly but steadily has met with public indifference—the sinister face of public tolerance. Displaced by art theory and surviving mostly in galleries and museums, art consciously embraces and appropriates this displacement by turning itself into its opposite: non-art. Agamben offers several examples where modern art shrinks into self-theorization, defining itself in purely negative terms. In the most obvious of these, Duchamp's readymades, art empties out its contents and reduces its relation to truth to the blank universal of formalization.[19] Still, Agamben argues that, even though the cost of art's free admission has been irrelevance and illegibility, art continues to give us glimpses into the truth of our predicament. Through its marginalization and ineffectuality, art points to the current void. And even though this disclosure of nothingness is itself hardly noticeable, it remains a disclosure: in Agamben's terms, it marks the coming into presence of privation itself (64).

In his article "Five Remarks on Aesthetic Judgment," which is concerned with the impact of Kantian aesthetics on modern art, Thierry de Duve defines the borders of modernity in terms of the limitlessness of its art: we are within modernity, "when anyone and everyone can be an artist" (24). This is admittedly not the Nietzschean world of art for artists only, the world of Dionysian frenzy and sweeping poetic passion with which Agamben begins his book;[20] nevertheless, de Duve and Agamben do agree on the point of modern art's limitlessness. Less exuberant in his diagnosis, however, Agamben remarks, "Limitless, lacking content, double in its principle, [art] wanders in the nothingness of the *terra aesthetica*, in a desert of forms and contents that continually point it beyond its own image which it evokes and immediately abolishes in the impossible attempt to found its own certainty" (56). The destruction of all limits comes at the loss of meaningfulness. Art's dispersal is no more the fecund dissemination of truth but a veritable dismemberment. Orpheus begets the man without content, the modern artist, whose creative experience amounts to the endless production of art without truth, without internal necessity. But to bring up the truth content and inner necessity of art at this point—the content (*Inhalt*) that Hegel reinstated as a correction to Kant's empty aesthetic formalism—means to bring Dionysus to the fore: it means to gesture toward the place of inspiration, of divine madness and poetic suffering, of the origin of art, without which no work could ever come to exist in the particular form it assumes.

It is to this distinction between origin and artwork that we now turn: "What does *originality* mean? When we say that the work of art has the character of originality (or authenticity), we do not simply mean by this that this work is unique, that is, different from any other. Originality means proximity to the origin. The work of art is original because it maintains a particular relationship to its origin, to its formal ἀρχή, in the sense that it not only derives from the latter and conforms to it but also remains in a relationship of permanent proximity to it" (Agamben 61).

According to Agamben, originality in a work of art has to do with the work's "particular relationship" to its moment of origination—a relationship, furthermore, of "permanent proximity." In order for the work to have a relationship to its origin, it must be that the work is different from its source, but their difference from each other is cast in terms of an indelible link—a kind of fidelity and affiliation in the sense of derivation (filiation) and an affinity in the sense of a permanent bond (connatural attraction). Since we have already discussed the relation of artwork to phusis, the following simile from nature may give us a sense of the kind of relationship the artwork bears to its origin: such relationship is much like the one between the blossom and its root. The blossom is permanently connected to its root; yet the root remains invisible below the ground; and when seen, it disarms the lay eye with its striking dissimilarity to its offspring, the flower. Thus, a work of art does not simply reduplicate its originating principle the way labor is mechanically reduplicated in a product. The work of art keeps its origin alive by literally transforming it: putting it into a new form. Inspiration is still the ground, the divine and fertile excess that initiates as it also stands in opposition to—even to the point of threatening to destroy[21]—the work, but the mediation of the artist's formal skill can only hope to keep this overwhelming experience at bay, thus also bespeaking its inexorable proximity.

The articulation of this precarious proximity between origin and artwork, which accounts for the subsequent difference between art as poesis and art as techne, had already preoccupied Plato and marked a certain rift between his thinking of art in the *Ion* and in the *Republic*. In the former work, the proximity between the artist, the work, and its origin in divine inspiration is so strong—indeed, it is described in terms of magnetic attraction—that any distance between them is collapsed. The artist and his work are divine just as the original inspiration that brought forth the work is divine. This cancellation of the distance rebounds in part to art's favor but with the proviso that art sacrifice its name.[22] That art qua skill is a misnomer for what Socrates seeks to define in this dialogue is emphasized by which art is under discussion: poetry. The privileging of versification owes to the fact that Socrates is interested in the event of poesis as creative making, which in Greek is synonymous with prosody, and not in the notion of art as skill. Socrates repeatedly attributes the rhapsode's virtuosity not to art (τέχνη) or knowledge (ἐπιστήμη) but to what he calls "divine power" (θεία δύναμις) (*Ion* 533d3) or "divine lot" (θείᾳ μοίρᾳ) (*Ion* 534c1).

Socrates thus explains to Ion, "This gift you have of speaking well on Homer is not an art; it is a power divine, impelling you like the power in the stone Euripides called the magnet, which most call 'stone of Heraclea.' This stone does not simply attract the iron rings, just by themselves; it also imparts to the rings a force enabling them to do the same thing as the stone itself, that is, to attract another ring, so that sometimes a chain is formed, quite a long one, of iron rings, suspended from one another" (533d1–e2).

Later on, Socrates again rebuts Ion's claim that his talent is an art based on knowledge: "So if you are an artist and . . . you only promised me a display on Homer in order to deceive me, then you are at fault. But if you are not an artist, if by lot divine you are possessed by Homer, and so, knowing nothing, speak many things and fine about the poet, just as I said you did, then you do no wrong" (542a2–7).

That poetry is not art in the sense of skill as is horsemanship, fishing, and so on, but divine lot, forms the crux of this dialogue.[23] It turns out that Socrates's main reason for distrusting the term "art" as an adequate description of poetic activity has to do with the uniqueness of creative practice, which exceeds the genus art—namely, the general gathering of the skills involved in a particular craft. Socrates emphasizes the singular character of poetry's divine lot, stating to Ion, "One poet is suspended from one Muse, another from another. . . . And from these primary rings, the poets, others are in turn suspended, some attached to this one, some to that, and are filled with inspiration, some by Orpheus, others by Musaeus. But the majority are possessed and held by Homer" (536a7–b5). Thus, from each specific combination of poets held together, various chains of poetic legacy emerge. One would suspect that all these chains would add up to the same species of art, the art of prosody, which would then be classified under the genus art (the fine arts), but Socrates resists exactly this gesture. Poetic voice cannot be subsumed under a common know-how the way that all fishing techniques—whether used on rivers, lakes, or the sea—form together the art of fishing, since poetry is not the result of know-how but of a spontaneous divine gift. This is why Ion is instantly moved by recitations of Homer but remains indifferent to discourses on any other poet. Homer attracts him for no *reason* in the strict sense of reason as rational cause. Homer is simply befitting to Ion's emotional sensibility. With this image of the rings, Socrates describes enthusiasm—the possession of the poet's and the listeners' spirits by the god—as a state of contagion.

Furthermore, it is only as such, as nontechnical divine gift alone, that poetry escapes the deception of which it could otherwise be accused, since it purports to know actions and events beyond its scope of expert competency. Though Socrates does not explicitly accuse poetry of deception in this dialogue, he does suggest repeatedly that Homer's description of other arts, such as medicine, charioteering, or fishing may be incorrect (*Ion* 538b2–d5). The reason, however, that deception is not much of a concern here has to do with the fact that poetry is viewed not as a techne, not as a product of conscious deliberation nor, therefore, as responsible for errors of intellection. In other words, in this Platonic scenario, Socrates rescues poetry from its delusional character by removing it from the realm of art qua techne and keeping it through this magnetic attraction as close as possible to its divine origin. Since techne does not mediate the divine frenzy that inspires the poet, he and his work are immediately coincident with their source. The divinely inspired poet is then celebrated for his gift, but the stage is now cleared for the next scenario, where poetic madness becomes a political liability.

Thus we come to this latter, more fatal of Plato's readings from his *Republic*, which is the one Agamben also quotes in the opening chapter of *The Man without Content* and which I have already begun discussing in the previous section of this chapter. In this passage, poetry is again synonymous with divinity, albeit this time the poet is not simply the light and winged and sacred thing that Socrates sees in the *Ion* (534b4–5) but a terrifying creature whose madness threatens the rational order of the city. I cite this passage once more:

> If a man, then, it seems, who was capable by his cunning of assuming every kind of shape and imitating all things should arrive in our city, bringing with himself the poems which he wished to exhibit, we should fall down and worship him as a holy and wondrous and delightful creature, but should say to him that there is no man of that kind among us in our city, nor is it lawful for such a man to arise among us, and we should send him away to another city, after pouring myrrh down over his head and crowning him with fillets of wool. (*Republic* 3.398a1–8)

His divine calling may earn him a precious moment of adoration but does not spare the poet from the exile to which the city must ultimately condemn him for his flights of fancy. Though the fate of the poet is markedly different from the *Ion* to the *Republic*, in both cases Plato's agon unfolds around the articulation of the relation between origin and artwork. I would suggest that it is this very proximity, the fine line between the two, to which Plato fell prey and so felt compelled to equate the work with the divine madness that is its source. And yet in thus falling prey to a quick immediacy, Plato was not so far removed from the truth when he spoke of art in terms of inspiration's terror: for as much as good skill is an asset to a successful artwork, no artwork could claim splendor on account of an uninspired but well-executed form.

It turns out that even though Plato dwells on the identity rather than the difference between the artwork and its origin, the intimation of this difference marks the strangeness of his own definition of art as imitation. Art in Plato's *Republic* is defined and condemned as imitation, as an incomplete, false, and illusory disclosure of reality, which corrupts the city. Still, as I have previously indicated, despite his association of imitation with deception, Plato is not against all imitation. In the *Republic* he distinguishes between good and bad imitation in storytelling, all the while encouraging good imitation for its pedagogical importance: "The stories on the accepted list we will induce nurses and mothers to tell to the children and so shape their souls" (*Republic* 2.377c2–4). Poetry would be allowed in the polis if it produced characters and values that would foster civic consciousness.[24] In fact, Agamben's citation of the poet's expulsion stops short of this exception Plato makes immediately afterward: "But we ourselves, for our souls' good, should continue to employ the more austere and less delightful poet and taleteller, who would *imitate* the diction of the good man and would tell his tale in the patterns which we *prescribed* in the beginning, when we set out to educate our soldiers" (*Republic* 3.398a8–b4, my emphasis). We want a poet, Plato seems to say, who is less of a divine creature and more of an ordinary artisan, a skilled worker in storytelling, an imitator, who knows how to obey certain rules in order to produce verses of pedagogical value. Strangely, the logic of the *Ion* is inverted in the *Republic*: whereas calling the poet an artist was a misnomer in the former dialogue, now Plato wishes for a poet who is an artist of sorts and, thus, a responsible pedagogue and citizen. Imitation, at least in its narrow sense of reproduction, can serve rational purposes and be subject to check—this is its goodness; divine inspiration is uncontrollable and, therefore, threatening.

Consequently, the problem of the *Republic* is that, more often than not, poets present us with bad imitations, in the sense of bad examples to follow. As I remarked earlier, it is actually *this* side of imitation—namely, poetry's pedagogical effect on others, its capacity to inspire young listeners to imitate dubious acts—that Plato finds worrisome. Let us note, however, that art's dubious effects are inextricably tied to its contents, which presumably originate in a divine source. The question immediately arises: how can we reconcile art's divine origin with Plato's critique of the tragic poets, who, with Homer at their lead, depict the gods as nefarious beings? Whence come the poets' terrible plots and unseemly characters? Plato's logic pushes us to expand his understanding of imitation further than its narrow definition as copy. If his critique of poetry as bad imitation does not always stem from its being a poor copy (from its not reproducing nature correctly), it must stem from his suspicion that art is not just a mechanistic reproduction and that its danger lies exactly in its potential autonomy. To be sure, Plato does criticize the poets for not knowing the specifics of what they describe, thus for indulging in poor reproductions. Revealingly, however, when speaking of the destructive influence that Hesiod's portrayal of the gods' wickedness has, Plato qualifies his understanding of both imitation and deception as well as of the ethics involved in these notions: he entertains the possibility that even if the deities were in fact as vicious as Hesiod describes,[25] the poet should have kept silent about their evil deeds, so as not to imperil the moral education of his audience (*Republic* 2.378a1–6). This implies, firstly, that art is no mere reproduction, since it can entirely transform what it purports to imitate, and, secondly, that deception—the very reason for which Plato denounced imitation as untruth—is not always unethical but, to the contrary, constitutes at times a necessary vehicle to moral conduct.

One way to elucidate this expanded notion of imitation is to frame it in terms of resemblance and analogy rather than reproduction. In other words, to say that art is an imitation of nature would not only mean that art copies natural objects but that art is *like* nature in another, more essential way. We need to recall at this point our earlier discussion of art's relation to phusis. Art is like nature in the sense that art too gives birth to something original, something that takes on a life of its own, so to speak. Thus, the morally dangerous aspect of imitation for Plato rests not so much in art's ability to reproduce external contents as it does in its power to imbue the world with its own life breath. We can now understand why Plato condemns Hesiod's and, most of all, Homer's unflattering depiction of the gods: Homer evokes and invokes the gods, and in this sense he is their origination. Granted, Homer's gift is divine in origin, and the bard himself recognizes this gift of inspiration in his first lines that apostrophize the Muse. But it is equally true that Homer enlivens the gods in his verses, for it would be impossible to copy down deities the way one is said to copy in painting a natural creature.

Here is summarily the abyss that art faces in these two dialogues: whereas in the *Ion* poetry is spared the verdict of deception through an insanity plea based on its identification with its mad, divine source, in the *Republic* art can only survive as the reproduction of an origin(al) that exists in a rather distant plane from that of divine mania—in the so-called empirical plane. The precariousness of this fine border between origin and work leads Plato's thought to these two extremes: utter coincidence in divine madness, which renders art holy but politically unreliable, or the impregnable hierarchy of a higher original in nature and its lower imitation in the work of art, which makes art appropriate for the average citizen at the expense of denying it its role in the disclosure of truth (and nature). In so contemplating the origin of the work, Plato faced the great problem that, locked in this paradox, art always risks being without content: without political content as a holy endeavor and without genuine truth content as a political prop. Today, it is also between these "withouts" that Agamben rehearses the whither of modern art.

Indeed, contentless art is the essence of art in our times: after all, as the modern mantra runs, what could be more artistic than "art for art's sake," art that does not look for a referent outside its own workings—modernism's dream of a comprehensive, self-reflexive poetics? Duchamp's *Fountain* exemplifies the issues surrounding art's absolute self-enclosure. Intentioned in large part as a scandal, Duchamp's piece raises a host of questions: By what criteria is it art or is it not; and what happens when art becomes the object of suspicion, the suspicion of not being what it says it is? The lowest object of utility, a urinal, claims the status of an aesthetic work, thus also claiming the space of an impossible universal—for what kind of truth or shared affect can such an ironic solipsism disclose? The question of affect is inextricable from the question of content, and this is why de Duve rightly points out that, faced with the hollowness of the readymade, one cannot speak about the content of one's affect but simply about the presence of an indeterminate "feeling of having something to do with art" (de Duve 20).

This is also for Agamben the enigma of modern art: Why is it that for all the politicization of art nowadays, our political institutions are hardly affected, let alone threatened, the way Plato was afraid they would be by a group of poets? De Duve's solution to the problem constitutes Agamben's question. For de Duve, modern art has the deictic function of the proper name. I baptize something as art—I say, "this is art"—where "the word 'art' is a proper name whose bearers one can only designate by pointing" (de Duve 19). Consequently, and in accordance with the Kantian nonconceptual nature of the aesthetic judgment, "'art' is . . . not a concept, but a collection of examples—different for everyone" (de Duve 20). In one's list of personal favorites, which dangerously alludes to the aesthetics of taste Kant attempted to eschew, Duchamp's urinal is established as art by virtue of metonymy and then analogy: in my list, it could be contiguous to Michelangelo's Sibyls, Mozart's *Requiem*, and so on, and this contiguity guarantees some sort of resemblance. Duchamp's *Fountain* is art just like its neighbor, the *Delphic Sibyl*; otherwise, it would not be on the same list. This metonymic chain almost recalls the Socratic chain of the poets, each hanging from the ring of his own patron divinity, each holding a ring for the next poet he has uniquely inspired: not a concept for Kant and not a techne for Socrates, art hinges for both on something profoundly subjective even as it promises to communicate something universal. All is well, it seems, with this subjective universal, except that, as de Duve's language already conveys, it is "a *collection* of examples"; the practical reality of post-Kantian subjectivity has less to do with the universal assent that Kant wished for and more with the solipsistic, consumerist attitude one detects in the image of the modern collector. A connoisseur whose interest in art is largely for the sake of acquisition, the collector figures for Agamben as a symptom of art's decline. The collector's appearance marks the moment when art loses its original relation to truth and becomes a commodity, a site for the exercise of taste, a symbol of the collector's financial and cultural capital, an endangered species to be rescued and appreciated on the dusty display shelf.

Furthermore, exemplarity is also at stake, since in de Duve's formulation, the exemplary is operative only within the subjective frame and logic of a single individual collection. An example legitimizes the link among the other listed items; it does not draw its force by being associated with them. In other words, the example stands as the representative of the collection by having a metaphorical rather than a metonymic relation to the whole. For Agamben, the withdrawal of art into the museum or the personal collection coincides with its withdrawal from exemplarity and meaningfulness. In revealing nothing else but the limitless subjectivity of the artist, who proceeds unaccountable to anyone, even to his or her own material, contemporary art lays bare the paradoxes of its existence: it becomes evident that such limitless freedom does not afford the artist any glory, as one might suppose. To the contrary, a look around quickly shows that artists are hardly modern society's cherished citizens. Artistic freedom rather emerges as the side effect of general indifference. Eventually, de Duve also admits to this double-edged sword of modernity: "The fact that one can be an artist without being a painter, or sculptor, or poet, or musician, [is] a fact that I still think one must not stop marveling at or worrying over" (24).

The Man without Content oscillates in this movement between marveling and worrying over the fate of art. As I have already underlined, the privileged instance through which Agamben contrasts art's earlier impact with its marginalized existence in modernity is the Platonic ban on the poets. This banishment Agamben correctly interprets not as a simply negative expulsive move but as Plato's profound understanding of the danger to which art exposes us and that may gravely affect the city's foundations. In other words, Plato the censor is actually touched and transformed by art. He cannot pretend to respect, appreciate, or judge art from a safe distance because he feels the shuddering truth of the artwork all too near. Over and against the tasteful but disinterested collector, the menacing censor emerges as an example of a spectator who is all too interested in the work, who participates in the upheavals of creation, and who, tormented by art, yields it its due by way of prohibition.

Indeed, the figure of the censor is the one that bridges the split between spectator and artist, a split Agamben attributes to Kant and to modern aesthetics in general. Whereas Kant's ideal spectator has a detached eye, Plato's censor is interested in the work to the point of being afraid that he will be swept away by it—and in a sense he already is. He thus confronts the work as his enemy. But the only other person who also sees in the work his mortal enemy is, as Agamben remarks, the artist: "For the one who creates it, art becomes an increasingly uncanny experience, with respect to which speaking of interest is at the very least a euphemism, because what is at stake seems to be not in any way the production of a beautiful work but instead the life and death of the author, or at least his or her spiritual health. To the increasing innocence of the spectator's experience in front of the beautiful object corresponds the increasing danger inherent in the artist's experience, for whom art's *promesse de bonheur* becomes the poison that contaminates and destroys his existence" (5). The censor is a powerful version of the dream of the spectator as artist. For, after all, which great artist would not be relieved to be rid of art? Plato and Rimbaud share the same dream, which is the same nightmare. To understand this creative logic of censorship means to also understand why Agamben begins *The Man without Content* with a reading of Nietzsche that reemphasizes the importance of the artist—namely, of the creative, productive principle—over and against the post-Kantian world of spectatorial reception.

It should be noted at this point that Agamben's reading of Kant is itself very interested and, in fact, strategic. Agamben espouses Nietzsche's refutation of the Kantian distinction between the empirical and the transcendental, which aligns the former with interest, contingency, and thus the need for concepts, and the latter with disinterest, universality, and thus freedom from concepts. Though Nietzsche finds Kant's valorization of disinterest to be responsible for the culture of indifference toward art, it should be said that, for Kant, this distinction between the empirical and the transcendental was meant to serve the opposite purpose: it was meant to foster a deeper engagement with art than that of bourgeois taste. For Kant, disinterest does not signify an indifferent, disengaged aesthetic experience; disinterest ensures that the work is not reduced to an object whose mere purpose is to satisfy the ever-particular spectator's subjective inclinations. Nietzsche attacks Kant because he sees that this actually does not work and that transcendental subjectivity is a stone's throw from relativistic egoism, the same bourgeois hallmark that

Kantian aesthetics attempted to avoid. In turn, Agamben follows Nietzsche's polemic because he too is less concerned with Kant's philosophical intentions at this point than with the discursive and cultural legacy Kantian thought generated—namely, the rise of public indifference to art that was concomitant with the systematization of aesthetic theory during the Enlightenment.

Thus, for Agamben, the split between artist and spectator, a split between risk and judgment, passion and detachment, gives way to a number of other splits in modernity, which I can only mention in passing here: the spectator/artist split produces a further split in the artists themselves, dividing them into "Rhetoricians" and "Terrorists."[26] While the Rhetoricians are concerned chiefly with form, much like the spectator is, the Terrorists insist on pure and unmediated content, much like the Platonic poet who, lacking techne, endures the terror of divine possession (Agamben 8). The spectator is also internally split. In a language that resonates with Marx's critique of the workers' alienation, Agamben describes the alienation of the spectator from himself and from the object of his judgment: "The spectator's is the most radical split: his principle is what is most alien to him; his essence is in that which, by definition, does not belong to him" (24). What does not belong to him is the creative experience, an experience he utterly lacks, yet the lack of which does not stop him from pronouncing judgments. This is judgment without justification, an inessential and illegitimate judgment since the judge cannot grasp what it takes to create the artwork he judges. The spectator cannot grasp this, not because of poor taste and lack of connoisseurship, but because art is not to be "grasped" in that manner of scientific know-how.

At any rate, the spectatorial judgment has been rendered virtually redundant by modern art, which makes self-commentary its sole content. As if all this were not enough and despite his power of judging, the spectator ends up a passive figure, relinquishing complete freedom to the artist, who ultimately proves to be his or her own best judge. Indeed, even if the common spectator does not deem Duchamp's found objects to be art, he or she would most likely concede that poetic license has no borders whatsoever. The artist is an artist who is a critic who is an artist, and this infinite tautology constitutes—or rather, evacuates—the artist's content. For Agamben, this modern collapse of the artistic and critical faculties lies at the heart of the political paradox of modern art—namely, the fact that art becomes politically impotent the more it is let free to invest itself with political urgency. To reframe this in relation to Plato: once the Platonic quarrel between philosophy and poetry was settled, the artist was ironically robbed both of art (art becomes non-art) and of politics (illegible art cannot have any shared truth content).

This is the case, of course, because the quarrel is all but settled. Plato gave it a try, and his solution was to side with philosophy and expel art from the city. However, expulsion is no settlement, and in this sense his failure is also to his credit, for a gesture as radical as his betokens the strife between these two realms as a difficult but necessary antagonism. Modern aesthetics too—with Hegel as its cornerstone—took wholeheartedly the side of philosophy, but this time not by expelling art but by subsuming it under philosophy. When the strife between the two was still on and the artist was held accountable by his public as by his material, art mattered, Agamben seems to say. In the present age of infinite aesthetic freedom, where everyone can be an artist, we are left paradoxically not with the abundance but with the poverty of art at both its producing and receiving ends. In Agamben's example, compared to Renaissance church paintings, the subject matter of which involved actively the clergy as much as the congregation, thus expressing the collective spiritual reality of their time (15–16), the call of political art today sounds like a voice in the desert.

Eternal Returns

Yet before some rush in to judge Agamben as retrogressive and others to commend him as an advocate of the classics, I should warn that neither is actually the case. Pursuing Heidegger's call to *decide* the fate of art after Hegel's pronouncement,[27] Agamben understands decision, no less than his mentor, to be anything but the taking of a position. In the expected Heideggerian vein of deferrals into the future, Agamben, like many fellow poststructuralists, avoids committing to any position, since any clarity of position is by nature a metaphysical trap, irremediably complicit with the violence of propositional thinking. Plato's philosophical commitment, which Agamben seems to favor over disinterested aesthetic judgment, *this* commitment is ironically the one ingredient contemporary theory lacks. Indeed, it would be quite fair to say that equating commitment with the lack of theoretical sophistication is by now de rigueur in poststructuralist discourse. Strangely, however, this aversion to commitment works to turn poststructuralism's critique of scientific objectivity and Enlightenment reason against itself: in its attempt to evade what it fears to be the pitfalls of propositional logic, much of poststructuralist theory reads as a new version of neutral, disinterested, even quasiscientific prose without, of course, the resort to the hard facts that at least science still affords to have.[28] This uncanny return of objectivity through the back door is one instance of what I call the untragic mode of contemporary thought: a writing without blood, without stakes, without content.

As such, Agamben may well engage Plato by way of imagining a possibly more meaningful existence for art in the past than its modern dead end, but ultimately he does not grant any certainty to this possibility. This despite the historical evidence that Greek art—with tragedy at its apex—did precede and exceed the metaphysical logos, that it provided the earliest food for philosophy's thought, and that it was its forcefulness (as Agamben after all suspects) that obliged Plato to subordinate it to politics. Nonetheless, Agamben insists on speaking of art strictly in its vicissitudes within the Western aesthetic narrative that culminates with Hegel and that reads all art heretofore retroactively as a sorry subject of metaphysics. We cannot ever make any pronouncement on the past outside Hegel's reading and Hegel's legacy. Eventually, Plato and whatever preceded him must only make sense in view of this apex of German idealism.[29] Therefore, to envision the future of art beyond Hegel's end, as Agamben wishes to do, requires the modern thinker to define this "beyond" as fundamentally exclusive of the past. "Beyond" is to be understood only as a new invention, as future, and as progress along the line that allegedly started with the Greeks. Surely, the past is cumulatively preserved as it is also canceled, Hegel would like to think; but this dialectical formulation can also be just a euphemism for rendering the past museal along with its art—both embalmed curios that prove ultimately irrelevant. The logic of historical accumulation is itself sequential and does not allow for the unpredictable rupture of past into present. It thinks of any such interruptive repetition as atavistic and ahistorical, just as it thinks that art can only exist accumulated in the museum, barred from reentering day-to-day life. The preservation of the past in Hegel works only to propel the historical spiral of the Spirit's passage, obeying ultimately a progressive or regressive line—depending on one's politics of reading. Spirals unfold around a central axis, and this linear axis remains far more prone to determinism than does the temporality of recurrence, which characterized Greek thinking and, most especially, tragedy.[30]

Thus, for all the interesting motivations and implications of Plato's ban on art and for all the examples of considering action poetically that Agamben finds in the ancients, Agamben's vision of art's future cannot include the Greeks in any substantive way. At best, the future of art must proceed from the Hegelianization of the Greeks—that is, from the retroactive but categorical certainty that all art ever was is what Hegel revealed it to be: a surrogate for the Idea. Has art *ever been*? Has art *ever existed* in any other way than in relation to two unsavory metaphysical alternatives—either as a servant to the concept (its Platonic curse) or as a merely sensuous thing designed to satisfy our taste (its post-Enlightenment predicament)? It is to questions of such spurious epochal nature that Agamben's no-longer/not-yet temporality of art adheres: "[Hegel's] is in no way a simple eulogy, but is rather a meditation on the problem of art at the outer limit of its destiny, when art loosens itself from itself and moves in pure nothingness, suspended in a kind of diaphanous limbo between no-longer-being and not-yet-being" (53). This passage is meant to highlight that Hegel's end is not the absolute last word on art but that it makes sense only as the conclusion of a specific narrative of art that we have had: the aesthetic narrative. Thus, Hegel simply announces the completion of "the circle of [art's] metaphysical destiny" (Agamben 54). But the not-yet does not really belong to the logic of the circle; and to be sure, any sense of cyclical time is already categorically foreclosed by the temporality of the no-longer. The not-yet is a furthering of the Hegelian ascent, an ultrabeyond of completion. Of course, it bears repeating that, if all this were true to begin with, if art had never been anything else but a servant to the Idea, Plato would not have had such trouble with it, nor would he have wished to contain it for the sake of his *kallipolis*.

We have, however, ourselves arrived full circle. We end with the tension—possibly more intensified—with which we began the introduction of Agamben into our discussion: a tension between Agamben's thought-provoking observations on Plato and the historical violence of revisionism that any grand epochal declaration such as his is bound to commit. Perhaps, however, ambivalence might not be so ungenerous a feeling toward a thinker like Agamben, who commended Plato precisely for his ambivalence. And since this latter point remains the one that most of all warrants our attention, as it brings the ancients to the heart of our modern quandaries, it would be appropriate to devote our last thoughts in this chapter to Plato's impassioned ambivalence—what I called his mimetic or cathartic reaction to art—which might offer an alternative model for experiencing art today. Even when he denounced art as illusion, Plato by definition thought of art in relation to truth. He thought of art qualitatively (whether truthful or untruthful, for then and always), not quantitatively (how much truthful) as did Hegel, who measured its truth only as a function of history and found it inadequate for now. In our world of commodity fetishism, where quantity and quantification reign supreme, the question of "how much truthful art is" sounds ominously less disclosive, and even less progressive,[31] than the more-hostile-sounding Platonism of whether art is truthful at all.

It is, if anything, this modern culture of commodity accumulation that lies behind Agamben's complaint that aesthetics cannot conceive of art in any other way than the "merely sensuous"—namely, than a material good. This complaint, despite Agamben's effort to extend it throughout the history of art, does not apply so well to the Greeks, not even to Plato, whose philosophical staple has been the subordination of the sensuous to the Idea. And yet for all his idealism, Plato saw that art presents another possibility to the antithesis of concept and matter. In art, the supersensuous does not have the Idea as its only and necessary synonym any more than it has sense as its only and necessary antonym. This thought-provoking but nonconceptual nature of art is its *poetic*, creative possibility. Let us remember that the divine lot of poetry Socrates was speaking about in the *Ion* refers exactly to this notion of art: divine mania is both sensuous (it takes over the poet's body) and supersensuous (it reveals something extraordinary), and in being both, it does not belong to the realm of concepts that regulate techne. The "merely sensuous" turns out to be never so "mere" for the ancients. Rather, this expression, "merely sensuous," is complicit with the logic of modernity, which, by way of philosophical atonement for its life of commodity fetishism, has decided to degrade everything involving sense, action, and matter to the register of the "mere"—a crude moralism that would have been incomprehensible to the Greeks, even to that great moralist Plato.

Whether Hegelian or post-Hegelian, aesthetics condemns or celebrates art for its sensuous aspects: for Hegel, the contingency of the sensuous renders it an inadequate mode for disclosing the Idea; for post-Hegelian aestheticians, most notably Theodor Adorno, the excess of the sensuous promises to relieve us from the oppressiveness of conceptual abstraction—though it is even arguable how embodied the Adornian sensuous is allowed to be. Still other poststructuralist thinkers like Agamben, who prefer the Heideggerian legacy, continue to devalue sensuousness to "mere life," even as they might also critique the Platonic or Cartesian metaphysical hierarchy of mind and body. In separating the sensuous from the conceptual, whether through celebration or condemnation, both modern branches of aesthetics fall prey to this typically Platonic hierarchy, albeit without Plato's troubled recognition of the supersensuous yet nonconceptual nature of art.[32] To face what Plato faced—and thus felt obliged to avert his eyes—is to face the unintelligible visage of truth, which art lets appear by virtue of its own irrational and asystematic character. There is a reason why the tragedians intensified at the utmost the conflicts narrated in the old myths, and the reason was not simply to indulge themselves in chaos and incoherence. Tragic conflict reveals a necessity, albeit a necessity that defeats the calmness of philosophical systematicity. Tragedy reveals necessity as a cosmic force that is always there ready to erupt into the course of human life. But even though its certainty is inevitable and its repetition evident throughout human history, each time, the conditions and form of its eruption prove as indeterminable as ever: a necessity that looks always like an accident even after its occurrence, a circumstance that makes no sense yet obliges the human being to respond to it with whatever sense is left.

This is what Plato knew but could not accept, because his highest concerns were the preservation of both public and individual happiness: the tragedians not only showed truth *through* nonrational means (poetry), but they imperiled truth by showing it *in* its indeterminacy, by showing that, for the most part, it cannot be accessed and responded to properly by humans. (Of course, in so showing the human strife toward truth's unattainable ideal, they resembled Plato more than anyone else did, for Plato too held human wisdom in not so high esteem.) Art imparts nothing less than truth, albeit the bitter truth, which the cosmos has *always* thrown ahead of unsuspecting humans faster than philosophy could ever dream of processing it. This "always" of experience—of suffering but also of rising above the worst of occasions—this "always," and not the no-longer/not-yet, reveals the time of tragedy as the time of truth.

II

FOR THE LOVE OF TRUTH

Habeas Corpus

FOUCAULT'S FEARLESS SPEECH

Michel Foucault understood that tragedy and philosophy are the undisputed protagonists (even as they are antagonists) of the scene of truth. This is why in his effort to write a history of truth through the modes of its attestation, that is, through various practices of truth-telling (parrhesia), he turned to Euripides and Socrates. Toward the end of his life, Foucault delivered a series of lectures compiled now in a slim volume under the title *Fearless Speech*,[1] where he followed ancient practices of truth-telling in order to trace the modern vicissitudes of truth and to propose truth-telling as a technique of the self—namely, as a way of comportment in the world today. Even though we may commonly think that the vocabularies of technique and selfhood are mutually exclusive, for Foucault techne as a process of transformation is also disclosive of the self in its transformative capacities: how the self cares for itself, how it molds, educates, and refashions itself, sometimes freely and sometimes out of necessity. At a time when truth and the self have become prominent targets of philosophical critique, Foucault turned to parrhesia as a practice that could potentially transform our wounded notions of truth and self.

But how does parrhesia actually bring about transformation? We may respond somewhat schematically that parrhesia first happens when excessive and unjust power compels one to speak up against it. The encounter with this external force transforms the individual, who feels obliged to resist at all costs. However, as this isolated intervention evolves into regular practice and as forms of governance pass from sovereign monarchies to democratic assemblies, the function of parrhesia itself changes: the concentrated power of the monarch against which it once spoke has now been diffused in the democratic state, and this new form of polity regulates the existence of parrhesia, transforming it from an exceptional moment of dissent to an institutionalized mode of opposition. To regulate parrhesia, moreover, entails not only the legal protection of the truth-teller (*parrhesiastes*) from sovereign retaliation but also the preparation and education of citizens so as to exercise effectively their right of free speech. It was in fact in this pedagogical arena that the battle concerning the status of truth was waged between Socrates and the Sophists, Athens's most celebrated teachers. Whereas the Sophists were famous for teaching the techniques of persuasion regardless of whether they themselves believed in the truth of their argument, Socrates sought to harmonize what one says with what one believes and, furthermore, with how one lives. This Socratic demand of an exemplary life that accords logos to bios is of paramount importance for Foucault's interest in the technique of the self: shifting from the purely political aspect of parrhesia, in which the truth-teller opposes a hostile sovereign, Socrates encourages his interlocutors to account for how their beliefs correspond to their way of life. With Socrates, parrhesia begins to be not simply a matter of oppositional speech to power but a way of living. Even so, it should be noted that, in turning parrhesia from political opposition to individual life path, Socrates's own last parrhesiastic gesture—his defense before the angered Athenians—marks a moment of political parrhesia, which reminds us that parrhesia can never be a safe discourse, any more than we can think of the Socratic life path as ever being divorced from political life.

While Socratic parrhesia will be the subject of the next chapter, I would like, at this point, to emphasize what for Foucault remains at the heart of all parrhesiastic speech, whether political or personal: the face-to-face encounter. Though Foucault does not use the term "presence" systematically to describe this encounter, there could be no substantive reflection on the care of the self without the simultaneous admission of this Socratic spontaneity of presence. Thus, what interests me in Foucault's classical turn is the urgent and unabashed reactivation of philosophical categories that have been variously condemned to the dustbin of contemporary thought.

Foucault ventures on his investigation of parrhesia by citing its etymology: *parrhesia* means "saying everything," from *pan* (everything) and *rhema* (that which is said) (12). It means telling everything that one holds in mind and heart to be the truth. Truth in this formulation is inextricably related to the process of its manifestation, which is this telling. This is why I think it important to reflect further on this rather self-evident aspect of parrhesia—namely, that it is not writing but speech (*rhema*). "Rhema" relates to *rhein*, which signifies flux, movement, transformation, change. When we speak, words flow out of our mouth. Our utterance can influence those whom we address, but they too can change our speech by asking questions, demanding explanations, disputing arguments, and so on. Hence, the change involved in the act of speaking is predicated on something else: on presence (*parousia*), the physical presence of the interlocutors to each other, the coincidence of the enunciation with the enunciator—what we call "full speech." What makes for change in a conversation is the fact that the speakers are readily available to each other and thus can be held accountable for what they say.

Yet presence in this sense of fullness is the philosophical term that most of all has endured the heaviest critical blows in contemporary theory: understood as coterminous with metaphysical fixation, it came to signify the delusions of self-mastery and the violence of self-sameness associated with the history of subjectivity and its attendant pitfalls. Additionally, insofar as speech is predicated on presence, it too had to undergo deconstruction—its primacy in the history of Western philosophy debunked by Derrida as either logocentrism or phonocentrism. With presence now a synonym for false coincidence, the speaking subject became a nebulous category, ensnaring anyone who dared appeal to its ethicopolitical potential into a web of impossibilities.

Psychological notions such as the unconscious and the unreliable nature of memory are but the most obvious reasons why the coincidence of subject and utterance has been shown to be precarious; the slipperiness of language that trips and traps the enunciatory subject is another. How could we ever trust that the intention of the speaker and the actual truth of what is spoken are one and the same, when a host of intervening factors have been shown to subvert both human intentionality and linguistic transparency? Can the subject itself even distinguish what constitutes its conscious intentions from what constitutes its unconscious desires? And if we could separate cognition from emotion, how can we expect that the person's actual speech will communicate transparently its intention, without any of the rhetorical plays and side effects that language inevitably entails? We soon begin to see that there is nothing masterful or fixed about this situation and that the integrity of both speaker and speech is set in doubt. This is not simply the doubt of skepticism, for this kind of doubt is relative to a particular situation, leaving open the possibility that another situation could be different. In this case, we are dealing with a far more fundamental doubt, one of epistemological and ontological nature, which dictates that the human being remains essentially unknowable to itself and that furthermore—in being defined by language rather than being language's master—the human being cannot guarantee linguistically the contents of its own communication. To quote Nietzsche's witty observation: "Where we ourselves are concerned, we are not 'knowledgeable people.'"[2]

With such a monumental shift in the thinking of subjectivity and presence—not even to speak of truth—the question of truth-telling and the presence it presupposes seems to have been declared moot. Because truth-telling beckons presence, because it is inseparable from a speaking subject who, moreover, insists on the ethicopolitical urgency of its discourse, Foucault's interest in parrhesia has larger implications for contemporary philosophical practice than being just another case study in discourse analysis.

Benjamin Pryor maintains that Foucault's understanding of parrhesia is not about the self-empowered, self-governed subject.[3] Pryor correctly points out that παρρησιάζομαι (the verb form of truth-telling) occurs in the middle voice, while reminding us that the middle voice "does not require a subjective agency but relates to oneself in an individual way." I concur to a large extent with his remarks, insofar as I too do not conceive of the power of the truth-teller in the egotistical and psychologistic terms of self-empowerment: truth-telling does not secure its agent any external benefits associated with power, nor is the truth-teller someone who speaks just to feel authorized or enabled. At the same time, however, I do not interpret this absence of self-empowerment to mean the evaporation of subjective agency, as Pryor does when he claims that through the practice of parrhesia "philosophy finds its speech at the place of the disappearance of the subject." After all, while it might be that whenever Socrates speaks, philosophy also speaks, it is not true that whenever philosophy speaks, Socrates speaks with it. To the contrary, as a truth-telling philosophical agent, Socrates would most probably reject the equation of his personal voice with the various conclusions of the ever-changing philosophical consensus. It was, indeed, against the accepted philosophical voice of his time that he self-consciously raised his own personal voice, in an open dissent that was deeply political in nature.

Consequently, while parrhesia does not *accrue* power *to* its agent, power, in parrhesia, *stems from* the agent's relation to himself or herself: it is the power of testimony, which involves the courage of publicizing an unpopular belief one could only hold privately and feel safe. In other words, parrhesia may not result in self-empowerment, but it does require powerful selves — namely, courageous human beings — to serve as its vehicles. That these human beings are *vehicles* — a mode of self-relation expressed by the middle voice of parrhesia's verb — does not compromise their degree of agency in the act of telling. Pryor's insistence on this middle voice hopes to enlist Greek grammar to effect another nonmetaphysical translation: namely, that courage inhabits us and truth commands us, contrary to the metaphysical view that it is the subject qua self who chooses to live courageously and speak truthfully.

But this translation does not carry over the middle voice, which in denoting self-relation (as Pryor himself recognizes) first and foremost presupposes a self — a self acting on itself, as both subject and object of the action. Pryor's translation keeps an active voice but simply invests agency onto the object: in place of "I tell the truth," now "truth tells me." This nonmetaphysical translation was not supposed to simply reverse the terms of the metaphysical binary, but inevitably it does so by espousing the logic of passivity as opposed to the logic of agency. Tragic logic, which binds fate (the outside, the object, the Other) irreducibly to character (the inside, the subject, the self-same), understands the middle voice of the verb παρρησιάζομαι better: though the predisposition to courage might come to a human being from the outside, it is still a *character* trait that this human being uniquely inhabits. In other words, it is this subject's mode of agency that makes the gift of courage show itself as either courage or a gift wasted on him or her. Eventually, it is this courage that lends parrhesia its transgressive character, its "excess," as Pryor calls it. This excess is not beyond or outside but part and parcel of parrhesia's emphasis on self-relation.

Hence, in fully agreeing with Pryor that philosophical parrhesia is transgressive speech, I understand transgression here less in the postmodern and poststructuralist vocabulary of the death of the subject and more in the tragic vocabulary of heroic choice. Heroic choice, though often ruining its agent (thus also superseding it), remains irrevocably owned by that agent — owned in both senses of this term: such choice is the hero's own, and the hero owns up to it while undergoing self-destruction. After all, one is a tragic hero — namely, one is extraordinary, *in excess of himself* — because he has chosen, just as much as he was chosen, to inhabit that kind of self-relation. To erase the subject from the scene of parrhesia would neutralize and even disarticulate the very connection Foucault draws between philosophy and tragedy through truth-telling, for there is no tragedy without human agents.

Even though Foucault's early work has contributed significantly to post-structuralism's declaration of the end of the subject,[4] it seems that in his *Fearless Speech* he does not settle for simply diagnosing such epochal breaks, nor does he relinquish the transformative possibilities of the subjective voice to being an illusory conceit. Thus, his interest in parrhesia is not without moral commitments, not without the acknowledgment that parrhesia is an ethically tantamount mode of speech that deserves to be taken up again, even as its specifications place it irremediably in the past.

In doing so, he also reveals the paradoxical temporality at work in the genealogical method: the ethical critique that motivates genealogical thinking resembles unwittingly the ancient commitment to truth and objectivity, even as the stated purpose of genealogical histories—to expose the ideological basis of all values—is irrefutably modern in its relativization of truth. The mark, of course, of this relativization is the turn from the vocabulary of truth to that of value. The paradox, though, goes even deeper. To expose that values are historically and ideologically entrenched requires that the genealogist step outside the very history these values proved themselves unable to eschew. It requires that he or she, for a moment at least, leap into the space once called Truth so as to see from there how human history has never involved Truth but only various competing values. This logical fallacy of perspective, I wish to argue, is genealogy's peculiar ethical mark—an ancient trace that continues in modernity to privilege moral content over formal logical consistency. Thus, as I hope to explain further below, genealogy practices a strange mix of subjective objectivity. It approaches objectivity through a subjective route, the main route available in the modern world of transcending the limitations of the subject.[5]

Since it was Nietzsche's critical account of morality in his *Genealogy of Morals* that furnished the model for Foucault's genealogical studies, my supposition regarding the ethical grounds of genealogy begs the various debates on the epistemic and metaethical nature of Nietzsche's moral claims. In other words, if Nietzsche decries the objectivity with which common morality falsely invests itself, does he himself claim an objective moral standard in order to justify his revaluation? If not, what are the grounds of justification for his elevation of the morality of the strong as opposed to that of the weak? Such questions are indicative, though by no means comprehensive, of this issue and have generated diverse responses in Nietzsche scholarship of both continental and Anglophone orientations.[6] Without discussing the merits or problems of these various positions, it will suffice to say that—regardless of their philosophical leanings—scholars who refute the normative basis of Nietzsche's genealogy do so on a common reasoning: that of Nietzsche's asystematicity. Accordingly, it is not that Nietzsche's writings lack consistently normative claims; it is that for every moral claim, one can find other passages where Nietzsche expressly refuses to be held accountable to an ethical standard. Scholars frequently attribute this asystematicity to the psychological dimension of Nietzsche's thought, which, by definition, cannot pertain to the absolute. If Nietzsche is a moral psychologist at best, then his morality cannot involve any such thing as an imperative, nor can it aspire to universal applicability. The absence of a universally applicable norm is the focus of the antirealist readings of his ethics, which emphasize that his morality is targeted only to the ones like him, the "higher types."

But one could read this moral antirealism differently, in a way that connects Nietzsche somewhat unexpectedly to the ancient thinker who, above all, pursued the absolute: Plato. The fact that Nietzsche reserves higher morality for the select few is actually not so different from Plato's view of morality. The latter's moral vision was also undemocratic in assuming the absolute as an impossible, but no less real, summit to which ethical beings remain drawn. Yet one would hardly describe Plato as a moral psychologist—at least not in the derogatory, relativist sense of the term. Plato could be considered a psychologist in the strict sense that his philosophy is a logos of the soul, but the soul is a category that actually escapes contemporary philosophy, political theory, and, revealingly, psychology itself. Just as for Plato the ascent toward the absolute was something few souls desired to undertake, let alone fulfill, so too for Nietzsche the life of noble suffering is fit, not for the many, but for the higher types, who can endure it and be elevated as a result of it.

It is generally understood that Nietzsche's confrontational rhetoric is meant less to provide clear guidelines to an ethics and more to inspire the gifted ones to a higher awakening. Accordingly, we must not exempt his fierce denial of moral standards and imperatives from this overall polemics. Such denial functions as a polemical and ironic strategy that distinguishes him from all that he disdains—namely, the hypocrisy of common morality that conveniently confuses its self-interested rules for the moral law. Hence my earlier claim that radical subjectivism might be the only path for gaining a glimpse in the modern world of what transcends the subject and the confines of moral psychology. Nietzsche's descriptive aspect (the fact that conventional morality is hypocritical because it claims an objectivity it actually lacks) collapses into a prescriptive aspect (all morality, including his own higher morality, cannot be objectively grounded), because in modernity only this kind of gesture would save him from being suspected himself of moral hypocrisy. Nietzsche, in other words, must fall victim in the very war he started for the betterment of humanity. This, of course, betrays his own taste for tragedy and his interest in Socrates, whose tragic performances will concern us in the next chapter. But what is this war that Nietzsche started? A war against objectivity.

Frequently shunned as naïve and anachronistic, objectivity is now only invoked as a specter to authorize relativism's ethical indifference. After all, if there is no longer any claim to objectivity, then at least we can all refrain from affirming our own subjectivity and thereby reach a semblance of universal neutrality. Objectivity no longer bears its primary meaning as an absolute measure, an outside. Modern theoretical reason's adoption of a purely historical (and thus, inherently cultural) logic forecloses any possibility of such an outside. Yet the critique of objectivity's allegedly false absolute does not prevent theoretical discourse itself from assuming a posture of detachment as a subterfuge for objective authority. I have in mind the textualist theoretical production that followed the linguistic turn and that, despite its ubiquitous references to ethics and politics, manages to keep a safe distance from addressing either at the level of actual content. The rhetorical acrobatics of so-called high theory—supported by an arsenal of puns, chiasms, neologisms, and ironies—may eschew classical objectivity's moral certainty, but it makes up for it by sounding ever more scientific in its formal, dispassionate parade of tropes. Refraining adroitly from committing to a position, the critic who writes after the end of the subject treats any hint of a strong position as nothing but the anathema of subjectivity in an age that should "know better." After all, how dare I insist that *this* is right? Is it not more objective to extend this logic beyond myself and recognize that the other, too, has an equally legitimate claim to assert his or her *version* of what is right? Or in a seemingly more impartial and universally objective fashion, to recognize that no one could ever make or has ever made serious claims to an absolute outside, since the simultaneously open and closed nature of language bars access to any content outside the linguistic play itself? This self-reflexivity may flatter my sense of logical progress, but it incapacitates me from deciding, creating, and in fact living meaningfully in this world.

In unearthing alternative histories (those of madness, punishment, sexuality, and so on), which expose the effects of power struggles in the formation of these concepts, genealogy cannot but bear the modern mark of relativism. How could it not, when Nietzsche, in whose steps Foucault followed, brought about a veritable tumult in the world of causes and effects, making the latter the parent of the former? And in so revaluating modernity's rationalism by privileging the noncausal tragic vocabulary of accident and fate as a better version of reality, Nietzsche himself translated tragedy's absolute into a modern theory of values?[7] Gary Gutting summarizes the Foucauldian genealogical project as follows: "Rather than asking what, in the apparently contingent, is actually necessary, [Foucault] suggests asking what, in the apparently necessary, might be contingent." Further down, Gutting continues, "The point of a genealogical analysis is to show that a given system of thought ... was the result of contingent turns of history, not the outcome of rationally inevitable trends."[8] By espousing historical contingency, genealogy gives up any pretense of presenting us with an objective exposition of breaks; its breaks cannot claim to be transcendentally valid, and they cannot serve as uncontested origins of official histories. Genealogy is by definition no official history, relying instead on the descriptive power of narration to trace the vicissitudes of a concept, practice, or institution. Certain moments in its narrations are particularly charged in the mind of the genealogist, who fixes on them to spawn *his* or *her* tale: they function as pivots, incitations, or defining turns; they are the prisms through which various concepts and practices become refracted. These originary moments illuminate as much the genealogical narratives they produce as they do the creative intellect of the genealogist, who picked them out from other potential instances to unfold his or her narrative.

All this is true enough. However, this does not mean that genealogy is mere whimsy and that its findings are of no serious concern. After all, in espousing historical contingency, genealogy recalls tragic time—a time that cannot be determined by the application of rational causality, but a time in which the human being must respond truly, that is, absolutely. The choice of reaction in tragic time must be ideal. The human being is urged to choose the "right" path despite the cluttering of all the power struggles that surround it. Is not the genealogist's effort similarly focused on clearing this ideological clutter? But to do so, to see behind the distorted causality of modern rationality, is to *believe* that there is an *outside* to rationality's workings. It is at this point that genealogy approaches what I have called above the ancient commitment to truth and objectivity. In the genealogist's very motivation to unravel what has been prohibited by power, in the commitment to speak what has been unspoken, one discerns the fate of a great moralist who could only exist as a modern by detesting morality: Nietzsche. Beyond the relative or ideological politics of genealogical thinking, which can surely be appropriated and tailored to fit specific agendas, there lies the ethical belief that something somewhere went awry and that this historical ill must be accounted for, given origins and legacies, that justice must be rendered.

To put this differently: what first appears as a subjective tale eventually relies on the very truth that underlies all genuine objectivity—and this is the notion of *belief*, the axiomatic structure of belief. Genealogy involves belief, the belief that *this* story is the true version, even in the face of knowing that it is contested. After all, Foucault's point is that truth-telling suffered the modern Cartesian blow when doubt replaced belief. Thus, genealogy's explanatory power lies precisely in its stubborn normativity, its scandalously subjective objectivity, not in the pursuit of abstract, conceptual exercises that offer only the objectivity of the relative. Because of their entrenched subjective nature, genealogies become sites of contestation and thus invested paths to truth, not philosophical pseudotranscendentals. Nietzsche, who understood that all philosophy is actually biography, practiced genealogy because genealogy admits to its investments, passions, and preferences.

Foucault too thinks that genealogy tells a story—the history of thought rather than of ideas, as he insisted on differentiating:

> The history of ideas involves the analysis of a notion from its birth, through its development, and in the setting of other ideas which constitute its context. The history of thought is the analysis of the way an unproblematic field of experience, or a set of practices, which were accepted without question, which were familiar and "silent," out of discussion, becomes a problem, raises discussion and debate, incites new reactions, and induces crisis in the previously silent behavior, habits, practices, and institutions. The history of thought, understood in this way, is the history of the way people begin to take care of something, of the way they become anxious about this or that—for example, about madness, about crime, about themselves, or about truth. (74)

The history of thought is not the linear progression of the development of ideas; instead, it involves the way that a field of experience suddenly loses its naturalness and becomes a cause of concern. By speaking of a "field of experience,"

Foucault extends the scope of thought beyond the limited horizon of ideas. Moreover, his interest in the symptomatic character of thought reveals two interrelated aspects of thinking: while the first part of this paragraph intimates that shifts in our thinking produce emotional responses, such as anxiety and unease, the second part tells us that the converse also holds true—namely, that people's emotional attitudes produce conceptual changes, that their anxiety about an idea results in redefining this idea. Foucault then writes the story of this anxiety—the anxiety of whether speech, presence, and thus truth-telling are possible—not the official narrative according to which these classical notions must prove essentially wanting to the intricacies of modern thought. But to think of the history of thought as the unfolding of an anxiety is the brilliant insight of an anxious mind, one that admits to its anxiety instead of elevating it to a discursive solution. As I have mentioned above, the admission of this emotional charge in thought is a fundamental premise of genealogical thinking. To equate taking care of something with the feeling of anxiety means to admit, and even to mourn, the potential mishandling of that something in the unsure hands of its anxious caregiver. That parrhesia will have lost some of its most compelling characteristics by the time it had become subject to institutional protection is the obvious conclusion of Foucault's narrative. Thus, like Nietzsche, who mourned Olympian beauty as he bade it a definitive farewell, Foucault too recognizes not only the historical necessity but also the ethical impoverishment of an age that has rendered the conditions of parrhesia impossible.

It is at this juncture of emotion and thought, anxiety and epistemological shift, that I believe Foucault's genealogical method offers a richer vision of transformation from past to present than various other pronouncements of ends.[9] His treatment of parrhesia specifically shows that Foucault takes the occasion of shifts to project them historically and zoom in on that aspect of the shift that constitutes a violent bending—a violence our time resists acknowledging, because if it did so, it would have to admit the sacrifice that such shifts require before they themselves become naturalized and inevitable, before they pose for us as the only place at which we must find ourselves. Shifts not only show what is necessary for us now; they hint as much about what was there before and perhaps, more importantly, *that* there was something else before.[10] I think that this loss, which accompanies all sudden revaluation of values, forms the core of genealogical inquiry, and if admitted, it might subdue the celebratory optimism with which much of contemporary theory views the epistemic project of our modernity as it submits anything and everything to critical interrogation. Put simply, the genealogical excavation recognizes as its origin the tragedy of thought, whether that be the violence of breaks or the anxiety of affirming this violence—an anxiety that itself often translates into violent suppression. Genealogy, then, is one mode of thinking tragically, while parrhesia, as we will see, is a mode of speaking tragically.

Let us focus closely on this anxiety that is particular to truth-telling and to the notion of the speaker's presence as well: to differentiate between who speaks and what is spoken is to sever truth once and for all from its axiomaticity, to sever the *belief* in it, and yet, strangely, to still consider philosophy a provenance of truth. But, in fact, the importance of full speech in truth-telling is less about the actual metaphysical coincidence of the subject and its enunciation and more about the heightened stakes that such a claim of coincidence yields for the truth-teller during this enunciation. Truth demands intensified stakes, and the claim to coincidence guarantees that the truth-teller is willing to set his moral authority and his bodily integrity under scrutiny and threat. In other words, though such coincidence is presupposed in the scene of truth-telling, it does not necessarily go unchallenged by the audience. Foucault turns to the Greeks—Euripides and Socrates in particular—because in the dialogic aspect of Socrates and tragedy, one can find the essence of speech as a movement between speakers: there would be nothing magnificent about a soliloquy displaying complete mastery of body and utterance, unless the display is meant for someone else. Thus, presence is not an end in itself. On the other hand, however, we should not rush to be done away with it. With no sense of presence, no one would be held accountable in any real and efficacious way. One must actually believe in an essential coincidence of who one is and what one says in order to generate any significant response. Otherwise, to challenge a subject who is self-doubting to the point of its own disappearance is not such a noble exercise.

The physical presence of the speaker in front of an audience encourages spontaneous interaction, and this spontaneity grants to speech an element of frankness. On account of this frankness, Foucault differentiates between parrhesia and rhetoric in a way reminiscent of the Platonic distinction between philosophy and rhetoric: "In *parrhesia*, the speaker makes it manifestly clear and obvious that what he says is his *own* opinion. And he does this by avoiding any kind of rhetorical form which would veil what he thinks. Instead, the *parrhesiastes* uses the most direct words and forms of expression he can find. Whereas rhetoric provides the speaker with technical devices to help him prevail upon the minds of his audience (*regardless* of the rhetorician's own opinion concerning what he says), in *parrhesia*, the *parrhesiastes* acts on other people's minds by showing them as directly as possible what he actually believes" (12). In Plato's vein, Foucault emphasizes that rhetoric differs from parrhesia in that rhetoric uses technical devices to affect the audience.[11] As the rhetorician aims at the emotional manipulation of the audience, his own speech is not emotionally frank. The rhetorician speaks *to* the emotions of others but not *of* his own emotions. The truth-teller, on the other hand, speaks from his own affect and his own experiential transformation, hoping that his audience will come to share his feelings; but this result is not guaranteed. In such an understanding of truth, truth's seat is not only the mind but the heart as well.

Plato too excised rhetoric from truth not so much because rhetoric did not yield true statements but because these were not necessarily frank statements. A Sophist may have defended a position that was objectively true, but he did not do so out of a frank and wholehearted attachment to this truth but mostly out of expediency. The appearance of Sophism in the democratic polity thus brought about a significant crisis in truth-telling, which carried over into modernity, where the preeminence of scientific thought drove that final wedge between truth and the truth-teller: truth for the moderns is utterly detached from the character of the truth-teller, having to do with evidence alone. Foucault illustrates this shift when he poses this anxious question on behalf of the moderns: "But does the *parrhesiastes* say what he *thinks* is true, or does he say what *is* really true?" (14). This is the question of the modern epistemological doubt that severs being from knowing. Foucault answers it, restoring the parrhesiastic claim that in the mind of the truth-teller there is no such split: "To my mind, the *parrhesiastes* says what is true because he *knows* that it is true; and he *knows* that it is true because it is really true. ... He says what he *knows* to be true" (14). Parrhesia presents this moment of ontological and epistemological coincidence, the coincidence not only between teller and telling but between personal belief and knowledge as well. The truth-teller believes that he knows that what he is speaking is the truth. Moreover, this truth is his own truth, a conviction to which he was led through his own experience, not a received opinion. Paradoxically, this deeply avowed subjectivity constitutes true knowledge: a private truth that can claim universal assent.

If democracy signaled the crisis of parrhesia for the Greeks by sanctioning even thoughtless speech as a civic right, it was Cartesianism that according to Foucault shook the modern confidence in parrhesia by doubting the subject's certainty of its truth claims (14). Modern science's response to this doubt was to align the domain of truth with that of evidence and objectivity, while rendering the notion of the truth-teller completely irrelevant. Truth's desubjectification in the modern era serves primarily as proof of truth's objectivity and universal validity. Science, which detests normativity, posits this detachment of truth from the teller by way of assuring a value-free and neutral proposition. Interestingly, however, the severing of truth from the person who speaks it is not limited to scientific discourse but finds a strange and unwitting ally in Heidegger, of all thinkers, who otherwise distances himself sharply from the totalizing and reifying aspects of scientific objectivity. Given the importance of Heidegger's thought for all poststructuralist problematizations of presence and for Foucault's own intellectual development particularly, I will offer some parenthetical reflections on this pointed distinction between truth and truth-teller—or to use Heidegger's own preferred terms, between ἀλήθεια (*aletheia*, or truth) and "sayer"—a distinction he establishes in his essay on "Hegel and the Greeks."[12]

As I have just mentioned, the insistence on bodiless aletheia cuts across both Heidegger's reimagining of a philosophy of Being and the scientific method for which truth must be universal regardless of the nature of its source. Of course, for Heidegger the source does matter, particularly insofar as it is aletheia itself that stands at the source of thinking—"Ἀλήθεια remains for us what is first of all to be thought"—and remains for him emphatically "*the* matter of thinking" (335). But still, in being so, aletheia can never be considered in its embodiment, for it is never the teller from whom truth originates. Defining aletheia as unconcealment, Heidegger refuses to ever commensurate the human being, through whom this unconcealment takes place or for whom it is intended, with the unconcealment itself. Heidegger poses the rhetorical question of whether unconcealment and presence (that is, truth and its teller in the terms of our discussion) belong to one another and in what way, and responds, "Presence is referred to unconcealment, but not vice versa" (334). Heideggerian aletheia, unlike Greek truth-telling as Foucault narrates it, is always prior to its contingent instantiation in the act of telling. As such, it thwarts any attempt at subjectifying it: "It has indeed often been remarked that there cannot be an unconcealment in itself, that unconcealment is after all always unconcealment 'for someone.' It is therefore unavoidably 'subjectivized.' Nevertheless, must the human being—which is what is being thought here—necessarily be determined as subject? Does 'for human beings' already unconditionally mean: posited *by* human beings? We may deny both options, and must recall the fact that ἀλήθεια, thought in a Greek manner, certainly holds sway for human beings, but that the human being remains determined by λόγος [logos]" (334).

Heidegger seems to differentiate between human being and subject, but whatever name he chooses to designate this presence that speaks, he concludes that this presence is derivative of what it says. In other words, this is another nonmetaphysical translation that subordinates subjective agency to truth's alterity, showing that what is intended for human beings and told by human beings is not ultimately *posited by* human beings. Preferring clear lines of demarcation between the underivable and the derivative, between priority and posteriority, Heidegger as the critic of anthropocentrism opposes any form of co-originariness, which would suggest a coincidence between truth and its teller and would thus elevate the human being to the place of truth.

While I agree that the history of the subject has placed the human being in a false centrality, divorcing it from anything larger than itself, the practice of truth-telling can and does at times open a unique plane of coincidence, where the human being and the truth that visits it appear together at once, each originary of the other. Truth-telling in this sense has to be understood as an exercise akin to the spiritual *askesis* Nietzsche describes,[13] a practice of self-discipline and self-sacrifice through which he superseded himself. This is in fact the reason Foucault thinks of truth-telling as a technique of the self—namely, as a mental and bodily discipline, a way of life (terms that evoke the project of *Lebensphilosophie* that Heidegger opposed) through which the self both sacrifices and exceeds itself in the pronouncement of truth. This is also why the truth-teller can only coincide with his or her *own* truth, a truth that is always individualized but never atomistic. Thus, what I find compelling in Foucault's analysis is the suggestion that once, at least for the Greeks, this coincidence of aletheia with personhood was more than a tangible possibility: it was a practice that, far from compromising the originary status of truth, helped it manifest itself.

Heidegger understands that, even though this primordial moment of aletheia constitutes the source and core of thinking, it withdraws itself from the horizon of thinking (335). To put it in simple terms, the Greeks could not think what enabled them to think in the first place, what gathered them around the philosophical project, or why Being disclosed itself to them in the structure of thought. It is because of this constitutive withdrawal of aletheia from thinking, Heidegger maintains, that the thought of the Greeks remains for us a "not yet," and not—as Hegel surmised—because the Greeks had not yet completed all the requisite mediations of the Spirit. For Heidegger, this "not yet" marks the fact that we too are and will remain inadequate to the kind of thinking this originary moment requires (335–36). Heidegger's understanding of this essential inadequacy merits a far longer elucidation than I can provide here, but I will briefly submit some remarks. Perhaps what for Heidegger has always been and will remain a "not yet" was actually not at all a "not yet" for the Greeks. And here I would employ vis-à-vis Heidegger in part the same logic he employs vis-à-vis Hegel: if the Greeks did not admit to the "not yet" of thinking aletheia, it was certainly not because they were unseasoned philosophers; it was also not because, as Heidegger suggests, they were—as we are today—inadequate to the task itself; and it was not because it was impossible to think what grounds thinking, since the ground lies by definition outside what it grounds.

Be that as it may, I would like to propose something along different lines than Heidegger—namely, that this impossibility may not have been an issue for the Greeks. Unlike us—for whom it registers *as* an impossibility because we admit to the logic of reflexivity as we privilege its abysses—the Greeks' inclination toward a philosophy of life had rendered perhaps this question inoperative,[14] redirecting it instead to its proper plane of address: the worldly plane of bios, not the plane of theory or logos. What cannot be thought can be exercised. I think this is exactly what Foucault means when he observes that, while for Cartesian modernity personal belief and truth coincide only through a mental experience of evidence, for the Greeks this coincidence occurred in the verbal activity of parrhesia (14). In other words, truth is not only a matter of pure ideality, but it is produced in an activity that involves a speaker. There would be no philosophic life for the Greeks without this sense that the one, the good, which still remained for them an absolute and likely inaccessible ideal, could be pursued and glimpsed by the human soul.

Of course, I said "perhaps." And this "perhaps" should not be taken lightly, since it betrays that now we can only engage the Greeks in speculation; but this should apply equally to Heidegger's claim of unveiling for us aletheia "in a Greek manner" (334). His too is a speculation or a dream. But if the dreams of our past say anything about where we wish to direct our present, then there might be something to my insistence on embodied truth versus the disembodied exteriority of Heidegger's aletheia. For the Greeks—who dared to see themselves in their gods—the logic of this constant domination of the outside on the human would have been unbearable, even though tragedy makes it plenty admissible (always, however, with the qualification that the human puts up a good fight against it).[15] As a people who cherished the world of appearances,[16] the Greeks could not but let withdrawal appear as well, and they did so through the perilous, tragic conduct of the truth-teller. Certainly, in the stubborn insistence of the truth-teller, we do not see immediately that withdrawal of which Heidegger speaks: we do not see aletheia's own withholding of itself from thought—that subtle and imperceptible movement by which truth actually conceals from thought truth's own concealing aspect. Rather, what we see is something of truth's effecting a withdrawal, which no less radically points to and externalizes this originary withholding: we see the withdrawal of the human beings who shut their ears over and over every time a truth-teller speaks. Why is truth so unbearable to listen to that the truth-teller risks his or her life to utter it? This fundamental aversion the human ear bears to truth is not simply a cultural or anthropological stance. It attests to something essential about the nature of truth as it holds itself in reserve from us, keeping itself inaccessible to the many who are not attuned to it. Yet the only way we can even perceive truth's essential withdrawal is by witnessing historically the intolerance, persecution, and aversion that truth-tellers qua nonconformist agents have unfailingly provoked.

Parrhesia in this sense offers an exemplary instance not only of collapsing the gap between ontological and epistemological difference but of collapsing the ontic-ontological difference: the truth-teller is what is spoken. This would be in fact the most radicalized understanding of the Socratic demand for a coincidence between bios and logos. Logos does not simply determine the sayer, but the sayer's presence is the witness of truth in the double sense of the genitive: the sayer is the witness of a truth that precedes and lies outside any individual's purview, but the sayer is also the embodiment of truth that others must witness. Uninterested in a logic of priority that does not necessarily translate into the good or happy life, the Silenic Greek philosopher may have hailed this co-originary moment in which the truth can only shine as such in the human face, his own face.

This is of course the reason why Socrates is the philosopher who does not (need to) write. While writing involves a systematic preparation, even a deliberate manipulation of one's thoughts to account preemptively against a possible criticism, speech may endanger even the most prepared speaker to fumble, stutter, and be unable to think on his or her feet while confronting an interlocutor. Immediacy, transparency, presence to the degree of risking oneself—these are the requirements of speaking, of speaking the truth, most especially. Habeas corpus. In speaking, there is only a body that sets itself vulnerably in front of an audience, a body that can be questioned, misunderstood, unheard, ostracized, injured, even killed. Speaking as presence is not about fixity and fixation but about movement as spontaneity, emotion, transformation, and even violence. To speak everything in one's heart and mind thus supposes a human being, a subject that may prove all too necessary in our postsubjective world. This subject is an exception by virtue of its speech, an exceptional subject in the history of the subject, for it comes to us from a time when the human was unthinkable outside its relation to something bigger than itself: the truth that it carries within it, a truth that weighs it, and that cries to come out.

The parrhesiastes is surely an anachronism, but no more now than in that remote antiquity that first launched him or her as an ethical figure. As a suitable protagonist for tragic plots, the truth-teller shares in the anachronism of the tragic genre, which at the height of Athenian democracy continued to be preoccupied with royalty and the oppositional forms sovereign power had provoked. Even though Foucault focuses on Euripides because it was he who used the term "parrhesia" for the first time, the other tragedians too provide us with a repertory of parrhesiastic characters: Oedipus, Antigone, and Prometheus are some of the most well-known examples. Above all, tragic structure itself relies on the parrhesiastic structure: tragedies often involve the risk of someone who dares speak otherwise to the powers that be. On the tragic stage of classical Athens, the tragic hero as truth-teller must have recalled an uncannily familiar yet already distant age with its bygone sense of ethics—a feeling of untimeliness that truth-telling seems to always evoke, even nowadays when the very image of a courageous human being is ridiculed as an ontological impossibility or a political fiction. It is as if parrhesia could emerge as an exemplary response to our crises only in its untimeliness. How can one's speech move me? How can it transform me? These Socratic questions become the Foucauldian exercises at a time where the logic of postsubjective structures remains inadequate in addressing real injustices and suffering in the world.

Parrhesia shows the power of speaking, which is strangely also the power of vulnerability, of the speaker's exposure to the whims of the audience. This is why parrhesia is marked by a fundamental asymmetry that, if balanced, would cause the speech to cease to be parrhesiastic and to become simple exposition. If I say that the sky is blue, what I say is truthful, but not much is at stake in my observation. If, however, I say to the Inquisition that the earth is not the world's center, this is a truth of a different order because it sets me in danger. Parrhesia links truth to danger in an essential and constitutive manner: How do I know something to be true? When it so compels me to speak it, regardless of the peril to which I expose myself by speaking it. Danger is the measure of truth, and in this sense, truth-telling admits inherently to a tragic structure. Parrhesia, however, is also a relation of love. Presumably, the truth-teller loves truth more than himself to be able potentially to sacrifice his well-being and even his life in order to tell it.

All this shows us that parrhesia's presence is not simply full presence in the sense of a positive and impregnable totality. But, again, we should not be hasty to assume that if it is not presence, then it is its opposite—some kind of an abstract absence, a discursive evaporation of the person that was just in front of me, or some watered-down idea of a fragmented, self-doubting trace of a person, some phantom-being that miraculously embodies presence and absence at the same time, as if it were a philosophical cipher. No, parrhesia requires a parousia that is an ordeal, the ordeal of a body that stands both sovereign and prostrate: sovereign in daring to speak everything, sovereign in knowing that this may mean its death, and yet prostrate, exposed, and vulnerable to the decision of the other sovereign, the one in power who is being addressed.

I find it felicitous that the title of the English translation of Foucault's lectures on parrhesia is neither "truthful speech" nor the widely accepted English translation of parrhesia as "free speech," but "fearless speech." This choice emphasizes not the content of the statement (whether true or false, right or wrong) and certainly not the notion of freedom in its casual sense of permission and permissibility. Rather, it says that truth occurs where the speaker freely risks his or her freedom to say what he or she must. In that instance, free speech is not guaranteed, but freedom shows itself in the speaker's will to utter it. The interestingly exceptional moment in parrhesia consists in the fact that though the speaker's body is threatened, the decision to speak truth to power is not vulnerable. The speaker's vulnerability never outdoes his or her own sovereign desire, and it is perhaps the reinscription of this heroism in Foucault's genealogy of truth that may have sounded strangely outdated to his colleagues.

In the remainder of this chapter, I will briefly survey Foucault's typology of parrhesia throughout Euripides. My purpose is to comment on several details in his discussion that illuminate further the practice of parrhesia and contribute to our impending reading of *The Bacchae* as a parrhesiastic play that dramatizes the shift of truth-telling from religion to rationality along with the tremendous violence this shift incited. In his analyses of the Euripidean plays, Foucault actually associates this shift with *Ion*, not *The Bacchae*. According to Foucault, the principal question of *Ion* can be summed up thusly: "Who has the right, the duty, and the courage to speak the truth . . . in the framework of the relations between the gods and human beings" (27)? Furthermore, it is only *Ion* and *Orestes* that, for Foucault, bear a particular significance to the practice of parrhesia, not so much the other tragedies where the term appears in passing and not with the full force of a "topic or *motif*" (27). Consequently, Foucault dismisses *The Bacchae* as one of these plays where parrhesia is invoked only momentarily by a messenger asking for permission to speak. While Foucault is correct to note that this particular scene does not constitute a significant intervention in the practice of parrhesia, I intend to show in the concluding chapter of this second part that the entire structure of *The Bacchae* dramatizes even more radically than *Ion* this important shift in parrhesiastic speech: the shift away from claiming truth as divine revelation to claiming it as a field of human rationality. But what is even more unique to *The Bacchae* is the strange and catastrophic conclusion this shift brings about—a conclusion that precipitates as much as paralyzes our need for ethical judgments concerning the nature of truth and truth-telling, whether human or divine, rational or mystical, philosophical or religious.

Foucault begins his commentary on Euripides's tragedies with the *Phoenician Women*, where he foregrounds the relation of parrhesia to power (28–29). This is indeed a relation of double bind, since the practice of parrhesia as a critique of sovereign power presupposes that the practitioner must already partake in the power structure to even be able to assume the parrhesiastic position. In other words, a slave does not enjoy the privilege of parrhesia, and this is why the play emphasizes that exile is the worst punishment for the Greeks. Equivalent to being a slave, the exile is also deprived of free speech, a value that, to the Greeks, sometimes proved even more important than life.

While the *Phoenician Women* underlines the importance of citizenship for the practice of parrhesia, the next tragedy, *Hippolytus*, lays out another requirement: honor and good reputation, that is, moral standing (30–31). I would argue, following Foucault's own description of parrhesiastic speech in his first chapter, that the requirement of *Hippolytus* precedes that of the *Phoenician Women*—or better, transcends it. In other words, if parrhesia is a form of speech that by definition sets the truth-teller in danger, then moral standing is even more primary than civic standing, since the parrhesiastes is always on the verge of renouncing his civic standing (his citizenship, his rights) for the sake of his moral standing (his beliefs). All that an exile would be left to risk in deciding to challenge power is his or her life, a danger from which even the parrhesiastic citizen is not exempt. Exile merely amplifies the conditions of risk that the parrhesiastes suffers even within his native environment, where his citizenship and good standing are supposed to protect him from possible retaliation. Though external requirements such as citizenship and good repute aid the practice of parrhesia, the experience of the parrhesiastes at the limit resembles that of an exile: at the very moment he speaks the truth, he may be stripped of all the rights and privileges the polis confers on its most honest citizens. Indeed, in his reading of *Ion*, Foucault does speak of natural versus institutional parrhesia (51)—namely, of a person like Ion, who is by temperament a truth-teller but whose social standing may obstruct him from exercising his parrhesiastic right. As we discussed earlier, it is exactly this split of parrhesia between natural disposition and institutional right that became exacerbated in the democratic polis, as it fueled suspicions concerning who was the *true* truth-teller among all those citizens democracy empowered to speak.

Next on the list, *The Bacchae* shows for Foucault an intermediary instance of parrhesia, where the messenger—not exactly a free man—enjoys the privilege of the "parrhesiastic contract" of a wise sovereign, who tempers his own power by accepting to hear inconvenient truths (32). This contract, Foucault observes, became an institutionalized practice in the late Greco-Roman world. With only this briefest of commentaries, Foucault moves on to *Electra*.

The situation becomes more complicated with *Electra*, as the institutionalization of the parrhesiastic contract results in a distortion of parrhesia. Foucault characterizes this distortion simply as a subversion of the parrhesiastic contract (36), during which the powerless parrhesiastes Electra ends up killing the sovereign, her queen and mother Clytemnestra, who initially granted her the privilege of parrhesia. However, I think that in *Electra* Euripides presents us with something more than a subverted parrhesiastic contract. He presents us with a pejorative form of parrhesia, one which is quite different from the mere chatter of *Orestes*—the only pejorative form acknowledged by Foucault. In *Electra* the techne of parrhesia shows itself in its degraded form, since techne here is reduced to sheer calculation and manipulation. Foucault begins with the scene of Electra's condemnation of Clytemnestra shortly before Electra and Orestes assassinate her in revenge for their father's murder. Electra asks for permission to speak freely, and it seems that Clytemnestra gives it to her in good faith. Of course, the subversion Foucault speaks about concerns exactly this point: Clytemnestra's good faith versus Electra's bad faith, a bad faith that is evident not only in the impending murder of her mother but more importantly in the previous moment of Electra's asking for permission to speak. Electra does not need this permission in any substantive manner but for the fact that, as Foucault already points out, she is playing the role of a slave to trick her mother (33), thus also elevating the dramatic stakes.

The scene subverts parrhesia by exposing its pejorative, degraded aspects. Parrhesia can descend not only into chatter but also into the complete opposite of truthfulness: deceptive demeanor, the dissimulation of weakness to cover the most pernicious of strengths. While Electra's literal utterance, her request for permission to speak, refers us to the linguistic nature of the parrhesiastic contract, her attitude as a parrhesiastes refers us to the split between logos and bios Socrates came to heal. By subverting the contract, she subverts much more than this contract's linguistic and institutional integrity: her moral stance recapitulates the Sophistic use of rhetoric, as it twists and turns circumstances into fitting its preordained ends. Foucault does not elaborate on this aspect of Electra's playing the slave to conceal the upcoming murder of the queen, but I believe that this scene constitutes a moment in Euripides that Nietzsche would later identify with the advent of "slave morality," the Judeo-Christian inversion and reappropriation of a strong value into its weak counterpart. The subversion, then, marks a shift that redefines radically the practice of parrhesia: from an instance of courage speaking against arbitrary power, parrhesia is transformed into an institutional tool that props its deceitful users in claiming power anew. The inner natural strength of the institutionally powerless, which once stood up against sovereign power and buttressed public concerns, becomes the political entitlement of the morally weak, which enables them to exact utilitarian ends for themselves—whether this is personal revenge, access to power, or any other benefit. In the first instance, parrhesia is earned; in the second, it is claimed. In the first instance, parrhesia challenges the power of rights; in the second, it becomes itself a right, thus abandoning its function as the quintessential cry for the possibility of speaking. Electra's scheme had already put her in a position of power, and the pretense of asking for permission serves only to enhance dramatic effects—a tragic-ironic underhandedness, an aesthetic ploy, not at all a necessary condition for speaking. In Electra's mouth what is shown forth is the technical-manipulative aspect of parrhesia: parrhesia as pure rhetoric.

Ion is for Foucault the parrhesiastic play par excellence: "It is primarily a story of the movement of truth-telling from Delphi to Athens, from Phoebus Apollo to the Athenian citizen" (38). That is, it describes the passage of truth-telling from the oracular space to the civic one. Apollo in this tragedy is the "hiding-god" (42). He remains inscrutably silent; and even at the end, when the human beings uncover the truth, "Apollo—the shining god—does not appear," Foucault writes (43). The withdrawal of the god of the visible will be in sharp contrast to *The Bacchae*, where Dionysus, the musical god and Apollo's dark counterpart, renders himself visible on stage throughout the duration of the play. Foucault compares the structure of *Ion* with that of *Oedipus Tyrannus* regarding the status of divine disclosure: in *Oedipus Tyrannus* Apollo tells the full truth, but it is the mortals who wish to dispense with it. Yet despite the blindness of mortals, the truth is exposed because of the divine will, and the reversal of the human fate is thus fulfilled. *Ion*, according to Foucault, works in the opposite direction, as the human beings discover the truth by interacting with each other, contrary to the god's concealment of the truth (41). Foucault's summary comparison sidesteps much of the complexity of the plays. For instance, Apollo's words are hardly ever transparent, and this holds for *Oedipus Tyrannus* as well. In contrast to the straightforwardness one expects from parrhesiastic discourse, oracular speech leads astray; it is both opaque and oblique, whether we look at *Oedipus Tyrannus*, *Ion*, or *The Bacchae*. This realization is not simply a thematic oversight, since it concerns the nature of parrhesia in this movement from the temple to the agora. It raises questions surrounding the very possibility of divine parrhesia: Can a god ever be parrhesiastes if the requirement for parrhesia, as Foucault pointed out earlier, involves speaking from a subordinate position (Foucault 16, 18)?[17] How can revelatory speech, which is by nature elliptical—Apollo's oracular emanation is Loxias, the crooked or oblique one—compare with the transparency and full disclosure expected of the parrhesiastic mode? And yet does not the martyric stance of the parrhesiastes recall the perseverance of prophets and saints, who often testify against great hostility and persecution? All these questions, which arise but are at most only tangentially addressed in Foucault's analysis of *Ion*, come into sharper focus in *The Bacchae*.

To these questions concerning the nature of parrhesia, I would append a passing but opportune remark Foucault makes on seduction in this play. This remark deserves attention because its significance extends beyond the limits of cultural commentary to illustrate the deeper problematic of parrhesia's relation to rhetoric that Foucault had underlined in the previous chapter. Commenting on Creusa's rape by Apollo that resulted in Ion's birth, Foucault mentions briefly a legal distinction in the ancient Greek world that would strike us as rather unseemly. For the Greeks, Foucault notes, seduction was considered more serious a crime than rape, because it not only assaulted the physical body of the victim but attacked the honor of the family—particularly the spouse—of the seduced, since the seduced forfeited her ties to her spouse for her seducer (39).

That rape is by no means a simply physical violation and that its effects are devastating both for the body and the psyche of the victim are surely by now obvious facts, regardless of whether the Greeks had or had not acknowledged them for their own reasons. Still, this disturbing distinction the Greeks made is instructive of the ways they understood the exercise of force in general. The rape victim does not will its predicament; its violation happens against its conscious will, and this will is important even as it appears to be discarded by the aggressor. In the case of seduction, however, what is at stake is the weakening of one's will through quasi-consenting, or even fully consenting, participation. In other words, while the rape victim suffers a complete disempowerment, one that modern legal thought equates with dehumanization and desubjectification, the Greeks allowed for that minimal but persevering internal will, that inner freedom, which knew this violation to be completely exterior to itself. This does not apply to seduction, which exercises itself in a way that muddles the mind of the seduced, so as to have no clear boundaries between what it wishes and what it is driven to wish. In this sense, seduction is linked to persuasion and rhetoric. We may say that seduction approaches in language the level of violation that rape effects on the body. The distinction reveals that the Greeks were more afraid of the insidious effects of covert coercion than the outrageous exercise of pure and unmitigated force. The reason is quite simple: sheer force invites resistance, but covert power neutralizes it. Covert power lures its victim to believe that there is no other way, no outside.

In light of this gendered problematic, we may also consider Foucault's analyses of two gendered forms of parrhesiastic discourse in *Ion*: Ion's is the exemplary masculine, civic form of parrhesia, speaking up against political power, while Creusa's is its feminine counterpart expressed in terms of indirect confession and as an emotional accusation against her divine rapist. It could be hastily argued that the male form of parrhesia ranks higher, stemming from a political sense of duty, whereas the female form of parrhesia, resulting from personal and emotional motivations, constitutes only a pathological form. But it is equally important, at least for the present play, that the former opposes mortal beings, while the latter takes on divinity. Furthermore, instead of dismissing the personal tone of Creusa's parrhesia, we should keep in mind that it resembles more closely the Socratic parrhesiastic model of offering a personal account than Ion's political parrhesia does. Foucault describes Creusa's parrhesia in almost identical terms to the Socratic one: "Creusa's truth-telling is what we could call an instance of *personal* (as opposed to political) *parrhesia*. ... Creusa's parrhesia takes the form of a truthful accusation against another more powerful than she, and as a confession of the truth about herself" (56). Socrates too was responsible for the shift of parrhesia from its political to a personal mode, as he aided his interlocutors in producing truthful accounts of their lives. Although Foucault maintains that "the forms of *parrhesia* we see in Euripides did not generate a very long tradition" (103), as Socratic parrhesia presumably did, we could say that Creusa's feminine form of parrhesia begat the enduring Socratic and philosophical model. After all, in Socrates's own life account in the *Apology*, philosophy was born to him out of his need to test the Delphic oracle's declaration that he was the wisest of all. Like Creusa, Socrates took on Apollo.

Finally, in *Orestes*, Foucault isolates the only instance where parrhesia appears in Euripides in the pejorative sense, as "ignorant outspokenness" (57). Parrhesia in this tragedy suffers from a split that is actually germane to the etymology of the word itself: to say everything (*pan*) can easily devolve to *athurostomia*, the state of mindless blather, in which a mouth cannot shut up. This internal linguistic split presents us with the following question: What is meant by saying everything, yet doing so in such a wise manner that everything is not always exactly *every thing*? Foucault's answer comes through

Plutarch: the everything of mindful parrhesia is not a quantitative modifier but a qualitative one; it refers not to every single thing that could be listed but to everything that is necessary for the pursuit of truth and that alone. Plutarch's example is clear, recounting the death of Theocritus as punishment for mocking a king's physical disfiguration (Plutarch qtd. in Foucault 64–65): parrhesia even as satire should serve to tackle issues not launch ad hominem attacks. Interestingly, the linguistic potential of parrhesia to mean its own opposite became actualized in the practice of pejorative parrhesia during the democratic institutionalization of free speech. The price of free speech is that freedom gets interpreted more often as license than as responsibility; and, correspondingly, truth-telling becomes demagoguery rather than duty. Thus, the Athenians grew anxious, sensing that parrhesia could no longer be left to the innate sense of courage, frankness, and wisdom of each individual, but should be cultivated through education. Teachers were needed to instruct the young how to distinguish the philosophical from the mundane, the ethical from the opportunistic. Enter Socrates.

IV

Plato's Courts

PHAEDRUS AND APOLOGY

Love and law have been long-standing adversaries in the history of literature—their most tragic battle marvelously staged in Sophocles's *Antigone*, which will concern us in part 3 of the book. But if literature is quick to see the rift, philosophy seeks to bridge it. By its very name, which pronounces its task and disciplinary law, philosophy is the discipline of love: the love of truth. In this chapter, I address two Platonic texts in which Socrates, philosophy's greatest lover, unfolds for us this necessary but often antagonistic relationship.[1] First, in the *Phaedrus*, Socrates distinguishes love of truth from obedience to law,[2] as he himself delights in the courtship of his younger pupil amid an evocative landscape. Second, in the *Apology*, the scene of the court of law, Socrates emerges as the emblematic parrhesiastes, accounting for his life as a lover of truth but accepting resolutely whatever unjust verdict of Athenian jurisdiction against him.

Upon first glance at least, the *Phaedrus* and the *Apology* offer us two opposite versions of love's (and philosophy's) relation to law: where the former dialogue decries the false authority of the letter of the law, the latter presents us with a Socrates resolved to accept even an unjust death sentence, because he refuses to violate the civil process no matter what its shortcomings. He grounds this decision on the fact that it would be equally unjust of him as a citizen to profit from the laws of a city when they favor him, while rejecting those same laws whenever they turn against him. However, the resolve to accept his political fate out of respect for citizenship does not mean that the moral content of his defense is itself innocuous or acquiescent to the law's injustice. That Socrates understands the civic necessity of lawfulness does not stop him from mounting a staggering critique of the particular laws and the political mendacity that produces and implements them. Thus, despite their seeming opposition, the two dialogues do not undo each other. They both speak in their own ways of the tragic nature of law's self-assurance that it is always just and always good—a self-assurance solidified by its appeal to longevity and convention and not by the continuing and honest strife to approximate the just and the good. In law's actual inability to protect the wise and the just man who, nonetheless, respects it in order to transcend its violence, we trace the visible outlines of a tragedy. Where Antigone chose to break the law for the sake of another—her brother's dishonored corpse—and accept the fatal consequences for herself, Socrates chooses to uphold the law, since it only harmed him and not another, and accept equally the capital punishment.

Interestingly, both dialogues transpire under the sign of divine presence; in both, Socrates attests to divinities inside him: he is ἔνθεος (enthusiastic), roaming around sacred groves in the former dialogue, and testifying for Apollo's word in the latter. If, as Foucault observes, Euripides stages the passage of truth-telling from the religious to the political realm while Socrates furthers it from political to personal parrhesia, I would add that the Socratic shift is actually twofold: insofar as the personal is the seat of the philosophical for Socrates, he simultaneously relays truth-telling from religion to philosophy while retaining the spiritual quality of truth over and against cold rationalism. Philosophy may supersede the need for religious rituals and the like, but philosophical truth-telling still assumes and restores religion's prepolitical identification of truth with the moral character of the speaker. Socrates's divine inspiration serves as the hallmark of his moral character, which, in turn, guarantees the truth of his speech. In the following two sections, I trace the Socratic pursuit of truth and its practice of truth-telling as it unfolds from the lighthearted and flirtatious misunderstandings of the *Phaedrus*—the exemplary dialogue of a personal parrhesia—to the tragic theater of the *Apology*, where Socrates's personal account, delivered from a public platform, meets only the deaf ears of his fellow men.

Phaedrus

> Here lies one whose name was writ in water
> John Keats

Foucault offers only a fleeting comment on the *Phaedrus*, but a weighty one nonetheless: "The opposition of *parrhesia* and rhetoric also runs through the *Phaedrus*—where, as you know, the main problem is not about the nature of the opposition between speech and writing, but concerns the difference between the logos which speaks the truth and the logos which is not capable of such truth-telling" (20–21).[3] This is an implicit but pointed response to Derrida's reading of the parable of Theuth in this dialogue as Greek philosophy's consolidation of the metaphysical prioritization of speech over writing.

Derrida's analysis in "Plato's Pharmacy" is well-known and celebrated for its keen insights into the sliding nature of signification and translation. Therefore, I will limit myself to only a few general observations about it that will be of immediate concern to my consideration of the *Phaedrus*. As a reader of linguistic slippages, Derrida authorizes his method somewhat cavalierly to perform another kind of slippage than a simply rhetorical one (but this is just the problem—rhetoric is never "simply rhetoric" for Derrida). Indeed, the slip between the two opposing meanings of *pharmakon* as poison and antidote, which occurs throughout Plato's medical metaphors of philosophy as a healing of the soul, is itself translated by Derrida into the key methodological device that alone sustains and explains the semantic difficulties of the *Phaedrus*. In other words, the rhetorical sliding between certain terms ends up reflecting the workings of the entire dialogue—in fact, of the Platonic corpus as a whole and of the metaphysical thrust of Greek philosophy that allegedly dictates fixed meanings as it also hides its own slippages. Not only is it impossible to assign a stable philosophical meaning to the words of the dialogue, but the question of translation is recast as an inevitability within the original language, as a foreignness in the native that begs self-translation before any other translation can take place. Yet this translation from Greek to Greek proves itself a daunting task. The *Phaedrus*, then, can say nothing more than language's originary dependence on translation, since translation does not follow an original, but the original is already an effect of translation. The *Phaedrus* means nothing more than the impossibility of signifying anything without simultaneously mobilizing a whole apparatus of suspicion. Given the performative dimension of Derrida's reading method in general, which professes to let the text rehearse itself, no shadow looms greater over this particular reading than that of reducing a work on love ("Περὶ Ἔρωτος," or "On Love," is in fact one of the subtitles of this dialogue[4]) to an exercise of suspicion.

Although as a commendation of the free and individual path to truth the *Phaedrus* presupposes the questioning of arbitrary authority, it should also be clear that Plato warns against the easy skepticism of suspicion—so often a sign of the kind of thinking that is anxious to make itself law and establish its pedigree, as G. R. F. Ferrari would say (217), rather than attend to what actually matters. With "pedigree," Ferrari describes the fetishization of sources that are in no way relevant to our assessment of an issue but that may be invoked alternately to lend a stamp of authenticity to our position or to destabilize opposing views by rendering them relative.[5] This fetishization of commentary best describes the modern espousal of a historicist notion of truth as opposed to the truth of Plato (and of the tragedians), which was absolute and immutable though never a law written in stone to be found ready-made. Platonic truth demanded to be sought by anyone desirous of it, each time in its own terms, independently of historical and exegetical emendations. It was always to be *pursued* in a human ascent but never to be imposed from its heights. Therefore, while no predetermined authority should be reverenced for the ascending journey to take place, the doubts and questions on the way should be candid. They should be real and in good faith—not abstract, hollowed-out formulas aimed to undermine more than to discover, to discredit others in their self-certainty while shielding themselves from the risk of offering anything positive for fear they might be considered naïve or held accountable in some other way.

Here are, in sum, the two main corollaries of Derrida's engagement with Plato. First, the dialogue has to be read not only *for*, but entirely *in*, its rhetorical dimension, thus rendered *absolutely* relative.[6] Otherwise, it dupes the reader rhetorically in its very insistence on dismissing rhetoric. Secondly, the prioritization of speech over writing admits to a problematic of presence that binds Plato to a metaphysical discourse of binaries and false hierarchies. Since the *Phaedrus* does treat the question of rhetoric among others, such problems are indeed to a large extent germane to it, and Derrida's reading is a testament to its difficulties: how to read the thought *in* and *out of* its figure; how to wrest truth out of myth and allegory; how to read truth in passion, perhaps most of all, in the passion of the figure, of the word. However, although I find many of Derrida's insights illuminating in several ways, it is also the unfortunate underside of his hyperlinguistic vision to obfuscate and foreclose matters that resist the purview of the letter and that are even tyrannized by the absoluteness of the letter. The *différance* Derrida reads in the pharmakon as an undecidable and ever-contaminating signifier does not couple with a correspondingly effective difference in the semantic field of the text, where Plato attempts to distinguish the love of truth from what is merely truth-like—namely, rhetorical seduction. Yet this distinction in the order of meaning should be poignant since the *Phaedrus* is very much concerned with philosophy's dialectical task of differentiating the manifold (division) before assembling it (collection).

I would like to suggest at this point that if Derrida's revisiting of the *Phaedrus* is at all performative of the insights of this dialogue, it is as a peculiar repetition of a Sophist's reading: I daresay that Derrida enters the scene of the *Phaedrus* as the text's absent Sophist, Lysias. Fully aware that deconstruction has already been accused of sophistry in critiques that may now sound even a tad trite, I hope not to be read as ungenerous to Derrida, since I redraw this comparison from a different vantage point. Firstly, despite my own critical gaze against Sophism in this project, I think it a philosophical error to dismiss its achievements in the history of Greek thought, including its influence on Socrates.[7] Secondly, what concerns me in this comparison is the issue of theoretical optimism that underwrites both the Sophistic project and some of Derrida's assumptions in his reading of the *Phaedrus*. Specifically, Derrida's insistence on the letter shares the theoretical optimism of the Sophistic primacy of rhetoric, a most likely unwitting optimism that, in rejecting any outside meaning to the materiality of inscription, substitutes the letter for the truth. In a certain manner, this insistence on inscription agrees with the democratic project of dissemination and openness: letters are available to be read by anyone. Democracy opens up reading, making truth widely available. But availability in one of its senses—as facile readiness—exposes the darker side of openness: just as parrhesia devolved into rhetorical manipulation, so the letter risks being fetishized for *how* it reads rather than scrutinized for *what* it means. With reading thus replacing meaning, there is only text with no action, letters with no spirit, words with no intentions, medicine with no blood, as all jolts and wounds disappear into the infinite linguistic slippages of différance, where no tragic conflict is allowed but where also there is no Socratic music to harmonize the real strife that always takes place in ethical life.

This faith in the letter, which is incidentally a very democratic faith, misses tragically—and I mean this in the full force of the term "tragic," with all its unconscious blindness as well as the terrible gain that ensues from the tragic error—the spirit of love and intimacy, these markedly nondemocratic states of mind that the dialogue rehearses. Away from the democratic milieu of the city, where the letter of the law ensures just and proper access through its institutionalization, the love of truth unfolds in the countryside, where law, civility, and the like are shown to be only effects of the rational mind (not necessarily bad for that), while it is the effervescence of the natural spirit that emerges as the source of philosophical thinking. It is, above all, my contention that this is a text of spirit and against letter. Lysias is about letters and regrettably all the more intellectually restrictive and self-absorbed for that, but Socrates and the surrounding nature are about breath and spirit.[8] This does not mean that Plato dismisses the good uses of writing any more than it means he turns a blind eye to the abuses of speech but that, for reasons that will become manifest later on, the letter is more prone to fetishization.[9] Ferrari illustrates this talismanic function of scripture in the example of Phaedrus's zealous possession of Lysias's speech. Phaedrus carries the script furtively, as if its mere presence under his cloak would save him in case he froze while reciting it by heart.

Hence, what I call the potential authoritarianism of the letter is summed up by Ferrari with this word "fetishization," which I find particularly apt for the modern readership of the *Phaedrus* given the sexual meaning this term has assumed after Freud. If fetishism consists in the displaced and anxious desire for a part-object that substitutes the person, then Phaedrus's relationship to Lysias's writing becomes paradigmatic of a misguided love: a love for the effects of writing (as well as of speech and of the philosophic life), to paraphrase Ferrari again (214, 217, 222–23), rather than for the philosophic life itself—an obsession with playing the part of the philosopher (Phaedrus) rather than being one (Socrates). Ferrari is also correct to point out that "Socrates does not say that writing inevitably lies; only that its truth is liable to get lost" (222). What makes it liable, however, is precisely its status as permanent authority. For as much as its longevity guarantees misappropriation, so much also its talismanic properties cannot protect it from being misread. In fact, it is the misreading that manages to emerge safely from behind the text as talisman. Plato seems to have seen in advance the day when we rejoiced that there is no Platonic text—meaning that there is no truth to any text (not just his own) outside what everyone can make, or make up, in the name of originality, democracy, play, or difference.[10]

If parrhesia in the *Phaedrus* happens under the more lighthearted tone of friendship, as opposed to the somber one of the *Apology*, it manages still to open up a tragic horizon in its reception: a passionate text, this defense of love was written as a committed refutation to Plato's own contemporaries who misread him (and Socrates) as mere rationalists.[11] Plato did not meet a much better fate at the suspicious hands of deconstruction and of poststructuralism in general, which all too easily internalized Derrida's authoritative voice on the metaphysical thrust of Greek thought.[12] An annoying riddle, a revenant, Plato's Socrates haunts Derrida's recounting: Socrates once again is misheard because over-heard (heard too much this time around, that is), misunderstood, and even disfigured in being "figured out" as the man of many figures. That Socrates is not rhetorical even when he appears to be using figures will become clearer, I hope, in my consideration of the *Apology*. For now, agreeing with Foucault's preference for the Platonic spirit over the letter, I will attempt to buttress this insight by focusing on the dialogue's link between love and speech—more particularly, the love of truth in relation to passionate speech. Looking past the self-preservationist attitude of conventional utilitarian morality, passionate speech is another name for parrhesiastic presence, the kind of presence that is impassioned with putting itself at stake. I will thus turn to the amorous aspects of the dialogue, concluding with a discussion of the Egyptian parable, which contrasts the empty fixity of law as convention and command to the fragile, yet profound, commitments of love. Just as the freedom of erotic love stands against the coercion of arranged marriage, so Platonic intellectual desire—involving a difficult but free search for truth—stands against blind obedience to whatever poses itself, at times threateningly, at times flatteringly, as the truth.

Already in the opening line, Socrates's salutation, "φίλε Φαῖδρε" (phile Phaedre), announces the subject matter of the dialogue: *philia* as not simply friendship but as eros (desire and love), as the philia of *sophia—philosophia*. Socrates's excursion to the countryside in the company of Phaedrus follows tirelessly the detours, twists and turns, and even dead ends that the path to truth involves. Loving truth more than oneself, the parrhesiastes, as Foucault noted, intends in sharing it with friends and foes alike. Making of duty, love and making of love, duty—truth-telling thus also connects the intimately personal with the public, the emotional with the ethical. Out of love for

Phaedrus and for the love of truth, Socrates's duty in this dialogue is to stand by his beloved for as long as it takes and assume all sorts of roles—even self-incriminating ones—if they help open paths for both of them to pursue truth. Truth demands this excursus, this going out of the way; and in one of these detours by the shady grove of Boreas, Socrates describes the two of them as ἐκτραπόμενοι, as the errant ones who digress (229a1). The word is significant in a larger context, since the Socrates of this dialogue is entirely outside his usual urban manner, inspired by the spirits of the place, and communicating this inspiration to Phaedrus through an anthology of myths and celestial images. Phaedrus too responds to this profusion of sacredness and natural beauty, addressing Socrates as the marvelous one (θαυμάσιε), in the sense of also being strange, or as he again calls him, ἀτοπώτατος, the most placeless one (230c8). For his part, the most Athenian of the Athenians, who knows nothing of the Attic countryside, fancies Phaedrus as his guide (230c7). Thus, the *Phaedrus* is no ordinary Platonic dialogue, if there is ever one; and it has been commended for its pronounced theatricality.

In the Cactus Philological Collective's introduction to the dialogue, for instance, the editors note how "the beauty of the landscape ... the sonority of language (the 'dithyrambic' rhythm according to the Alexandrians), the almost childlike naïveté of the interlocutors, and the clear movement between lyrical, descriptive, and dialectical parts" all contribute to the theatricality of the dialogue. This effect is enhanced by the fact that, "frequently throughout the dialogue, both Socrates and Phaedrus react to each other as if they were in front of an audience" (22, my translation). Theatrical, dithyrambic, and lyrical in alternation, the dialogue unfolds as a praise of love and its changing moods and seasons symbolized by the sun's shifting position in the firmament throughout their walk.

Plato develops his theory of love through an examination of the erotic bond between two lovers, which, both in the Sophist Lysias's speech and in Socrates's two responses to it, takes the form of an older man courting a younger boy. In stark opposition to love, Plato tackles the question of rhetoric, or persuasion qua seduction, by testing the way Sophistic rhetoric speaks about the scene of seduction itself: in Lysias's speech, erotic seduction and rhetorical seduction coincide in that they are both emptied of even the slightest hint of love. The former is pure lust aimed at the self-satisfaction of the more powerful of the partners, while the latter is manipulation lacking any passion for the truth and any personal conviction on the part of the speaker. To put it in different terms, Lysias's picture of erotic and rhetorical seduction exhibits the form of love but is wanting in content. It lacks the crucial ingredients of vulnerability, exposure, risk, and self-sacrifice that intimacy entails. The absence of vocatives, which Seth Benardete astutely notices, makes this speech generic, "spoken by anyone to anyone" (*Rhetoric of Morality and Philosophy* 116). While this abstract formalism befits the utilitarian and self-preservationist logic of Lysias's rhetoric, according to which everyone is for oneself, love for Socrates (love of truth, most of all) contests this logic. Love is not love without the risk of being rejected, even of perishing. This is why Socrates elevates the lover far higher than the beloved: in loving without the expectation of return, the lover refuses to reduce love to a profitable transaction. Of course, the theatricality of the dialogue is intensified in that such theoretical questions of seduction are dramatized in the amorous exchanges between the interlocutors, as the older Socrates courts the younger disciple.

An impressionable youth, Phaedrus praises Lysias, whose speech on love he has recently heard. In fact, Lysias's speech is actually not speech at all but written oratory of the epideictic genre. The speechwriter (λογογράφος) has crafted it carefully in advance and delivered it to an audience that was impressed partly because of its completed form. This alignment of sophistry with writing and untruth serves as an early point of anticipation for Plato's later hierarchy of speech over writing that Derrida finds problematic. Still, it might be instructive to consider the reasons behind Plato's aversion for *this* particular written speech before deciding either for the Platonic preferences or the Derridean apprehensions concerning speech and writing in general: something of the solipsistic character of this writing is repeated in the narcissistic lover Lysias describes, and this impermeable self-certainty and self-aggrandizement must have been insufferable to a philosopher who insists on dialogue. Hence, Derrida's objection to the fixity of presence as metaphysical philosophy's unassailable condition of possibility for truth might find in Plato a strange ally rather than an archenemy: at issue in Lysias's writing is exactly its preexistent completion, its fixity, which obstructs contestation by precluding anyone else from speaking. The dialogue's extensive length and Socrates's double attempt at refutation can be seen as narrative devices that indicate the amount of work it takes to dislodge such fixed presences, particularly in their absence. Almost perversely, the Platonic text suggests that Lysias is more present through this speech than if he were actually on scene, because his written word — as if actually written in stone — becomes authority and shelters him. This is indeed the case with Phaedrus's firm belief in Lysias's grand style.

Hence, when Socrates expresses interest in hearing the speech, Phaedrus fears that his memorized recitation will not do justice to the Sophist's great writing, though as an aspiring pupil of oratory, he loves the chance to show off his skills. Less interested in the youth's rehearsal and more in Lysias's letter, Socrates detects the script hidden under Phaedrus's cloak and asks him to read it. Why hear the speech through Phaedrus's memory when Lysias himself is "present" (παρόντος δὲ Λυσίου) (228e2)? This is not simply a matter of writing being aligned with absence as both take backseat to the privileged categories of voice and presence. Socrates's words intimate that this script establishes a presence more entrenched and more totalizing than any bodily coincidence between speaker and voice could effect: a kind of presence that is always already axiom, law, and first principle before it even presents itself, and whose authority actually relies on its disembodiment, following a logic not so different from Freud's superegoic internalization of the voice of the dead father. To dispel this curse of disembodied authority, which transmutes absence into full presence, the *Phaedrus* offers presence as a homeopathic recipe: the scene of embodied togetherness. In other words, the companionship of Phaedrus and Socrates displaces the authorial centrality of Lysias.

Thus, it is worth emphasizing that Plato's discomfort with Lysias's physical absence from the scene should not be hypostatized as a metaphysical judgment against absence in general. Plato is not yet the systematic Western philosopher to have made of absence and presence conceptual categories, any more than he did so with speech and writing. Instead, he is after Lysias's lack of conviction and desire, which makes oratory formulaic and empty—in the colloquial sense of vacuous. It is extremely important to grasp that, for Plato, the problem is not necessarily that rhetoric fails to address logically the holes of an argument but that it compensates for the absence of subjective faith in the argument by its very thinker. In other words, Plato worries less about bad logic and more about deliberate manipulation and the institutional mechanization of thinking. We can infer that one's faith in the argument may even inspire a more elegant formulation (a better rhetoric), particularly if the arguer is well educated, than the mechanistic obedience to the rules of rhetoric that generically apply to an argument regardless of the arguer's presence (belief) in it.

Lysias's speech exemplifies mechanization, having been written as an exercise in repeating the same thing variously (235a5–6)—namely, the advantages of the non-lover. It does not obey an internal logic but relies on a collage of different phrasings (278e1), with its transitions moving mechanically rather than causally (ἔτι δὲ [moreover], καὶ μὲν δὴ [and then too]) (231a8, 231c1, 231d7, 232a8, 232b7, 232e3, 233a6, 233d6, 233d10). The loose connections of Lysias's speech, along with its indifference to its own truth content, are symptomatic of a deeper problem in the causality and temporality of rhetoric that puts the cart before the horse: as Socrates explains, rhetoric confuses the persuasion of its audience (the end) for the determining ground (the origin) of its thoughts.[13] Prior to convincing others, the orator should instead engage in self-persuasion: he should be committed to his thought as a necessary and inevitable result of his search, not as a convenient product. This minimal condition is the bottom line of all philosophical thinking. Yet, Socrates observes, the logic of precedence between persuasion and philosophy has been reversed. The structure of Lysias's speech illustrates this reversal: "For he has begun not from the beginning, but is swimming against the tide of the argument, from its end toward its beginning" (264a6–7).

The focus on the stylistic poverty of a rhetorical speech is a performative move on Plato's part that shows how a rhetorician who remains unconvinced by his own thesis cannot really make a vivid argument.[14] Lysias's speech is exposed as being not so much about love, or any such actual topic, but about formal concealment, about the occlusion of the topic behind a generic form of argumentation. Thus, while the Lysianic thesis appears to be against the lustfulness of the lover and for the advantages of friendship, it ends up as a recipe for gratifying sensual desires without the risk of love. And just as the form operates in a utilitarian fashion, offering itself as an available mold that can enclose any content, so the content of the speech repeats the same callous utilitarianism even as it addresses a sensitive domain of human life—that of intimacy. The gist of the speech tells us that the non-lover is preferable for the beloved because he does not care simply for immediate pleasure but also for future advantage, and all this because he is in control of his emotions and not a victim of love (233a6–b2). But make no mistake: the non-lover cares for the future advantage of the beloved not out of altruism but because such advantage will be advantageous to him as well. Lysias concludes his speech by exhorting mutual advantage and complete symmetry in the exchange of pleasures. Utility is the name for exacting perfect symmetry out of human relations. No favor should go unpaid.

Mistaking Socrates's critical commentary for a desire to correct Lysias, Phaedrus expects him to reconfigure Lysias's argument through a more competent rhetoric. For Phaedrus, the argument's validity is still a question of rhetorical arrangement alone. Patiently, Socrates accepts the misinterpretation and assumes the task of defending Lysias. But his defense is minimal, upholding—and this only temporarily—the tenet of Lysias's thought that is acceptable to common sense: the rational should be preferable to the irrational. Socrates's reluctance to proceed even with such minimal defense is captured by Plato in a theatrical image that stages the tension between truth content and rhetorical figuration: ashamed of the speech he is about to deliver, Socrates insists on being cloaked (ἐγκαλυψάμενος) while speaking (237a4). We must recall that Socrates had earlier extorted Lysias's speech from under Phaedrus's cloak. As Phaedrus concealed the presence of Lysias, so Socrates is now concealing himself, posing as another Lysias. And as Lysias's rhetorical style covered over the lack of belief in his own argument, so Socrates will cover his own face while delivering covered meanings. The bodily cloak obscures the speaker who speaks obscurantisms.

At the same time, however, the cloak functions paradoxically, since it illuminates even more than it obscures. On the one hand, it shows Socrates's discomfort, marking a temporal disjunction in space: by concealing himself, Socrates desires to be in absentia while speaking, since he is not *with* what he is saying. As such, the cloak sets Lysias and Socrates in a chiasmatic relation whereby Lysias is present through his writing, while Socrates wishes to absent himself from his speech. On the other hand, in contrast to Socrates who wears it out of a sense of shame, the cloak hints at the shamelessness of those who indulge in irresponsible speech because they are sheltered (by the cloaks of deliberate or fortuitous absence, rhetoric, power, and so forth) from showing their faces. Consequently, the image of the cloak implies the ethical dimension of presence for Plato: only a covered face can say things that cannot be accounted for, that do not have genuine logos; the bare face is the locus of responsiveness.

Further, Socrates's veil unveils the function of rhetoric itself as veiling. Though Plato will grant rhetoric its disclosive force as a tool of philosophy, we are asked, for the moment, to focus on its problematic function as concealment. Rhetorical turns and twists are shown to be the masking of untruth as truth (234e5–9). Though Plato does not explicitly observe this, it should be noted that rhetorical embellishment is not limited to covering over falsities alone. It can also usurp the place of meaningful absences and silences, becoming itself the very superfluity of presence, while obstructing the more fruitful—if also more disturbing—possibilities for genuine communication that such absences and silences promise. Thus, contrary to the common opinion that thinks of rhetoric as linguistic beauty, Socrates concludes that rhetoric is not beautiful speech. Hamlet's distinction between the beauteous and the beautified,[15] though in a different context, is on target here: something like language's lipstick, the rhetoric that cares not about its contents involves more beautification than beauty.

Lastly, the act of cloaking intensifies the drama of love that the dialogue stages: the old man is charmingly embarrassed because his philosophical contestation of Lysias is not only intellectually but also erotically invested, expressing the rivalry between Lysias and himself for the love and education of Phaedrus. In this context, we should again recall the sexual connotations of asking Phaedrus what he hides under his cloak.[16] Even though Socrates's love for Phaedrus is not explicitly sensual, the amorous tone of the dialogue justifies the blush Socrates may wish to hide from the young man.

After the completion of this first speech, the time of the palinode and of the unveiling of Socrates arrives at high noon. Under the rays of the meridian sun, the philosopher begins the bacchic hymn to love by announcing the presence of his daemon's sign (σημεῖον) (242b10–c1). Ironizing his own prophetic mood, he first compares himself to a lesser seer, whose understanding of signs is as limited as a poor scholar's mastery of letters (γράμματα) (242c5–7). Although this contrast between σημεῖον and γράμμα makes for a passing remark, it anticipates the later juxtaposition of speech and writing. An unexpected occurrence, the divine sign does not comply with the logic of correspondence that governs linguistic signification; thus, the sign cannot be read as a text. If interpretations of omens often fail, as they do in tragic drama, it is because the nature of the omen is to strike humans with a corporeal immediacy rather than ask to be read.[17] Yet because of this immediacy, the sign invites human beings to respond spontaneously to it, to rise to its occasion, whether obediently or disobediently. In contrast to the sign, which—as in the case of Socrates—sets the human being in the presence of the gods, the letter sets a barrier, separating the human body from the authority that commands it. The letter mediates and delimits, requiring to be deciphered rather than experienced, obeyed rather than communicated. As we will see, whether sign and letter or speech and writing, the contrasts help Plato establish philosophy's live discourse as an erotic discourse and thus as a fundamentally antiauthoritarian and antiabsolutist endeavor. Plato protests not only the dogmatic but also the utilitarian thrust that the letter of the law imposes on ethical life, so that instead of questioning its tyranny, humans find in its fixity the comfort of ready-made solutions.

However, as Socrates's self-ironic comment suggests, the sign too risks becoming letter in the hands of a diviner who, instead of being stricken, prefers to read and interpret (most likely for a reward), thus resembling a bad scholar (most likely the Sophists, who teach virtue for a fee). Yet if sign falls into letter as the great oracle gives way to the mediocre one, what does Socrates's analogy entail for the good scholar's relationship to letters? This question points again to the upcoming Egyptian story on the origin and use of writing. Already, however, we may entertain an answer. Given Socrates's inspired state, it is likely he would expect the good scholar's treatment of letters to be imitative of the good seer's treatment of signs: just as the seer refuses to submit the divine sign to the mere use of fortune-telling, the inspired scholar exceeds the didactic function of the letter, rejecting the letter as an instrument of command. The good scholar writes *not* the letter of the law. This ultimately also means, in an imitation of Socrates's own radical practice, that the good scholar dispels the hold of the letter for the spell of the sign, a practice exemplarily shown in Socrates's refusal to write. For Socrates, the easy exchange of the semiotic for the grammatic constitutes not simply bad scholarship but an act of impiety, an ethically injurious act. It is for this reason that he acknowledges the error of his first speech with the following quote from the poet Ibycus: "I might be buying honor from men at the price of sinning against the gods" (242c9–d2). His first speech was still too close to Lysias's intellectual specifications not to risk sacrificing the sign (the spirit, the truth content) in favor of the letter (the empty but all-intimidating form), thus sacrificing his ethics for popularity.

In light of our present discussion on divination, it is worth noting Socrates's defense of madness, which he bases on an etymological explanation of the art of divination. To stress the point that madness can be a divine gift, Socrates maintains that in earlier times the practice of divination was called manic art (μανική), from mania qua divine possession; but later, people have added the letter "t" because of ignorance and called it mantic art (μαντική) (244c1–6). This little etymological derivation, most probably fictitious, serves a double purpose: it not only places inspired thought higher than rationality, but it itself allegorizes the history of the corruption of truth-telling through the corruption of the oracle from divine possession to sign interpretation and rationalized augury. We could say that the "t" is the bearer of a différance, or the locus of translation from a present to a past—and probably imagined—form of prophecy. However, all this deconstructive verbiage, which insists on meaning's instability and the impossibility of origin, would deny the purposely unambiguous function of this letter as a symbol of thought's decline for Plato. I consider this "t" not a deconstructive mark but a genealogical origin that propels Plato into a critique of this decline. In fact, this whole etymological explanation rehearses a transition from oracular to evidentiary truth similar to Foucault's analysis of parrhesia in Euripides's *Ion*. Whether the etymology is itself correct, erroneous, or an outright fiction on Plato's part, it serves as evidence of a fact that exceeds puns and language games, a regrettable fact that must have shaken Plato's world: the degradation of truth from inspired to formulaic discourse, and the concomitant eclipse of parrhesia by normalized and self-interested institutional practices. The "t" points to the mournful realization that there *was* another way of relating to truth. It also shows the temporality of this "before" to be more inspiring of better futures than is the present's absorption in its own "afterness"—a solipsism that has now become the hallmark of modernity as it copes with its anxiety of influence by reducing the past to a huge retroactive imaginary construction.

To return to Socrates's praise of divine mania, it follows that philosophy as a pursuit of truth should belong to a *manic* logos: while it should yield rational accounts, these should stem from inspired, not simply rationalistic, motives. Put differently, philosophy should be a *practice* of one's own free inquiry, during which one questions, though not out of sterile skepticism, but during which one also refuses to submit in fear and slavishness to self-proclaimed authorities and fixed laws. What rescues truth from ossifying into truism is exactly this living desire of the human being toward it, the palpable intimacy and presence that truth as question requires from us, an intimacy that risks as much as guarantees the ascent.

Thus, we have at last arrived at the parable of Theuth as an exemplification of philosophy's contrast between love and law. Let us begin with three crucial points Benardete observes about it, which will help us pinpoint the story's main philosophical concerns: firstly, writing is considered not in general terms but in a particular modality—as law; secondly, the story is Egyptian—namely, Oriental, not Greek;[18] and thirdly, Socrates is interested in the uses, not the origin, of writing (*Rhetoric of Morality and Philosophy* 187–88).

The first point, concerning legal writing, introduces the problem of figurality in relation to truth, at least truth qua objectivity. It thus also serves as a link between the first part of the dialogue addressing rhetoric (linguistic figure) and the second part addressing dialectic (philosophic truth). Far from dismissing the figurative, the *Phaedrus* is critical of the contemporary legislative discourse in Athens regarding the supposed neutrality of written law: "The fact of written legislation had made writing in itself neutral and left open the question whether writing could ever be beautiful regardless of how beautifully written the laws were" (Benardete, *Rhetoric of Morality and Philosophy* 187). Because legislators considered rhetorical embellishment dangerous to law's objectivity and universal applicability, they favored a kind of writing that was soulless and indifferent to the beauty of its own articulation. Naturally, this legal objectivism impacted the rhetorical practice of the Sophists, who had to present their arguments as if they were objective truths as well. In other words, although rhetoric had its sources in passion, its forensic efficacy would have been undermined unless it had espoused the pretense of objectivity and concealed itself as passionate speech. This is perhaps the most crucial of rhetoric's concealments — namely, that it hides its own origin as committed speech. Contrary to the common belief that rhetoric serves persuasion alone, Plato shows that when rhetoric forgets its origins in desire and sets persuasion as its sole aim, it actually forgets itself. Consequently, the accusation that Plato professes an objective truth without admitting to the oblique effects of (his) tropes is hardly immanent to his mode of thinking,[19] since his understanding of truth, particularly as it was laid out in Socrates's palinode, rejects a priori objectivity's pretense of dispassion and neutrality. Plato's conception of philosophy as desire and his linkage of both philosophy and desire to beauty could never deny the figurative as the site of passion and beauty in language — provided again that we keep passion separate from ulterior motive and beauty separate from beautification.

Still, the question remains why it was *written* law that precipitated this problematic in Plato's Athens. Why was it that written law brought about this rigidification? Benardete's second point, concerning the story's location, is key. Plato tells a tale about gods, but not about the beautiful Olympians. It is a tale about Theuth, the Egyptian scribe-god and god of the dead, and about Thamoun (Ammon), the god-king ruler of Egypt:

These gods are inconceivable as the objects of eros.... Herodotus tells us that the Egyptians knew of no god in human shape in 11,340 years, but they said gods had ruled in Egypt and dwelt with men before this time, and the last god to rule was Typhon. We are to imagine, then, a time when gods ruled men directly, and there was no need for legislation as memorials of a one-time theocracy; but we are also aware, through the existence of Egyptian writing, that the gods have long since withdrawn from the earth. The forgetfulness and seeming wisdom, which Thamoun realized were unavoidable concomitants of writing, must not have outweighed the advantages of written law. To be reminded of the gods through the law, though all living memory must be lost with their absence and a seeming wisdom about the gods inevitably reign, is radically different from the divine reminders of Greek poetry, which link eros and the beautiful and subvert the law. The withdrawal of the gods or the hiddenness of the gods must accompany the promulgation of the divine law. The presence of the gods in the form of ourselves cannot but prevent the establishment of divine law. The most sacred laws among the Greeks are called unwritten laws. (Benardete, *Rhetoric of Morality and Philosophy* 187–88)

Benardete pairs the anthropomorphism of the Greek gods with the Greek propensity for unwritten law on the one hand and the withdrawn Egyptian gods with the need for written codification of moral life on the other. The mimetic reciprocity between gods and mortals in the Greek world fostered a relation of mutual presence between human beings and higher principles, which suggests that moral laws had for the Greeks a living resonance: they were venerated and contested through an individual's moral dilemmas, not obeyed as distantly dictated statutes. In contrast, as the Egyptian gods ceased to appear among mortals, they began emitting the last faint traces of their existence through dictations of laws. In the effort, then, to memorialize and secure these higher statutes for all human beings alike, writing had to assume an impersonal—potentially despotic—form of articulation: didactic recording. Meanwhile, the receivers of the laws became passive practitioners rather than active seekers. Yet being interested eventually in Plato's vindication of writing, Benardete surmises that Thamoun found the advantages of writing outwinning its disadvantages and so accepted Theuth's gift. This, of course, is the necessary conclusion one is led to by the historical evidence of ancient Egypt as a scriptural culture, but it is not the conclusion of Socrates's story.

Indeed, Thamoun's reaction to Theuth's invention expresses reservations concerning the adverse effects the use of writing may bring to his subjects. Despite Theuth's good intentions, the inventor of the art may not be the most impartial judge of its merits, thinks Thamoun (274e8–275a2). While Theuth believes writing will assist human memory and wisdom, Thamoun fears it will do just the opposite: with everything available in the form of letters, his people will not exercise their own memory; they will grow forgetful and, worst of all, falsely self-assured in their seeming wisdom (275a2–b3). Writing does not improve memory qua mindfulness; it works as a mnemonic device that gives the impression to its users of being wise when they are in fact regurgitating. To give a rather timely example, consider the difference between a pupil who understands the material and is capable of rewording it in his or her own words and the pupil who memorizes a formula to reproduce the information and obtain a good mark. As Ferrari suggests, Thamoun's anxiety about the written letter is none other than the anxiety of self-reflection and belatedness, of the "loss of innocence": Thamoun worries that Theuth's "formalisation of the arts" (writing is only one among others Theuth invented) will prevent his subjects from reaching wisdom personally, transforming whatever native capacity they have into pretense (216) and opening wide "the gulf between the pursuit of wisdom and the pursuit of the effects of wisdom" (217).[20] If in this age of innocence people lived wisely without being conscious of their wisdom, then at least they were closer to the Socratic epistemological ideal we will encounter in the *Apology*—namely, that the wise ones do not think themselves so wise. Thus, if the letter kills—lest we forget, the scribe-god is also the god of the dead—it is only in this specific sense of imputing a distorted idea of self-reflexivity, one that is actually not reflexive enough, but rather solipsistic, as it never fails to aggrandize the one who professes it.[21]

Still, if writing risks becoming an empty mnemonic formula, how plausible is the proposition that the unwritten is not threatened by forgetfulness? I suggest that Plato does not mean to say all unwritten things are not forgotten. They can be, and often they are. But this then also means they were insignificant to begin with. On the contrary, things of value are not forgotten even if they are not written down, for they live in the soul—the seat of love, not of fetishization.

We could say that the treatment of writing in the *Phaedrus* raises *avant la lettre* the same problematic that Heidegger's essay on technology has raised in the last century[22]—namely, not simply the problem of the use of technology but the ways in which that very use dictates a way of being for the users, a new ontology. Writing was for Plato a technological mode that irrevocably changed the ontology of his time: by interfering with personal memory as the way to knowledge and by letting time threaten and distort the truth of its sayings, writing issued forth an essential change in the way of being human. Choosing to express his reservations about writing in writing does not make Plato a self-reflexive player in a game of irony, even though he was certainly aware of what he was doing. I suggest that this choice reveals another tragic fold of his thinking: turning to writing by necessity, he did not accept unquestioningly all its effects any more than some of us who are now obliged to live digitally think of this as a paradisial reality.[23]

That for all these reasons the sacred laws of the Greeks remained unwritten is the main theme of *Antigone*, as we will see in an ensuing chapter. Antigone exemplifies the courage of living and dying with the full responsibility of one's own intimate interpretation of a higher law—namely, the mortal responsibility to freely engage with what is held to be absolute. Even though such laws are larger than oneself, Antigone shows that their value shines forth only when human beings reach them through their own conscience. To obey the laws simply because it has been said so or written so—as Ismene's fearful obedience of Creon's edict amply shows—degrades the laws from offering glimpses into a higher consciousness to being an apparatus of threats. The story of Theuth repeats this tragic truth of *Antigone*: law for the Greeks was inner duty (duty as love) not external command (duty as fear).

The importance of embodiment behind this ethos of joining freedom to responsibility is thus evident: because the Greeks thought mimetically and thus proximally—letting their gods assume a human shape and appear as incarnate principles—they approached their gods through a relation to beauty. Beauty, Plato explained in the *Phaedrus*, is the singular Form that kindles human desire for the idealized and the transcendent; and as such, it serves as the sole vehicle through which human beings may gain access to other ethical principles. The point of all of this again is that the attainment of ethical conduct proves worthy only when enacted out of desire rather than fear, out of freedom rather than coercion. Benardete calls this the "antinomian" aspect of eros that traverses the *Phaedrus* (*Rhetoric of Morality and Philosophy* 157). Presence, then—which has been strangely inverted by deconstruction into an abstract metaphysics, a vague and contingent empiricism—must be put back to stand on its feet: as embodied appearance, presence is the place of contestation, the place where ethics is arrived at, not given, the place of an immanent self-transcendence. And let me clarify (if it seems I am setting up a problematic ontology/ethics binary) that to arrive at an ethics does not make this ethics derivative; to the contrary, the personal desire bespeaks the elevation of this ethics as one's own inalienable circumstance, as the highest summit, rather than an external burden. Thus, Socratic presence is not static but dynamic, not abstract but concrete—painfully and jubilantly concrete. Against any law written in stone, the antiauthoritarianism of the Socratic voice confronts the ontology of absence, whose obsession with the letter fosters an ethic of an a priori obedience to any command—no matter how meaningless its directives or how spectral its source. Transforming the nothing into the all, this ethic recognizes only the arbitrariness of the letter and the despotism of its author as the marks of wisdom. Such reification of absence, however, ironically yields a nihilist metaphysics of presence, one far more entrenched than that associated with speech. After all, what could better attest to fleetingness and finite temporality than words that content themselves in simply being uttered without the conceit of print, "words of air" as Claudia Baracchi calls them, because they disappear into thin air the moment they are spoken?

The *Phaedrus* is the only dialogue where Socrates comes to the human soul from the world of nature, which he notoriously dismisses everywhere else. If this basic Platonic hierarchy is reversed in this dialogue, how much can we hypostatize the binary of speech and writing without missing the point? We would be well-advised to heed Ferrari's warning:

> In the particular case of the valuation of speech over writing, the effect of Plato's presentation here is to show that we who now prize the capacity of conversation to encourage genuine rather than manipulative communication do so not in the belief that speech in its very orality can bring about this result at a stroke—to believe *that* would be to do exactly what writing encourages us to do: treat the external trappings of communication as a talisman—but rather in the belief that only after we have appreciated that speech does not merit its superior place on the basis of orality as such, does speech in fact come to merit its superior place. (219–20)

In other words, speech should not be revered qua speech even when it does not do the work of thinking; this would be to treat it as an empty law—the worst effect of writing. As I hope to have shown, the critique of writing is based on what Plato may have identified in his time as another sterile hierarchical thinking—the one of this Oriental theology, whose god is never part of oneself, whose nature is never around oneself the way this sacred landscape surrounds Socrates. And so perhaps we can conclude with Hölderlin and Nietzsche again that, yes, the Greeks were religious, and mad for all of that. But at the same time, their form of religiosity, though certainly not Occidental, is hardly Oriental. This is also to say that the truth of anything cannot be written into generalized typologies of this sort any more than Socrates can be written into a law-making tradition. The murmur of this text says repeatedly that the most courageous ones wish to have their name writ, not in stone, but in water.

Apology

> After all, what would be the value of the passion for knowledge if it resulted only in a certain amount of knowledgeableness and not, in one way or another and to the extent possible, in the knower's straying afield of himself? There are times in life when the question of knowing if one can think differently than one thinks, and perceive differently than one sees, is absolutely necessary if one is to go on looking and reflecting at all.
> Michel Foucault, *Use of Pleasure*

As if anticipating the intellectual upheavals that the encounter with Socratic thought would produce in his own work (*The Care of the Self* follows *The Use of Pleasure*), Foucault describes the pursuit of truth in markedly Socratic terms: true knowledge has little to do with mastery of skills and information, while truth's itinerant seeker is perpetually on the verge of losing every familiar comfort. In the *Apology*, Socrates portrays himself as such an errant man, wandering from human being to human being, questioning them about self-knowledge, until he realizes it to be the descent into non-knowledge. His parrhesiastic model of self-examination and the tragic end[24] he meets on account of his parrhesia involve the exposition of this fact: knowledge is not true knowledge unless it leads us away from the safety of our assumptions.

Standing before a large number of Athenian citizens who act both as judge and jury, Socrates elides for the most part the current accusations and takes an eccentric route to his defense. Uninterested in the mere legalese of the court, Socrates prefers to unveil the Athenians' lack of subtlety in receiving his ideas, and the overall hostile political climate that has indelibly marked the specifics of his case. In this choice lies the genius, truthfulness, but also forensic inefficacy of his speech: it is authentically parrhesiastic in saying everything, in uncovering deep-seated prejudice and mendacity, rather than engaging in the refutation of mindless particulars to win his case. However, in dismissing the current charges as mere symptoms and exposing the source of the problem in the phantom accusers of years past, Socrates acts in a deliberately counterintuitive manner that expands rather than minimizes the scope of the charges. In lieu of a defense, his response emerges as a kind of autobiographical account (apo-logy), through which he reveals himself and his philosophical project. He thus performs for others what he has continually asked them to do for themselves: to account for their lives.

Socrates begins by juxtaposing persuasion with truth, remarking that his accusers must have already affected the audience emotionally through their rhetorical style. Surely a lot has been written about this Socratic critique of rhetoric as being itself rhetorical and most misleading in insisting that it is not. I will tackle this criticism against Socrates more thoroughly later on, but for now I will offer only a tiny clue as to why I believe otherwise than his critics. If Socrates is being at all rhetorical, he is certainly practicing a peculiar kind of rhetoric, a rhetoric that defeats the purpose of rhetoric, an antirhetoric: dissuasion rather than persuasion, an ineffectual discourse designed to turn people away from the result the speaker ostensibly wished to obtain. Why would anyone use such antiutilitarian rhetoric when the very purpose of rhetoric is to produce self-interested results? In many ways my reading of the *Apology* unfolds as a humble attempt to answer this question, but for now I will return to Socrates's first gesture of dissuasion: he dissuades the Athenians from believing in his eloquence.

Equating eloquence with untruth, he protests that if he is eloquent, it is only because he speaks plainly. In other words, he is not really eloquent, but for this reason he is all the more compelling. The word δεινὸς (awesome, fearful) (17b3) splits the difference: while Socrates uses δεινὸς to describe the power of a cunning rhetorician, the word could also evoke the fearlessness of someone who speaks the truth. Contrary to the accusers' premeditated charges and speeches, Socrates presents his apology as a series of "improvised arguments" (17c3). The Greek ἐπιτυχοῦσιν, connoting this sense of improvisation, is salient. Socrates will leave his defense to chance (τύχη). The most careful thinker will abandon his words to whatever comes to be of them. I think this is an apt characterization of the parrhesiastic demeanor as the frankness of the face-to-face encounter. The parrhesiastes speaks in the present, not in previously arranged words, and thus opens himself up to whatever fortune or misfortune awaits him. Socrates implies that the time of righteous speech is not bound by past deliberation. Righteous speech is always righteous speech and can be detected as such—that is, as truthful content and solemn intention—regardless of the awkwardness of its articulation. Contrast this to Socrates's wording when he describes the deliberate and prepared untruths of the specific charges as *writing*: "Μέλητός με ἐγράψατο τὴν γραφὴν ταύτην" (literally, Meletus wrote against me a written charge) (19b1–2).

The portrait of language emerging out of Socrates's remarks is quite different from the one we have inherited after the linguistic turn. Language for Socrates must always say something beyond itself. Far from being a solipsistic medium folding and unfolding on itself,[25] Socratic language is the medium of exteriority, a pointer to the place where events occur, and not only events of language at that. A stance, a gesture, the language of the body, the timbre of the voice—all these are important events surrounding language, and they are the reasons why the presence of the speaker is vital to any parrhesiastic scene. This is also why Socrates proceeds to distinguish between λέξις and φωνή (word and voice) (17d4–6). Stating that he is a foreigner to courts and unskilled in their language (ἀτεχνῶς οὖν ξένως ἔχω τῆς ἐνθάδε λέξεως) (17d3–4), he will assume the voice and manners with which he was brought up—namely, the voice that is native to him, not the artificial and manipulative techne of rhetoric.

Apparently, Socrates is unskilled not only in legal etiquette but in the very profession the Athenians ascribed to him: teaching. He reminds them that he himself has never purported to be a teacher and has never received compensation for such a service (33a6–b2). In fact, he insists that he does not believe there is anyone who can profess such expertise in human apprenticeship. Socrates recounts the story of Callias, who entrusted his children to the Sophist Evenus, whose fee was quite modest for his renown. Unconvinced that the Sophist lives up to his reputation, Socrates suggests that while a horse trainer knows how to groom his horses, taking care of a human being is an altogether different affair, for which there exists not a fixed profession or a specific techne (20a8–b6). Of course, taking care of a human being is not an act of inspiration and enthusiasm either, the realm claimed by the poets (22b10–c5). This would seem to contradict Foucault's designation of parrhesia as a *technique* of the self. (Parrhesia's aversion to the manipulative techniques of rhetoric, which Foucault had noted, was one such example of its nontechnical nature.) Yet Socrates may be interpreted to say somewhat paradoxically that this technique of becoming a proper human being is itself *atechnos*, a nontechnical techne. The training of a parrhesiastic individual is thus located at the threshold of a nature that is not simply genius and inspiration and of a techne that is not exactly skill or science.

What, then, enables Socrates to practice this nontechnical techne of education on the youth of Athens? Charged as an atheist, Socrates answers this question with a peculiar piety that combines faith with doubt: he claims it was the Delphic oracle that led him to his philosophical practice, because upon receiving Pythia's words that he is the wisest of men, Socrates felt he had to verify the oracle rather than simply accept it. By way of a brief parenthesis, I would like to stress how essential this doubt is and that it cannot be explained away as the usual Socratic irony. In fact, if we are not to take his insistence on the divine mission lightly, which I certainly do not do, we cannot dismiss this doubt as ironic ploy either. Thus, in light of my later emphasis on Socrates's divine mission, it is important to keep this issue clear and well-balanced from the start. His doubt attests to personal freedom, to the human prerogative not to take the word for granted—significantly, not even when the word flatters and aggrandizes him. Imagine how many other human beings would gladly step into his shoes and be eagerly faithful to the god's word upon hearing such an omen. To wish to eschew divine approval is reserved for the ones who are not simply humble and pious but also free and obstinate, those unwilling to yield to predetermined self-definitions, preferring instead to arrive at them through their own terms. The god's word may eventually be fulfilled, but not without the interlude of human revolt. Moreover, without revolt, Socrates would hardly be the wise man of the oracle; if he did not doubt Apollo's word and embark on a self-examination, he would be like all the others who thought themselves wise when they were not. Like any other tragic hero, his wisdom too rests in consciously opposing the god, because he feels this is what he must do *for himself* regardless of the terrible outcome. And Apollo, it turns out, will reward him for this impious stubbornness—not by sparing him the death penalty but by reserving for him this precious place of a free being.

Thus, Socrates was prompted to question the knowledgeable men of his time—politicians, poets, and artisans—to check whether there may be someone wiser. While the politicians proved themselves utterly unwise, the poets—though inspired by gods and nature—did not have self-awareness of their wisdom either. Regarding his negative judgment against the poets, we should keep in mind that his interest is in human wisdom (ἀνθρωπίνη σοφία) alone (20d10). The poets are unwise in the sense that their wisdom originates outside themselves; it is not human wisdom but a kind of divine breath. Poets are thus closer to soothsayers (22c3), whose truths need to be interpreted, demonstrated, and attested just as Socrates has been doing with Pythia's words. Socrates's conclusion that poetic inspiration needs philosophical explication implies the passage of truth and truth-telling from religion to philosophy: God's word needs to be interpreted for human ears, and the interpreter must be, above all, a person of moral fortitude, for without care for one's comportment in the world, philosophical logic would be just as empty as poetic genius. Socrates may have learned from the Sophists the skills of language and argumentation, but he embodies an earlier understanding of truth-telling in which truth is inextricable from the moral nature of its speaker.

His insistence that the divine and poetic words must be supplemented by and renewed in philosophical thinking has to do with the fact that religion, much like the thoughtless recitations of Homer, had by his time devolved into formal custom and ritual commonplace, evacuated of any genuine meaning. Socrates alludes to this shift as he responds to Meletus's charge of impiety, which contradictorily calls him an atheist and accuses him of believing in different divinities than those of Athens. Benjamin Jowett translates the Greek νομίζειν ("to hold as a custom" or "to practice") not with "believe" but with "recognize": Socrates may believe in divinities Athens does not recognize (26c4). The translation proves quite apt in this context. Knowing that, for Plato, recognition is unthinkable without recollection, the gods Athens does not recognize could be said to be the gods Athens cannot remember, such that when Socrates speaks of them, the Athenians see them as foreign deities, as unauthorized "spiritual novelties" (27c5–6). Because the gods have been reduced to customary usage, they are no longer recognizable in their essential forms. Socrates turns the Athenians into someone like the Cadmus of *The Bacchae*—an old and pathetic people, worshiping their gods more out of a self-serving principle of continuing ancestral traditions than an inner imperative to reach a deeper truth. In thus anticipating *The Bacchae*, the question for us is whether Socrates's critique of religion is aligned with the side of Pentheus and his unrepentant rationalism or the side of Dionysus and divine madness that demands real faith instead of empty ritual. For many reasons, I am compelled to think that this old, dignified man has more to do with the young, maddening Dionysus than one would think, and his devotion to Dionysus's counterpart, Apollo, is an added proof. At the end of the first part of his speech, we get more glimpses of Socrates's religiosity, which then climaxes in the prophetic speech succeeding the verdict.

Before returning to these prophetic aspects, a few remarks are due for the last group of people Socrates cross-examined, the artisans. It turns out that they too confuse the knowledge of a particular techne for the totality of knowledge. The question is posed again: what is that nontechnical techne that is neither ecstatic possession nor sterile specialization? If the shape-shifting of the poet is dangerous in purporting to know too much, is not the narrowness of the expert equally dangerous in shrinking the world to the confines of his craft? The Delphic oracle has apparently led Socrates to bring about the crisis of knowledge—not simply any knowledge, but the knowledge of being human. Socrates's testing of Apollo, which seems to justify the charges of atheism against him, turns out to be the fulfillment of the divine word. "The wisdom of men is worth little or nothing," says Socrates (23a8–9); instead of overestimating themselves, human beings should take heed of their limitations. In Socrates's recalcitrance to accept Apollo's assurance that he is the wisest of men, the god shows indeed that the wisest is the human being who understands the poverty of his wisdom. It should be no surprise by now that such tragic wisdom belongs, above all, to Apollo's counterpart, Dionysus, whose terrible lesson in *The Bacchae* is exactly this: "You do not know what your life is or what you are doing or who you are" (line 506).

As I mentioned above, the concluding part of Socrates's first speech resonates with subtle but distinctly religious overtones, giving us more clues into the significance of the Delphic story as an explanation of the way philosophy now takes over the truths religion can no longer deliver. Parrhesia is what stands at the threshold of this passage from religion to philosophy. In conjoining the love of truth with a specific kind of ethical character, parrhesia provides the very structure through which truth passes from being divinely revealed to being thoughtfully pursued. Indeed, Socrates offers numerous portraits of himself as parrhesiastes throughout the *Apology*, in effect equating the function of the philosopher with that of the truth-teller. Firstly, he assures the jury that the best proof of his telling the truth is their hatred of him (24a7–10). Parrhesia, in other words, is visible in the reaction of the audience as well as in the face of the truth-teller: the more infuriated the audience, the more truthful the testimony.

In another example, Socrates foregrounds the inherent tension between parrhesia and group mentality, a tension that prompted him to turn from political to personal parrhesia. Sensing in the jury's hostility one of those homogenizing feelings that punishes anyone who differs from the herd, Socrates admits that there is no purpose in even trying to defend himself; rather, it makes more sense to exercise parrhesia once more, even if this means paying dearly for it: "I have said enough in answer to the charge of Meletus: any elaborate defense is unnecessary. You know well the truth of my earlier statement that I have incurred many violent enemies; and this is what will be my destruction if I am destroyed—not Meletus, nor yet Anytus, but the envy and slander of the multitude, which has been the death of many good men, and will probably be the death of many more; there is no danger of my being the last of them" (28a2–b1). Envy and slander, two particularly nonparrhesiastic behavioral patterns, are specific to multitudes. In contrast, Socrates is by nature someone who individuates, who enters a group to break down the assumptions of its members. Of course, such gesture does not flatter the multitude; and when the multitude has been authorized to hold power, as in the case of Athenian democracy, it will avenge its wounded pride. Socrates's remark is prophetic, announcing that no prophet and no parrhesiastes will ever find hospitality in his own land: other men like him will also die in the future. It is the fate of the parrhesiastes to be destroyed—and more radically still—to self-destruct willingly.

Lastly, the most famous image of Socrates as parrhesiastes is that of the gadfly sent by the god to wake a sluggish steed (read, "the city of Athens") from its slumber and revitalize it (30e1–6). Socrates states that the steed is sluggish owing to its great size, intimating once again that great numbers are not conducive to the honest but judicious practice of parrhesia. This is why he insists on the format of individual examination rather than political address.

Indeed, Socrates did not use the traditional venues of religion or politics (temples or assemblies) to carry out his philosophical project, even though his truth resonated with both prophetic wisdom and political urgency. While he was comfortable discoursing in the agora, he refused his services to the assembly, where political life proper took place (31c5–33a1). For Socrates, addressing multitudes by definition misses the fine points of an issue as it does the nuances of each individual soul. The structure of the assembly forces people into an organized group with a prearranged agenda, as the genre of political oratory exchanges mindfulness for propaganda and expediency.

Contrary to the predominant democratic ethic, which assumed that civic excellence was proven before the assembly, Socrates thinks that such political performances are empty and do not expose the speaker to the right kind of scrutiny. Instead, they are designed to accrue benefits for the speaker through the flattery of his audience. Thus the assembly turns the politician into the opposite of the parrhesiastes.[26] Socrates's city, then, has little to do with the prearranged procedures and fixed techniques through which public discourse maintains its power. His city happens in the everyday, in the free-floating life of the streets, where those minute, private details in every human soul assume all sorts of unexpected outward expressions, transforming the surroundings and being transformed by them. The ideal city is not arrested in an abstract, metaphysical grid but is produced through the Socratic conversation, through the continual striving and renewal of each soul in its relation to others.

In fact, the Athenians' version of democracy sounds a lot like the hasty modern readings of the Platonic Ideas as ethereal forms suspended from the clouds, waiting to be emulated. Just as the hasty metaphysician fails to detect the intricacies beneath Plato's mimetic binary, so the unseasoned Athenian citizen—an equally bad metaphysician—produces civic-minded statements that mimic the forms of a patriotic performance but amount only to groundless demagoguery. Beyond simple copies and metaphysical adequations, the Socratic call for self-contestation relocates the transcendent Ideas in the core of the human soul and activity: this is another way to understand the harmonization of logos and bios—for instance, whoever values the Idea of courage, should be able to embody in words and deeds this Idea. The transcendentality of the Idea, which is due to its prototypical nature, is reconfigured as exemplarity in a concrete and bodily prototype: Socrates, the exemplum of truth-telling, the prototypical philosopher.[27]

Having acknowledged the fatal end that truth-tellers invite on themselves, Socrates wraps up the first part of his speech by stating that he does not view death with fear. This passage anticipates the way Socrates will handle the question of death when he revisits it in the speech following his verdict. His account of death is brilliantly strange. On the one hand, we see the philosopher in his safe Apollonian distance from everything, submitting even the fearful mystery of death to reason: logically, one should fear only things one knows to be fearful, and about death one knows nothing. After all, only ignorant people profess judgments about things they do not know (29a6–8). This tranquil Socrates denies that fear is often the irrational fear of the unknown.

On the other hand, Apollonian serenity veils a mad, Dionysian side: Socrates is drawn to his death, much like Achilles, to whom he compares himself (28b10–d6), and Antigone, of whom he does not speak but who too dies a religious martyr.[28] To die as soon as possible is second best to never having been born.[29]

Socrates, the critic of all things poetic and Homeric, identifies himself with Achilles, a hero who elsewhere in Plato's work has been denounced for his desertion and his effeminate mourning—both stances undesirable in a warrior. Socrates, the old, homely man, suddenly places himself on par with Greece's fairest youth. What connects the two? Parrhesia. Even though this is not the aspect Socrates visits in this comparison—he focuses instead on Achilles's fearlessness of death—parrhesia is what connects them. Achilles too spoke truth to power, and the *Iliad* proceeds as the catastrophic effect of power's unwillingness to yield to parrhesia. Death forms the litmus test of ethical consistency, and Socrates implicitly commends the terrible harmony between Achilles's words and deeds.[30] Socrates's antipolitics and Achilles's desertion reveal their eagerness as truth-tellers to forfeit social ties in order to preserve their own ethical integrity. Conversely, through this comparison, Socrates establishes parrhesia as the new form of heroism, much as he shows parrhesia to have been heroic even in the archaic time of the Greeks. However, whereas parrhesia needed additional war deeds to supplement it during that archaic, mythopoetic age, the new hero does not need such external wars to reach glory. The new heroism is reserved for the philosophical being that dares examine the depths of itself, war with its own soul, and confront its limitations. In this sense, Socrates surpasses his own model: he will not desert his station, the way Achilles once did (but, then, Achilles deserted the war in the name of what he thought was the truth).[31] The pursuit of truth becomes for Socrates the only pursuit worthy of honor, the only pursuit we cannot afford to quit in life. He thus describes it once again in terms of divine duty: "[If] I were to desert my post through fear of death, or any other fear—that would be indeed strange, and I might justly be arraigned in court for denying the existence of the gods, if I disobeyed the oracle because I was afraid of death, thinking that I was wise when I was not wise. For to fear death is indeed to pretend to be wise when not, since it is to pretend to know what is unknown" (28e5–29a6). Similarly, he speaks of his greatest civic service as coincident with his divine service (30a6–7),[32] while insisting that to abandon philosophy would amount to forgetting and disobeying the god. Serving the city as a kind of high priest, Socrates draws ever stronger the link between divine word and philosophical examination.

Let us examine this link closely. Socrates says that it would be unfaithful of him to quit the god's command on account of fear of death, thinking he was wise when he was not. We see in this formulation that the delusion of self-knowledge is intimately tied to the delusion of possessing knowledge about death, which is the absolute unknowable. Hence, the abstract dictum in the earlier recounting of the Delphic story—namely, that one knows little or nothing—takes on now its proper content: death. Death defines the horizon of human knowledge while remaining completely outside that horizon. Knowing that one knows nothing is a performative statement whose contradictory formulation shows that all human contradiction, distortion, and inconsistency stem from a deeper ontological limitation—namely, mortal temporality. The greatest question to which mortal temporality lacks access is the nature of death, and the human beings who can admit fearlessly to this incompleteness of knowledge are alone the knowledgeable ones. Socrates assures the jury that he would never cease his commitment to this kind of knowledge and to helping others reach it, not even if this were the only condition that would grant him acquittal. The man whom Nietzsche saw as the most negative manifestation of spirit is strangely a yea-sayer. Socrates unveils the affirmative logic of an eternal return: no matter how many times he would have to live this life of poverty and persecution, he would choose the same path all over. Yet he does so in negative terms: "I shall *never* cease from the practice and teaching of philosophy" (οὐ μὴ παύσωμαι φιλοσοφῶν) (29d5, my emphasis). This insistence, which Socrates associates with love not only of truth but of his fellow countrymen as well, makes him the caretaker (ἐπιμελούμενος) of the soul of Athens, a soul that has been neglected and is in urgent need of cultivation. Hence, he prophesies that his death would also signal the death of Athens, as his personal fate converges with the destiny of the city. In this link of the oracular to the civic, and the personal to the public, lies the key to understanding the new form of parrhesia Foucault sees in Socrates.

Moving to the next portion of his speech, which negotiates the nature of his punishment, I will focus on Socrates's use of rhetoric, to demonstrate an earlier claim I made concerning the nonrhetorical dimension of his language that fits his parrhesiastic demeanor. Contrary to a well-established scholarly opinion that Socrates is a sleek master of tropes and thus the greatest of the Sophists in his use of rhetoric,[33] I would like to advance the argument that his language—at least in the *Apology*—is quite literal, exactly as he says he intends it to be. My main examples involve, firstly, the hyperboles Socrates employs in his counterproposal to Meletus's request for the death penalty and, secondly, his rebukes against his condemners.

Instead of attempting to convince the jury of a less severe punishment, Socrates suggests that he should be rewarded. But is this counterproposal a hyperbole, or should we take Socrates at his word? Socrates anticipates the quandary: "Perhaps you think that I am displaying arrogance in what I am saying now, as in what I said before about the tears and the entreaties. But this is not so. Rather, I speak this way because I am convinced that I have never intentionally wronged anyone" (37a2–7). Aware that he may be read rhetorically as being purposefully boastful, Socrates urges his audience to take him at face value, as they should also have taken him when he insisted that he would not cry and plead to change their minds. Crying and entreating are bodily postures that operate similarly to rhetorical tropes in language, since both are used to alter the emotional state of the jury. Thus, Socrates assures them that he will not resort to such tropes; furthermore, he asks of them to believe that his incessant condemnation of tropes is not itself a trope. If we think that there is more to Socrates than irony and deception, which I do, we must take this demand seriously, no matter how peculiar it sounds, and attempt to understand it. I suggest that this demand stems from the strange place he occupies as a human being in relation to language. He speaks from a place where the figure has become realized, such that the harmony of logos and bios becomes in him pure music: what he says appears *as if* it were a figure when in fact it is not, because his life brings to presence and concretizes that ineffable thing the figure was meant to evoke. Socrates ends up looking too figural because he is too literal, not because he really needs figures. He does not exaggerate; he is an exaggeration. But this claim deserves further elucidation in terms of the particular textual examples.

Socrates confronts the task of finding a proper counterproposal (ἀντιτιμήσομαι) to the verdict (36b4) and finds that the *counter* of the counterproposal is not just another type of verdict but something that counters a verdict altogether: he takes τιμή, a frequent Homeric word, not just to mean any value as in the monetary worth of bail, or its equivalent in prison time, but in another of its Homeric dimensions—its moral resonance (ἀξία), as in what one deserves. Engaging the ethical rather than economic semantics of τιμή, Socrates is bound to conclude that he is not simply innocent with respect to *these* charges. He has been unrecognized for his service to the city and has been wronged by the city long before these charges were filed. Consequently, if this court is to decide on him, it should decide not on this particular case alone but on what he deserves for his entire life. Socrates strangely augments the authority of this court. This is the court of life; and if it fails him, as it does, it is because Socrates exposed it to be something it does not yet understand itself to be, though it acts as if it does: the court is always on the verge of judging arbitrarily as the law always risks becoming dead and deadly letter—a "law in force without significance."[34] Socrates's death will emerge as a testament to the law's arbitrariness. By obeying the law, the philosopher in fact performs an act of civil disobedience, shattering the law's transcendental claims and revealing instead its self-maintaining violence.

What does the philosopher deserve according to Socrates? If we think that intelligence should work to obtain the lesser sentence, we immediately see that Socrates has put himself in a bind. Dedicated to speaking the truth, he is condemned to say what he really thinks, not what is convenient. Careless (ἀμελήσας) of all the extraneous things the majority cares about—money, speaking at the assembly, inciting conspiracies and rebellions—Socrates insists on the care of the self, which apparently is not so valuable to the Athenians. What then can such a strange man deserve? Obviously, Socrates deems his service to be invaluable, in that no monetary value can be assigned to the ethical function he has performed for the city. The free lunches at the Prytaneum serve as the symbolic reward (36d6–37a1). This counterproposal is read either as boastful exaggeration—the jury certainly read it this way, deciding as a result not to spare him—or, in Kierkegaard's vein, as a whimsical suggestion in light of no other real alternative.

Stephen Rojcewicz,[35] combining historical details around the Prytaneum meals with the cultic significance of divine feasts, has uniquely argued the point to which I have also arrived: Socrates is being neither ironic nor superfluous. His proposal, like everything else in this speech, admits to parrhesiastic honesty, which only offended ears dismiss and punish as arrogance. Noting that free dining at the Prytaneum was a distinction accorded to Olympic victors, council members, foreign ambassadors, and distinguished citizens such as descendants of heroes who restored democracy to the city, Rojcewicz remarks, "Socrates is suggesting a comparison with all these groups: he is as valuable, or more valuable, to Athens as an Olympic victor, he would benefit the city by advising the members of the Council, he is an ambassador not from a foreign city but from the god, and he is restoring not democracy, but truth and virtue to the city" (190). But if this sounds still like another self-aggrandizing gesture on the part of Socrates, Rojcewicz takes his argument further by introducing the significance of the divine mission, which dominates the logic of the *Apology* and which I have also emphasized throughout my analysis. The free lunches are not intended as signs of Socrates's self-entitlement. Inasmuch as Socrates's questioning of his fellow men serves Apollo's word, the Prytaneum offers a free and open space where the philosopher—with the god present inside him—hosts everyone in a divine symposium rather than being fed gratis by the city: "The city is not the host for the free meals, the city merely is providing the occasion. Socrates, and ultimately Apollo, the divine presence, can be seen as the true hosts for a festive occasion, and the Athenian citizen body as the guests. The Prytaneion can be seen as an example of . . . the threshold, but only if the Athenian citizens freely agree to have Socrates as a presence among them, instead of having him executed. Entering the Prytaneion to meet with Socrates, who is acting in service to the god, is to enter a sacred space" (Rojcewicz 190). Rojcewicz concludes thus:

> The antitimesis proposal by Socrates is not an insult, a provocation, or an afterthought, something proposed in passing because he "might just as well" merit a reward. The counterpenalty offered by Socrates is analogous to what he has practiced throughout his life, but now made potentially available to the entire city in fulfillment of his desire to make the citizens virtuous and happy in reality. It is an invitation to create festive occasions structured by a host-guest relationship, linking the world belonging to mortals to the world belonging to immortals. Socrates offers dialogue leading to truth and virtue, and the presence, in some sense, of the god. Through his offer of a counterpenalty, Socrates summons the citizens of Athens to co-create with him a threshold into a sacred place where, on behalf of the god, dialogue can lead to a revelation of the self. Socrates has proposed a Feast of the Gods. (190–91)

For a city, however, that has lost sight of this function, Socrates is not worth anything, not even worth living. It is this meaning of "worth" that Socrates evokes in his famous phrase "the unexamined life is not worth living" (ἀνεξέταστος βίος οὐ βιωτὸς ἀνθρώπῳ) (38a5–6).[36] The essence of being human—that is, the essence of human worth—is self-examination, and no other value can be attached to this than life itself. To live without self-examination is not to live a human life. This is why, by nature, he cannot have any other counterproposal and why the counterproposal is not merely rhetorical posturing.

After the verdict, Socrates addresses the jurors who have just turned out for the death penalty, infuriated by what they mistook as his self-indulgence. This is his last address to the Athenian citizens before he moves to his cell to wait for his execution. Appropriately, this speech begins prophetically, its language marked by a distant and otherworldly tone that places Socrates in that dark plane of those about to depart. Socrates assures the Athenians that history will hold them responsible for the death of an innocent and that people who wish for the city's destruction will exploit Athens's blunder. In other words, his death, which was decided under the sway of rhetoric, will become a powerful rhetorical weapon at the hands of the city's enemies. He warns the city of forcing him into the position of being a martyr (in Greek, *martyr* means "a witness," and Socrates is the witness of truth), when in fact they could be prudent and wait a little longer for his natural death, since he is of advanced age.

Addressing those who have condemned him, he emphasizes again that his conviction is not due to his lack of arguments but due to the profound inability of the many to hear the truth:

> Perhaps you think that I was convicted for lack of arguments [ἀπορίᾳ λόγων] of the sort that would have persuaded you—I mean, if I had thought fit to leave nothing undone or unsaid. Not so. I was indeed convicted by a lack, but not of arguments—rather, of brazen temerity, and impudence, and the inclination to address to *you* the kind of thing that would have been sweetest for you to hear from me, as I wept and wailed and lamented, and said and did many things of the kind that you have become accustomed to hear from others, but I maintain to be unworthy of myself.... I would rather die having spoken in my manner than live in the manner you like. (38d3–e7)

Socrates lacks neither arguments nor words. He lacks, however, the rhetoric that makes people listen—the rhetoric that, once scrutinized, often leads to impasse (ἀπορία) but that, when unexamined, manages to find a backdoor entry into the human soul. Truth is austere for Socrates, and it requires the listeners' effort to attune their faculties to the unexpected modulations of this austerity, an effort the Athenians refuse to make. Their preference for rhetoric betrays their mental laziness, since rhetoric's primary usage, far from challenging the audience, was to flatter and propitiate it. In refusing to engage the Athenians rhetorically, Socrates refuses recourse to athurostomia, to irrelevant postures and embellishments that could have manipulated the jurors to his benefit. His is a fearless speech, not a free speech; and in speaking fearlessly, he exposes, among other things, that the athurostomia of rhetoric is the only surviving model of parrhesia in democratic Athens: emotional outbursts, entreaties, and exhausted figures.

In guarding himself against the indignity of meaningless figures, Socrates not only defends the status of parrhesia but keeps vigil over the figure's proper use. Meant to capture something extraordinary for which we have no readily available words, the figure is degraded by rhetorical overuse. Hackneyed phrases make language overly porous, lessening its aporetic potential and, with it, the potential for genuine disclosure. Why do we need figures to explain everything that is plain, all too plain? This is not the way to live an honest life — not honest to others and not honest to language — Socrates warns. Refusing to wear the figure as a vestment, he instead inhabits it, lives in it, and transfigures it.

The conclusion of the *Apology* reprises the issue of heroic duty: as in war, so also in court, one should never cowardly machinate (μηχανᾶσθαι) to do anything just to avoid death (39a1). But as usual, in drawing an analogy between the courage of an innocent victim of the court and the courage of a warrior, Socrates pushes the steadfastness of the Homeric hero way beyond the war code in which glory is the reward exacted for feats of killing. If Homer's heroes bravely disregarded their lives in pursuit of victory, Socrates's fearlessness of death involves something entirely different from military prowess: Socrates understands that death deceives us by distracting us from fulfilling our destiny. We are so busy scheming and strategizing to evade death that we evade ourselves, forgetting to lead a proper life. Again, there is nothing figurative when he says that "the difficulty ... is not to avoid death; it is much harder to avoid unrighteousness, for that runs faster than death" (39a8–10), even though the masterful alliteration of the latter part of this phrase enacts this speed in its own condensed procession: "θᾶττον γὰρ θανάτου θεῖ." Θᾶττον (quicker, speedier) sounds too close to θάνατος (death), and θεῖ (to run) sounds uncannily close in the Greek ear to θεός (god), under whose purview this entire speech takes place. Yet this is no mere rhetoric. Socrates means quite literally that it is not difficult to avoid death; for most people would attempt to avoid it, although death comes anyway. What is difficult, however, is to avoid the avoidance of death. In disjoining us from our destiny, the wish to avoid death turns us into unharmonious beings consigned to a state of badness (πονηρία) or wickedness (κακία) that runs faster than death. Using his own life as an example, Socrates gives us a glimpse into this precarious mortal race that takes place over the course of our lives, the outcome of which determines whether we are harmonious beings or disjointed ones. He himself is old and slow, but death, which is slower than our evasions of it, has overtaken him in his resistance to running away. The accusers, on the other hand, are quicker than Socrates, but not only in imposing death on him; they are quicker in trying to evade their own deaths, which is the fastest way to wickedness. While they condemn him to corporal death, they are condemned to the death of the soul precisely by trying to avoid the death of the body. The care of the self is the technique that comes to replace this mortal techne or *mechane* of evasion.

The very last point of this concluding speech is reserved for the maledictions against his condemners and the benedictions for his friends. Socrates explicitly characterizes this part of his speech as oracular (χρησμωδῆσαι), since men who are near death acquire that penetrating vision of what comes ahead (39c1–4). He warns his accusers that if they think they have avoided accounting for their lives by killing him, they will be asked to account in an even more pressing way by the future generations and ultimately by history itself. To his friends he offers a visionary consolation, claiming something miraculous has befallen him (θαυμάσιόν τι γέγονεν) (40a4). His inner daemon (θεοῦ σημεῖον) (40b2) too appears for the first and last time as an affirmative force, giving no counterindications to his fate. The verdict, in harmony with the daemon's wish, serves as a good sign about the nature of death: death is either the end of all sentience or a migration to another space (40c1–11).

If it is the former, death is an improvement over the sufferings we undergo because of our sentience: "a sleep like the sleep of someone who is undisturbed even by dreams" (40d4–5), the sleep Hamlet wished for but was afraid may not be guaranteed by death either:

> To die, to sleep—
> To sleep, perchance to dream, ay there's the rub;
> For in that sleep of death what dreams may come.
> (Act 3, scene 1, lines 64–66)

Socrates imagines that death offers the resting in pure nothingness. If, however, death is a migration to another place (ἀποδημῆσαί ἐστιν ὁ θάνατος)

(40e5–6), the philosopher is ready and serene for his departure, delighting in the opportunity of infinite philosophical conversations not simply with the everyday man but with the heroes of old. A brief remark is due on this poignant description of death as the soul's *apodemia* (literally, away from the community). In signifying this departure from demos, death heralds its own peculiar kind of democracy. Death snatches human beings away from a particular polis regardless of their civic standing; and to truly understand what it means to be in an earthly demos, human beings must first understand what it means to be without it. This is the reason behind Socrates's insistence that people must first take care of themselves and then of the city: only in taking care of themselves—that is, in considering their death without evasion—can they actually understand democracy in terms of a shared mortality before proceeding to handle the issues they have in common.

Thus, the divine feast ascends from the threshold-space of the Prytaneum to its proper sphere, as the religious and heroic aspects of Socrates's speech converge one final time. The philosopher as poet, prophet, lover, and truth-teller is the last creature to join this splendid banquet where gods, demigods, and heroes sit around one table and share. Socrates's choice of company in the other world is, nonetheless, revealing. He starts with Minos, Rhadamanthys, and Aeacus, the judges of the underworld, as well as Triptolemus, a just Eleusinian prince—all of whom enjoyed a great position in the afterlife because of their earthly commitment to justice. He then passes to the poets, mythological and historical—Orpheus, Musaeus, Hesiod, and Homer. After the poets, he reaches the heroes, but specifically heroes who have suffered injustices as he did: both Palamedes and Ajax, emblematic of intelligence and strength respectively, were unjustly undercut by the cunning Odysseus, who managed to invest himself with their excellence.[37] The harmony between mind and body that Palamedes and Ajax signify is broken by a manipulative intelligence that exacted undue rewards. These heroes allegorize the Socratic experience, and Socrates imagines sharing with them their common lot. The rest of them, unworthy of the designation of "hero," simply await among the other dead for the Socratic cross-examination that would counteract their unexamined life: Agamemnon, Odysseus, and Sisyphus—the names of unbridled power, deceit, craftiness, and avarice—were avatars of the nonparrhesiastes, figures whose lives were filled only by dreams of power, the most commonly used techne of avoiding death.

We have started with Foucault's tracing of parrhesia as courageous speech and its subsequent shift from political dissidence in the time of kings to personal account in Athenian democracy with Socrates standing at the threshold. Both the *Phaedrus* and the *Apology* presented us with an antipolitical Socrates, a man for whom everything connected to Athenian civic life (rhetoric, written speech, desire for flattery and popularity) is an obstacle to producing an ethical self. In contradistinction, presence, spontaneous speech, and passion for the inconvenient—namely, the defining categories of truth-telling—are offered as sites of ethical cultivation. For all of Derrida's righteous indignation about the primacy of such categories in the history of Western thought and the need for their deconstruction, it may be even more instructive to notice the continuous hostility that they met with from the time of Socrates to Derrida's own corpus. Is not this hostility, among other things, the very mark of their affinity to truth, and does it not account for the tragic fate of fearless speech in a self-servingly political world as Socrates prophesied in the *Apology*? Recanting his earlier work on irony, Kierkegaard too came to admire the tragic over the ironic Socrates, wholly embracing the Socratic antipolitical imperative. In a late journal entry in *The Concept of Irony with Continual Reference to Socrates*, Kierkegaard remarks, "Influenced as I was by Hegel and whatever was modern, without the maturity really to comprehend greatness, I could not resist pointing out somewhere in my dissertation that it was a defect on the part of Socrates to disregard the whole and only consider numerically the individuals. What a Hegelian fool I was! It is precisely this that powerfully demonstrates what a great ethicist Socrates was" (453).

We have also started by remarking that Foucault understood tragedy and Socratic thought to be two exercises in truth-telling. Though Socrates and tragedy may make for strange bedfellows, they both share a parrhesiastic mode with an antipolitical thrust that nonetheless expresses an alternative understanding of politics.[38] This antipolitics is what the last of the tragedies performs.

V

Euripides's Verdict

THE BACCHAE

This, Aristotle knew better than Nietzsche: Euripides may still be the most tragic of all tragedians, not least because he gave tragedy its last blow, as Nietzsche later concluded. Excessive dialectics, deus ex machina, whatever else smacks of rationalization in many of Euripides's tragedies—it is hard not to concede to Nietzsche his point.[1] Nevertheless, Euripides may claim the title of the most tragic poet not only by default but in a substantive way, and he may do so through his last tragedy alone. *The Bacchae*,[2] his swan song, written in exile and performed posthumously, marks also the last work left of the three great tragedians. Finding the beginning in the end, *The Bacchae* enacts the Nietzschean drama par excellence, showing "the founding myth of the theater itself," as Froma Zeitlin remarks (136), by staging its birth in the Dionysian cult.[3]

Here is a brief summary of the play: An exile god, Dionysus returns from his Asiatic wanderings to his native Thebes to set the record straight about his lineage and punish his Theban family for dishonoring his mother's name and ignoring his divinity. In this conflict, his antagonist is Pentheus, the young prince of Thebes and Dionysus's maternal cousin. A man of rationality, Pentheus rejects the ecstatic nature of Dionysian worship. The god's faithful followers make up the chorus of slave women, the Bacchae, who exalt him as their liberator. Since the god has possessed the Theban women, who have taken to the mountains for a fertility rite, Pentheus feels taunted to go spy on them, capture them, and restore order. Dionysus's terrible revenge is to take over Pentheus's mind as well and to use the latter's specular fantasies of the mountain orgy against him. Convincing him to disguise himself as a woman so as to watch, Dionysus parades Pentheus through Thebes to the mountain whereupon he is torn to pieces by his own mother, Agave, who confuses him for a wild beast. The House of Thebes is completely destroyed as the god concludes his revenge by banishing even Pentheus's old grandparents, Cadmus and Harmonia, despite Cadmus's professed faith in him.

For the first and last time, the god of tragedy appears on stage,[4] rehearsing the most quintessentially tragic themes: the quest for origin and identity on the one hand and the veneration and vindication of the family dead on the other. Returning from exile to his native land, the young god seeks to establish his matrilineal heritage, prove his divinity, and impose rites of worship on his faithless kin. His tribute to the tomb of his mother, Semele, which opens the play, is followed by the oath to avenge her sullied name and restore her true reputation as Zeus's consort. While the god's search for origin enacts the genre's own genealogy, Pentheus's dismemberment commemorates the terrifying rituals of Dionysus Zagreus and reveals the symbolic structure of all tragic suffering to be the atonement of a mortal sovereign at the hands of divinity: tragedy's antipolitical impulse takes center stage as two incommensurate discourses, two irreconcilable modes of truth-telling—the ecstatic and the civic—confront each other to the latter's complete annihilation.[5] In what follows, I will concentrate on the exchanges between Dionysus and Pentheus, which put forth two modes of truth and truth-telling. While the prophetic mode of Dionysus's speech is enhanced by the god's duplicity, the rationalist mode of Pentheus's rebuttals demands a straightforward attitude. Yet Euripides's mastery of reversals turns the tables in time: just as the liberating god speaks his prophecies shackled, so the straightforward Pentheus falls victim to the god's duplicity and, masking himself as a woman, participates unwittingly in his own demise.

Given Foucault's interest in the transition of parrhesia from the oracle to the agora in Euripides's *Ion*, where Apollo refrained from speaking parrhesiastically, I would like to consider this same transition in *The Bacchae*, where Dionysus speaks, but in a doublespeak that proves as deceitful as Apollo's silence. *The Bacchae* should be read as the companion piece to *Ion*, if only for the reason that between the two plays, the question of parrhesia's transition from the temple to the city is rehearsed between the pair of oracular gods who claim Delphi: Apollo and Dionysus. In *The Bacchae*, as I have mentioned above, divine duplicity upsets even the basic definition of parrhesia as a discourse against the powerful, since the god, disguised as an initiate, acts the vulnerable party, while the resisting Pentheus, being the mortal sovereign, appears initially in full command. Although the true power differential is evident to the audience from the beginning, it is almost impossible to say that Pentheus ever comes to know it, since its consciousness coincides with the moment of his death. By the end of this tragedy, it becomes clear that such duplicity is the exemplary mode of divine truth—a truth that impacts mortals but that is not designed to be grasped by them. By the end of this tragedy, we are also left unhinged as to whether we can speak of any transition from oracular to civic truth-telling, since the human world is utterly destroyed, unlike in *Ion*.[6] *The Bacchae* complicates Foucault's notion of parrhesia, but by turning truth-telling into a scene of catastrophe, the tragedy does not necessarily suggest we give it up. Rather, it foregrounds through Pentheus's form of parrhesia the ethical stakes of the human lot. As straightforward, courageous, but also responsible speech, parrhesia remains a human prerogative, for the gods need not submit to any such requirements. In this sense, truth-telling is also open not simply to being abused (as it is by Pentheus) but to becoming the very agent of catastrophe (as Dionysus makes it).

The first hints of Pentheus's athurostomia, of his inability to check his speech, come in the second choral ode. Agreeing with Cadmus and Teiresias, the chorus introduces Pentheus with the image of a mouth without reins (ἀχαλίνων στομάτων) (line 386), the hubristic mouth that cannot restrain itself from speaking its excesses. Soon thereafter, the chorus shifts to a description of Dionysus, extolling him for the gift of wine, which is notably a symbol of equality: wine is given equally to rich and poor, high and low (lines 421–23). This egalitarianism of the god, however, unravels as the mark of his violence. Turning the orders upside down and leveling everything out, Dionysus embodies the promissory but violent aspect of democracy that also underlies tragic truth: the extraordinary meets eventually the same end as the ordinary. Piously and cautiously, the chorus concludes by distancing itself from the over-wise (περισσῶν) and by aligning its beliefs with those of the common people (πλῆθος) (lines 427–31). The word πλῆθος invokes again the link between tragedy and democracy. Yet democracy in the sense of this πλῆθος is neither a juridically defined polity that protects individual rights and differences nor a contractual discourse on being together. For one, this chorus of foreign women slaves could never aspire either by status or by gender to belong to such a polity. The chorus must refer to Dionysian ritual collectivity, which, outside the prescribed laws of civic coexistence, involves the risk of being together, the risk of renouncing individual boundaries to become one through common worship.

Though clueless about Dionysus's nature, Pentheus gives an evocative description of the god, who stands before him as a captured devotee (lines 451–60): speaking of his youthful beauty, Pentheus emphasizes its feminine qualities. Dionysus is not born a wrestler, not in the athletic sense of a disciplined exercise. Pentheus almost grasps, but not quite, the fact that Dionysus's fights are not the organized games of civic competitions but primeval revolts and bloody festivals spurting out from the shadowy realm of desire. In the ensuing stichomythia, Pentheus conducts himself as an ambitious parrhesiastes. An adamant believer in rationality, he demands from his prisoner a virtual show-and-tell, interrogating him about the Dionysian cult practices. When denied access to the mysteries, for they are unspeakable (ἄρρητα—the opposite of parrhesia) to the uninitiated (line 472), Pentheus still expects nothing less than full disclosure. To the god's statement that the mysteries unfold by night because night adds solemnity, Pentheus responds that night also adds deceit and lewdness. Dionysus counters that the day too can produce shameful deeds, but Pentheus accuses him of sophistry (lines 486–89). Ironically, Pentheus, whose conception of truth is far more informed by the Sophists' democratic principle of equal access, calls ecstatic truth sophistic. If the Dionysian collective represents the spontaneous but potentially dangerous undercurrent of democracy as ecstatic fusion, Pentheus represents democracy's other side: a rational, deliberative polity of individual rights and access that secures its transparency by excluding mysteries and secret societies. As opposed to the god who suggests that the truth of darkness may be even more illuminating than some truths of the day, the rational, civic leader demands evidentiary truth.

Euripides well deserves the designation of the most tragic of the poets, since in grasping and staging the high stakes behind this exchange, he revealed nothing less than the very essence of tragedy as a Greek genre—a genre that summed up the inherent paradoxes that riveted the ancient Greek world and perhaps even brought it to its end. The rivalry between Pentheus and Dionysus—the civic and the sacred, the transparent and the hidden—allegorizes the fragile balance that the Greek experiment of tragedy tried to reach as an aesthetic *and* moral exercise. Greek tragedy attempted to give shape, no matter how transiently, to another precarious opposition, which has divided modern scholarship perhaps no more than it had already torn asunder the experience of the Greeks themselves—namely, the opposition between the Occidental-Hellenic passion for clarity, presence, and full disclosure and the Oriental-Hellenic acceptance of the mysterious force of fate. Yet even in such a contrast, it is notable that Dionysus does appear on stage—that is to say, the dark and fateful god is not a distant voice but a present and embodied form.

Returning to the question of truth-telling, however, I would like to elaborate further on the god's oblique mode of testifying and on whether it can be properly called parrhesiastic. While the fact that Dionysus is initially a captive of Pentheus seems to fit Foucault's definition that the parrhesiastes speaks from a position of risk, this is actually not the case. Playing with the unsuspecting mortal, Dionysus deliberately presents himself in the guise of an initiate who testifies in the god's name. Thus, when Pentheus speaks and acts transgressively, Dionysus reminds him obliquely of the god's nearness. The god performs his self-splitting linguistically in a prophetic statement reminiscent of the structural duplicity of Apollo's oracles: "καὶ νῦν ἃ πάσχω πλησίον παρὼν ὁρᾷ" (the god is watching what I now suffer) (line 500). The first person verb "suffer" (πάσχω) contrasts with the third person verb "sees" (ὁρᾷ), reinforcing Dionysus's essence as the suffering god, as the god who spectates his own suffering. The statement is prophetic in that it foreshadows the god's witnessing of another's ordeal, that of Pentheus, whose name means sorrow and who will die for the god's honor as the god's sacrificial double.[7]

This duplicity intensifies, leading to Pentheus's ordeal. Dionysus wreaks havoc in the palace with earthquake and fire, a fire that leaps up from Semele's tomb, as if repeating the scene of the god's birth. The Bacchae sing in awe about how he walks triumphant amid the disarray (line 602). When Dionysus boasts of his ploys, he speaks of the phantom world he created for Pentheus, who, struggling against it in vain, is exhausted. Imagining he is fighting the captive, Pentheus fights a bull instead; the flames on Semele's tomb, illusory in fact, defeat Pentheus in his effort to extinguish them. The palace eventually falls; but amid its ruins, the destroyer appears again only as the phantom representation of the captive. We may say that instead of being deceitful, Dionysus's justice is poetic justice indeed: if Pentheus thinks the god to be nonexistent, the god responds with a phantom universe. The question Euripides raises is the same one Nietzsche bemoaned in Plato, because the modern saw in it the origin of the decline of Greek thought: Are *what is* and *what appears* one and the same thing?

Truth and phantasm split and mingle on Pentheus's fateful walk to the mountain. Throughout the entire play, Pentheus's only epiphany occurs during this walk and coincides with a moment of terrible distortion and irreality: hallucinating two suns and two cities, he also catches a glimpse of the monstrous emanation of the god as predator (θήρ) (line 922). Notably, it is the sun and the city that Pentheus, as a prince, sees redoubled, both belonging to the world of rationality that now fails him. What are these doubles, though? Are they shadows, reflections, mirages, or simply intensifications of what is already there but which Pentheus could not see unless it became exaggerated? In this dissimulation, he confronts the truth of the tragic realm of Dionysus. Truth's double, which is not necessarily untruth, is the truth of tragedy. The world of the cave has been brought out into the broad daylight of the double sun. Pentheus did not think that the daylight could be shameful, yet now—a debased reveler like the old Cadmus and Teiresias he earlier scorned (line 250)—he exposes his madness and his shame under excessive light.

The other double, of course, is himself in the company of the god who commands this shadow world.[8] Dionysus tells Pentheus that the god accompanies him as his ally (ἔνσπονδος) (lines 923–24). Liddell-Scott-Jones defines ἔνσπονδος as "included in a truce or treaty," because treaties were sealed with libations to the gods (σπονδή). Peace is declared with wine, the gift mortals gave back to the gods, which they got from *this* god. But knowing Pentheus's end, peace is not what comes to mind. We could say again that Dionysus is traitorous, which would be certainly as valid as the fact that all alliances are subject to betrayal, but the play takes us elsewhere: the god's plans for Pentheus are cruel but also glorifying. This ennobling aspect of tragedy, however, will have to be slightly postponed, so as to lead us to the conclusion. For now, some further remarks on parrhesia are due.

Dionysus's duplicitous mode of revealing has several repercussions for parrhesia. His split identity undermines parrhesia's presumed coincidence of teller and telling. Yet the deity that he is demands mortals to accept him both as presentation and representation of the godhead: as an initiate he represents the god but, at the same time, the god presents himself as nothing but representation—a mask, the tragic mask.[9] In this context, we should recall that the god first enters the stage as a ritual performer: he comes to his mother's tomb to establish her cult before performing his own rites. Dionysus is simultaneously a mortal initiate who suffers and a divine being who initiates the cult that will commemorate both divine and human sufferings. Therefore, his duplicity cannot be reduced only to its deceptive aspects, because it also reveals what Walter Otto saw as the essence of this god — namely, paradox: the man-god, the native-foreigner, the latecomer who was one of the earliest gods of Greece.

If, on the one hand, this duplicity undermines the straightforwardness of parrhesia, on the other, it heightens parrhesia's reliance on passionate belief. By posing as a reveler, Dionysus taunts the civic-minded Pentheus to consider other modes of speaking than the dispassionate, rational mode of persuasion. Put differently, the initiate's commitment to his god could itself be proof more powerful than the rational arguments Pentheus expects to hear. Thus, in doubting the existence of the god, Pentheus also degrades the initiate's testimony, planting that seed of doubt Foucault saw bearing fruits in the modern secular world, where truth is thoroughly extricable from its teller. That the civic temperament is particularly offended by the sensuous and excessive nature of the Dionysian cult is further shown in the messenger's recounting of the fertility rites. The messenger tells that the spying herdsman who proposed to capture Agave was himself a city goer and linguistically skilled (κατ' ἄστυ καὶ τρίβων λόγων) (line 717). Against this civic skepticism, only the Bacchae prove consistent in their piety, weaving seamlessly their song in between the god's emanations: they somehow seem to understand that the initiate serves the god but that this god is first and foremost an initiate.

By way of drawing some conclusions about the parrhesiastic ethics of tragedy in general, I will turn to the dramatic exchange between the two young rivals on their way to the mountain, the place of Pentheus's sacrifice. That their bond is a sacrificial one is alluded to in the stichomythia right before Pentheus falls entirely under the sway of the god. Euripides highlights this turning point with an alliterative chiasmus (lines 794–96). In the first two verses, Dionysus advises Pentheus that it is better for mortals like him not to anger the god but to sacrifice to him: "θύοιμ' ἂν αὐτῷ μᾶλλον ἢ θυμούμενος / πρὸς κέντρα λακτίζοιμι θνητὸς ὢν θεῷ." But Pentheus hubristically challenges the god's command by threatening to sacrifice the women revelers: "θύσω, φόνον γε θῆλυν." He even accuses the god of excessive speech: nothing — neither suffering nor any other measure — will silence this stranger, exclaims Pentheus (line 801). From this moment on, Dionysus begins the final stage of his vengeful scheme, the "mechane" as Pentheus recognizes it (line 805), or the "techne" as the god calls it (line 806). As the god hypnotizes him with a visualization of the Maenads, Pentheus is overcome by his desire to see them — a desire that leads him to his fall. Dionysus prophesies Pentheus's fate while announcing to the audience the essence of his paradoxical divinity as most terrible (δεινότατος) and gentlest (ἠπιώτατος) unto humankind (line 861)—the hunter who is also hunted (Otto 105).

Mesmerized by the god and at the height of his pride and confusion, Pentheus declares that he is the only man in the city to dare such a feat as to spy on the Maenads: "μόνος γὰρ αὐτῶν εἰμ' ἀνὴρ τολμῶν τόδε" (line 962). Because he is a prince, Pentheus undertakes this risk for the good of his city, at least as far as he believes. He is alone, because he is also unique, special, the *archon basileus*. Dionysus too is an archon basileus,[10] but of a different kind; still, he too acknowledges Pentheus's mortal uniqueness: "All alone you bear the burden for this city" (μόνος ... ὑπερκάμνεις) (line 963), Dionysus concurs, adding that a fatal but great struggle awaits the mortal prince (lines 971–72). Through the god's recognition, Euripides foregrounds something essential to the tragic genre—namely, that the fate of transgression and atonement belongs only to such extraordinary human beings. We begin to see that Pentheus is not just any impious youth but serves as Dionysus's mortal double. Pentheus's overstepping matches the paradoxical essence of the god as the predator who turns prey. The victim and the executioner are one and the same, for the god would never seek for himself an unworthy foil.

Euripides's contrapuntal language conveys dramatically this fearful symmetry: "I go" (ἔρχομαι), says Pentheus, toward his fate—"carried" (φερόμενος), answers the god, he will return (lines 967–68). The unwittingly willing victim expresses himself in a middle-voiced verb only to stand corrected by the god's passive participle. That Pentheus stands as the god's double is made further explicit as Dionysus describes him with the same adjective he had earlier used for himself: δεινὸς, which is used threefold (line 971), as if to compensate for its single superlative form (δεινότατος) with which Dionysus had described himself (line 861). Aside from Euripides's mastery of tragic irony and reversal, this is a substantive equation the god implies with his victim. It is true that in the struggle Pentheus wages against the god, the god will be the victor. But let us not underestimate the seriousness of Dionysus's words—namely, that the struggle is great (ἀγῶνα μέγαν) (line 975) and that this greatness cannot be diminished by the mortal's eventual defeat. At the moment tragedy wanes as an aesthetic form in Athens and near his own death, Euripides writes a play that performs the very essence of tragic truth.

Here is the blueprint of (this) tragedy: an extraordinary human, a prince, transgresses. He exceeds himself in words and deeds of pride and impiety, which for him are nonetheless marks of courage and responsibility. In so taunting the god who also taunts him, he becomes one with him in the strife that ensues. The cost is high: dismemberment. But the glory is also great: the victim will be glorious not just on earth but in the heavens too (line 972). Dionysus uses the Homeric word κλέος (glory) to describe Pentheus's heroic ascent, a word used for warriors. Pentheus will have also won a victory—perhaps not as sizeable as the god's but one not so small for humankind. He is the chosen one, the one whose blindness is always more acute than seeing, the one whose confusion is more disclosive than clarity, the one whose mistaken speech is more responsible than any wisdom.

Tragedy is shown to be the logos and bios that resist, the attitude that cannot help but stand out, reach beyond itself, and atone for its daring—an attitude not so different from what Foucault saw in Socratic parrhesia. Pentheus is a parrhesiastes because he is ἄθεος, ἄνομος, and ἄδικος (atheist, unlawful, and unrighteous) as the chorus condemns him (line 995)—all condemnations Socrates had faced as well. Even though he lacks Socratic self-knowledge and even though his youthful intransigence cannot rank next to Socratic wisdom, he remains a protagonist in the dangerous scene of parrhesia; for regardless of the validity of his claim, he reveals the nature of parrhesia as passion. Actually, he bears its mark: he is ἐπίσημος in the god's words (line 967), the one citizen who manifestly bears the sign of chosenness. His mark of parrhesia is his disregard toward the very foundations of the social order—its gods, its laws, its moral customs. Of course, here again Euripides complicates the power play of parrhesia, since Pentheus *is* the social order, albeit at a moment of rebellion, when power wishes to renew itself and blast the weight of tradition. Still, though Pentheus is a firm believer in his truth, the truth of evidence, his ordeal strikes one as tainted and his parrhesia marred because—unlike Socrates—he remains clouded by his own ulterior motives of power and control.

On the other hand, regardless of the good or bad faith of Pentheus, Dionysian truth is bound to run the course of terror. This is what Otto means when he writes, "Only because Dionysus, himself, is not merely the enraptured one but also the terrible one, has the terrible demanded him as its victim. That sinister truth which creates madness shows its horrible face in his actions no less than in his sufferings" (105). The truth of the mad god, of the "dark Being," casts its shadows over humanity no matter what (Otto 40), yet humanity does not deserve its name unless it struggles to renew itself, as much through the acknowledgment of as through the confrontation with this imminent danger. Thus, the play ends with yet another parrhesiastic clash between the avenging god and his surviving victim, Cadmus, who reproaches him for behaving as barbarously as humans, though a deity (line 1348).[11] It is surely lines like this that make Nietzsche accuse Euripides of Socratism: Cadmus's demand for divine justification signals for Nietzsche the weak Socratic morality that wishes to subject everything to reason. But whether Cadmus's response is morally weak or brave, it does not actually matter. *The Bacchae* concludes neither with the restoration of reason nor even with the vindication of the pious chorus, whose fate remains unclear after Pentheus's demise.[12] Dionysus declares in his fury that Cadmus and Harmonia will be transformed into serpents, and heading a barbarian army, they will wander in Greece ravaging temples and cities. What of the chorus, then? Will the slave women join the barbarian attacks against Greece, headed still by a Greek victim of Dionysus? How free is this freedom? Or will they remain in Thebes after Cadmus's exile? The protagonists (at least as far as the title goes) are left with their barbarous cheers at the death of their oppressor, their overblown hopes of liberation, and their ambivalent—if not despairing—last words: "What heaven sends has many shapes, and many things the gods accomplish against our expectations. What men look for is not brought to pass, but a god finds a way to achieve the unexpected. Such was the outcome of this story" (lines 1388–92).[13]

The play's last word is πρᾶγμα (*pragma*)—a thing, an outcome, but also an event, a praxis, the *dromenon*. This event came to pass, tells the chorus, but what really is this event? Euripides has left us with the aporetic confrontation of two truth claims that engage in an age-old and irreconcilable struggle, both being equally necessary to human life even as they rend it asunder: in modernity we call this the struggle between faith and reason, the religious and the secular. Oddly enough, this could be the founding play rehearsing the separation of church and state, which, despite all our modern legislative and juridical assurances to the contrary, remains (and most probably will always remain) a site of fateful contestation, much like the one between Dionysus and Pentheus. Atheist Euripides died leaving us an oracular work to interpret[14]: How can we pursue the truth behind its enigma? How can we decode his verdict? Is he telling us that if tragedy has always been the great conflict of right versus right, it can also be that of wrong versus wrong? Or is he saying that tragedy consists in the urgency of living a committed life—a life consistent with oneself, a parrhesiastic life—even as the world admits no just verdict to the ones who live it? And is parrhesia's underside this terrible reality that if one can die for what one believes, so one can kill for (not) believing? If so, this would be the antirational and antipolitical truth of Dionysus: that tragic ethos lies necessarily and always beyond good and evil, beyond divine justification. Yet there is another side to this tragic ethos—one that is even darker but all the more ennobling at the same time: despite the lack of any such guarantee, the human being must still find the resources to make decisions, speak them forth, act them out, and suffer the consequences responsibly.

The tragedy of parrhesia and parrhesia as tragedy converge in this passion for consistency that seeks to harmonize logos and bios, *rhesis* and praxis. Commitment to one's own truth makes parrhesiastic speech tragic speech as it makes tragedy a parrhesiastic genre. Thus, we are far from the Hegelian conception of tragedy as the balancing of two equally legitimate claims. Tragedy surely uses antithetical principles for its plots, but what it communicates hardly rests within the bounds of a disinterested understanding of this antithesis. Such neutral cognizance is the prerogative of self-reflexivity. In contrast, tragedy's antitheses serve to bring into ever-sharper focus the riveting effect that the "one" position has on whomever comes under its grip. After all, what would be the purpose of our understanding that both Dionysus and Pentheus are right? That both Creon and Antigone are right? Even if this were the case, their principles are necessary but also thoroughly irreconcilable with each other. To understand them dispassionately does not mean to have transcended them in any effective sense; it means, more likely, avoiding the responsibility of taking a decision. In any case, it is not that Antigone, for instance, does not *understand* why Creon behaves the way he does; it is merely that she does not accept it, that she has decided otherwise. Tragedy requires a decision, which irremediably tips the balance that sustains it. Balance can only be admitted in books. In real life one must choose. Admitting this choice and living up to it is what conjoins the ethics of tragedy with the ethics of parrhesia.

Socrates, who can easily be presented as the counterexample to this tragic choice—being himself the man of reflection not action, the philosopher not the statesman (Nietzsche often thought of him in such terms)—he too appears more tragic than philosophical insofar as he acts as a parrhesiastes: How else could we understand his fatal decision to scourge the Athenians in his *Apology*, thus deliberately undermining any potential lenience they may have had toward him? And how could we make sense of the still-stranger decision virtually to seek out the death penalty for himself by refusing all other alternatives as unethical concessions? Does this look like a calm, negotiatory stance of the kind we now invest in our philosophers? No. Socrates, the philosopher, sought his own death through his words *no less actively* than did Antigone, the allegedly hubristic heroine, through her deeds. Their "insolence" rests precisely in their contempt for balances and bargains, for the so-called rational negotiations that quickly purchase self-preservation at the cost of moral self-effacement.

It takes a cursory glance around to realize that negotiation is most frequently nothing but a euphemism for unilateral surrender; at best, it results in a sizeable asymmetry of gains and losses and very rarely—if ever—does it describe mutual concession. Unilateral surrender would have certainly been Antigone's option, had she decided to sit at the table with Creon: What could she have negotiated—really—when the desecration of her brother's body was decided a priori? Or should she have repented after her deed, in hopes of appeasing the king and avoiding punishment?[15] Perhaps we tend to overstate the moral necessity of negotiation as we understate the obvious fact that the morality of negotiation sanctions, and often requires, the apology of the one who is right to the one who has might. Socrates's parrhesiastic defense exposes this moral falsity that we often take for granted and even have come to expect from a philosophical consciousness. In his unapologetic *Apology*, Socrates transports onto the philosophical stage the passion for truth and truth-telling that tragedy has been showing all along—a passion that not only undermines but actively despises self-preservation.

The link Foucault forges between Socrates and tragedy through parrhesia can thus be strengthened if we try to comprehend Socrates's tragic predilections rather than if we philosophize tragedy, as Hegel and post-Hegelian theory has tended to do. In other words, it is tragedy that lends itself as the model for philosophical parrhesia, not vice versa. Socrates spoke up and he chose accordingly—that is, he acted tragically. He, along with Euripides and the other tragedians, showed us that the harmony of the parrhesiastes, as of the tragic hero, is not in *reflecting* on the coexistence of striving principles but in the courage of *choosing* and *acting* consistently with this choice in the face of the opposing principle.

PASSIONS

VI

Ῥίζα Αἱματόεσσα

ON *ANTIGONE*

> All this is very different from the usual presentation of the
> play as a Hegelian or post- or pseudo-Hegelian clash of ideas:
> family vs. state, religion vs. secularism, and the like. Ideas do
> clash in the play, but they are as near or far from the center
> of the action as ideas generally are in real life. Sophokles'
> conception, that the clash is basically a matter of *gods* and
> *blood*, is closer to reality as he knew it and we know it.
> Gerald Else, *The Madness of Antigone*

A Tragicomic Misreading?

Despite the startling in medias res with which Antigone pulls us into her act, she is hardly an immediately approachable figure. To approach her from our present moment proves multiply difficult: it requires not only our attunement to a way of thinking and of being that manifests itself only obliquely to us but also our engagement with the many other Antigones she has engendered. For even though this young girl of the myth died unwed and childless and even though her very name means anti-generation, she has reproduced herself in various guises throughout centuries of literary, critical, and philosophical production.

My own remarks here were formed, at least on a preliminary level, as responses to a relatively recent, poststructuralist Antigone—that of Judith Butler. However, instead of attempting a systematic commentary on Butler's reading—which is itself deliberately not a close reading of Sophocles, even though it offers several rhetorical analyses of the play—my chapter takes only certain cues from her work, cues that prompt my own turn to Sophocles's tragedy. In other words, just as the Sophoclean *Antigone* served for Butler as a springboard for questions that exceed the scope of Sophocles (and they exceed it not in the sense of existing outside Sophocles's horizon but rather in the sense that Sophocles may have—for essential reasons—kept a certain reserve from them), so Butler's text offered me a similar springboard to reread *Antigone* as a guidepost toward a modern problematic. I have already identified this problematic with the consequences of a profoundly untragic vein that runs through the heart of what we call contemporary theory, whether it is allied to cultural studies, critical theory, or the poststructuralist ethicojuridical discourses Butler follows. The latter discourses are in fact embellished and "improved" forms of social construction and identity theory that, by displacing agency into "performativity," thinly veil, but do not actually abandon, the determinist pitfalls of such sociocultural outlooks.

Butler's reading of the play as a critique of law's exclusion of the nonnormative family implies a larger theoretical assumption according to which theory can isolate specific problems, identify their social determinations (let us note that in her case, at least, the determinations are invariably sociocultural), and thereupon undertake the project of improving the world (mostly by attempting discursive redefinitions of already existing political and juridical categories). Despite its good intentions, the optimism of Butler's social voluntarism is not without problems, problems that begin with her textual and thematic misreadings of the play. Of course, it could be argued that these misreadings, offensive as they may be to classicists, are fruitful updates of Sophocles, and Butler herself admits that she is interested not in a philological exercise but in the philosophical implications of the play's treatment of kinship.[1] However, one cannot expect textual misappropriations and omissions not to affect the philosophical meanings one elicits from a text. Therefore, beyond its specific philological oversights, Butler's heterodox reading of the function of the law in Sophocles's play points to a larger issue concerning the place of tragedy in modern thought: the theoretical failure to understand tragic logic in general—namely, the logic of the indeterminate par excellence, the logic that exists beyond justification and in which "bad things happen to good people," so to speak.

Despite its obvious unfairness and callous arbitrariness, which proves off-putting to our modern sensibility, this ancient logic allows for more profound differences among human beings than social construction does, even when the latter, like much of contemporary theory, claims difference as one of its central concepts. Tragic logic highlights human beings' singularity in the unique way each one responds to unexpected adversity. Thus, while I understand the democratic spirit of social construction when it comes to addressing the civic nature of things, I submit that tragedy offers the site where the hard question of what exceeds civic—and hence, human—determination is at stake. In the precinct of the tragic, we cannot claim that all relations—blood commitments, commitments of love, cries of jealousy or betrayal, and so forth—can or should be leveled out.

In distinguishing the unwritten and inevitable law of *atē* qua mortal fate from that of the written, immanent law of juridical right, I thus attempt to show the priority of tragedy's law. Subsequently, I turn to the notions of blood and incest because they both introduce the question of nature (phusis), which the theory of social construction elides but which remains germane to tragedy for important reasons: beyond any simple determinism, nature is the field of accidents and contingencies, and as such, it presents us with the limits of the human capacity to explain, control, or improve the world around it.[2] Before Heidegger's devastating assessment of humanism that resulted in the so-called antihumanist trend of modern continental philosophy,[3] it was Attic tragedy that put the idea of the human on trial. The anthropocentrism of Greek culture did not oppose but, on the contrary, fostered this tragic principle by which the human being was brought to its limit: only a worldview that invests the human being with such passion for elevation as did the Greeks could see how terribly vulnerable the human being is to the whims of fate.

In tragedy, the human subject is not at the center of the world above all other beings but instead exists as the site of strife between opposing forces that exceed it. Thus, if the tragic subject is privileged at all, it is in this minimal sense: the human being is the only being who cognizes itself as the site of this fatal strife and who *suffers* the consequences of its defeat. Through this suffering, as Nietzsche notes, the human being grows deeper but not necessarily better.[4] The depth consists in the learning of a strange lesson—namely, that there is nothing to learn that could purposively improve one's actions; one can only hope to realize that the actions themselves, regardless of how they are chosen or what their content may be, are worthy of one's fate. It is with this understanding in mind that I develop my reading of Butler and Sophocles:

instead of illustrating prior theoretical questions through Sophocles's play (questions concerning the tragic or untragic consciousness, questions concerning law, kinship, obligation, the state, and so on) as Butler chooses to do, I insist that the play—and particularly its heroine—stipulate in advance for us the very language from which these questions can emerge.

Butler begins by acknowledging the play's long critical reception, her discontents with which led her to take it up once again in what will presumably be a new and different way. This is not an unlikely beginning to the study of an enduring text. Quite the contrary, in his preface to *The Madness of Antigone*, Gerald Else also acknowledges the "vast literature" on *Antigone* (8) but sidesteps extensive documentation in favor of a narrow focus on textual details, so as "to bring forward a number of aspects and bits of evidence which have been overlooked, to the detriment . . . of our understanding of the play and its heroine" (7). In another example, George Steiner opens his comparative motif-study *Antigones* with a triply framed quotation, thus underlining the oblique path through which we approach the play. Steiner cites Montaigne's implicit reference to Plato's description of the rhapsode in the *Ion*: "We are 'only the interpreters of interpretations'" (1), suggesting the distance and mediation that separate us from Sophocles's original.

Regardless of admitting to its exhaustive citation, however, critics, philosophers, and ordinary readers alike are drawn toward this work in an original manner—not only in hoping to find something new and distinct from the previous analyses but, more importantly, in being drawn above all to Antigone herself, to encountering her directly as if for the first time.[5] Thus, Else underlines Antigone's force of attraction by comparing her to "a tidal wave of energy which cannot be stemmed," adding that she claims "the lion's share of our attention" (80). Jacques Lacan too saw this exclusive attention she commands and spoke of it in terms of fascination (252), a fascination that draws us toward the bare minimum of what makes her be, the bottom ground—which is also to say, it draws us toward the very beginning: who is she really, and what does she stand for?

Each time, a reading begins more or less guided by these two questions (and significantly so in this sequence, as we will see), and each time, the heroine seems to demand originality and daring from her readers. Thus, even though her distance and reserve are essential aspects of her grandeur, they are simultaneously markers of an invitation. That this invitation is often missed owes to the very slippage in the sequence of the two questions we just have posed: "Who is she?" seamlessly recedes during the interpretive process behind the question "What does she stand for?" Slipping from presence to representation, the reader forgets who Antigone is, reducing her instead to some sort of political representative. Antigone is, but also *is not*, only what she represents. The most emphatic sense of this negative copula can be seen in the fact that Antigone's being is given over to death from the beginning of the play: she is she who is (about) *to be not*. It is in this sense of a primordial fatality that we should be hearing her proper name—the one who does not generate. Antigone is the name of the futureless, of the one who dies for blood relations while rejecting her own chance for offspring.

Nevertheless, this death that prevents Antigone from generating her own children is a death that, instead, generates meanings: as a tragic death, hers is by necessity a meaningful death, a death consciously decided—a death *for* something. Antigone's loss is not a nothing yielding another nothing: this is the moral taboo she poses for the modern theoretical outlook, which in the aftermath of two world wars has deemed that tragic death is simply mythic death, that there is nothing worth dying for, and that in order not to exploit the other's death—or, in Nancy's terms, not to put the other's death to work for our purposes—we should drain even self-sacrifice of all its meaning. Theory offers the banality of death as the moral corrective to the immoral aestheticization of death it disapproves of in tragedy.[6] But in dispelling the draw of death, banality also absolutizes death in a peculiar manner: alien to and feared by theory, real death has to be avoided at all costs. Most of all, it has to be avoided by theoretical investigation itself, which, instead, resorts to speaking of death only in textual and rhetorical terms.[7] Hence, the tragic logic of fatality (a logic bound to the inevitably actual as much as to the actually inevitable nature of mortality) is replaced by the poststructuralist logic of finitude (a logic of limits between beings, limits whose scriptural and mediating nature appears to be theoretically inevitable but is actually quite negotiable).[8] Grasping Antigone's choice, then, requires a difficult correspondence between her essence as a human being who is unafraid of her death and the meaning or representation of this death—namely, the reasons and circumstances that bring her to this sacrifice. In other words, just as she harmonizes duty with desire, consciousness with passion, and words with deeds, so the reader must be able to harmonize her presence with her representation, her being with her meaning. It is at this juncture, I think, that the play tests our critical originality.

Butler's revisitation of this tragedy is largely in keeping with this desire for an original encounter, which often translates into a critical assessment of previous analyses. Indeed, *Antigone's Claim* begins by distancing itself from the philosophical, psychoanalytic, and existing feminist tradition of reading Antigone, on the grounds that they all reduce Antigone to the question of representation. However, in evoking legal rhetoric in its very title, *Antigone's Claim* is already situated within a long tradition of interpretation that has established this play as the quintessential example of law and literature, at least since Hegel. Even though Butler's critique of the law and the political implications she draws from this critique problematize this tradition, her analysis encases and even reproduces the principal argument she critiques—namely, Antigone's representativeness.

I will be returning to this remark in more detail later in this chapter, but it deserves a brief explanation for the time being, since it does counter Butler's explicit intents. Wishing to distance herself from the history of representative readings, which rely on the mimetic fallacy that a fictional character like Antigone can be a real representative of something, Butler writes, "Indeed, it is not just that, as a fiction, the mimetic or representative character of Antigone is already put in question but that, as a figure for politics, she points somewhere else, not to politics as a question of representation but to that political possibility that emerges when the limits to representation and representability are exposed" (2). Thus, the symbolic function of Antigone is undermined not only by her fictionality but also by the crisis of the theories of representation themselves. Yet as her study progresses, Butler depicts Antigone somewhat paradoxically as a spokeswoman for those who question representation's limits. Butler's Antigone appears before the law of Thebes to challenge the limit of the state's conception of law as representation. As such, she opens up a space for what law, insofar as it is thought within representation, does not or cannot represent.[9]

From here on the problematic of representation reinscribes itself in Butler's account. For even though, strictly speaking, this reading beyond representation should not be so easily pinned down, it turns out that it has many and readily available names and can be identified with various existing constituencies and their juridical, or quasi-juridical, status: persons of same-sex desire, disenfranchised AIDS patients, alternative families, and so on. This is precisely why Antigone, this time as Butler's fiction, is sought "as an example of a certain feminist impulse" (1)—that is, in the service of a political agenda that, no matter how carefully framed at the limits of representation, remains largely within the scope of representation. In other words, Butler's Antigone too is representative, but she represents what politics has not yet managed to voice because of its hegemonic misidentification of the political with the representational.

However, Antigonian politics is much more eccentric than Butler's politics of inclusion allows for, though not in the sense of legitimizing the socially deviant, or of accepting eccentricity, so to speak. This is instead the politics of contemporary theory, which, enamored by the idea that the Other must be approached precisely in its threatening difference, avoids addressing the practical—that is, political—difficulty of this imperative. Satisfied either with its own, *self-reflexive* guarantee that theory is also praxis or with the notion that the potential is more important than the actual,[10] contemporary thought turns a blind eye to the obvious fact that the relation to the Other as Other has been always ridden—and most likely will always be ridden—with conflict and suffering. At best, the acceptance of the Other depends on the neutralization of the threat it poses to the social order: the Other is practically divested of its difference, which is then euphemistically preserved in official discourse. The rhetoric of accepting alterity in its difference—namely, the discourse of tolerance—serves as the antitragic, and eventually antieccentric, mark of contemporary theory that, nonetheless, relies heavily on the notions of eccentricity, the nonidentical, exorbitance, excess, and so forth. The play's politics, on the other hand, is eccentric in *not* legitimizing deviance: that Creon orders Antigone's death is paradoxically a salutary fact for Sophocles, in that it shows the incapacity of any institutionalized form of power to normalize, assimilate, sanitize, tame, incorporate, or even accept in their difference those truly revolutionary aspects of human nature that refuse to yield and to be "reasoned with."

Indeed, to embody the antistatist impulse Butler searches for in this play (Butler 1), Antigone must remain forever socially illegitimate, an outsider who delegitimizes everything except her relation to herself. This notorious autonomy of hers attests to another kind of law[11]—one that, as we will see, the Greeks wisely kept outside the realm of the polis and the technologies of writing that civic organization imposed on legislation.[12] The unwritten character of this Antigonian law is, in fact, essential to a nonrepresentational vision of politics. In short, Antigone's eccentricity is her *tragic* nature, which Butler's reading undoes, wishing to correct tragedy with tragicomedy as my section title above suggests: Butler's antitragic argument assumes that had the state allowed for nonnormative kinships, Antigone would not have had to die.[13]

Consequently, despite other drawbacks to Hegel's assessment of this tragedy in the *Phenomenology*,[14] he is basically correct when it comes to the nature of Antigone's political existence: like the category of the family whose claims she defends, Antigone is prepolitical in that she both founds the state and is excluded by it.[15] The family for Hegel is the founding cell of state organization, but when its chthonic demands impose themselves over and above civic obligation, Hegel sides unambiguously with the state as the only guarantor of universal, objective, and actualized—not merely subjectively contingent—ethics: in the figure of Antigone, who stands for familial duty, the state supersedes and excludes its founding unit. Here I would emphasize Antigone's precedence over politics in a manner as explicit as possible: Antigone not only precedes the modern sense of political organization, to which according to Hegel she also remains utterly inadequate and thus outdated, but she is even prepolitical with respect to Greek politics, which Hegel considered to be unreflexive and primitively one-sided. In other words, she is prepolitical to any politics—ancient or modern. Or to borrow Loraux's vocabulary again, she is antipolitical.[16] Given that Butler's interest in the play stems from her interest in an antistatist kind of feminism as opposed to a recent wave of feminism that seeks "the backing and authority of the state to implement feminist policy aims" (1), I find that Antigone's prepolitical (or antipolitical) character may be more relevant to her argument than the politics of social construction. Nevertheless, in trying to go beyond Hegel's instrumental reading of the play for the purposes of his own statist philosophy, Butler's argument posits an Antigone who shares in Creon's legalese, thus compromising the heroine's antistatism.

At any rate, in this discussion of Antigone's representability, the issue at stake is the peculiar repetition that marks so many readings of *Antigone* and that is actually not contrary to but constitutive of the text's originary character. Perhaps this is one way, and an ironic one at that, to understand Hegel's notorious statement that Antigone shows woman as the "everlasting irony ... of the community" (*Phenomenology of Spirit* 288). Perhaps he recognized in Antigone an irony not just against any community but against the community of scholars most of all, as she relentlessly turns them (as she turned Hegel too) into someone like her own father-brother, the ambitious but eventually defeated theoretical investigator. For, like Oedipus, the critical reader must similarly overcome his or her predecessors and solve the enigma of Antigone, only to end up blinded by his or her own method. And just as the Sphinx's mystery owes mostly to the patency of her riddle—she asks about that which is most proximate to humans (their mortality) and hence most illegible to them also—Antigone's mystery too owes to her elemental simplicity, to a peculiar obviousness in her that erects a theoretical stumbling block.

Yet the particular position this work occupies in the Western canon *as* a political text necessitates its continued prominence. It is because we desperately want this text to reveal a radically new political possibility for the present that we revisit it every so often. And the more the world remains largely unaffected and the more distant Antigone grows from our political horizon, the more drastic the intellectual need for her retrieval. As such, no matter how each critic qualifies his or her entry into this text, one is compelled to repeat the assumption that since this is a text about politics (other issues—religion, kinship, love, and death—are always subsumed by politics), Antigone must be a representative of something or other: religious martyrs, feminist agitators, rebels against the state, even terrorists may find in her their symbolic prototype.

Let me clarify: I am not suggesting by any means that we abandon this political line of inquiry, nor do I actually believe we can do so with a play like this, which so obviously begs the question of what politics is—its scope, its task, its provenance. On the contrary, I myself consciously conclude my book with a political—hence representative—understanding of Antigone's legacy in later Greek history. However, in anticipation of such a political interpretation and of my critical reading of Butler, I am also appending the following qualifiers: instead of claiming that there can be a politics beyond representation, as Butler seems to suggest, we should perhaps admit to the *actual* inevitability of representation and of what this inevitability entails. Is not this real inevitability, which theory can afford to elide only discursively, a tragedy in itself? Is not this inevitability the Platonic fact, in other words, that we cannot exit appearances and representations? That this is why we are bound to always fall short of truth, even though it should never become the reason why we should stop pursuing truth? Politics is inevitably enmeshed with representation. This is politics' tragic underside, and this is why Socrates—an Antigonian figure himself—never trusted it but never stopped engaging with it in his own oblique way. It is because of this inevitability that any action resisting representation becomes suspect and has to be punished (as Creon does with Antigone) or has to be read and recuperated into being itself a form of political and legal—that is, representational—rhetoric (as Butler does with Antigone).

There is, however, another way of thinking of Antigone (and her antipolitics) representatively: in this case, representation does not signify the hegemonic usurpation of the singular voice by a symbolic proxy, but the representative stands for the exemplary,[17] the singularly outstanding that nonetheless compels us universally into its orbit, making us part of it. I contend that such an understanding of representation cannot be reached so much through reading or analyzing her but through exposure to the extremities of her tragic situation. Arriving at this exposure was the very reason why the ancient Athenians did not read tragedies as texts but *witnessed* their representations in a vivid imitation on their tragic stage: to reach the state of compassion, which is not the same as the faculty of cognition. A sacrifice is not a piece of writing to be read, and the richness of its meaning does not consist in eliciting various discursive explanations from the spectator but in overwhelming and short-circuiting the spectator's cognitive faculties. If simply read, this sacrifice looks only menacing, irrational, primitive, horrible: in one word, tragic, and derogatorily so. Such acts of blood (and I insist on *acts*, not words) ruin any attempt to make sense out of them without first coming under their grip, for they make sense only in their own absolute terms and not in terms of a retroactive philosophical logic that shuns whatever does not obey its self-reflexive and self-interested economy of survivalism.

We can now return to Butler's problematic of legal and political representation under this light: it is not categories such as the alternative family, persons of same-sex desire, racialized others, refugees, and so on that state legislation eventually refuses to represent. Legal history is filled with the gradual extension of the law to include minoritized categories, no matter how unjustly belated this inclusion always seems to be and how inadequate still the law remains in its understanding and treatment of basic issues surrounding these identities. Rather, what state legislation *should not* and *cannot* represent is something else, something much more elemental than any identity traits a particular society might deem outlandish and wish to outlaw: it cannot legislate over the fearless desire of a person to die, to sacrifice oneself for a cause that presents itself unpredictably—no matter how painstakingly human institutions have tried in advance to account for it. This exorbitant revolt, which always takes as its object something that can become retroactively political, does not in itself stem from the realm of politics. Antigone's capacity to see in the desecration of her brother's corpse a good reason to forego her life—this peculiar capacity of a human being to give meaning to life by snatching it away from herself, the strongest weapon in any resistance—springs from the deep well of human intimacy, from the certainty of one's own presence to oneself and to first principles, not from any civic attachment or obedience to conventional law. It certainly has nothing to do with the kind of inclusive politics of tolerance to which Butler points, even as she carefully avoids words like "inclusion" or "tolerance" because of their neoliberal tint.

To sum up, if Antigone is political at all—and I think Hegel, again, is far more prescient than Butler on this point in considering Antigone prepolitical—she is in a radical, that is also to say antipolitical, way. Her antiauthoritarian stance is first and foremost her refusal to be mastered or understood not only by Creon and his city but also by philosophy and politics in general—namely, by the official discourses of immanence and instrumentality. To think of Antigone radically, then, which seems to have been Butler's aim, one has to think of her at the root and as a root. One needs to take the chorus at its words when it describes Antigone as "ἐσχάτη ῥίζα"—the last root of the house of Oedipus (lines 599–600/653). Further, one needs to take this description as pointing in another direction: as the last root of the accursed, of the bestial and godly family,[18] she is also the first root of what is properly human. She marks the origin of the human insofar as she has shared in and cleansed, through her deed, the blood of the inhuman. Hence, we cannot dismiss the questions of blood and root as biological anathema, as essentialist or deterministic remnants of mythical violence, but we have to consider them radically—that is, at the root of the human and its ethical horizon.

The Unwritten Law: *I* Shall Act as *I* Have Come to Know It to Be Right

Before considering the issues of blood and incest and the ways in which they open up and delimit kinship in Sophocles's play, I would like first to discuss the notion of law in this tragedy, particularly since the law's relation to kinship forms the crux of Butler's argument. While I commend Butler's political vision "to extend legitimacy to a variety of kinship forms" (74), the fact remains that reading the figure of Antigone in the service of this agenda obscures what is at stake in the text. At stake in Sophocles is law not as juridical procedure—that is, as part of the instrumental discourse of right—and not even as the more primal psychoanalytic prohibition issuing from and protecting the family structure itself. At stake is law in its most primary and necessary sense as the origin that dictates what human beings are: mortal beings, exposed to unrelenting fate, taunted to make decisions that exceed them but that must be made if the human being deserves to be called human at all.

Responding to Creon's interrogation of how she dared violate his edict, Antigone fearlessly insists that there are other principles whose gravity is far greater than a tyrant's proclamation. I cite an excerpt from her speech both in Greek and in English for the benefit of noting its sonority along with its semantics, since her words resonate as oracular sayings rather than as a legal defense:

> οὐ γάρ τί μοι Ζεὺς ἦν ὁ κηρύξας τάδε,
> οὐδ' ἡ ξύνοικος τῶν κάτω θεῶν Δίκη
> τοιούσδ' ἐν ἀνθρώποισιν ὥρισεν νόμους,
> οὐδὲ σθένειν τοσοῦτον ᾠόμην τὰ σὰ
> κηρύγμαθ' ὥστ' ἄγραπτα κἀσφαλῆ θεῶν
> νόμιμα δύνασθαι θνητά γ' ὄνθ' ὑπερδραμεῖν.
> οὐ γάρ τι νῦν γε κἀχθές, ἀλλ' ἀεί ποτε
> ζῇ ταῦτα, κοὐδεὶς οἶδεν ἐξ ὅτου 'φάνη.
> τούτων ἐγὼ οὐκ ἔμελλον, ἀνδρὸς οὐδενὸς
> φρόνημα δείσασ', ἐν θεοῖσι τὴν δίκην
> δώσειν· θανουμένη γὰρ ἐξῄδη, τί δ' οὔ;
> κεἰ μὴ σὺ προὐκήρυξας. εἰ δὲ τοῦ χρόνου
> πρόσθεν θανοῦμαι, κέρδος αὔτ' ἐγὼ λέγω.
> (Lines 450–62)

> Yes, it was not Zeus that made the proclamation;
> nor did Justice, which lives with those below, enact
> such laws as that, for mankind. I did not believe
> your proclamation had such power to enable
> one who will someday die to override
> God's ordinances, unwritten and secure.
> *They* are not of today and yesterday;
> they live forever; none knows when first they were.
> These are the laws whose penalties I would not

incur from the gods, through fear of any man's temper.
(Lines 494–503)

Even though the translation of this passage begins with an affirmation[19]—the "yes" referring to Antigone's admission of transgressing the edict—the Greek text begins with two parallel negative constructions, explaining the reasons behind her disobedience: neither Zeus nor Justice were the authors of this law. The repetition of these negatives structures her response less as a defense and more as a denunciation. Instead of justifying her act, Antigone speaks parrhesiastically, accusing Creon of hubris: his edict disregards the laws of the gods. The Greek audience would know that it also violates civic law, which often allowed for the burial of criminals and traitors outside the city walls. In the terrible unjustness of Creon's decision, Antigone recognizes the faulty thinking of a mortal mind that is too anxious to consolidate its power and authority at a time of political unrest. Anticipating Teiresias's prophetic speech later on in the play, Antigone thus reminds the king that human ordinances cannot overrule the laws of the gods, which she characterizes as both unwritten and secure.

This connection she forges between the unwritten character of the divine laws and their security is noteworthy, as it could be understood in the strongest terms of cause and effect: the divine laws are secure from corruption *because* they are unwritten, for an unwritten law calls only those who are freely drawn to it and whose intent is thus to protect it from distortion. The unwritten law, in other words, is the voice of their own conscience, a decision at which they have arrived of their own accord, not out of fear or coercion. In contrast, the written law, readily available to everyone who may or may not agree with it but who feels coerced into obeying it, risks continually its own distortion: its letter can be cunningly misinterpreted and tailored to fit corrupt needs. This is, after all, the most usual pattern by which a law drafted out of a just cause turns out serving unjust ends, transforming itself into legalism, empty form, and callous technicality. The letter's polyvalence, available on the page to be variously exploited, offers an unwitting cover for the corruption of the law's spirit. As such, human or written law cannot be protected from unjust changes and amendments that often favor those with the power to draft them. Divine law, however, is secure in its immutability, in the *always* (ἀεί ποτε) of its temporality, because it speaks moral absolutes not historically contingent juridical rights.

Notably, κήρυγμα, the word Antigone uses to differentiate Creon's order from the unwritten divine laws (νόμοι), itself designates an oral proclamation. However, this does not necessarily undermine her overall distinction between the unwritten first principles and the secondary civic laws, for her distinction does not refer to the particular *means* of publication of the law but to the *nature* of its source. Being issued from a contingent source, human laws, even when orally promulgated, produce the contingent effects of the written law. On the other hand, divine laws scarcely need to be written, since their only significant means of expression remains the moral conduct of their agents: the very idea of a divine law that is not practiced, but holds true only in a book, is a contradiction in terms. Hence, divine law for Antigone can only be unwritten: a law that is already desire not obligation, living presence not formal command—an inner voice that sings the harmony between one's acts and one's avowed principles, a celestial guide to human acts that could never reduce itself to becoming a recipe.

Antigone's negative certainty that it was neither Zeus nor Justice who dictated such an unjust law culminates in yet another statement whose negative grammatical construction paradoxically heightens, rather than undermines, the powerful affirmation she expresses about the origin of the divine laws: no one even knows when they first manifested themselves—this is how absolute and primordial they are. The implication is that they came to be before even Zeus himself, since it was no secret to the Greeks that Zeus was not the father of the gods from time immemorial. These laws precede the divine order itself and perhaps even legislate it. They have no origin, because that would render them derivative and detract from their moral efficacy.

Still, while the source of such laws might be as elusive as time immemorial, it becomes clearly visible in Antigone's presence and in the presence of all those who attune their lives to these laws. Though hard to locate in terms of origin, since human consciousness remains inadequate to cognizing the infinity of the "always," the temporality of divine law can be expressed in terms of a paradox: though it exceeds the human in its force—hence, it is divine—this law does not precede humanity in a sequential sense; rather, it has always manifested itself within the human heart, having its seat in individual conscience. This is also to say that divine law is nothing else but the awareness of something great, an awareness through which the human being shows itself to be human in having the very capacity to transgress the conventional (civic, written, formal) laws it imposes on itself. To be free of oneself and of one's own self-imposed limits—this is the law that constitutes our being human, and it cannot be written down if it hopes to retain this constitutive efficacy and not end up as another mundane regulation.

Loraux writes of the suggestive homophony between the Greek *aei*—a word that means "always" and that was the hallmark of political speeches proclaiming the polis as eternally victorious—and the Greek *aiai* of tragedy, which is a mournful interjection, the cry of mortal suffering (35–38). For Loraux, the political *aei* signals human hubris: it usurps the infinity of divine temporality and relies on the false certainty that humanity can be forever invincible. Sharply contrasted to this civic *aei* that divinizes the human polis is the tragic cry that bespeaks another kind of "always," the one most properly belonging to mortals: the persistence of human suffering, the always we have been sharing from time immemorial in tears and cries of loss. Antigone's mortal certainty of the eternal immutability of divine law foregrounds this double register of the always in the political and tragic realms. Far surer in her beliefs than the political man she confronts, Antigone puts the civic *aei* to its proper, secondary place: it is not Creon's law that carries within it the force of this *aei*, but it is the divine law, which she serves—interestingly, through an antipolitical act. The divine laws live forever (ἀεί ποτε ζῇ ταῦτα), she insists, as they become concrete in the conduct of people who choose to remember rather than recite them, affirm them rather than obey them, believe in them rather than fear them. Antigone's gods would bequeath us only this *living* law, which is more of an oracle than a command: one must find the law unto oneself; one must find, not the order of the "Thou shall not," but the desire of the "I shall do." It does not mean that the road is easy, as Antigone herself knows that she will pay for it. And as if Creon's punishment of her were not enough, she continues to pay in the world of interpretation: it is typical of Hegelian and post-Hegelian criticism to construe her transgression as a hubris symmetrical to that of Creon—a construal that ignores the many elements of the tragedy that suggest otherwise.

To freely come to see what is right—this tragic path of moral autonomy is also the one Socrates was trying to show to Phaedrus and to virtually every other human being with whom he entered in conversation. The desire to reach the good through one's own means is the dynamic that underlies all the Platonic dialogues, and it furnishes the main reason why Socrates criticized writing as a mnemonic aid in the *Phaedrus*: to avoid authoritarianism—in fact, the representative impulse of the law, whose didacticism simply dictates but does not inspire. In being written down, the didactic aspect of the law is inherently bound to representation and to becoming just another resource at hand. Even the Hebrew god, whose written commandments have been sharply contrasted to the dark and ahistorical mythic laws,[20] first spoke to Moses before his words were engraved on the tablets. Earlier still, before his covenant with Abraham was sealed in the bodily inscription of circumcision, the same god gave his first command to Abraham orally.

Certainly, the fear that human beings will forget the law—namely, they will forget their own self-awareness as humans—necessitates legal writing, which is aimed at reminding them of their duties. But soon the menacing power of the law as a formal, abstract command takes over as well, targeting exactly those who expose its violence. Antigone's answer to Creon, which Butler reads legalistically because she (dis)misses everything about the oracular tone of Sophocles's words, repeats on the tragic stage what Socrates had related to Phaedrus about the law: the law should be remembered because it is inscribed on the human soul first and foremost, not on any other external surfaces. This is not necessarily a generic condemnation of written legislation. Instead, it implies that written legislation should proceed from the consciousness of these inner laws and not vice versa. Antigone's autonomy enacts tragically this Socratic wisdom: she abides freely to a principle that is larger than any human or even divine author, yet this same principle is one that only human beings have the great privilege to sometimes glimpse. I am referring to the sense of responsibility that, for reasons I will shortly discuss, belongs exclusively to the human lot.

Since *Antigone* relies heavily on this practice of autonomy that sets in relief the tension between fate and individual disposition and since the contemporary destabilization of any experience of self renders autonomy ethically moot, I will offer some further remarks on the function of these notions in this play. First of all, Sophocles's understanding of autonomy is not synonymous with human mastery, as contemporary theory often charges this term to mean: Antigone is capable of her judgments only because she knows that she cannot control her destiny—namely, the fact that she will one day die. She says that much to Creon, and I will return to this realization of hers again soon. It is not she who behaves as if she is all-powerful and immortal; it is Creon, who, in the name of the city's security, pursues his own dreams of invincibility and self-interest.

But this is not the end of the story. The play has in store potentially more unsettling reasons for its focus on the self than are allowed by my own, theoretically safe explanation, which aligns Antigone with the modern subject who is devoid of any mastery. (This explanation nonetheless remains valid, since the tragic subject's succumbing to fate has an affinity to the modern subject's lack of self-mastery, as I mentioned in my introduction.) Still, there may be other implications of the Sophoclean relation between self and other that run counter to our current theoretical assumptions. For instance, no critic who pursues the ethical dimension of this work should let go unnoticed the play's emphatic repetition of composite words starting with "auto" or "homo"—prefixes designating the self and the self-same. In light of the current philosophical discussions concerning the Other in ethics, which for the most part eclipse and even efface the gravity of the self in its ethical relation to itself, this drama's insistence on the self and sameness is paramount. Among the many binaries that *Antigone* elaborates (family versus state, particular versus total, woman versus man, divine versus civic), this of the self (and the self-same) in relation to Otherness should also be considered.

Therefore, in addition to the word "autonomous," which exemplifies Antigone's ethics in the most explicit manner, I cite a few more examples where ethical notions are inflected through their referral to the self. In the opening verse of the play, Antigone addresses Ismene with a notoriously untranslatable expression, hoping to enlist her participation in the act of burial: "Ὦ κοινὸν αὐτάδελφον Ἰσμήνης κάρα" (line 1/1–2).[21] The play's apostrophic beginning—the address to the other—is an immediate return to the self, to Antigone's possessive expression "my own sister." Through a double citation of sameness (κοινὸν αὐτάδελφον), Antigone emphasizes their blood relation in the figure of a sisterly head shared in common by both. Being of the order of the self-same, blood kinship might translate into sharing the same moral attitude toward the dead brother. Only because the two sisters are in common with each other and with the dead brother, who is also αὐτάδελφος, can Antigone hope to find a collaborator in Ismene. Interestingly, that Ismene's choice is different from Antigone's does not lead the latter to revise her opinion about the moral efficacy of the self-same: it is not that the self-same proves incapable of the right ethical decision; rather, Ismene's moral weakness is recast as precisely her *difference*—the fact that she is not a worthy descendant of the family of Oedipus, that she is "ἐσθλῶν κακή" (base, although of noble parents) (line 38/44). She is not one of them. She has incurred the enmity of both Antigone and the dead man (lines 93–94/109–11); and at this crucial moment, Antigone disowns her.[22]

This also shows that commonality and self-sameness are not exhausted by the biological determinism of shared blood, as we will see in the next section, but refer to a moral nature shared in common: Antigone and Ismene should be self-same because of their blood bond but are actually different because they do not share the same moral attitude. Such a difference, however, can never become a reflexive object of celebration of democratic pluralism for Antigone: it is simply morally untenable. (This is one example of the unreflexive moral attitude of Antigone that Hegel, in turn, finds historically untenable.)

In another example, when Ismene lists the evils of the house of Oedipus trying to dissuade her sister from her fatal decision, she refers to their father as αὐτουργός—someone who acted on himself, taking with his own hands his very own eyes, after having detected and exposed his own crimes (αὐτοφώρων ἀμπλακημάτων) (lines 49–52/56–60). The implication is that Antigone's choice makes her also αὐτουργός, as she too will bring disasters on herself. Passing on to their mother, Ismene emphasizes how doubleness becomes sameness, as Jocasta was mother and wife to Oedipus at once: "διπλοῦν ἔπος" (two names in one) (line 53/61). Further accentuating the intransitive nature of the Oedipal family while implicitly separating herself from it, Ismene describes the mutual fratricide with the verb αὐτοκτονοῦντε, which translates as mutual suicide: to kill the brother is to kill oneself (line 56/64). Creon, in his turn, will position the two brothers in a mirroring, self-reflexive relation as "πληγέντες αὐτόχειρι," striking and struck by each other's hand, each defiled by the other's blood (line 172/190). Echoing Ismene, he too will speak of doubleness becoming oneness, as the double death of the brothers marks one indivisible fate in time: "διπλῆς μοίρας μίαν / καθ᾽ ἡμέραν ὤλοντο" ("they met their double fate upon one day") (lines 170–71/189).

Αὐτόνομος, αὐτουργός, and αὐτόχειρ will be the triple characterization of Antigone, who, following the path of self-determination, brings her fate on herself, taking at the end her own life. The chorus adds the adjective αὐτόγνωτος (line 875/927), someone who is self-willed, who knows her own self, and who is thus responsible for her fate. Although the chorus is accusatory, chastising Antigone for reaping what she has sown, the positive Socratic undertones of this adjective should not escape us: Antigone's self-knowledge is intricately bound to her noble conduct, to her acting consistently with her principles. As with Socrates, harmony of words and deeds proves to be the essence of Antigone. Appropriately, it is inconsistency and fragmentation, the split between act and speech, that Antigone denounces in Ismene when the latter offers belatedly to share her fate: "λόγοις δ' ἐγὼ φιλοῦσαν οὐ στέργω φίλην" (I do not love a friend who loves in words) (line 543/597). Even though Antigone's sense of autonomy serves different ethical purposes than the mostly selfish and despairing acts of her kin, it is nonetheless this emphatic self-relation that ties her to Oedipus, Jocasta, and her brothers, leaving Ismene again outside family resemblance. Antigone affirms repeatedly her familial belonging, explaining her devotion to Polyneices in terms of his being her ὁμόσπλαγχνος, one who sprang from the same womb as she (lines 511–13/559–61).

Whereas this emphasis on the self-same makes sense in a work that aims at foregrounding the importance of the family as opposed to the inherent variance of the state, its ethical significance is not exhausted by this thematic requirement alone. What if the Sophoclean understanding of self-sameness suggests this theoretically inconvenient fact: even as we are expected to act ethically not just to our blood kin (namely, not just to the naturally self-same), this still implies a relation to an other who is in some way already of our kind? What if the very movement of compassion brings the other (whether human or inhuman) inadvertently into the horizon of the self and its identifications, of resemblance and connection, rather than of alienation and alterity? Symmetrically, what if the current one-sided focus on difference as the only tenable ethicopolitical figure risks becoming blind to the fact that difference can turn—and has already turned—into historical exclusion, political discrimination, and social disenfranchisement, perhaps even more quickly than moral universalism can turn into totalizing hegemony?

Whether or not we can ever know what Sophocles actually espoused, we should still attempt to register the various manifestations of the self in this play and their ethical significance. At the very least, two experiences of self become pronounced, engendering antithetical moral legacies that seem to have been conflated by the current sweeping critique of selfhood and self-certainty: on the one hand, the egotistical self of Creon, from whom proceeds a delusional ethics of control and domination that contemporary theory has aptly and rightly critiqued; on the other, the tragic self of Antigone, who also professes self-certainty and self-mastery, but of another sort. Whereas Creon's self-certainty stems from a narrow experience of the self—the self confined to an atomistic existence—Antigone's sense of self is expansive, fueled by the immense fire of primordial principles, almost cosmogonic in its vastness. And whereas Creon's self-certainty serves his own ephemeral purposes, Antigone's serves something absolute and someone other than herself. Hers is a self larger than itself—this is why it can afford to sacrifice itself—and its self-certainty is directed generously toward the other: it is in fact *through* her that the other enters the ethical world of Sophocles and attains its importance in this play.

Modern thought may not be able or willing to sufficiently discriminate between these two notions of self and self-certainty; worse, modern thought may even deem the resoluteness of Antigone hubristic, since such determination exposes the mediocrity of those who cannot master it and at the same time does not excuse those, like Ismene, who excuse themselves with claims of helpless and inevitable victimhood. This is an instance of what I have tried to call our tragic blindness. And here is the unbearable hegemony of Antigone's self-certainty for us: her criteria for acting, for sheltering friends and denouncing enemies, are not fluid categories of the sort that establish political and other ephemeral, instrumental alliances, nor are they self-reflexive mirages produced by thought experiments—they are actual moral standards, something that is inadmissible to our modern, relativist outlook. Consequently, for all the recent critique of dominative reason, Creon's cunning version of self-mastery as self-interest might still be preferable to us moderns, since at least it does not make any metaphysical demands on us as does hers: his civic triumphalism is immanent and thus manipulable by critique, in contrast to the theoretical threat her moral absoluteness poses. This might account for why, from Hegel onward, theory, in its historicist turn, has been trying to Creonize Antigone rather than Antigonize (or should I say antagonize?) Creon. Butler's Creonization of Antigone constitutes, in this sense, a profound Hegelianism, even though she wishes to avoid a Hegelian reading.

After this extensive parenthesis on the notion of autonomy, let us now return to Antigone's understanding of the law as the voice of conscience. To identify the voice of conscience with law is in some sense already a misnomer: the voice is not an inscription meant to address anyone *abstractly*; at the limit, it may not even be meant *for* others as the object of their approval or disapproval. Antigone does not intend to persuade Creon. She is not mounting a legal defense, as Butler thinks (11), any more than Socrates's apology should be reduced to a forensic document meant to exonerate him. The *Apology*, as I hope to have shown in an earlier chapter, is not an apologetic statement in the sense we mean this word today. Socrates knew the hostility he would encounter, and he exacerbated it in exactly the same way that Antigone knows what awaits her but goes on to challenge and infuriate Creon all the more. Both of them are taunting their persecutors; they are not defending their acts so as to extract a lighter sentence. Their discourse is about revelation, not persuasion. As such, their logos is indebted to poetry and prophecy, not to rhetoric. What Antigone reveals to Creon and also to the elders of Thebes—who are too cowardly to proclaim it, though they hesitantly admit it at various moments—is the moral foundation of the law, which the law inevitably forgets the very moment it cognizes itself as an externally imposed command. In other words, law as a dictate *representing* external requirements forgets its sources in the higher register of a person's desire to do right. Antigone's act reminds her audience of the bitter truth that, although the law should be the child of the voice of conscience, it often functions as the sanctioned venue through which this voice is silenced.

But why is it that only certain human beings are capable of this attunement to the voice of conscience? Antigone's speech gives us some insights: she knew she would die one day, with or without Creon's edict. The edict merely shortens a life already destined to an end: the implicit, but all-important, question is what kind of end her life would meet. With this statement, Antigone unveils for us the law of mortality, the *aei* that belongs to the human sphere. She, like any other mortal being, cannot escape the inevitable. She does, however, have a choice: she can strategize to prolong her life at the expense of her moral integrity, or she can refuse this self-interested, survivalist instinct that betrays everything worthy about her existence. She decides for the latter, and in doing so, she shows that only by accepting fate, by facing mortality with no cunning schemes, do we also reach the sense of responsibility that ennobles human life. Responsibility is our only freedom; it is the manner in which we choose to act in *this* life, which is the only life given to mortals. This is why, as I suggested earlier, responsibility is the exclusive destiny of humanity, since gods do not die and need not account for their acts. Antigone's moral capacity to disregard Creon's punishment is a direct correlate of her understanding of the primordial law that governs the human condition: mortality, what the Greeks called fate. Only human beings who hearken to this law of atē are capable of the self-sacrifice she has committed.

Nevertheless, concerning the necessity of Antigone's death, Butler asks, "Is her fatality a necessity? And if not, under what non-necessary conditions does her fatality come to appear as necessity?" (27).[23] The nonnecessary conditions that appear as necessary are for Butler the laws of blood and kinship—the incest taboo in particular, which, having been transgressed by Oedipus, returns to haunt and punish Antigone. Butler critiques Lacan, whose conception of the symbolic law in terms of inevitability delimits kinship arbitrarily, thus legitimizing Antigone's death as the necessary conclusion of these allegedly necessary limits within the kinship structure: "The law that mandates her unlivability is not one that might profitably be broken" (40), Butler writes of the Lacanian paradigm, implying that there may and should be other conditions under which Antigone's death can be avoided. We need only think of Antigone's ironization of this Creonic rhetoric of profit—she openly chooses death as more profitable than life (lines 461–62/506–7)—to fathom the ethical dissonance of Butler's own rhetoric at this point. More importantly, however, at issue in Butler's questioning of law's necessity is not simply the specific reason behind Antigone's death, or Polyneices's dishonor and so on, but the very ontological necessity of fatality as such. Put differently, this specific way of politicizing Antigone—namely, in the context of interrogating the arbitrariness of the law, while at the same time proposing inclusion ad infinitum of the unrepresented, thus infinitizing the law—is tenable only at the expense of the tragic, since in tragedy the law is by nature inevitable.

Butler's reading outside the law of fate, or rather her reading from the infinite extension of juridical law, forms a rationalist—and potentially totalizing—project of secularist inclusion. When rationality is brought to bear on deeply conflictive matters, the hope is that things will be resolved calmly and that strife will be neutralized. This resort to rationality is of course the tragic-ironic predicament of the modern thinker, who knows rationality to be anything but beyond suspicion. Martha Nussbaum recognizes how this rationalist tendency of modern thought eschews the tragic disposition:

> The avoidance of practical conflict . . . has frequently been thought to be a criterion of rationality for persons—just as it has frequently been thought to be a condition of rationality for a political system that it should order things so that the sincere efforts of such persons will regularly meet with success. . . . And it has become firmly entrenched in modern thought, pressed even by some who defend a "tragic view" of individual cases of practical conflict. It has profoundly colored modern criticism of ancient tragedy. For the claim is that the human being's relation to value in the world is not, or should not be, profoundly tragic: that it is, or should be, possible without culpable neglect or serious loss to cut off the risk of the typical tragic occurrence. Tragedy would then represent a primitive or benighted stage of ethical life and thought. (51)

Indeed, what could belong more to the night of human culture than blood? What could be more primitive than the law of the blood tie, the law that originates in the taboo of burying the dead, thus separating the human from the animal?[24] For if the law did not have such bloody origins, who would expect that rationality would demand the erasure of law's limits? To read untragically, then, is rationality's attempt to cleanse these bloodstains of culture. But such a reading also does away with the originary law according to which human culture happens, *the law* according to which the human being emerges as a creator of culture, becoming both a bearer *and* critic of one's own *laws*. To read untragically is to read ἐκτὸς ἄτας (beyond fate), for the law is first and foremost atē—the law not simply of blood and the tragic genre but the law that declares tragedy to be the humans' essential disposition.

Resourceless Antigone: Fate, Blood, and Incest

Despite his arguably tenuous translations of the Greeks, Heidegger's reading of *Antigone* in his *Introduction to Metaphysics* rests at least on the following tragic principle: the human attempt to respond to the overpowering knowledge of our mortal predicament renders us creators, makers of a world through work, but at the same time exposes us to the futility of such projects and to imminent perdition. The second choral ode, offering the background for Heidegger's reading, starts as praise to the skillfulness of human works but concludes with the declaration that every such skill pales in front of death. Such works, admirable though they may be, function as ephemeral distractions aimed to turn the human being away from the death that confronts it; they are accomplishments that come to naught as death makes of them a mockery.

Heidegger recasts the classical relation between fate and will in terms of two kinds of violence that respond to each other. On the one hand, there is the violence of fate, which he also calls the violence of the "overwhelming sway" and which he identifies with *dikē*. Dikē taunts the human being, who, thus provoked, responds in kind through the violence of its will, by conquering and transforming the natural world into its proper habitation. This second kind of violence Heidegger aligns with techne, the resourcefulness of industry that allows human beings to create a world for themselves but that also misleads them into thinking they are masters of their fate, putting them always at risk and exposing them to perdition: "But neither perdition nor its possibility first occur at the end, when the violence-doer does not succeed in a particular act of violence and mishandles it; instead, this perdition holds sway and lies in wait fundamentally in the opposition between the overwhelming and doing violence" (*Introduction to Metaphysics* 173). In other words, perdition is not contingent upon the human being's way of handling the situation; it cannot be avoided by a more efficacious application of techne. Rather, the human being becomes a creator by way of this violence—that is, by way of techne—by rising to the challenge of the overwhelming sway and risking the fall in this very confrontation. The risk of perdition is the necessary condition of possibility of being human.

Antigone is the uncanniest (δεινότατον) of all violence-doers, not because of what she does since her violence hardly involves a material transformation of the world of the kinds listed in the second choral ode. She stands as the δεινότατον because of who she is—the "resourceless" one (ἀμήχανος), as Mary Whitlock Blundell calls her (112n26). She is the one without skills to dodge the death that awaits: "εἴκειν δ' οὐκ ἐπίστανται κακοῖς" (She does not know / how to yield to trouble), says the chorus of her lack of techne (line 472/516–17). Drawn by death and the dead alone, she obeys only the law of dikē, thus engaging in the most exemplary form of violence by radicalizing the daring, and making this uttermost contestation most immediately manifest in her refusal of techne. The chorus apostrophizes Antigone shortly before her lamentation:

προβᾶσ' ἐπ' ἔσχατον θράσους
ὑψηλὸν ἐς Δίκας βάθρον
προσέπεσες.
(Lines 853–55)

You went to the extreme of daring
and against the high throne of Justice
you fell.
(Lines 908–10)

Seth Benardete articulates this daring in the following terms: "Antigone shows all the artless intensity of life itself in her devotion to the heartless coldness of the law about corpses" (*Sacred Transgressions* 16).[25] She does not simply bury Polyneices; she does so in a zealous pursuit of her own death. To stand by the dead on the risk (or, better, on the guarantee) of one's own death—this is Antigone's noninstrumental and sovereign *nomos*, a nomos that exceeds all violence-doing by accepting and facing head-on the overwhelming sway. She thus makes sure to be caught, as if to show Creon that it is not really he who catches her but something else — something beyond any human agency, something whose force he comes to glimpse only after his own ruin.

This ontological law of perdition, which Heidegger formulated through his reading of the second choral ode, is given a more explicit articulation in the third stasimon. Sophocles warns here that it is impossible for mortals to remain for long outside ruin, or atē:

τό τ' ἔπειτα καὶ τὸ μέλλον
καὶ τὸ πρὶν ἐπαρκέσει
νόμος ὅδ'· οὐδέν ἕρπει
θνατῶν βίοτος πάμπολυς ἐκτὸς ἄτας.
(Lines 611–14)

For the future near and far
and the past, this law holds good:
nothing very great
comes to the life of mortal man
without ruin to accompany it.
(Lines 662–66)

Else, who also wishes to consider Antigone beyond her discursive generality as conscientious objector and in her poetical particularity as the last root of an accursed family, writes of this indelible connection between blood, kinship, and atē, a connection that issues from and attests to the passage of time and the inheritance of this law of perdition from one generation to another: "the race, the γενεά, has no respite; its *atê* marches on" (Else 13). Atē is the congenital condition of human existence, and in exposing the human to the awareness of mortality, it renders him or her an ethical being, a being that understands its limits in relation to the world.

Nevertheless, Antigone's exposure to death is not simply a passive abandonment to fate. It is a noncalculating but absolutely deliberate decision that, for instance, Ismene could not make, since her *nature* was not capable of it, as she admits:

ἐγὼ μὲν οὐκ ἄτιμα ποιοῦμαι, τὸ δὲ
βίᾳ πολιτῶν δρᾶν ἔφυν ἀμήχανος.
(Lines 78–79)

> I will not put dishonor on [the dead], but
> to act in defiance of the citizenry,
> my nature does not give me means for that.
> (Lines 90–92)

Surely enough, death (the great Other) is confronting Antigone in the corpse of her brother, in the memory of her lost parents, and in the face of her own execution. But it is she who actively aligns her desire (for death) with her destiny and duty (to bury her brother)—she who chooses not to shrink from this destiny the way her sister does and the way all of Thebes did. That fate is character (or nature, alternatively) proves to be the algorithm of the play: fate is not simply an external determination to which one yields—it is an admixture of uncontrollable circumstances *and* of one's characterological disposition. Free choice, on the other hand, does not mean freedom from fate's consequences.

However, as I have tried to argue, Butler's version of Antigone consists in avoiding and even denouncing the realm of fate and in recuperating tragedy within a discourse of conditionals, corrective possibilities, and alternative endings. Butler's heroine is the fantasy of a reader who wishes to have read an *Antigone* by Aristophanes (or, at the least, a tragicomic Euripides) rather than Sophocles. Such a reading is tenuous not only because it is not faithful to Sophocles but because it forecloses essential—if unsettling—questions posed by tragedy itself. Contrary to her optimistic interpretation, I would stress that in tragedy the province of atē, of the accursed inheritance of generations—"οὐδ' ἀπαλλάσσει γενεὰν γένος" (No generation frees another) (line 596/650)—delimits precisely this: the law of fatality is the hallmark of mortal life, that individuals come to an end as do entire generations. Houses and empires alike fall, but history goes on to repeat itself. As such, tragedy cannot provide lessons for improving legislation or for helping us learn (at least discursively) from our mistakes. Tragedy marks the impossibility of doing otherwise; if it teaches anything, it is only this: that tragedy is the mark of the inevitable. Note, for instance, the fate of Creon, the man who certainly believes in lessons: Creon—who learned from the civil war and thus wished to curb further unrest by setting an example through his desecration of the rebellious Polyneices—ended up producing yet another catastrophe, both civic and familial. "The essence of tragedy," writes Blundell, "is often precisely that moral conflict is insoluble or soluble only at enormous cost" (11), a reality that can hardly be mitigated by any socially constructed voluntarism.

Antigone's law is consistent with the law of fate. In her very first words, Antigone is the character who acknowledges the role of fate, as she speaks to Ismene of the "evils" that have fallen on the house of Oedipus (line 2/3), though she seems to separate the misfortunes sent by Zeus from those sent by mortal rulers. Antigone's law, then, has to be thought outside the register of right, which is, properly speaking, Creon's sphere. Her law is sovereign not in the sense of a political, instrumental sovereignty, like Creon's, but in the sacred sense of excess and expenditure: she acts so as to expend herself, to join the dead, to go to waste.[26] Yet her act signifies everything but a waste of meaning. In our modern world, in which everything is negotiable and, thus, every act of dying for something is a priori relegated to blind irrationalism, Antigone's sacrifice can be reduced to the meaningless, self-destructive impulse of a young mad girl. But these sorts of insights hardly exhaust the moral depths of such an act. Far from meaningless, Antigone's choice is one whose overwhelming meaning is all the more difficult to grasp, since it violates the safe categories of conceptual thinking, requiring us instead to witness it not through the eyes of intelligibility but through those of truth and conviction. Accordingly, her language resonates in prophetic tones that reach well beyond the particular time and place of her enunciation, not as an example of legal rhetoric that mirrors Creon's performance by "assum[ing] the voice of the law in committing the act against the law" (Butler 11).

Loraux's argument that the *aei* (always) of tragedy is different from the *aei* (always) of the assembly—the former expresses the eternal anguish of mortals while the latter proclaims eternal political triumphs—could be instructive. The bifurcation of this *aei* suggests that the language of tragedy is essentially different from the language of politics even though they are both using the same word. Tragic experience is not equivalent to political representation. This is why when Antigone uses the same word for law (nomos) as Creon, her voice—blending a sense of moral plenitude, indignation, and despair at her fate—remains incommensurate to the discourse of political opportunism and ideological harangue. To push further Loraux's contrast of tragic voice and political logos, Antigone cries to us to hearken to her voice, whereas Creon orders us to understand and obey his logos.

Antigone buries her brother not because of any dictated law. Her law is not a law given to her in advance that she applies, but this does not mean that she is lawless either. To the contrary, as I have already emphasized above, she is αὐτόνομος (of her own choice), in the words of the chorus (line 821/882).

She exceeds the province of the civic nomos, which is by nature derivative, reflecting particular demands and changes in the social fabric. Law for Antigone is *ethos*, a way of being, her very character; only secondarily is it also a civic—and even divine—convention, since the divine too becomes quickly another convention. She is the source and giver of her own law; or one could say, law comes to show itself through her nature and her act. Strictly speaking, then, she does not obey any law. Rather, she exists exemplarily, which means that she illuminates for us the ontological condition of being human—namely, the acknowledgment of mortality: the mortality of others to which one is exposed as she is to her brother's decaying corpse but also the mortality of one's own, which enables her to act the way she does, as she says to Creon. That she knows she will die one day makes it possible for her to shorten her life for the sake of someone she loves—her implicit but powerful question to Creon's power-thirsty attitude being, do you not know that you will die one day too?

This is the meaning behind the achronological temporality Antigone ascribes to her laws as she is brought to stand before Creon: "οὐ γάρ τι νῦν γε κἀχθές, ἀλλ' ἀεί ποτε / ζῇ ταῦτα, κοὐδεὶς οἶδεν ἐξ ὅτου 'φάνη" (They are not of today and yesterday; / they live forever; none knows when first they were) (lines 456–57/500–501). Antigone is not a solipsist who cannot abide by the laws of others—the immanent laws of the state and its citizens—but rather shows in her autonomy the true sources of the law that precedes every lawmaker: to exist is to be perpetually confronted with the corpse of Polyneices as much as to be confronted by the death of oneself. To forget this ontological dimension of the law is tantamount to missing the most important aspect of the tragic: what is actually at work in the tragic is not merely the staging of unfortunate events that could be avoided by the drafting of improved legislation but an evocation of this state of exposure that requires the possibility of perishing.

With this general understanding of the law of fate, we can begin to think through the themes of blood and incest. I will try to consider the role of blood in the play away from the usual notions of determinism and biologism, and as a metaphor for accidental nature, for the realm of contingency that demands ethical treatment. Blood ties mark a moment of arbitrariness, in the sense that one does not choose one's bloodline; thus, to act ethically to the kin means also to act ethically because that kin is simply another human being, not necessarily one we have chosen to be with but one whose uncanny closeness to us and simultaneous otherness most of all exemplifies the arbitrariness of living with others. Being of the same blood with someone turns out to be as much a figure of dislocation as of self-sameness. Polyneices's criminality serves to show exactly this: Antigone buries him despite his treason, because he is her brother, which also means that she acts ethically toward him even if she might not condone his behavior.[27] Tending to the brother is also tending to someone with whom she may not have freely chosen to be related. To further illuminate this argument, I will turn to two interrelated moments in the play and their reading by Benardete. Both instances reveal how Antigone moves from the benighted category of blood to the universal site of the moral law: the first involves Antigone's distinction between the world above and the world below, while the second involves the distinction of civic affairs from what she calls "τῶν ἐμῶν" (my own) (line 48/54).

In her confrontation with Creon, Antigone refuses to assume that the justice of the dead corresponds to that of the living. Where Creon sees a seamless continuity between the city of the living and the earth below, Antigone sees a sharp distinction.[28] Benardete writes on this point: "The city must for him keep itself intact below. 'Below' therefore cannot be more exactly determined; it is only an extension in depth of Thebes. For Antigone, however, who with Ismene alone specifies that below means below the earth, burial means a removal from Thebes and its concerns. The city is restricted to the surface of the earth" (5). The city as a site of convention—namely, the city that is solely politically determined as in Creon's definition—is the place of boundaries and restrictions. What counteracts this restrictive character of civic life is not a discursive extension or abolition of its boundaries, as Butler suggests. It is, rather, the earth below, the oldest of the gods, unperturbed by the machinations of man who tills her surface (lines 337–41/374–76). The earth, and not simply the land, refers to the chthonic principle of nature associated with blood and roots as the nondiscursive markers of human togetherness, for all humans are rooted in the earth.[29]

As *autochthon*, the family is *of* the earth; it is different from the citizens of Thebes, or any other particular city built *on* the earth. In other words, while the chthonic is the condition of possibility of the polis built above it, the reverse does not hold. After birth, we are raised to be citizens of a state. But upon death, we do not return to a state; we return to the earth. Family marks this suspended state, out of which one emerges to partake in social and cultural conventions but to which one returns by way of nature, or blood. Put differently, one dies as a man or a woman, as someone once loved by his or her kin, not as a citizen or a traitor. The vastness of the earth below, unregulated by borders and indifferent to human values such as honor and dishonor, receives equally everyone, regardless of their marks of cultural identification.[30] The family—which in Butler's account constitutes a determinist, hierarchical, and exclusive cultural construct, insofar as it is based on the fixity of blood rather than the mutability of its own constructedness—shows itself in its chthonic determination to serve inclusion and to disregard all social and civic hierarchies.

The ethical centrality of the blood tie as φιλία can also be surmised in Antigone's response to Ismene's charge that she will be guilty of disobeying Creon's decree: how can attending to her own—that is, to what does not belong to the civic sphere—involve disobedience to civic law? That Creon does not know what properly belongs where is no reason to charge Antigone with disobedience. Let us focus on these words: "my own." These words characterize the near and dear—friends and family. In fact, as Else maintains, φιλία does not mean just friendship, since "it originally referred to *close blood relations*, and that sense is the only one Antigone ever employs. Kreon, on the other hand, consistently uses φίλος in the derived sense: 'friend'" (30). Whether we deem Else's reading of Antigone's φιλία to be restrictive, it nonetheless discloses the ethical significance of the blood tie. Of course, the move from such narrow understanding of φιλία to the larger field of ethical relations can be made, but such a move—though it may transcend—should not erase the significance of blood as an ethical figure. To the contrary, I suggest that moral obligation in general is arrived at by way of a transmutation or transfiguration of the blood tie into human relations qua extended kinship. Indeed, Antigone's remarkable step is that she moves from kin to friend, from necessity to freedom, from chthonic duty to responsibility, without, however, renouncing the friend's rootedness in the chthonic world. Creon, on the other hand, in not recognizing this rootedness, ends up using φιλία only in its derived—and I would add, instrumental—sense as friendship. For him, friends are friends only because they are useful for the security of the state and the welfare of its citizens. In Nussbaum's words, Creon "replaces blood ties with civic kinship" (57), with no trace of the former in the latter—a move not so different from Butler's.

But how is it that Antigone opens this passage from one form of φιλία to another? Benardete gives us a clue: "She will lie with those who love her through what she does for them, and she will lie with those who already love her. She must first, to rejoin her own, acquire them as friends. Antigone proves her right to be by deed what she already is by birth. She reconstitutes the family as something into which one freely enters. The love of her own almost becomes a matter of choice. It is this to which Antigone partly owes her awesome uncanniness" (12–13). The family dead, who can no more demand anything on their own behalf, are now exposed to the decisions of the living kin, decisions free of any requirement. Antigone's devotion to her dead, far from being elicited or demanded by them, is the result of her choice to do well by them as one would do by the friends one wishes to please. Antigone does not take her kin for granted by assuming they would forgive her even if she does not act rightly just because she shares in blood, as Ismene does. Instead, she who stands for the irrevocable family bond gives herself the strangest test and passes it: before reuniting with them in the underworld, she proves herself worthy of their love as if this love could be revoked, the way one always risks losing love in friendship. It is therefore this peculiarly reversed—that is to say, Oedipal—temporality, to which Creon does not have access, that allows for this passage between kin and friend. Antigone comes to what is prior and to what she has always known as prior (the kin, the root, the necessary) by way of decision and action—that is, by way of freedom. Nothing could show better the priority of the prior than such a backward path of reaching the necessary via the detour of deliberation. This dislocating, ecstatic, and achronological effect of blood kinship is what Benardete calls Antigone's uncanniness.

Having discussed the ethical importance of blood beyond its immediate associations with determinism, I would like to briefly address the related problematic of incest Butler raises. For Butler, Antigone's burial of Polyneices cannot be understood outside the matrix of incestuous desire that defines Oedipal kinship, particularly since the curse striking both brothers and Antigone herself is bound up with the incest taboo: the curse comes to these children as the price of the father's incest. Such a punishment, however, by no means cements the incest taboo as a successful prohibition or guarantor of the normative family. To the contrary, Butler warns, the incest taboo "does not simply prohibit incest but rather cultivates incest as a necessary specter of social dissolution" (66–67)—hence that "certain amount of horror" (57) with which the normative family looks upon such kinship. The horror, in other words, is due to the resemblance or kinship the normative family bears to its Oedipal exemplar, as the incest underlies the family's "ownmost possibility" (Butler 67) by virtue of its prohibition. Butler's dialectical temporalization of desire and taboo, however—in which the taboo produces the desire just as much as (if not more than) it is produced by it—is of paramount theoretical importance. It forecloses again the tragic possibility that the taboo, like any other human law, is a work of techne responding to something outside the human, something whose excess cannot be explained away immanently as the retroactive construction of the human taboo. This something belongs to the order of dikē, and no matter how thoughtful and calculating our mortal responses to it can be, they cannot preempt the calamity to which dikē exposes us.

We should of course be mindful of the articulations this prior tragic law takes on in the play, articulations involving the sexual, the gendered, and the generational, all of whose tenuous political associations and ramifications rightly concern Butler; however, we should also be equally mindful that this tragic law supersedes these articulations. True, blood as a mark of generational inherency within the natural family serves to figure this tragic law of exposure, which is also inherent to the human, but this process of figuration happens in the most revealing sense—namely, in a way that illumines what lies beyond the figure rather than simply figuring it out. In this sense, the figure sheds its purely rhetorical trappings and ascends—one might say, transfigures itself—to actually become indistinguishable from what it first represented. This is a movement from the realm of representation, where a concept represents and dominates a thing, to the proper poetic realm of presentation.[31]

Regarding the figurality of blood, which concerns us here, the figure of blood reveals tragic necessity only when it exceeds being coterminous with the actual liquid substance running through a person's veins. If we simply think of blood as this liquid substance that inheres in a biological family, and as that alone, it would signal a false necessity in the play. However, if we think of it through the logic of this transfigured figure, blood reemerges from being the mark of biological essentialism to become the mark of our shared mortality—our most unchallengeable condition, lest we forget it is only gods who are bloodless beings.[32] In this vein, so to speak, it is telling that Haemon, Antigone's lover and cousin, whose name means blood, forms the nodal point between her, Creon, and the concerns of the citizens—that is, between erotic love, filial duty, and political responsibility. As I have already observed in note 29 of this chapter, Haemon assumes the difficult function of showing blood to be not only the price paid in civil war and not only a biologistic marker of the natural family but also the flow of a possible convergence between opposing desires and conflicting duties. In the end, that he bleeds by Antigone's body, emptying himself both of his blood and of his name—in effect, emptying himself of himself in this scene of love, empathy, and despair—should help us envisage more concretely this process of the transfiguration of the figure: in the literal shedding of blood, Haemon, the name that figures blood, sheds itself of its figurality as well, thus presenting (rather than representing) the moment of shared mortality.

Likewise, incest and its prohibition follow a similar figural logic that now, however, discloses the necessity of positing boundaries. The incest taboo marks in the human world of convention the drawing of an arbitrary line that, according to Butler, fatally confuses its arbitrariness for a transcendental requirement. I suggest, instead, that the incest taboo figures most poignantly the necessity of a boundary precisely because of the ambivalence involved in its arbitrary drawing. Such a boundary serves to separate first and foremost the mortal from immortal spheres, since, after all, it was only in the realm of the gods and their cosmogonic stories that incest was not simply permitted but sanctioned. Incest is the modality par excellence of coupling and generation of the inhuman. Incest points to the inhuman beginning, out of which and in contradistinction to which the human emerged. It is this affinity to origins that renders the domains of the sexual and the generational into privileged figures for the expression of a primordial law such as the law of our tragic predilection. Hence, while it is fruitful to question with Butler the particular place where the boundary is chosen to be drawn, and to flesh out the unspoken reasons and unthought effects of choosing that place, what remains unquestionable is the necessity of positing the limit at all—a necessity imposed *on* the human, not *by* the human. In other words, the positing of a limit has an ontological priority; though its expression is restricted to convention and thus to arbitrariness, the requirement of its postulation remains irreducible to particular juridical, legislative, or symbolic acts.[33] As such, I cannot follow Butler's conclusion that the play, in questioning the incest taboo as a false necessity that sets off a chain of horrible events, "requires a rethinking of the prohibition itself" (67).

In denying the tragic law its ontological priority and in thinking blood and incest strictly within a juridical and symbolic matrix rather than as figures of mortality, Butler's nonrepresentative intention becomes ensnared in a representative project that finds in Antigone the dismantler of yet another limit: the incest taboo as guarantor of heteronormativity. Far from actually determining and producing all forms of legitimate kinship as it ostensibly claims to do, the incest taboo, Butler argues, only guarantees that kinship is biologically determined, thus, only heterosexually reproducible: "From the presumption that one cannot—or ought not to—choose one's closest family members as one's lovers and marital partners, it does not follow that the bonds of kinship that *are* possible assume any particular form" (66). To mistake the incest taboo for a transcendental requirement of kinship is to bind all kinship structure to the biological in a false a priori. The horror of incest, then, bespeaks nothing else but the horror against an other-than-biological kinship structure, a kinship that one enters into rather than is born into. *Antigone* serves for Butler as a cautionary tale that shows the horrific ramifications of mistaking the incest taboo for a transcendental determination of kinship, and of subsequently misrecognizing the social punishments against the nonnormative family for inevitable calamities.

According to Butler, the play's locus of interrogation of the incest taboo is the overdetermined body (and name) of Polyneices,[34] a name that Antigone does not pronounce but substitutes with the kinship term "brother." For Antigone, however, her father is also her brother and her brothers are also her nephews, so that the term "brother," rather than being singular, veils the condensation of Polyneices, Eteocles, and most of all Oedipus who—Butler reminds us (60)—cursed Antigone before his death to remain loveless, loving no man but him alone. Butler links Antigone's love for Polyneices to Oedipus's exclusive claim of her love, maintaining that this paternal/fraternal incestuous desire both haunts and precipitates her deed: "Thus she betrays Oedipus even as she fulfills the terms of his curse. She will only love a man who is dead, and hence she will love no man. She obeys his demand, but promiscuously, for he is clearly not the only dead man she loves and, indeed, not the ultimate one. Is the love for the one dissociable from the love for the other? And when it is her 'most precious brother' for whom she commits her criminal and honorable act, is it clear that this brother is Polyneices, or could it be Oedipus?" (60).

Incest emerges as the causal determination of Antigone's devotion to Polyneices and of her death. Antigone remains committed to Polyneices because he exemplifies the locus of her peculiar desire: not simply her explicit double desire for the father-brother Oedipus and his sons but a deeper yet not fully articulated desire for any such potential "transposability of the terms of kinship," to use Butler's own phrasing (78). Regrettably, since such desire has no place in a legal code grounded in the incest prohibition, she must die and die loveless as well. Despite Butler's force of argument in this quasi-literalized scene of incest that she draws between Antigone and Polyneices, the play suggests otherwise. After all, in forgiving the old Oedipus and becoming his eyes throughout his blind wanderings,[35] Antigone might be the least of Oedipal daughters. This is most likely why, even though Ismene survives her in Sophocles's version, it is Antigone who is called "the last root" of the house of Oedipus: she is the one who refuses to continue the Oedipal legacy, and her physical death functions as the consolidation of this stoppage.

But even if we are to entertain the relation of Antigone to Polyneices in terms of incest, the temporality of her love for him suggests other reasons for her devotion than incest: it is important to note that, once again, this is a reverse temporality that recalls the uncanny manner in which Antigone rejoins her kin through φιλία. Antigone's love for Polyneices is heightened after his death. She loves him not only because he is lost to her but because of the dishonor he suffers even as a dead man. At stake is not simply his irreproducible place in the kinship structure, as Carol Jacobs points out, since the honored Eteocles too could be said to be an irreproducible brother for Antigone.[36] Moreover, at stake is not simply Polyneices's criminality, which connects him to Oedipus—Antigone's other incestuous object of desire, according to Butler. (Eteocles is also criminal in not ceding the throne, even though Antigone keeps silent about it.) At stake is the irreversible loss of dignity effected by the ordeal of his corpse, by the public prohibition of even private mourning. Polyneices is much more than a life not worth living; he is a man not worthy of being dead—the essence of the unlovable, of the one who deserves to be ritually dehumanized in death more than in life, a fate he shares neither with his incestuous parents nor with his equally accursed brother, Eteocles. This utter dehumanization is what ignites Antigone's love and drives her to transgress. However, in her incest theory, Butler does not explain why Eteocles never makes it as Antigone's object of desire, even though his position in the kinship structure is identical to that of Polyneices.

That Polyneices's name or kinship position condenses Antigone's other criminal kin does not at all compromise the uniqueness of his body and its afflictions: he alone of the family undergoes a punishment that far exceeds any crime he may have committed or even inherited—a punishment all the more illegible in the language of the civil code in which it is pronounced, since it is directed against a corpse. Thus, his two burials by Antigone, more than signifying a belated burial of Oedipus along with him (Butler 61), mark another kind of surplus in this economy of redress: it is as if the abomination suffered by Polyneices needs more than one burial, yet no burial is enough to restore to him what is due a priori to the dead. Revealingly, the two burials add up to no mound. After all, Oedipus's death (if we can even call it that in *Oedipus at Colonus*[37]) took place under the sign of the gods with all due rites and purifications and with the deceased's chosen bystander, Theseus, as witness. Jocasta's was a self-inflicted punishment, while the fratricide Eteocles was given due burial. What summons Antigone, then, is the exceptional fate of the body of Polyneices, and his alone, as it lay helpless and exposed.

Likewise, Creon does not legislate her mourning because of the impossibility of her incestuous desire, but rather his edict precipitates the trajectory of her desire and makes it possible. Whatever Antigone's erotics might be (incestuous or not, toward Polyneices, Oedipus, or Haemon), it is death that she most longs for, and this is perhaps the only claim on which Antigone, Ismene, Creon, and the chorus all agree. Creon gives her that gift of death, so to speak. At the end, the play has little to do with hierarchical binaries such as kinship versus state or man versus woman and more to do with illuminating the rare desire of a human being to live toward its death, to incline toward it. In this consists Antigone's uncanniness: that she relates to death in a terrifying immediacy, with no need for the distractions that cater to our evasion of death. When she says "my own," we should take her to mean not only her family affairs but also the way in which Polyneices's burial leads her to her own death, her owning of herself in death.

If this catastrophic stance—which dispels the political dream of immanence wherein human law can preempt tragedy—appears theological to Butler (75), I am inclined to think that it is, instead, social construction that runs the utopian-theological risk of slipping from emancipatory project to totalitarian status quo. What state could be deadlier and more repugnant to Antigone than the one that would pretend to save her from "her own" (death)? George Orwell had this in mind when he outlawed tragedy from his vision of the totalitarian state, precisely because tragedy is tied to the personal and the unlegislatable, because it marks the site where not everything in a human life is politically and socially determinable. In the thoughts of his hero, "tragedy ... belonged to the ancient time, to a time when there were still privacy, love, and friendship, and when the members of a family stood by one another without needing to know the reason" (31).

Crystal (Un)Clear

The figure of Antigone demands less explanation and more admiration, or maybe even reverence. If this sounds worrisome and a bit anachronistic in its religiosity, one should not forget that tragedy was a sacred genre for the Greeks, witnessed not only by the mortal spectators but by their gods as well. Nietzsche reminded us of this sacred function,[38] and Sophocles's own position as a high priest should only add credence to it. Admiration, reverence, fascination—these are the terms that come to my mind, not explanation or interpretation.

But what exactly commands this reverence at the outset? It is not only what she represents, such as ethical conduct in extremis, personal responsibility, fearlessness, generosity, and so on, but also how she holds back: her secrecy and reserve. For Antigone does not only keep several secrets: her silence about the civil war initiated by her brothers, the secret ways in which she performs Polyneices's funeral rites and changes her hate of Ismene into compassion, the secret of her death. Beyond these secrets, which remain detectable in the telling silences of the text, there is another, more profound reserve. The ethical resolve for which we admire her is enabled by something that must remain hidden—not something she consciously hides in order to draw power from it (which could otherwise be divulged)—in order to shine forth in her presence. It is this mysterious, recessive force that she approaches when she tells Creon that the order she obeys precedes the divine order itself, having been upheld from time immemorial. It is this darkness lost in the mists of time that she, however, also comes to illuminate and make visible.

Secrets, though, are not concepts, nor can we entrust them with political possibilities. This does not mean that secrets do not inform and even threaten political life; it means that they are reducible neither to philosophizing nor to politicizing. Of course, we can tailor our definitions of philosophy and politics to account for a secret, which may all be for the improvement of philosophy and politics in a way, but it impoverishes, nonetheless, the experience of what remains unaccounted for, the experience not simply of privacy but of privation as well. This is why Antigone's secrecy cannot be thought from within the contemporary theoretical frameworks of complexity. Belonging to the utilitarian and mechanistic vocabulary of networks and circuits, the obsession with complexity has nothing to do with the stony opacity of Antigone. The chorus is right that she is savage and raw like her father (ὠμὸν ἐξ' ὠμοῦ πατρὸς) (line 471/515–16), but she is neither complex nor convoluted, as he is. Unlike Oedipus, who provided the very definition of a complex, Antigone stands for a certain mysterious purity. What makes her infinitely opaque is, in fact, her transparency: a crystalline hardness, impenetrable but diaphanous. Benardete said it best when he wrote, "Perhaps, then, the ultimate conflict does not consist in that between Antigone and Creon, or even between the family and the city, but between Antigone and Sophocles, of whom one is always what she shows herself to be, and the other is never what he shows himself to be" (21). It is Sophocles's complexity in drawing such a transparently elemental character, among other things, that confuses us. Else too concurs, stating that Sophocles's "vision is ultimately mysterious and paradoxical. . . . Like the god of Delphoi in Herakleitos's phrase, Sophokles 'neither declares nor conceals, but gives a sign'" (8). His sphinxlike sign is Antigone herself: the enigma of transparency, of rootedness even in the most extreme deracination—a problem that proves insurmountable for our optimistic, theoretical age of mediation.

VII

Antigone's Children

Κι όσο τρώει την ύλη ο καιρός, τόσο βγαίνει πιο καθαρός

ο χρησμός απ' την όψη μου:

ΤΗΝ ΟΡΓΗ ΤΩΝ ΝΕΚΡΩΝ ΝΑ ΦΟΒΑΣΤΕ

ΚΑΙ ΤΩΝ ΒΡΑΧΩΝ Τ' ΑΓΑΛΜΑΤΑ!

And the more time erodes matter the clearer

the oracle comes out from my face:

FEAR THE WRATH OF THE DEAD

AND THE STATUES OF THE ROCKS!
Odysseus Elytis, *The Axion Esti*

Hölderlin, Again: Xanthos

At the turn of the eighteenth century, Hölderlin composed an alcaic ode entitled "Stimme des Volks"[1] ("Voice of the People"), invoking the famous Latin phrase *vox populi*, which describes the shared, spontaneous opinions of the general public. Although Hölderlin's title omits the second part of this phrase that paratactically adjoins the first — *vox populi, vox dei* (the voice of the people [is] the voice of god) — the poem begins by equating the two voices:

"Du seiest Gottes Stimme, so glaubt ich sonst / In heilger Jugend; ja, und ich sag es noch!"[2] Provoking rivers to hasten their course and to impetuously seek rest in the all-dissolving sea, the voice of God proves fatal when it is followed equally impetuously by human beings.[3] The experience of divine immediacy, which underlies human desire for union with the all-encompassing, is in fact a death wish.

The poem thus unfurls as a questioning of the very equation Hölderlin affirms in the opening verse, an equation he otherwise claims to still uphold past his own fiery youth: Is the voice of the people the same as the voice of God, as the paratactic connection between these two terms has been interpreted to mean? Indeed, this entire ode may be read as an elaboration on the problems of the syntax of parataxis itself, of which Hölderlin was a great poetic practitioner.[4] Parataxis often propels the logic of identity, as in this Latin phrase: what follows the comma is what preceded it, even though the lack of definite syntactical connection between the juxtaposed parts should allow for a space of ambiguity. The copula "is," which interpretation inserts into the saying, creates the very sense of immediacy that makes Hölderlin uneasy.

In questioning this immediacy and the historically impossible connection it forges for the modern age (for how can human beings even hear the divine voice, when the divine has absconded?), Hölderlin produces yet another paratactic identification, at least as fraught as he thinks the previous one: describing the human desire for death, which becomes intensified in moments of extreme danger, the poet compares it to a natural phenomenon—namely, to the rivers that impulsively seek rest in the ocean. This comparison does not stop at the level of metaphorical resemblance but runs deeper in order to reveal nature as the unreflexive, blind structure of some human acts. Through a catachrestic use of personification, Hölderlin not only likens but actually equates the way in which rivers—against their wish (*wider Willen*)—rush seaward following the sacred call and the way in which human beings unthinkingly—with no sense of self-reflection (*selbstvergessen*)—follow blindly a shortcut (*die kürzeste Bahn*) to their destruction, overtaken by holy fire in the form of a death wish (*Todeslust*). The human becomes one with nature, as both act with no reference to reason.

Except, of course, a river does not have a will to begin with, from which the god drives it to go astray. If anything, the essence (*not* will qua intention) of running water is to follow a path that leads to a lower point where it can pour itself; it is not to wish for alternate routes so as to prolong its individuality as a specific river on the map before it fuses with other waters in the ocean. I am not trying to be unnecessarily tedious with hydraulics here but, rather, to make a point that will prove crucial in grasping what is at stake in Hölderlin's valuations. The phrase "wider Willen," then, is a catachrestic personification, which fleetingly, albeit strongly, suggests there may have been another *choice* of course for the waters to take. Yet whatever the rate of speed with which the river plunges into the sea and whatever the shortness of its itinerary through a particular landscape, its course is always predetermined and its destination always fixed.

Human destiny, on the other hand, is a different story altogether. In contrast to the rivers, the human being could potentially have another destiny than the one it actually chooses; but as tragedy shows us, "could" is different from "is." Humans cannot always, in reality, take the decision that hypothetically exists for them as a possibility. Nevertheless, the sheer fact that an alternative course of action is possible at the same time that it is not feasible for them should, in turn, make us think twice about how tragic choice is arrived at. The poet too must think not only about the path taken but about why the other one could not be taken, or perhaps even should not have been taken.[5] If, by conflating the rivers that lack intention with people who either are not able or refuse to take the course of action deemed more human and less instinctive, Hölderlin aimed at suggesting precisely that human beings should behave differently from nature, then his communication is not very clear. His own onrushing analogy obscures the fact that this yearning for self-destruction can only be a human desire, for nature cannot desire. "Todeslust" is a psychic wish, one not always so unconscious. We need only recall Antigone, whose death wish was itself a manifestation of *conscious*—albeit spontaneous and immediate—will, not just a mysterious abyssal longing that had neither visible causes nor internal necessity. Her madness, which was a choice as much as was Ismene's careful deliberation, emerged *practically* as the only alternative left to her in the face of the unbearable. To judge which path is less terrible than the other terrible one is not an easy thing; in a tragic situation such as the one Hölderlin's poem describes, the mad choice is often saner than the seemingly sane one.

Tragedy also shows that this disjunction between the theoretical possibility and practical impossibility of a particular alternative choice often hinges on an unfortunate coordination between character and circumstance: big and small character flaws, combined with unforeseeable external circumstances, often lead us to decisions *retroactively* seen as hasty, self-destructive, and irrational. The question, however, that tragedy asks us is, just because a decision appears afterward to be irrational (read, "unthinking"), is and was this necessarily true? Moreover, does such a decision lack in truth because it was not the fruit of conceptual reflection, and is it therefore inadmissible to and unworthy of our age that sees truth only in reflection? Put more succinctly, this is the core question the tragic absolute poses to the age of Hölderlin, the modern age: is truth really *that* historical?

Furthermore, what do we really mean by the irrational or by holy madness? If not something pathological and clinical, then why is this mode of existence, which Hölderlin otherwise recognizes as lofty and worthy of "the Highest," kept carefully outside the fence of thinking? Why should thinking be the exclusive prerogative of conceptual reflection and linguistic mediation? My contention in this chapter will be that, just because some decisions look disturbingly violent or irrational to us, it does not mean their "illogic" is not the product of thinking—though, admittedly, of a thinking of a different kind. It is true that will, desire, unconscious fantasy, and conscious deliberation are all intricately interconnected behind every human act, and often it is hard to split them apart and see which ingredient is more essential to an act. However, this is exactly where tragedy does not value conceptual determination as higher thinking than the profound desire that accompanies it. The nature of this madness is, after all, the question, not the answer. Whether such sacrificial acts become pathologized in the eyes of those who prefer not to commit them or of those who, like us moderns, happen to be spatially and temporally removed from the scene of the actual plight, and whether there is a meeting ground between madness and intention—these are difficult questions. Reflection might insist on its privilege of never being able to answer them, but actual human beings cannot afford not to answer each time they are called to decide over something significant in their lives. And even as we take heed of Hölderlin's own advice for cautiousness and self-reflection, we should also wonder whether it is he who also rushes to ascribe to the heroic choice only madness and not intention, only passion and not intelligence.

In her holy madness, Cassandra too gained actual knowledge and foretold not only the Trojan defeat but her own perishing under Clytemnestra's sword. Yet the zeal with which she looked forward to this moment of self-destruction, because it also meant the death of her oppressor Agamemnon, and the vindication her words offered to the Trojan slaves—these too are forms of knowledge and modes of thinking. And Oedipus, did he not see more clearly and more deeply when, in his mad despair, he plucked out his own eyes? Is he not the best counterpoint to that line of Hölderlin that describes how once-seeing mortal beings took the rational path with eyes open (*offnen Augs*) but, overwhelmed by the voice of God, abandoned reason and poured themselves into destruction like a river pouring into sea?

While the above discussion has laid out some general issues that Hölderlin's poem raises, it is important to explore them in further detail by taking a closer look at the poem itself, a work full of tensions and questions that, as we will see, leap out at us from the pages of the *Iliad* as they do from those of *The Bacchae*. My entry into the poem followed Hölderlin's own beginning—his assertion and ensuing questioning of this equation between the voice of the people and the voice of God. As it turns out, however, the question that really preoccupies him in all this involves the nature of the poetic voice: what kind of voice is the voice of the poet, who should be concerned both with preserving a place for the holy in our era and with responding to worldly political events?[6] That this is the poem's actual concern becomes obvious in its final stanza; but in order to reach his conclusions, Hölderlin first recounts a peculiar story in which the immediate relation assumed by *vox populi, vox dei* is put to the test.

The story refers us back to an incident of a city's destruction narrated in antiquity by Herodotus and cited again in Plutarch: the Lycian city of Xanthos was first invaded by the Persians circa 540 BC, and in their unwillingness to surrender, its inhabitants decided to commit mass suicide.[7] Centuries later, around 42 BC, they repeated the same act in their resistance against the Romans, and it is this second episode that Hölderlin's ode describes. Their way of dying, throwing themselves into an all-consuming fire, became significant for Hölderlin, who admired the philosopher Empedocles and had even written a tragedy about him.[8] Empedocles proposed fire as one of the four equiprimordial elements, and legend tells us that he fell into the volcano of Mount Aetna.[9]

Fire for Hölderlin was sacred, and in his early years it served as the immediate way to the divine. By the time he writes the letters to Böhlendorff, however, another way of thinking has begun to settle in. I have already discussed his first letter, which speaks of the Oriental holy fire of the Greeks, which they could not master. Still, the second of these letters opens with the poet's claim that Apollo's light had struck him with inspiration.[10] Fire was the means of mortal Semele's union with the divine Zeus, and the poet revisits this myth in "Wie wenn am Feiertage" ("As on a holiday") (*Hyperion and Selected Poems* 192–97) to show that—similar to Dionysus, who is the fruit of a mortal-divine marriage—the poet is an intermediary between God and humanity. The word "intermediary," then, becomes the operative one in discussing the more mature Hölderlin. "Stimme des Volks," like "Wie wenn am Feiertage," exemplifies this turn in Hölderlin's thinking: a move away from the impulsive and fiery desire for immediacy toward a more mediated, earthbound way of thinking—a passage from the dangers of collective dissolution to the safety of self-reflexive individuation. The poet emerges as an intermediary between ancient fire and modern earth, between gods and mortals. As human beings do not have direct access to the divine anymore, they are in need of the poet to keep alive the memory of the god who absconded and to be the messenger of the coming god. Only the poet, who alone withstands the terrible absence of the divine, can sustain us in these godless times and prepare us to receive the holy if and when it returns in the future.[11] This turn, the famous Hölderlinian *Kehre*, instantiated much of contemporary theory's suspicion of any sense of immediacy and active decision making, of self-certainty in the decision one takes, and finally, even of self-sacrifice.

Nevertheless, in taking this turn, Hölderlin himself—still a passionate believer in the ideals of the French Revolution—reserves some words of praise for those who follow the holy fire's call all the way to their self-destruction, even as he decidedly separates his path from theirs (*meine Bahn nicht*): his is not the vehement flow of rivers looking for the shortest way to the ocean but the more reflexive, convoluted path. Still, he calls the Xanthians heroes (*Helden*) and compares their death to the sacrificial offering of the first fruits of the harvest (*gleich den Erstlingen der / Ernte*), echoing the tender similes of early blooms that Homer used in order to describe the premature departure of young warriors. (In one such simile, the bard laments the fall of a young man by comparing him to the drooping arch of a poppy under the rain [*Iliad* 8.306–8].) In yet another image of praise, Hölderlin parallels the prostration of human beings overcome by prayer to the surrender of the artist who destroys his work in honor of the heavenly, suggesting that it is in response to our honoring the gods through sacrifice that they too return the favor by sparing the rest of us the terrible destiny of destruction. Even though destroying one's work is not exactly suicide and even though the mystery of prayer does not always lead to the holy madness of martyrdom, the poet recognizes that such sacrificial acts are necessary for the reciprocal relation of gods and mortals. Indeed, both versions of this ode retain the stanza that praises divine love, which often intervenes to obstruct the human desire for self-destruction and to make mortal life longer. This tension between the divine voice that summons us to self-destruction and the divine love that pays us for our sacrifices by prolonging our days on earth recalls Achilles's speech to Priam about the two urns of Zeus from where the father of the gods distributes our fate (*Iliad* 24.527–33): to some falls the portion of sheer suffering, to others an admixture of pain and joy.

Furthermore, describing the first conflagration during the Persians, the poet writes of the Xanthian ancestors:

Die Väter auch
Da sie ergriffen waren, einst, und
Heftig die persischen Feinde drängten,

Entzündeten, ergreifend des Stromes Rohr,
Daß *sie das Freie* fänden, die Stadt.
(my emphasis)

Reading the "sie" (they) to refer to the Persians and "das Freie" (the Free) to designate an open, cleared earth, both Michael Hamburger and Nick Hoff translate these lines to mean that the Xanthians rushed from the rivers to set the city ablaze so that their enemies will find scorched earth. However, in the syntax of these lines, "sie" can refer to "die Väter" (the Xanthian ancestors) as well, while "das Freie"—as such, a rather clumsy word choice for destroyed earth—has profound connotations in Hölderlin's poetics when translated as "the Free": recall, for instance, Hölderlin's poetic preoccupations with the "free use of the national" in the first letter to Böhlendorff—namely, with a culture's free mastering of its native capacities.[12] What Hölderlin might be saying is that by destroying their city and themselves, the Xanthians found the Free, which in the language of the Böhlendorff letters means that this first Xanthos emerges as an example of a people who practiced freely and spontaneously their nature, excelling in holy pathos.[13]

Though Hölderlin's poem grows skeptical of the second Xanthos's claim to this innate spontaneity on account of time's passage, I suggest that the path of immediate spontaneity could and should remain a human prerogative that is not thoroughly foreclosed by history's linear progression: just because an act was already accomplished in the past, it does not mean that the second time around its authenticity and spontaneity are by definition marred. This possibility, in fact, is preserved as the weaker pole within Hölderlin's own double conclusions: we need such sacrificial acts to remind us of the Highest; but mostly we need interpretation and mediation, tells the second version. The first version, fierier perhaps even in its brief chronological precedence to the later one, reverses the order of importance: the poet praises the state of human tranquility but immediately adds the wish that this calmness may not slide into stagnation and complacency.

Therefore, even though his choice of the earthly path is clearly stated in both renditions, Hölderlin does not conceal his admiration for the courage of those who chose fire. Like a modern Achilles, the poet presents us with a twofold fate: to live a short and intense life that quickly leads us back to our heavenly source,[14] or to live the contemplative, terrestrial life—the life of *this* world—that requires us day in and day out to endure both its petty and its great trials and tribulations.[15] Though Achilles wavered, he took the glorious path; but his dead spirit told Odysseus that, *retrospectively*, he would have chosen otherwise.[16] Hölderlin may not quite waver, but he certainly acknowledges the splendor of the fiery course, much like Odysseus himself, who lived and went even to battle cautiously but who, confronted with the great shade, could only envy its eternal glory. This is why as Hölderlin turns toward the earth, he concedes that the direct path of holy madness is surer (*gewisser*) than his own meanderings: those who take the quick flight upward to rejoin the heavens enjoy an absoluteness that is lacking in the terrestrial wanderers, who perish not in the battlefield of eternal ideals but undergo quietly everyday life's wounds and ambiguities.

Of course, our postmodern perspective can easily relativize this poetic assessment too: *Surely*, we are not to think that the poet endorses the certainty of the direct path as an absolute condition! *Surely*, this surety is sure only for those passionate ones—a naïve construct for whoever wishes to believe in it, a subjective belief and nothing more. I cannot express more pointedly the internal contradiction (or irony, as postmodernism would say) that underlies such type of criticism. Nonetheless, even if we concede to the historical fact that our post-Nietzschean world can only be a relative one and that truth has currency only inside quotation marks,[17] the manner in which Hölderlin expresses his ambivalence remains more analytically astute than any *immediate* theoretical hypostatization of uncertainty that elevates uncertainty to a new absolute: the poet's preferences are genuinely divided between these two ontological orientations, which he finds necessary but mutually exclusive. That he leans toward the earthly life of ambiguity is itself to a large extent an inevitable symptom of his own modern, indecisive nature, not necessarily a free-willing celebration of the decidedly better path. Part of what he mourns in gaining the pleasures and nuances of immanence is the lack of conviction, the worst consequence of which might be this: Lacking any standard of measure, any transcendental reference—how can this immanent course ever legitimize itself as the better course to begin with? This tension, which undermines any clear conclusion the poet attempts to reach, is in fact foreclosed by the self-contradictory theoretical certainty that there is no certainty.

After all, to question the certainty with which this verse praises the steadfastness of the passionate souls, one is logically obliged to question equally Hölderlin's other certainty, which, however, has now emerged as the theoretically privileged conviction. Toward the end of the first version, Hölderlin reevaluates the order of surety attached to each path: instead of the "gewisser" path of the rivers and the ones like them, he designates as "sichrer" ("more certain," in Hoff's translation) the terrestrial way of mortal hesitation, of convolution and uncertainty. This new position, which dovetails with the postmodern claim of the certainty of uncertainty, cannot, however, be neatly separated in the poem from the opposite principle in the earlier verse. Let alone that in its explicit formulation, the firmness ascribed to the terrestrial path in the first version is omitted entirely from the second. If we presume Hölderlin's historicist perspective that the second event should always bear a reflexive mark of difference from the first, would this not mean that his own second version is more reflexive than the first? Thus, in removing the assurance of the terrestrial path but preserving that of the heavenly one, is the poet trying to intimate something of the ethical force and necessity of tragic decisions? It seems to me that Hölderlin might not know *what* is the sure but he surely admits *that* there is (or there ought to be) something of the sure: therein lies the measure of a human life whether its essence is heavenly immediacy or earthly mediation. Theory, on the other hand, knows only how to critique the passion of such tragic decisions and to delegitimize any sense of necessity behind them, in the manner of Butler's reading, for instance, which casts doubt over the necessity of Antigone's death.

Back to the story of the Xanthians, though, who first destroyed themselves at the invasion of the Persians and then eagerly repeated their sacrifice against the Romans. This second destruction occurred during the Roman civil wars, when Brutus arrived as the new conqueror. When a fire broke out and Brutus offered to help the Xanthians extinguish it, they refused his help, giving themselves and their city over to the conflagration. Plutarch, a Romanized Greek historian, has written of this incident in his *Lives*, and I will momentarily quote his account at length, since it offers poignant instances of comparison and contrast with Hölderlin's poem.[18] Given the moralist nature of the *Lives*, which forges biographical parallels between noble Greeks and Romans, Plutarch casts Brutus in a positive light and scolds the Lycians for stubbornness and madness, as if anticipating Hölderlin's similar assessments seventeen hundred years later. Hölderlin not only takes Brutus's kindness and nobility for granted but supposes that it was the Roman's kindness that provoked the Xanthians' feat of madness: "Es *reizte* sie die *Güte* von Brutus" (my emphasis). His choice of the verb "reizen," which also designates the provocation of an animal, suggests yet again the natural state of the Xanthians, who—as I have already discussed—emerge in this poem as part of an extended simile that compares human longing for death to savage rivers rushing to merge with the open sea.[19] Just as these waters remain unconcerned with human wisdom (*Um unsre Weisheit unbekümmert*), so the Xanthians are unmoved by the generosity of their conqueror and, instead of yielding to his humanity, rush on illogically and savagely to their death the way a river seeks rest in the sea.

Plutarch also emphasizes the contrast between Brutus's civilized conduct and the Xanthians' wild response. Admiring Brutus's mastery of the Greek rhetorical style of the apopthegm and laconic brevity (224), Plutarch quotes one of his letters, in which the Roman statesman describes epigrammatically his thoughts on the Xanthian response to his siege: "The Xanthians, through their madness in rejecting my kindnesses, have made their country into their grave" (225). No matter how eloquent Brutus's statement is, its rhetoric should not dupe anyone into ignoring its problematic contents. First of all, a certain tone of condescension is unavoidable in any imperial claim of benefaction such as this. More importantly, however, the problem lies with the fact that once the Xanthians are subjugated, Xanthos is not *their* country anymore. Thus, in setting it on fire, they are not merely devastating their own land but are making it unavailable for their enemy, while exposing at the same time the actual violence that underlies such rhetorically disingenuous claims of help and cooperation directed from above.

Be that as it may, when the "obstinate" Lycians did not appreciate "Brutus's humanity and kindness," writes Plutarch, the Roman "forced the most warlike of them to take refuge in the city of Xanthus, and then besieged it" (195). Afterward, the following events transpired:

> The people tried to escape by swimming under the surface of the river which flowed past the city. But they were caught by nets which had been stretched across the channel and fastened to the bottom, while the tops had bells attached to them, which gave the alarm as soon as anyone became entangled. After this the Xanthians made a sortie at night and *set fire to some of the siege-engines*, but they were seen by the Romans and forced back to the walls. Then, when a strong wind began to blow the flames back towards the battlements and some of the adjoining houses caught fire, Brutus, who was afraid that the whole city would be destroyed, ordered his men to help put out the blaze.
>
> However, the Lycians were suddenly seized with a terrible and indescribable mood of *despair*, which can best be defined as a *passionate longing for death*. Every inhabitant of the city, women and children, free men and slaves, people of every age and condition hurled missiles from the walls at the Romans, as they struggled to help the citizens to overcome the flames; and meanwhile the Xanthians with their own hands brought up reeds, wood, and every kind of inflammable material and so spread the fire throughout the city, feeding it with all the fuel they could find and doing everything possible to increase the strength and fury of the conflagration. As the fire rushed onwards, encircled the city on every side, and wrapped it in a sheet of flame, Brutus in deep distress rode round the walls, and in his eagerness to help implored the Xanthians with outstretched hands to spare themselves and save their city. Not a soul listened to him, but men and women alike sought only for the means to destroy themselves, so that even the little children with cries and shrieks leaped into the flames or flung themselves headlong from the walls, or offered themselves up to their fathers' swords, baring their throats and begging them to strike. After the destruction of the city a woman was seen hanging in a noose. She had a dead child fastened to her neck and was holding a lighted torch to set fire to her house. The sight was so tragic that Brutus could not bear to look at it, and *burst into tears* when he heard of it; he also proclaimed that a reward would be given to any soldier who succeeded in saving a Lycian.

All but one hundred and fifty, we are told, escaped the Romans' efforts to save them. So it came about, after a long lapse of time, that the Xanthians had the *courage* to repeat the disaster which their ancestors had suffered, as though they were fulfilling some *predestined cycle of destruction*: for the same people in the time of the Persian Empire had likewise burned down their city and destroyed themselves. (*Lives*, 250–51, my emphases)

Several aspects of Plutarch's description should be elaborated in relation to Hölderlin's poem if we are to grapple with the ethical and historical repercussions of powerful yet horrible episodes such as this. First of all, the Greek historian emphatically tells us that the fatal event was preceded by conscious efforts to resist Brutus through other, less destructive means. People tried to escape the city but were trapped by the Romans; thereupon, they decided to sabotage the siege by setting the siege engines on fire, a fact that shows the beginning of the fire to have been an intentional act of defense and, thus, not an unusual act in warfare. Only then, when an accidental wind caused the fire to expand and Brutus decided to come to the rescue—perhaps not only out of altruism as Plutarch would have us believe but also because it was not to his benefit to inherit scorched earth—did a wave of madness take over the Xanthians, who proceeded to destroy themselves and their city all over again.

Hölderlin, as I observed in my discussion above, crucially bypasses any sense of deliberation in the acts of the besieged, preferring to begin and end with the utter accidentality and madness of the incident. Unbeknownst to anyone, Roman or Xanthian, a fire started somewhere in the area, and then something extraordinary happened: an immolation where past and present, fiery human disposition and natural flames, collapsed into each other in an uncanny repetition. It is as if nothing preceded this wind, as if despair and madness fell upon the Xanthians out of the blue, like some dark forces that cannot be understood in any other way outside their blind unreadability. Though this reading is true, it is only *partly* true—its partiality being illustrative of Hölderlin's modernity. Plutarch, whose judgment is harsher on the Xanthians, could still see a more integrated picture than the one Hölderlin in his modern turn allowed himself to see. The historian saw the tragic unfolding and blending of two forces: human courage and historical fate, rational intention and accidental doom. Again, this is not because the poet misses the solemnity of the act, and I need not repeat all the citations of Hölderlin's praise of the

Xanthians. It is, rather, because these acts of holy fire, great as they may be, remain for the modern poet mutually exclusive—not complementary—with logos and intention. Hölderlin can see only the chaos of fusion and not that the deliberate rejection of individuation can be a form of resistance. Spontaneous will and immediate action are not part of deliberate thinking, the modern outlook tells us; they are not part of thinking at all. Only careful, mediated reflection is.

But even if we follow this other, unconscious explanation, we will see that it also obeys a certain logic of intentionality. In this scenario, as if outer accident precipitated internal desire, historical fate met once again national character, and the Xanthians repeated unconsciously the act of their forefathers as a result of an accidental provocation. I should add parenthetically here that the poet's silence about the nature of the forefathers' act is deafening: Was the first revolt conscious in the sense of being deliberate? The brief description of the citizens rushing from the rivers to return to Xanthos and set it ablaze suggests such a plan; but at the same time, their metonymic connection to the rivers sinks them back into the same unconsciousness with which these waters are said to rush to their end. Could it be, then, that this first revolt was unconscious as well but justifiable as such because it was a first occurrence?

It is true that the poem does not deal much with the first episode. More importantly, it is also true that the poem is not concerned with the plight of Xanthos at all, neither the first nor the second time. Its real interest in Xanthos is only as an allegory for our modern way of thinking historically: the second Xanthos is to us what the first Xanthos was to the second one. How can we, in moments of danger, learn from our forefathers (the second Xanthians) by avoiding the mistakes they made with respect to their forefathers (the first Xanthians)? The lesson is essentially historiographical: through reflection and interpretation, we should try to avoid the unconscious repetition of such terrible historical precedents. But insofar as we do not even know what the first Xanthos was and, thus, what it also meant *for* the second, we can only construct our own image of the second Xanthos as an automatic and mistaken repetition of the first and then attempt to extract an objective, practical lesson out of our own mirage of the past. No surprise, then, that compared to this one-dimensional and spectral Xanthos of the epigones who desperately repeat the acts of their ancestors without understanding them, we the modern epigones—too aware of our belatedness—will emerge higher in the ladder of reflection. While an objective relation to the past is sought out for the sake of this lesson, it is also immediately intercepted. Once again, the poem throws us back to the *mise en abîme* of the Böhlendorff letters: we do not really know the nature of the past except in our own retroactive imaginings of it, yet this mirage is turned into an actuality against which we assert our objective difference.

Closing this parenthesis, I return to Hölderlin's problematic portrayal of this disaster as sheer happenstance: we do not know whether the Xanthians would have themselves started the fire as their ancestors did, but since it was offered to them as a kind of horrible yet liberating divine gift, why not fall in it again? Even if this is the case, contra Plutarch's variant description, their decision is not necessarily the result of illogic but, on the contrary, illustrates the very foundation of tragic logic: tragic logic is the logic of those kinds of accidents that impose on human beings the strictest sense of deliberation and responsibility. More strongly put, it is the logic that takes advantage of accidents, as the Xanthians are said to have done in this case by seizing the weapon chance offered them. Their logic, relentless and even monstrous from our modern perspective, is not dissimilar to Hecuba's gratitude to the god who crushed Troy, a gratitude equally incommensurate with modern consciousness: if war did not come to Troy, Troy may have suffered a fate worse than its military destruction—oblivion. The future may have never heard of its existence; but burned to the ground, Troy in its valiant self-defense became the stuff of legend.[20] Indeed, the legends of which Hölderlin speaks in his closing lines would not be available to the poet if not for these acts, which even in their "unconsciousness" betray a profound understanding of history and future inheritance.[21] So Xanthos, like Hecuba's Troy, has already become a poem, as Hölderlin *repeating* Euripides—who wrote *The Trojan Women* as an allegory against the Melian massacre—wrote of Xanthos as an allegory for our times. And if the Xanthians did not explicitly speak Hecuba's self-reflexive prayer about the historical meaning of Troy for the future, we should not assume that their sacrifice was not motivated by this historical foreknowledge.

Hence, Plutarch's conclusion of the incident reads markedly different from Hölderlin's: whether we are to believe the sincerity of Brutus before this mass suicide or not, he was certainly haunted by the tragic image of the hung mother intent on setting her house ablaze. In his tears, we may have the first and only assurance that his eagerness to save the Xanthians—though still contrary to their wish of self-determination—now stems out of admiration for their courage and sympathy for their plight, rather than self-interest and arrogance, as when he intercepted their secret escape to prove his power over them. Unlike the modern poet, the ancient historian sees no contradiction but, on the contrary, complementarity between the impulses of the human soul and the workings of fate: for Plutarch, the event is both an act of courage (τόλμη) — a word that accounts for its deliberation and for its future historical meaning (it confirms the bravery of the Xanthians) — *and* the fulfillment of a fate that he brilliantly articulates in the language of tragic temporality as cyclical destruction (εἱμαρμένην περίοδον διαφθορᾶς ἀποδιδόντες).[22]

This idea of cyclicality puts into question Hölderlin's sense that repeated events are not authentically spontaneous but tainted by time's passage. Additionally, it also casts doubt over the efficacy of reflexivity in preventing tragedy. For one, reflection does not even always lead to a moderate decision: generals may reflect for a long time on their strategy, but this does not mean their decision is benevolent. For two, who could guarantee that if the Xanthians took the middle road of collaboration with Brutus, tragedy would not have struck them in a different manner? What of their humiliation, subjection, and even the likelihood of retaliation from the Roman army for their initial efforts to resist? Yet while Plutarch remains firmly within tragic temporality, Hölderlin, who was drawn by tragedy, opts for the modern linear temporality of retrospection, which inevitably reads progress *in* chronological progression. Indeed, reflexivity (introspection) is often another name for the retroactive reading (retrospection) that constructs the present as the future completion of an inadequate past.

Whereas his first ending, assuming the tone of prayer, asks from the heavenly ones to safeguard civic peace from falling into apathy, Hölderlin's second version, assuming an openly didactic tone in the last stanza, concludes that we need not only great legends of popular resistance but also consummate interpreters.[23] Such a conclusion implies that it was for lack of poetic interpretation (which alone for Hölderlin founds history by separating it from legend) that the Xanthians repeated their past unreflexively, having learned nothing from the time interval between the two events. Yet such a didactic point could only be made if the poet first removed — as he did in contrast to Plutarch — any intentionality from the Xanthians the second time around. Without assuming that Plutarch is correct about all his facts — and I have warned that we should take his own moralist claims with a grain of salt — it seems more likely that "despair" and "passionate longing for death" might in this case be a legitimate response to a very rational and understandable fear of conquest: when all other solutions failed, the only viable choice for the Xanthians, who were unwilling to surrender, became self-destruction. This madness, in other words, is not just a myth in need of elaboration. It happened in distant actuality (*in* history and *as* a historical response), but it had to first become myth for us, in a series of two retroactions, so that it could then be explained by us for the "first" time.

To remove this intentional aspect of this second suicide means to eclipse the historical facts that precipitated it, to overlook the causal chain of events that set in motion the Xanthian despair. This elision of history qua fact facilitates, in turn, Hölderlin's claim that the Xanthians lacked in historicity—that is, they lacked a proper understanding of the underlying conditions of their history. With no cause behind this event, the modern poet can invest *language* with the power to confer reason (logos) on alogical *acts*. The poet's own productive oversight translates seamlessly into the Xanthians' blind spot. Yet the Xanthians are not the only ones afflicted by the compulsion to repeat; so, too, is Hölderlin in his attempt to announce a modern era no more enslaved to the past. His privileging of reflection over spontaneity is an old Greek topos and recalls another ancient figure who, however, thought poetry was not reflexive enough: Socrates, who charged the tragic poets for not really knowing the meanings behind the immediacy of their divine inspiration. But where philosophy, for Socrates, came to reflect on the poets, poetry, for Hölderlin, comes to reflect on history and to endow it with meaning. (In considering poetry a higher instance of reflection than philosophy, Hölderlin differs not only from Socratic reflexivity but from his own contemporary, Hegel, as well.)

For Hölderlin, the Xanthian people remembered their past too well, and in not forgetting anything, they destroyed themselves: had they forgotten something, they would have behaved historically—they would have put their past retroactively into perspective, responded differently the second time around, and thus entered historical consciousness. In contrast, by repeating themselves, they remained ahistorical, undifferentiated from their past, stuck forever in the atemporal eddy of myth. Viewed through the Hegelian lens, which sees truth only in history qua historicity, their standing outside historical reflection makes the Xanthians stand outside truth altogether. Or to be more generous, we can say that they simply stand outside modernity and its assumptions of what counts as history and truth—assumptions Marx astutely satirized in his dictum about history being first tragedy and then farce. For the Xanthians, history was tragedy both the first *and* the second time. Lacking in modernity, which has forgotten some of the most constitutive of human ideals, rather than lacking in thinking, they managed not to "ascend" to the stage of farce.

Interestingly, Hölderlin's conclusion attenuates, if not contradicts, its own grounding assumption: to say that poetry founds history by interpreting sagas betrays the originary role of the legendary act, as opposed to the derivative process of linguistic reflection that he attempts to foreground. The act of holy madness is poetic in the most primary sense: it enjoys both a temporal and a creative precedence to any later interpretation of it. The poetic resonance of this madness is evoked by Plutarch's characterization of it as "δεινή," the same adjective that Hölderlin seized from Sophocles's *Antigone*, interpreting it to signify the ecstatic destiny (*das Ungeheuere*) of human beings who can never be at home in this world.[24] The uncanny for Hölderlin lies, then, in this catastrophic chasm between divine destiny and human will, between the terrestrial imperative to dwell in this world with other mortals and the revolutionary dream to fly toward the heavens.

However, as my previous chapter has suggested, this principle of strife is not what structures Antigone's act. The most radical innovation Sophocles effects in the tragic outlook is that, through the sacred madness of his heroine, he shows the deep harmony that underlies all strife. Earthbound and ecstatic at the same time, desiring the company of Hades and obeying the will of Zeus at once, Antigonian madness, much like the Xanthian suicide, is all the more uncanny because it does not pose fate against will but, rather, passionately wills its fate. Antigone is deeply rooted not in Creon's polis but in her family and in the earth. Her terrestrial absolute certainty—that she belongs to the earth, even if Thebes treats her as an outcast—is what gives her the power to act in the ecstatic, heavenward manner that she does. Her deed too obeys not only the laws of the underworld: this law is not Zeus's law, she says of Creon's edict, intimating that she respects Olympian justice. Mortality and divinity, rootedness and ecstasy, earth and heaven all meet in her in perfect resonance, and for this reason alone Antigone does not exactly fit the classic Aristotelian scheme of the fallen hero, as Oedipus does, for instance. Were we to follow more faithfully this scheme, the tragedy should have been called *Creon*, as many have already observed. He is the one with the conflicting demands between being a family man and a civic leader and between obeying divine laws and imposing his own laws—antithetical principles he desperately tries to conform to each other but cannot.

In terms of his lifelong inquiry into the nature of tragedy, Hölderlin's turn to earthbound reflection in this poem could be read as the abandonment of the Silenic wisdom the chorus speaks in *Oedipus at Colonus*:

> Not to be born is best of all;
> when life is there, the second best
> to go hence where you came,
> with the best speed you may.
> (Lines 1410–13)

Birth is a curse and not a blessing; but once here on earth, dissolving back into the all is the most cherished path: this is what Hölderlin's poem sets out to question. "Stimme des Volks" has traveled so far away from this tragic insight that the poem's concluding reflections in both versions begin to sound alarmingly like other parts of the Greek chorus: those slightly more hackneyed and formulaic parts, I dare say, where the chorus, detaching itself from the excesses of the protagonist, expresses pity for him or her while sanctimoniously praising its own convenient neutrality as a form of wisdom.[25] Such moralistic parts support the political interpretation that the chorus in general represents the average public opinion, the quietist *vox populi* that cares about order and self-preservation—an interpretation Nietzsche attacked, preferring to think of the chorus in its sacred, intoxicated origins as an ensemble of Satyrs. Going back to Antigone, it seems that in this poem, we hear very little of her voice and much more of that of her reluctant chorus—the gathering of old Theban men who stand uniquely in opposition (in age, gender, and beliefs) to the heroine, a chorus so largely unsympathetic to the sufferer that it forms an exception in the extant tragic repertory—as if Sophocles created it in order to highlight the political solitude and moral elevation of his heroine. Like this cautious chorus, who reflects but is little moved, Hölderlin remembers duly the ones sacrificed but "wisely" removes himself from their blood-stained path.

Disenchanted with the fiery disposition and convinced that we lack the proper skills to think and to live tragically, Hölderlin completes the story of Xanthos with a gesture that could now be said to define poststructuralism's new ethicopolitical imperative: from now on, for such thoughtless disasters not to happen again, the poet (or, currently, the literary critic) is needed to interpret and thus *to change* the legend. Hecuba's logic is turned on its head: the act is no more there to be immortalized by the poet; the poet is there to explain and prevent an act from happening. I suggest that the following is one way to sum up the difference between ancient (tragic) poetry and the modern lyric: The former commemorates not only by theorizing and moralizing but by affirming the ineluctable necessity of terrible choices that, nonetheless, are never entirely devoid of human radiance. Euripides's Hecuba, who knows firsthand that war is violence and lamentation, knows also that the memory of those who have fallen cannot simply be questioned and superseded by the superior reflexive logic of those like her, who—left behind—now "know better." This is why, despite her sufferings, this old heroine of the most modern, self-reflexive, and pacifist of the tragedians is capable of statements worthy of epic heroes. The modern poet, in contrast, thinks of himself as preemptor of tragedy, as mediator of the terrible message of divine absence, rather than as singer of what simply happens. In his inverted world, it is not history as the unavoidable reality of human suffering and grandeur that necessitates poetry; it is poetry that writes and reveals history.

What, then, is the moral of the story of Xanthos, according to Hölderlin? That only ahistorical people are capable of such holy fire. Seduced by the force of repetition and unable to see history as difference, they present us with something that verges on monstrosity: absolute sameness,[26] something illegible to the modern consciousness, which aligns difference squarely with progress, as it subsequently elevates all difference to an a priori progressive (good) value. From this perspective, the second Xanthos and any others following its path—those children of Antigone as I call them—look by necessity like primitive anachronisms, impossible ontologies in need of correction and differentiation. Xanthos becomes for Hölderlin the example he needs to repeat linguistically in order that it not be repeated in actuality. As the Hesperians (the Germans, in particular) come to define their own peoplehood, they ought to reflect on this ancient act; and steering clear of its violence, they may still honor its dead from a safe distance. We have finally reached the kernel of Hölderlin's concern with the poetic voice and its task. The terrible dilemma the modern poet has to voice turns out to be the same aporia that plagued Euripides—Greece's own belated poet—in his *Bacchae*: seduced by the glory of holy fire, we risk the depths of Dionysian barbarism, but too accustomed to orderliness, we risk apathy and soullessness, let alone the other kind of irrationality that follows from the deification of reason.

Hölderlin's reservation about the romanticism of Xanthos's self-destructive immediacy strikes us as all the more relevant from the point of view of our own historical retrospection, as we look back into the excesses of Hitler's Germany. Unable to cope with the eruption of this demonic fire in the midst of civilized Europe, the theoretical gaze—consumed now with its desire for redress—forgets the essential difference that separates those events from the story of Xanthos: the murderers and the murdered in our recent history do not form a neat parallel with their correspondent categories in the ancient incident. In other words, the holocaust of Xanthos happened again, but it was not the Hesperian Germans who were attacked, nor was it they who willingly destroyed themselves by way of resisting.[27] This suggests that not all instances of holy fire must become *immediately* suspect but that holy fire can and does also refer to that which remains the freest and the most human in the human. Nonetheless, as disasters often impose their darkness over the clarity of distinctions (is this not Hölderlin's lesson?), so the postwar theoretical imperative dictates that we forego such distinctions between holy fire and deluded grandeur, between resistance and fatalism, even between Dionysian Greeks and fascist Germans. These distinctions are now deemed irrelevant and are suspected to undermine the new moral authority, which condemns all forms of collective desire as dangerous nationalisms.[28] To insist on drawing such lines risks the charge of missing or even trivializing the all-appropriative yet all-silencing capacity of fascist terror.

Indeed, the idea that any collectivity based on passion is essentially mythic and fascist forms the thrust of Jean-Luc Nancy's reflections on community, which develop as a critique of Georges Bataille's theorization of community as communion and fusion.[29] Inspired by Nietzsche's loathing of the self-interested, narrow-minded, bourgeois individual, Bataille thought of the desire for communal fusion in terms of a profound human yearning to expand beyond the egotistical, utilitarian, and petty confines of the self. However, in Nancy's work, the expansiveness of this desire, still caught in the myth of the heroic subject in search of transcendence, threatens to derail itself into the frenzy of a fascist mob.[30] For Nancy, the only possible community worthy of the name—and not surprisingly a community yet to come—is based on shared finitude. The members of such a community do not share anything in common but simply *are* in common: they share the space in between them. They share not something that connects them but something that differentiates them from each other: those finite contours that render them discrete, singular beings. According to Nancy, only this nonfusional community could be truly "inoperative" (*désœuvrée*), thus fulfilling Bataille's vision of a nonutilitarian collectivity—namely, of a collectivity that does not exploit human relations by reducing them to benefit-yielding structures. In rejecting communion, this community rejects, above all, the myth of heroic, transcendental subjectivity that, by idealizing death, exploits someone's actual loss for the benefit of the greater good. In Nancy's version of community, there is no place for a heroic or tragic death (66), for such deaths are simply mythic: they are illusions invented to confer a false infinity on the finite human being.

My response to Nancy's conclusion is twofold: Firstly, if a human being's existence is not simply monadic but relational—and Nancy does define it as relational, as "Being-with" (from Heidegger's *Mitsein*)—then both its life and its death may well have meanings for the others who were in relation to it. Furthermore, the fact that its death is meaningful (idealization being one of such meanings) is not a priori reducible to naked instrumentalization any more than Nancy's demythologization of death could be said to serve nihilistic purposes: if death means nothing, why should life really mean anything either? Secondly, I would bring Nietzsche as a thinker of community to bear on Nancy's critique of tragic death as an illusory, mythical construction. Nietzsche, I imagine, would ask Nancy, so what if the idealization of death is an illusion invented in order for humans to withstand death's darkness? Indeed, this is the gesture Nietzsche admired in the Greeks, who, according to him, invented Olympian beauty as a veil over darkness (*The Birth of Tragedy* 42). Still, in inventing this illusion, by no means did they delude themselves that the abyss existed no more. The very definition of tragedy for Nietzsche involves the superimposition of the aesthetic on the real as a way of coping with what remains unbearable in existence.

If poststructuralism finds this aestheticization ethically offensive in the face of real horror, then I submit in turn the following provocative consideration: either the reality of the unbearable cannot be *that* unbearable, or, more likely, it is, but in filtering it through this veil of beauty, human beings have managed at times to transcend even what appears as impossible. For there is no other way to explain the actual fact that humanity—despite all the current philosophical talk to the contrary—has existed and continues to exist in its viciousness as it does in its radiance. No matter how exceptionally rare its instances of radiance and no matter how distasteful to the theoretical piety my insistence on these exceptions, they remain part and parcel of the human experience. I am thus in complete agreement with Nietzsche, who saw in the traditional philosophical condemnation of myth and illusion—of which Nancy is also guilty here—little more than sanctimony. After all, it is because these moments of radiance are so exceptional that they should merit all the more our consideration rather than our scorn.

To return to Nancy, his antitragic theory of community conforms to another poststructuralist assumption that proves relevant to my discussion of Xanthos—namely, that one cannot choose one's death, that the existential prerogative of suicide is another heroic myth to be debunked. The most notable proponents of this idea are Maurice Blanchot and Emmanuel Levinas. For both of them, death cannot be thought in terms of self-relation, which is exactly what Heidegger proposed in *Being and Time*: "Death reveals itself as that *possibility which is one's ownmost, which is non-relational, and which is not to be outstripped*" (294). These three conditions can be explained as follows: death stands before each being (*Dasein*) exclusively as that being's possibility and no one else's. Thus, "being toward death" (*Dasein-zum-Tode*) does not mean the empirical death of a being but constitutes the mode of that being's existence in the world—the way in which it comports itself because of its relation to its own mortality. In short, this first condition tells us that death individuates us, offering us the most authentic moment of self-relation. As such, the second condition insists that one's death cannot be related through the death of another but that one relates to the death of the other only by referring it back to one's own death. Finally, death's inevitability cannot be surpassed by any other possibilities open to being: death is being's "uttermost possibility" (*Being and Time* 303), which is to say that death marks the impossibility of any other possibility.

Influenced by Heidegger's existential analytic of death, Blanchot's analysis of suicide concludes that one cannot meet one's death but that it is death (the great Other) who meets each of us.[31] Death, in other words, can never be a subject's intention. It is arguable that Blanchot's analysis was motivated by the theoretical concern that making death the object of human will would undo Heidegger's third condition: to intend one's death would mean to outstrip death as the unsurpassable condition of being and render it an option among others. Yet intending one's death does not necessarily entail death's neutralization but, rather, its affirmation as the inevitable. "Todeslust," in other words—the attitude we found in Antigone and the Xanthians—is the most authentic form of *Dasein-zum-Tode*, since it does not seek to avoid death or trivialize it as a distant option somewhere in the future but acknowledges its constant proximity to us from the moment of our birth. Let us recall what Antigone said to Creon:

> I did not believe
> your proclamation had such power to enable
> *one who will someday die* to override
> God's ordinances, unwritten and secure.
> (Lines 496–99, my emphasis)[32]

Antigone recognizes her death as her only inevitability, as the most defining of all conditions of her existence, and announces to Creon that no mortal punishment or threat will be enough to make her turn away from what lies definitively ahead of her. To the contrary, she will go half the distance.

A student of Heidegger and a lifelong friend of Blanchot, Levinas finds the Heideggerian understanding of death as self-relation too narcissistic.[33] Insofar as Levinas advocates an ethics dictated from the other, death for him could never be thought from within the phenomenological categories of subjectivity and intention, since such categories still keep us within the contours of the self-same. Only the death of the other can impose itself on a subject as an ethical requirement and oblige him or her to respond.

In his essay "*Il y a*: Holding Levinas's Hand to Blanchot's Fire," Simon Critchley offers a good summation of both thinkers on this issue. Of Blanchot, he writes, "Dying transgresses the boundary of the self's jurisdiction. This is why suicide is impossible for Blanchot: I cannot *want* to die; death is not an object of the will" (109–10). And of Levinas, he adds:

> The ungraspable facticity of dying establishes an opening onto a meta-phenomenological alterity, irreducible to the power of the Subject, the will or *Dasein*.... Dying is the impossibility of possibility and thus undermines the residual heroism, virility and potency of Being-towards-death....
> ... If death is not a self-relation, if it does not result in self-communion and the achievement of a meaning to finitude, then this means that a certain plurality has insinuated itself at the heart of the self. The facticity of dying structures the self as Being-for-the-other, as substitution, which also means that death is not revealed in a relation to *my* death but rather in the alterity of death or the death of the Other. (110)

Of course, insofar as the "other" (*autrui*) of Levinas refers to a personal alterity, death as a relation to this other turns out to be still in relation to a *subject*, albeit now the relating subject is no more selfish, while the related subject—the other—is prioritized because it is not one's self. Levinas's other is deeply personal, since only as personhood can alterity have the strong ethical grip that he maintains it should have. Thus, Levinas's notion of alterity, as Critchley sums it up, ultimately refers to "the alterity of the child, that is, of the son, and the alterity of illeity, of a (personal) god" (Critchley, *Il y a* 111). Levinas cannot really unfasten death ontologically from the relation to *a* subject because this would destroy death's ethical force: if *my* death cannot concern me, because death is by nature not something to which *any* subject can relate, then the death of the *other* subject cannot concern me either. Hence, Levinas remains well within the bounds of subjectivity, but by rendering each subject prostrate in front of the other. In fact, the only other way around this contradiction of a nonsubjective yet subjective relation to death is to pronounce death itself as the absolute Other. In this second alternative, Blanchot's impersonal other and Levinas's personal other meet in their theologization of death: death, this invisible and ungraspable alterity, is the god that emerges after it has killed God. The death *of* God evolves naturally into death *as* God.

It is exactly against this type of untragic thinking that I have structured my argument of intentionality both with respect to Antigone's and Xanthos's choices. For tragedy—which is not just an aesthetic act, as it is often accused of being, but an enactment of living communally and historically—involves not only fate but choice as well, including the choice of how one goes to one's death. One certainly cannot will to die or not (there is effectively no "or" in this sentence); however, it remains the tragic prerogative to choose the moment and the manner one dies. Willingly and of your own choice you go to your death (lines 882–84), says the chorus to Antigone; and the Greek word αὐτόνομος (autonomous) stands solemnly and prohibitively against the Levinasian understanding of death as absolute heteronomy that can never become a person's choice. Additionally, instead of submitting to Creon's punishment by slow death in the cave, the heroine chooses in her own manner to commit suicide by hanging.[34] Heroes, after all, are not necessarily selfish just because they bear a strong relation to their self. On the contrary, as with Antigone, they are often more likely to expend themselves for the sake of others. On the other hand, I am not sure that the same generosity is shared by the contemporary antiheroic ethic, which uses the deaths of others—heroic or not—in order to cement its own theoretical incontestability. For all the talk about death being inoperative, I see it working tirelessly at the wheels of theoretical sanctimony.

Like any philosophical trend, the current antitragic and antiexistentialist brand of theory is also historically embedded, responding to what it perceives as historical exigencies. Seen through such a historical lens, the philosophical impossibilization of suicide may turn out to serve some insidious ends, though most probably without intending to: affected by the largely antiheroic response of Europe during World War II and trying to belatedly atone for the inability of many to resist Hitler's death machine, theory feels now ethically authorized to blanket charge every other human response to atrocity as a senseless, cheap show of "virility," offering us in honor of Europe's dead an ever-more-passively thanatophilic and thanatocentric ethics. In the name of redressing victims, it also kills again ruthlessly the other dead, those of other histories and other times who dared fancy their death otherwise, who thought they chose it and thus gave it meaning. Those are the mistaken lives, the lives now easily deconstructed, disfigured, and dismissed as philosophically incorrect. We now know better, having outgrown the infantile delusion of the heroic and tragic death: no one has the right to die anymore or even to think it, in the aftermath of postwar Europe. Thinking otherwise constitutes the ultimate hubris and total historical irresponsibility.

The enormous oppressiveness with which this new ethical imperative imposes itself is in fact unfathomable and might well require the same light years to be truly understood as the ones Nietzsche thought we would need to understand the death of God. While I cannot emphasize enough the ways in which two world wars have justifiably shaken Europe and its so-called human values, I also think it important not to grow too quiet—as the poet warns—with our new philosophical (un)certainties. We should see in this new imperative of absolute passivity not only the virtues of saintly prostration, nonviolent thoughtfulness, and political maturity of a reformed postwar modernity but also its underside of complacency, blind obedience, and ultimate acquiescence: a politically and now philosophically sanctioned docility, a quietism that has its own marked relation to violence, since the violence of a silent *vox populi*, as the same recent history has shown, might be the deadliest accomplice of them all.

Beyond any attempt to reclaim a systematic ethics of resistance, which would fall mostly on suspicious or deaf ears as a delusional and complicit humanism, I would like to return to Hölderlin's poem in light of this discussion of death and intentionality in order to underline the deeply problematic character of any corrective, historicizing reading of the Xanthian suicide—a reading I have detected in Hölderlin himself. I want to stress that Xanthos cannot be subsumed easily under any philosophical or formal-poetological imperative, and even less can it become an ethical lesson for others to follow or not to follow. Its irrevocable allegiance to tragedy consists precisely in the antididactic thrust of that kind of experience. One cannot teach another how to die. One cannot demand from another not to want to die or not to think of that death as inaugural of something else. One cannot tell, and *does not have the right to tell*,[35] anyone any of that—particularly in the name of morality, piety, and concern for otherness. To assume such a moral prerogative could constitute the worst of all fascisms. If death is indeed this inoperative and ungraspable notion that every other contemporary theorist seems to think it is, it can hardly grant anyone the moral imprimatur to judge and regulate the loss of those who do not conform to this or that philosophical definition.

This is the contradiction, or perhaps embarrassment, of any systematic, ontological impossibilization of suicide that Xanthos presents. Xanthos exposes reflection's callousness at the moment reflection tries to be all-too-tenderly ethical. Why would we need to tell the saga and make the Xanthians historical? Because making them historical would spare them—in fact, would spare us moderns, who are allegorized by the second Xanthos—another self-destruction. Of course, the unspoken assumption here is that the preference for a communal life in subjection over a communion of death is the great discovery of our worldview, which, in its rush to relativize everyone else's values, ignores that it itself must be as relative and as much a subject to historicization. Insofar as the Xanthians themselves are concerned, all that historicization would do is teach them what they already knew: necessity (represented in their case by Roman aggression) will kill or enslave them anyway, and thus, why rush to their own death rather than wait for the great comer? But by the same token, they would respond, why *not* rush to their death? The nihilism that now goes by the name of historical reflection asserts that between the two necessities (the Roman death and their suicide) there is no difference, because the result is identical either way: it is death who comes and not we who go to it, as Blanchot claimed.

Obviously, none of this has anything to do with Xanthos, as I have already signaled earlier on. It has to do with what its story *signifies* for us now. Were I to rephrase this, however, in terms of our discussion of death's inoperativity,

I would say that it has to do with working the Xanthians' death toward a better present and future for us. Apparently, it may turn out that the distant, now-legendary dead *can* be worked on and with a sufficient rationale for it, too: since they themselves believed in heroism, they have irrevocably offered their death up to such working. By believing in a tragic death, they have rendered themselves legitimate exceptions to the theoretical claim that death is inoperative. This is one of the potentially sinister implications of the injunction to historicize sagas, since it is in the nature of reflection to neutralize history's tragic structures. Reflection rationally says that if the end is the same, the means do not matter. Tragedy, on the other hand, passionately insists that when it comes to the human being—precisely because the ends are not in his or her hands—all that matters is the means. It is how a human being chooses to walk to its death that makes it the unique being it has been in this world.[36] Therefore, I repeat that no one who stands apart, protected from this passion, is in a position to prescribe whether a person or a community can or cannot will its death. It is simply not a matter of prescription or inscription or transcription; this kind of act is not scripture and refuses to be read. It is a volcanic irruption, the fulfillment of time in one instant.

Xanthos is pure peril, and if it became so remarkably repeatable, it is because in its core it contains something of the unrepeatable: one cannot repeat it, but equally cannot not repeat it, according to some political, moral, philosophical, or even poetic specifications. The Xanthian act attests to the most dangerous, but also most revelatory, sense of poetry as creation: it shows creation as destruction and regeneration, for the meaning of the act lives on and does not need any further commentary to enhance it, attenuate it, or complete it. Hölderlin's own last couplet suggests as much as this. The poet-interpreter reflects on these events to mold a history for his people, but poetic writing must acknowledge, in turn, its own volcanic, perilous origin: the act-turned-myth—myth qua original truth, not myth in the pejorative sense we use it today.[37] Selfless and full of self at the same time—selfless in annihilating the boundaries of the self in conflagration and full of self in insisting that the most disastrous but free decision is better than coercion—it is this tragic act that fuels poetic reflexivity.

Xanthos, the Lycian town, belongs to the time of the aorist, a uniquely Greek tense that means "indefinite." While in the indicative mood, the aorist, like the simple past, connotes an action completed in the past, its aspect—that is, the kind of action to which it refers—is not limited to the past: it describes the sense of totality captured in an instant, though an indefinite instant, whether in the past, present, or future. Lorenz Gyömörey writes of the aorist as the indefinitely absolute dimension of the momentary: "absolute—but never absolutist" (57, my translation). Unconcerned with the act's temporal duration, the aorist brackets the agent outside time for an infinitely discrete moment, an indefinable and absolute moment at once: infinity's cut into the finite. It is the action pure and simple, yet without boundaries.

Gyömörey continues:

> The fact that no other language ... —even after the evolution of philosophy during the French Enlightenment and German Idealism in particular—has the means to bracket the momentary event, the momentary action from the linear scheme of past-present-future, to detach its agent psychologically and let freedom's *indefiniteness* occur in the margins of past and future, is something that from its linguistic roots separates Greek consciousness from others. ... We can say that the aorist expresses the Greek's relation with time, with existence in time, in the moment where one is freely situated in the past or the future without being interested in duration. Here and There, Now and Then, always in the absoluteness of free will and fate. (57–58, my translation)

What Gyömörey identifies as "Greek," I prefer to align with tragic time: the time where free will and fate coincide in a terrible yet splendid moment. I thus find in this indefinite absoluteness of the aorist the most compelling linguistic encapsulation of the Xanthian suicide. Its instant totality, which may still recur in the indefinite future, cannot be absorbed by any philosophical or historiographical assimilation but only caught in the intensity of the act itself.

Little would Hölderlin have known that a mere two years after his poem was written, autonomous groups in the land that is now called Greece, in their disparate efforts to sustain their communities free from the impositions of empire, would not have chosen the terrestrial road *at all costs*. In the vein of what I have already theoretically elaborated, I will merely sketch two Xanthos-like events from the nineteenth-century Greek struggle for independence, hoping also that these brief descriptions will do the work of thinking more justly than any reflexive analytical apparatus I could graft onto them. Most of all, I wish to conclude with this gesture of remembrance, since these incidents are not only theoretically but also historically significant in the context of discussing German idealism and romanticism: highly familiar and inspiring to the literary and intellectual circles of that time, both these events and their dead—like so many other dead—have now been forgotten and thrown in the dustbin of popular lore.

Souli

Souli is an isolated mountainous location in Epirus, in the northwestern part of Greece. The Souliots moved there in the beginning of the seventeenth century, after an unsuccessful insurrection against the Ottomans in Ioannina in 1611.[38] Following the Ottoman retaliation against the revolt, several Epirotic families decided to relocate to the natural fortress of Souli's mountains (Tsolis 31), where they established the first four villages (the Tetrachori: Souli, Kiafa, Avarikos, and Samoniva), to which others were later adjoined. Thus, the Souliots were originally shepherds from neighboring villages who, determined to avoid Ottoman rule, came to this area because its inaccessible landscape allowed them to live freely.

Although the Souliot bravery has become a hallmark of the national struggle for Greek independence, it should be noted—as with other such attempts at freedom from imperial rule—that the initial desire for autonomy was expressed locally rather than organized around the vision of a nation-state. In other words, what guided the actions of the Souliots were the family ties within and between their village communities, the sharing of local customs, and an intimate relation to the landscape that provided them both refuge and a means of livelihood no matter how harsh. Demetris Stamelos, whose ethnography aims at drawing uninterrupted lines of continuity between the Souliot life under Ottoman occupation and the values of the Homeric world, offers a number of examples of this reliance on family and unwritten law, along with a strict observance of the honor code, among the Souliots. He mentions, for instance, how the Souliots, having cosigned a treaty to allow several Muslim Albanians out of a monastery where they had sought refuge, fought to protect them from other Greeks who broke the oath and ambushed them (34–35).[39] Whether this type of community is Homeric as Stamelos claims, an immediate democracy as Michalis Tsolis insists, or merely feudal or tribal as some more neutral interpreters might view it, the important point in all these suppositions remains the localized, proximate bond of responsibility that sustains its members.[40]

This contrast between a national and a communal vision of the struggle for self-determination becomes even clearer when we consider the fact that the villages surrounding Souli used to pay taxes to Souli in exchange for defense by the Souliots. Overall, more than sixty villages contributed either currency or agricultural products to the Souliot Confederacy (Stamelos 60). In effect, these Greeks were subjects both to the sultan, to whom they paid capital tax (a tax on each head), and to the Souliots, to whom they paid taxes for their protection from the Ottoman forces.

The uniqueness of Souli, which had made it world famous through foreign travelogues at the time of the occupation, was that they put up a successful resistance against an empire—a resistance that was described as "the epos of Souli."[41] Though they were few in numbers, the Souliots were trained very young; and by using their inhospitable natural surroundings and their passion for self-governance, they took on the Ottoman army for nearly a century (Tsolis 11). Despite Souli's community being ethnically hybridized, consisting chiefly of Greeks and Arvanites, their common determination as a small group to resist an empire has been compared to moments of ancient Greek history where the notion of the few fighting successfully the many constitutes a distinctive motif, with the Persian wars providing the most famous example. Hence, several European intellectuals and travelers interpreted the Souliot self-determination as a modern reverberation of this ancient spirit of resistance. Tsolis cites such foreign observers who called the revolt of Souli a "miracle" (40), while quoting excerpts from various poets, travelers, diplomats, and literati who portrayed the Souliots as continuing ancient heroic traditions. The French historian and philhellene Claude Fauriel, for instance, remarked that "the adventures, achievements, heroic deeds, and misfortunes of the Souliots resemble old heroic myths, which by mistake were inserted in the history of modern peoples" (Fauriel qtd. in Tsolis 18, my translation).

I offer here a cursory review of the wars that led to Souli's ultimate fall on September 26, 1803, and the act of sacrifice that finalized the three-year siege in December 1803.[42] Upon receiving an order from the sultan to quell the Souliot uprisings, Hadzi Achmet Pasha invaded Souli in 1731 but was defeated. From then onward, the Souliots began to be officially persecuted and considered to be at war with the empire. The war by Mustafa Pasha in 1754, the 1759 invasion led by Dost Bey, and the war by Maxut Aga in 1762 all ended again victoriously for Souli. Started by Suleiman Tsaparis, another war broke in 1772, during which the Souliots took hostage Tsaparis, his son, and his close associates, all of whom were later freed through negotiations, during which the victors exacted ransom. The Souliots defended themselves successfully against Mustafa Kokka and Kurt Pasha around 1775 and against Bekir Pasha in 1780. A returning Suleiman Tsaparis declared yet another war but was defeated a second time. The wars against Souli were continued by Ali Pasha until its eventual fall in 1803. Ali Pasha was an Albanian appointee of the Ottoman Empire known for his courtly splendor, his political shrewdness, his cruelty as a despot,[43] and his thirst for personal power that eventually undermined the empire. Ali's first war against Souli in 1792 resulted in a humiliating treaty for the pasha, who had to pay ransom for the Turkish hostages as well as war reparations to the Souliots (Tsolis 80).[44] However, his second war led to the fatal siege of 1800–1803, which concluded with the conflagration at the Koungi monastery and the mass suicide of several Souliot women, who fell off the cliff of Zalongos in order not to be captured.

With no external support and exhausted by the siege, the Souliot clans broke down, with the prominent Botsaris family leaving Souli. The remaining Souliots withdrew to the fortresses of Kiafa and Koungi, where they lost their last battle on December 7, 1803. In an immolation reminiscent of Xanthos, the monk Samuel, surrounded by Ottoman troops at the monastery of Saint Paraskevi at Koungi, set the gunpowder barrels on fire, blowing up the monastery, himself, and those who remained with him. On December 12, upon the Souliot surrender, a treaty was signed that promised them safe release to relocate with their property and weapons. However, as the fleeing Souliots took their paths to exile on December 15, the Ottoman troops violated the treaty, caught up with the group heading for Zalongos, and attacked it. It was at this site that the second incident of communal self-destruction took place. The protagonists are reported to have been primarily, if not exclusively, women. As the exiles were encircled, some were killed, others were forced to retreat, but a group of about twenty-two women with their infants and children chose to turn toward the cliff's edge rather than surrender. Throwing their children over, they themselves followed after them. Though accounts differ as to the exact number of the women, with one account including several men as well, they all agree that infanticide and suicide took place.

Opposite the movement at the end of "Stimme des Volks" by which old legends become historicized, the event of Zalongos became legend *as* it entered history: it was reputed that the women did not simply fall to their deaths but that they formed a dance—the "Dance of Zalongos"—and on each round, its leader fell. Perhaps, as Alexis Politis's demythologization of modern history insists,[45] the dance itself never took place; certainly, it could not be empirically attested in an era that lacked video cameras and embedded journalists. Yet if the element of dance is just a legend added to this terrible moment of dying, then this legend is not simply a sentimental and manipulative embellishment, as Politis seems to suggest, but provides a fitting interpretation for such an event. In a Hölderlinian reversal, the legend here interprets history rather than the other way around: the dance expresses the Dionysian frenzy of the women who took a shortcut to their deaths, but in its orderly formation, it also shows the other side of this madness, which is pure deliberation. Thus Tsolis writes, "The glorious Epos of Souli is not the fruit of a momentary enthusiasm, nor an explosion of despair, but a mature and steadfast choice and deliberation for a free life, with its cost—if needed—even death itself. It is not a vain delirium, but an unshakable faith in life's values without concessions and conciliations. The Souliots wish and decide to live freely, with honor and dignity, respect and their humanity" (40, my translation).[46] This deliberation does not characterize only the official wars waged between Ottomans and Souliots; it can also be found in the suicides of both Koungi and Zalongos.

After the destruction of 1803, the surviving Souliots went into exile in Parga and Corfu. They returned to Souli in 1820, enlisted by their former enemy Ali Pasha to help him in his conspiracy against the Ottoman Empire. A second exile came after 1822, when they left for the Ionian Islands. During this second exile, which coincided with the full force of the revolution in the mainland, they dispersed throughout Greece to help the rest of the rebels.[47]

Arkadi

After the sovereignty of Greece was officially recognized by the great powers (Great Britain, Russia, and France) in the 1830 London Protocol, a large part of what constitutes the present territory of the country was not yet included. With the Arta-Volos line defining Greece's northernmost frontier, the liberated territories were limited to the central and south mainland, while the regions farther north and many islands, including Crete, still belonged to the Ottoman Empire. For this reason, insurrections that aimed to achieve union with the free Greece continued to take place in those parts.

In 1866 such an uprising led to the holocaust of Arkadi, a monastery in Rethymnon, Crete, that repeated Samuel's 1803 explosion of Koungi.[48] Here are summarily the preceding historical events[49]: The 1669 surrender of Heraklion to the Ottoman Empire signaled the occupation of Crete, which lasted for roughly one and a half centuries without any opposition. The Cretans participated in the Greek Revolution of 1821; and even though, after the conclusion of the revolutionary war in 1829, the rural areas of Crete were under the control of the rebels, Crete was not included in the territories of free Greece by the London Protocol. The Ottomans handed the island to Egyptian rule between 1830 and 1840 as a gesture of gratitude for the Egyptian assistance to the empire's wars. Despite his initial efforts to keep order by disarming Christians and Muslims alike and to benefit the island with the construction of public works, Mustafa Pasha's heavy taxation provoked much resentment among his subjects, who were already exhausted by long-standing military operations. Thus, in 1833 about seven thousand Christian civilians with the support of many Turkish Cretans gathered to protest the heavy taxes, but Mustafa's army dissolved the demonstration and executed some of its leaders.[50]

In 1840, when the great powers returned Crete to Ottoman rule, many Cretans who had relocated to the free territories decided that the time for revolution was ripe. They arrived in Crete with organized militias, and in 1841 the revolution was declared, albeit without official support from the Greek government, which was obliged by the great powers to keep a strictly neutral position on the Cretan question. The revolutionary atmosphere in Europe around 1848 reverberated in the island, while the Crimean War (1853–56) resulted in the sultan's issuance of the Hatti Humayoun, an imperial proclamation that guaranteed freedom of religion, personal freedom, and the right to property for the Christian population of Crete. Since many of the local pashas did not implement effectively this reform charter and since taxation remained unbearably high, another protest movement arose in 1858, addressing the consuls of the great powers, which concluded with some further measures beneficial to the rebels such as amnesty, the right to bear arms, the revocation of certain taxes, and the recognition of local senates of elders as arbitrators in legal affairs pertaining to the Christian population. The revocation of some of these rights after 1861 by the new administrator of Crete led to the revolution of 1866–69, which was marked by the events at the monastery of Arkadi.

As several revolutionary groups fortified themselves in various areas of Crete, one such group stayed in Arkadi, which was considered a stronghold for rebels, as it had already hosted Panos Koronaios, the Greek military leader of operations in the island. As Arkadi's fortifications were very strong and its storage was rich both in food and ammunition, it made a haven for the rebels, though the fact that the rebels did not tear down the adjacent buildings was a fatal mistake, since these structures provided launching places for the Ottoman artillery that had surrounded the monastery (Psilakis 238). Once again, the exact numbers of the besieged differ in various accounts. In his travelogue of Crete published in 1881, the doctor Josef Hadjidakis writes of two hundred fighters, eighty volunteers, and one hundred families (Karellis 7–8). Giorgis Manousakis mentions six hundred women and children and about three hundred armed men (17). Vasileios Psilakis also estimates the number up to 950 people (240). But we also have estimations in official consular documents. The Greek consul at Chania, Nikolaos Sakopoulos, in his report to the Greek minister of foreign affairs dated November 20, 1866, cites 540 people in total, of whom 343 were women and children and the remaining 197 were armed men, civilian men, and monks. In his later and presumably more informed report, dated November 28, 1866, Sakopoulos raises the total population to 966. Of these, 325 were men, of whom only 250 were fit for battle while the others were old, sick, or wounded. The rest were women and children.[51]

Whatever the exact number, upon hearing of the gathering, Mustafa Pasha ordered a siege on November 8, 1866. Asked to surrender, the besieged refused, choosing to fight instead. The strong monastery walls provided protection for the first day, obliging the pasha to send for help from Rethymnon. The next day, reinforced with heavy artillery, the Ottoman army bombarded repeatedly the gate, which eventually fell in the evening hours of November 9. However, the rebels had barricaded the gate from the inside with stones and all sorts of items. When the Ottoman troops entered, they faced a long battle around the gate before they could march farther into the building. Abbot Gabriel, who had earlier refused the Ottoman invitation to surrender, is reported to have blessed the rebels' backup plan—namely, the mass suicide in case of defeat—and he himself died from a bullet, fighting on the walls. Thus, when it seemed that all was lost for the Cretans, they retreated to the ammunition storage room, where a young man, whose identity is disputed (traditional accounts propose Kostis Giampoudakis, but new evidence points to Emmanuel Skoulas[52]), shot the gunpowder barrels and exploded the monastery with most of his comrades and many invading troops. Of the few who survived, the volunteers were executed; the women and children were relocated to Rethymnon, where they were imprisoned for about eleven months; and some of the injured and the weak died on the way to their imprisonment. Despite popular support for union with the mainland, Crete was obliged by the great powers to remain an autonomous territory under the suzerainty of the sultan until the conclusion of the Balkan Wars in 1913, when upon defeat of the Ottoman Empire, Crete finally joined the Greek nation-state.[53]

Still, much as a free Greece was the stated purpose of these revolutionary acts, official national identity can never absorb in its stately, rational interests the passion for autonomy that had motivated these communities of rebels. To function at all, the state must be a rational entity and an avowed enemy of passion in the long run, as Plato knew well: it appropriates and rationalizes sacrifices to justify its establishment (was not Antigone the sacrifice Creon needed to authorize his accession to the throne?) in the same way that it can also revise and even question these sacrifices when they no longer work to its benefit, when they remind it of terrible conflicts that inconveniently intercept the way to new alliances. Karellis is not wrong to observe that the nation-state's current official histories are often too quick to conflate the historical imperative for factual accuracy with present political demands for outright revisionism—the latter now serving the new national interests better than memory would (17). To his observation I would add that, in the irony (or the farce, as Marx would say) of our times, the oppositional intellectuals who do this work of demythologization might well turn out to be themselves producers of an official history, albeit this time a history dictated by different—that is, *multi*national and corporate rather than merely national—ideological concerns. It is known that history is always written by the victors; and even though on the small scale the victors of the revolution were the Greeks, the great powers and their interests in the region perhaps have not changed all that much. In any case, there is indeed something both insidious and contradictory about trusting a nation-state, whatever its guise and its historicopolitical motives, to undermine its own potential nationalism.

For all these reasons, I prefer to conclude these citations of remembrance not by way of subsuming them into the rational, grand-scale narrative of the nation-state, into which they have already been assimilated and which is by now ready to disgorge them in order to promote its current interests. Events such as Zalongos and Arkadi cannot be submitted to the particular and contingent interests of nation-state narratives, whose rationalism will inevitably fail them, any more than the sacrifice of Antigone could be subsumed by Creon's state.[54] Instead, I would like to let them shine not only as examples of independence but as independent examples—acts that stand on their own as moments of a tragic consciousness that atones as it overreaches, in the terrible manner the Aeschylean chorus has described from ancient times. Blood on blood, accursed but necessary for all sides involved—blood of all wars past and future, between nations and within families alike—pouring out from the haunting lines of Aeschylus's *Agamemnon*:

> Here is anger for anger. Between them
> who shall judge lightly?
> The spoiler is robbed; he killed, he has paid.
> The truth stands ever beside God's throne
> eternal: he who has wrought shall pay; that is law.
> Then who shall tear the curse from their blood?
> The seed is stiffened to ruin.
> (Lines 1560–66)

But this same Aeschylean chorus who saw the ruin that fate makes of humans, whether high or low, conquerors or conquered—this same chorus also detested political tyranny and sang of death not only as the terrible sign of fate but as the liberation from human despotism: "Better to be killed. / Death is a softer thing by far than tyranny" (lines 1364–65). If tragedy is the only place that has understood these kinds of acts, it is because it has never tried to explain them but has simply presented them as expressions of the creative and destructive principles that make up (poiein) the cycles of human life. Portentous acts such as Arkadi do not need further commentary: "Des suicides prodigieux comme ceux d'Arcadi se passent de commentaires."[55]

Thus, in a final juxtaposition to Hölderlin's counsel for interpretation and commentary, I conclude with excerpts from another poet, a Greek contemporary of Hölderlin who also was moved by revolutions: Andreas Kalvos. His poetry incites rather than mediates, resists rather than negotiates. And when it reflects, it also vindicates; but this does not make it any less philosophical. First, in his ode "Eis Samon" ("To Samos"), Icarus's fatal flight, often viewed as an immature and irrational overreach of a youngster against the sound advice of his experienced and measured father, is cast in a completely new light:

> Those who feel the bronze hand of fear
> weighing heavily upon them,
> may they bear the yoke of slavery.
> Freedom requires

excellence and daring.

[Freedom] (and the myth hides a sense of truth)
gave wings to Icarus;
and though winged
he fell and drowned
in the sea,

from high above he fell
and died free.
If you become a tyrant's
dishonored prey,
consider your grave to be terrible.
(Lines 173–81, my translation)[56]

And to Hölderlin's choice of the terrestrial path that does not wish for quick drowning in the sea or for consumption by the holy fire, this is Kalvos's tragic answer in the first stanza of "Ai Euxai" ("The Wishes"):

Better for the sea's
swollen waves
to drown my country
like a despairing,
deserted ship.

Over land and over islands,
I would rather see
a pouring flame,
devouring cities, forests,
peoples and hopes.
(Lines 193–99, my translation)[57]

Appendix

"Stimme des Volks" [Erste Fassung, ca. 1800]
BY FRIEDRICH HÖLDERLIN
(from *Sämtliche Werke, Kleine Stuttgarter Ausgabe*, 2:50–52)

Du seiest Gottes Stimme, so glaubt ich sonst,
In heilger Jugend; ja und ich sag es noch!
  Um unsre Weisheit unbekümmert
    Rauschen die Ströme doch auch, und dennoch,

Wer liebt sie nicht? und immer bewegen sie
Das Herz mir, hör ich ferne die Schwindenden,
  Die Ahnungsvollen, meine Bahn nicht,
    Aber gewisser ins Meer hin eilen.

Denn selbstvergessen, allzubereit, den Wunsch
Der Götter zu erfüllen, ergreift zu gern,
  Was sterblich ist und einmal offnen
    Auges auf eigenem Pfade wandelt,

Ins All zurück die kürzeste Bahn, so stürzt
Der Strom hinab, er suchet die Ruh, es reißt,
  Es ziehet wider Willen ihn von
    Klippe zu Klippe, den Steuerlosen,

Das wunderbare Sehnen dem Abgrund zu,
Und kaum der Erd entstiegen, desselben Tags
  Kehrt weinend zum Geburtort schon aus
    Purpurner Höhe die Wolke wieder.

Und Völker auch ergreifet die Todeslust,
Und Heldenstädte sinken; die Erde grünt
Und stille vor den Sternen liegt, den
Betenden gleich, in den Staub geworfen,

Freiwillig überwunden die lange Kunst
Vor jenen Unnachahmbaren da; er selbst,
Der Mensch, mit eigner Hand zerbrach, die
Hohen zu ehren, sein Werk, der Künstler.

Doch minder nicht sind jene den Menschen hold,
Sie lieben wieder, so, wie geliebt sie sind,
Und hemmen öfters, daß er lang im
Lichte sich freue, die Bahn des Menschen.

Und wie des Adlers Jungen, er wirft sie selbst,
Der Vater, aus dem Neste, damit sie sich
Im Felde Beute suchen, so auch
Treiben uns lächelnd hinaus die Götter.

Wohl allen, die zur Ruhe gegangen sind
Und vor der Zeit gefallen, auch sie, auch sie
Geopfert gleich den Erstlingen der
Ernte, sie haben ihr Teil gewonnen!

Nicht, o ihr Teuern, ohne die Wonnen all
Des Lebens gingt ihr unter, ein Festtag ward
Noch Einer euch zuvor, und dem gleich
Haben die anderen keins gefunden.

Doch sichrer ists und größer und ihrer mehr,
Die allen alles ist, der Mutter wert,
In Eile zögernd, mit des Adlers
Lust die geschwungnere Bahn zu wandeln.

Drum weil sie fromm ist, ehr ich den Himmlischen
Zu lieb des Volkes Stimme, die ruhige,
Doch um der Götter und der Menschen
Willen, sie ruhe zu gern nicht immer!

"**Stimme des Volks**" [Zweite Fassung, ca. 1801]
BY FRIEDRICH HÖLDERLIN
(from *Sämtliche Werke, Kleine Stuttgarter Ausgabe*, 2:53–55)

Du seiest Gottes Stimme, so glaubt ich sonst
In heilger Jugend; ja, und ich sag es noch!
   Um unsre Weisheit unbekümmert
      Rauschen die Ströme doch auch, und dennoch,

Wer liebt sie nicht? und immer bewegen sie
Das Herz mir, hör ich ferne die Schwindenden,
   Die Ahnungsvollen meine Bahn nicht,
      Aber gewisser ins Meer hin eilen.

Denn selbstvergessen, allzubereit, den Wunsch
Der Götter zu erfüllen, ergreift zu gern,
   Was sterblich ist, wenn offnen Augs auf
      Eigenen Pfaden es einmal wandelt,

Ins All zurück die kürzeste Bahn; so stürzt
Der Strom hinab, er suchet die Ruh, es reißt,
   Es ziehet wider Willen ihn, von
      Klippe zu Klippe, den Steuerlosen,

Das wunderbare Sehnen dem Abgrund zu;
Das Ungebundne reizet und Völker auch
   Ergreift die Todeslust und kühne
      Städte, nachdem sie versucht das Beste,

Von Jahr zu Jahr forttreibend das Werk, sie hat
Ein heilig Ende troffen; die Erde grünt
   Und stille vor den Sternen liegt, den
      Betenden gleich, in den Sand geworfen,

Freiwillig überwunden die lange Kunst
Vor jenen Unnachahmbaren da; er selbst,
   Der Mensch, mit eigner Hand zerbrach, die
      Hohen zu ehren, sein Werk, der Künstler.

Doch minder nicht sind jene den Menschen hold,
Sie lieben wieder, so wie geliebt sie sind,
Und hemmen öfters, daß er lang im
Lichte sich freue, die Bahn des Menschen.

Und, nicht des Adlers Jungen allein, sie wirft
Der Vater aus dem Neste, damit sie nicht
Zu lang ihm bleiben, uns auch treibt mit
Richtigem Stachel hinaus der Herrscher.

Wohl jenen, die zur Ruhe gegangen sind,
Und vor der Zeit gefallen, auch die, auch die
Geopfert, gleich den Erstlingen der
Ernte, sie haben ein Teil gefunden.

Am Xanthos lag, in griechischer Zeit, die Stadt,
Jetzt aber, gleich den größeren, die dort ruhn,
Ist durch ein Schicksal sie dem heilgen
Lichte des Tages hinweggekommen.

Sie kamen aber, nicht in der offnen Schlacht,
Durch eigne Hand um. Fürchterlich ist davon,
Was dort geschehn, die wunderbare
Sage von Osten zu uns gelanget.

Es reizte sie die Güte von Brutus. Denn
Als Feuer ausgegangen, so bot er sich,
Zu helfen ihnen, ob er gleich, als Feldherr,
Stand in Belagerung vor den Toren.

Doch von den Mauern warfen die Diener sie,
Die er gesandt. Lebendiger ward darauf
Das Feuer und sie freuten sich und ihnen
Strecket' entgegen die Hände Brutus

Und alle waren außer sich selbst. Geschrei
Entstand und Jauchzen. Drauf in die Flamme warf
Sich Mann und Weib, von Knaben stürzt' auch
Der von dem Dach, in der Väter Schwert der.

Nicht rätlich ist es, Helden zu trotzen. Längst
Wars aber vorbereitet. Die Väter auch,
Da sie ergriffen waren, einst, und
Heftig die persischen Feinde drängten,

Entzündeten, ergreifend des Stromes Rohr,
Daß sie das Freie fänden, die Stadt. Und Haus
Und Tempel nahm, zum heilgen Aether
Fliegend, und Menschen hinweg die Flamme.

So hatten es die Kinder gehört, und wohl
Sind gut die Sagen, denn ein Gedächtnis sind
Dem Höchsten sie, doch auch bedarf es
Eines, die heiligen auszulegen.

Voice of the People [First version, last three stanzas only]
BY FRIEDRICH HÖLDERLIN
Translated by Nick Hoff
(from *Odes and Elegies*, 229–30)

Not without the blissful joys of life
Did you perish going down, O dear ones,
There was a celebration day before you,
And the others have found no day like that.

Yet it's more certain and greater and more than she
Who is all to all, of value to mothers,
Hesitating in her rush, with the eagle's desire
To soar the winding way.

Therefore since she's devout I honor the gods
For the sake of her the people's voice, the calm and rested one,
Yet for the sake of gods and men
May she not always rest too gladly!

Voice of the People [Second version]
BY FRIEDRICH HÖLDERLIN
Translated by Nick Hoff
(from *Odes and Elegies*, 107)

You were the voice of god, so I believed,
In my holy youth; yes, and I maintain this still!
But the rivers also rush onward
Unconcerned with our wisdom, and yet

Who doesn't love them? And they always move
My heart when I hear those fleeting ones far away
So full of foreboding, they don't follow my course
But rush more surely down into the sea.

For mortal beings forget themselves, and once they've
Wandered their allotted paths with open eyes,
They're all too ready to do what the gods
Wish for them, and too eagerly

They take the shortest way back to the All; thus do
Rivers plunge, searching for peace and rushing,
The wondrous longing for depths
Drives them against their will

From rock to rock, utterly blind;
The unbound depths seduce, and lust for death
Might seize whole peoples too,
And a holy end strikes bold towns

That have given their best, year after year
Pursuing their work; the earth grows green,
And art that's long lies under stars
In silence, like a man in prayer

On his knees in the sand, willingly vanquished
Before that matchless one; man himself,
The artist, he smashed his work
With his own two hands to honor the high ones.

Yet they aren't less inclined to hold man dear,
They love us back as they are loved
And often block man's course
That he might long enjoy the light.

And not only does the eagle throw
His young from the nest so they won't stay
With him too long; he who rules
Drives us out too with a fitting prod.

Praise be to those who went to rest
And fell before their time, for even they,
Sacrificed like first-fruits
Of the harvest, even they have found their lot.

The town lay on the Xanthus' shores in Grecian times,
But now, like the glorious ones who rest there,
Fate has snuffed out
The town's holy light of day.

The people of Xanthus didn't die in open battle
But by their own hand. And as the wondrous legend,
Reaching us from the East, describes,
What happened there was dreadful beyond measure.

The kindness of Brutus incensed them. For
When the fire had broken out, he, though leading
His troops in a siege of the gates,
Offered to aid the town,

Yet the servants he sent were thrown
From the walls. The fire flamed
Higher and the Xanthians rejoiced,
And Brutus stretched his hand to them,

And they were beside themselves. Hue and cry
Arose and rejoicing. The men and their wives then
Threw themselves on the flames, and boys
Plunged from rooftops or on their fathers' swords.

It's not wise to defy heroes. But
It was prepared long ago. The town's forefathers,
When they were once besieged,
And the Persian foe pressed hard upon the city walls,

They too grabbed river reeds and set the town
Ablaze so the Persians would find mere open land instead of town.
And the flames that flew to holy Aether
Took house and temple away, and the people too were taken up.

The children had heard all this, and doubtless such
Legends are good, for they remind us
Of the highest, yet still we stand in need
Of one to interpret the holy lore.

Voice of the People [Second version]
BY FRIEDRICH HÖLDERLIN
Translated by Michael Hamburger
(from *Friedrich Hölderlin: Poems and Fragments*, 239–43)

The voice of God I called you and thought you once,
In holy youth; and still I do not recant!
No less indifferent to our wisdom
Likewise the rivers rush on, but who does

Not love them? Always too my own heart is moved
When far away I hear those foreknowing ones,
The fleeting, by a route not mine but
Surer than mine, and more swift, roar seaward,

For once they travel down their allotted paths
With open eyes, self-oblivious, too ready to
Comply with what the gods have wished them,
Only too gladly will mortal beings

Speed back into the All by the shortest way;
So rivers plunge — not movement, but rest they seek —
Drawn on, pulled down against their will from
Boulder to boulder — abandoned, helmless —

By that mysterious yearning toward the chasm;
Chaotic deeps attract, and whole peoples too
May come to long for death, and valiant
Towns that have striven to do the best thing,

Year in, year out pursuing their task — these too
A holy end has stricken; the earth grows green,
And there beneath the stars, like mortals
Deep in their prayers, quite still, prostrated

On sand, outgrown, and willingly, lies long art
Flung down before the Matchless; and he himself,
The man, the artist with his own two
Hands broke his work for their sake, in homage.

Yet they, the Heavenly, to men remain well-disposed,
As we love them so they will return our love
And lest too briefly he enjoy the
Light, will obstruct a man's course to ruin.

And not the eagle's fledgelings alone their sire
Throws out of eyries, knowing that else too long
They'd idle — us the Ruler also
Goads into flight with a prong that's fitting.

Those men I praise who early lay down to rest,
Who fell before their time, and those also, those
Like first-fruits of the harvest offered
Up — they were granted a part, a portion.

By Xanthos once, in Grecian times, there stood
The town, but now, like greater ones resting there,
Because a destiny ordained it
Xanthos is lost to our holy daylight.

But not in open battle, by their own hands
Her people perished. Dreadful and marvellous
The legend of that town's destruction,
Travelling on from the East, has reached us.

The kindliness of Brutus provoked them. For
When fire broke out, most nobly he offered them
His help, although he led those troops which
Stood at their gates to besiege the township.

Yet from the walls they threw all the servants down
Whom he had sent. Much livelier then at once
The fire flared up, and they rejoiced, and
Brutus extended his arms towards them,

All were beside themselves. And great crying there,
Great jubilation sounded. Then into flames
Leapt man and woman; boys came hurtling
Down from the roofs or their fathers stabbed them.

It is not wise to fight against heroes. But
Events long past prepared it. Their ancestors
When they were quite encircled once and
Strongly the Persian forces pressed them,

Took rushes from the rivers and, that their foes
Might find a desert there, set ablaze their town;
And house and temple — breathed to holy
Aether — and men did the flame carry off there.

So their descendants heard, and no doubt such lore
Is good, because it serves to remind us of
The Highest; yet there's also need of
One to interpret these holy legends.

Notes

INTRODUCTION

1. All citations from *The Trojan Women* in this introduction refer to the Richmond Lattimore translation of the Chicago edition unless otherwise noted.

2. Nicole Loraux makes a similar argument in *The Mourning Voice*, as she compares Euripides's *Trojan Women* to Sartre's modern rendition of it. She situates Sartre's modernity in the partisan fervor with which his victims blame their conquerors. In contrast, the ancient playwright refrains from engaging in wars of words and concentrates on mourning as the counteruniversal to violence. See the first chapter, entitled "Greek Tragedy: Political Drama or Oratorio," 1–13.

3. This is the adjective used by Hecuba to describe Cassandra's madness (line 170).

4. One could find numerous examples of this gesture in contemporary theory, as well as ascribe to them different genealogies. I limit myself to a well-known and oft-cited instance: Walter Benjamin's remark that fascism is the aestheticization of politics in his essay "The Work of Art in the Age of Mechanical Reproduction" (242) has generated an abundance of commentary that reads any visionary moment of supraindividuation as a potential alarm of fascism. Giorgio Agamben cites Pierre Klossowski's account, according to which Benjamin himself had accused Georges Bataille and his Acéphale group of "working for fascism" because of the importance that myth and sacrifice had in their social philosophy (*Homo Sacer* 113). Agamben sides with this criticism as well, but it is Jean-Luc Nancy's *The Inoperative Community* that cements it. Taking up the question of myth and community that preoccupied Bataille, Nancy suggests that any impulse to transcend oneself risks becoming a mythical (and as such, delusional and violent) attempt to elevate humanity into an infinite state, thus denying mortality through acts of self-aggrandizement that, at the limit, lead to fascism. For a detailed analysis of this, see also Nikolopoulou, "Elements of Experience."

5. Loraux writes of tragedy's challenge to civic rationality in the epigrammatic summary of her third chapter: "Tragedy, as opposed to civic discourse, expresses ineffable grief by means of the oratorio" (26). Later she adds, "By inviting the reader to listen to the mourning voice in tragedy I wish not only to emphasize listening over seeing in theatrical representation, but also song over discourse (*logos*)" (54).

6. E. P. Coleridge's more literal translation renders this even more acutely: "O woe is me! trembling, quaking limbs, support my footsteps! away! to face the day that begins thy slavery" (27).

7. Eagleton reads the history of tragedy along political lines, distinguishing and critiquing two modern traditions that have pronounced the end of tragedy: the conservative one, which he aligns with Nietzsche, laments that tragedy is no longer possible, while the progressive one has traditionally thought tragedy to be undesirable, since it risks legitimizing suffering (21). His project, similar to some extent to mine, is to recuperate tragedy's progressive political possibility for our world; however, in sidelining Nietzsche's end of tragedy as a conservative misappropriation of tragedy, Eagleton himself falls prey to an optimism that thinks that the understanding of the tragic is a means toward social amelioration. While this might in part be the case, tragedy exceeds the social project, since it refuses to conceal the real in favor of pointing only to the ideal. Both Marxism and poststructuralism—the former at least actually committed to social change, the latter only theoretically preoccupied with it—converge in the discourse of amelioration. They are both versions of messianism, of "the impossible," in contrast to tragedy's realist pessimism, which shows human nature as it is and not only as it will (not) come to be.

8. As this book will go on to address, the same critique of tragedy is offered by many thinkers grouped under the rubric of poststructuralism, who are themselves also idealist in many respects. Where Marxism at least still dares to entertain pragmatic solutions for a better world, however, much poststructuralist rhetoric often discourages and disables any programmatic engagement with worldly problems, for whose sake, nonetheless, it claims to launch its critiques.

9. Anguished by her daughter's madness, Hecuba is ashamed to show her in that state to the Greeks, who will further humiliate her (line 171).

10. See Marx, "The Eighteenth Brumaire of Louis Bonaparte": "Hegel remarks somewhere that all great, world-historical facts and personages occur, as it were, twice. He has forgotten to add: the first time as tragedy, the second as farce" (594). This text was published initially in 1852.

11. The list of thinkers and artists belonging to each of these camps in France, Germany, or England could be quite long, although romanticism alone, with its diverse philosophical and artistic corpus both in England and the continent, can upset such a neat mapping. However, I employ this term "romanticism" for heuristic purposes insofar as it signals a decisive turn in late modernity. Without attempting a thorough list, I will mention a few representative names of the eighteenth century in Germany, since these thinkers are discussed to some extent in the book: Johann

Joachim Winckelmann is neoclassicism's most famous proponent, while Gotthold Ephraim Lessing, Friedrich Hölderlin, and Immanuel Kant count among its detractors.

12. Nietzsche concludes his essay "On the Uses and Disadvantages of History for Life" with the Greek example.

> There were centuries during which the Greeks found themselves faced by a danger similar to that which faces us: the danger of being overwhelmed by what was past and foreign, of perishing through "history." They never lived in proud inviolability; their "culture" was, rather, for a long time a chaos of foreign, Semitic, Babylonian, Lydian, Egyptian forms and ideas, and their religion truly a battle of all the gods of the East: somewhat as "German culture" and religion is now a struggling chaos of all the West and of all past ages. And yet, thanks to that Apollonian oracle, Hellenic culture was no mere aggregate. The Greeks gradually learned *to organize the chaos* by following the Delphic teaching and thinking back to themselves, that is, to their real needs, and letting their pseudo-needs die out. Thus they again took possession of themselves; they did not long remain the overburdened heirs and epigones of the entire Orient; after hard struggle with themselves and through protracted application of that oracle, they even became the happiest enrichers and augmenters of the treasure they had inherited and the first-born and models for all future cultured nations. (122–23)

13. See Nietzsche, *The Birth of Tragedy*, first published in 1872.

14. Elsewhere in *The Birth of Tragedy*, and in other works, Nietzsche understands that Socrates is as much the tragic as he is the theoretical man. This position is more consonant with my reading of Socrates in this project: Socratic philosophy and tragedy are complementary. That the Ideas can never be achieved in human life is the philosophical equivalent of the following tragic truth: human reason and language can never fully explain or dispel the larger forces that govern mortal life. To think this would be hubristic—the delusion (*Wahn*) of theory Nietzsche describes. I have thus amended Kaufmann's rendering of *Wahn* (illusion) with "delusion."

15. Opposing modernity's "theoretical optimism," Nietzsche preferred Hellenism's "pessimism of *strength*." Nietzsche uses this expression in his preface to *The Birth of Tragedy*, titled "Attempt at Self-Criticism" (17), to describe a temper that affirms the abyss instead of resorting to the coping mechanisms of denial and rationalization of life's terror.

16. Nietzsche's appeal to poststructuralism owes largely to his attack on classicism as tradition. However, this requires overlooking the ways in which theory itself has by now come to resemble the barren antiquarianism Nietzsche so disliked in nineteenth-century classicism. To realize this turn of events requires us to *become* Nietzsche rather than to apply Nietzsche. On Nietzsche's critique of the idealist bias underlying the methods of nineteenth-century classicists, see Porter, *Nietzsche and the Philology of the Future*. Porter explains that Nietzsche attacked the classicists for thinking that they could reconstitute a total—namely, ideal—object out of archaeological

fragments without reflecting on the hermeneutic circle of their method: archaeology reconstitutes Greece from found artifacts; yet to ascertain what is Greek about them, the archaeologist must have a prior idea of Greece (201). Thus classicism is a cryptomodernism, suffering from a presentism it wishes to conceal (Porter 202). However, Nietzsche's attack on idealism does not avoid idealist-romantic pitfalls, and for this reason I do not entirely agree with all of Nietzsche's extremes. To assume that problematizing the archaeological method leaves us knowing nothing of the Greeks—to the point that the Greeks are reduced to being only a topos of philosophical speculation—is the other pole of the same (Hegelian) idealism by which all historical facts disappear and history is reborn as a subject of idealist philosophy.

17. Except, apparently, Plato's epistemology. In his reading of the *Phaedrus*, Giovanni R. F. Ferrari argues that Socrates raises myth and mythical explanation to the status of an epistemological model (12).

18. See also Vassilis Lambropoulos's "On the Notion of the Tragedy of Culture," in which he defines the tragic as being "not a continuation of ancient theatrical practices but an adaptation of dramatic theory for metaphysical purposes" (233).

19. Even though within the general humanities the term "theory" often functions as an exclusive synonym for this other, less philosophically rigorous poststructuralism—namely, the literary theoretical, or critical theoretical kind—I forewarn the reader that I use "theory" in both these registers: while it sometimes designates specific approaches within the post-1960s landscape of literary and critical theory, it mostly signifies the reflexive mode of inquiry that includes philosophy and all other fields relying on discursive accounts, in contrast to the sphere of tragedy, art, and creativity in general. I do hope that the context around each of these instances makes it sufficiently clear when I refer to theory's limited, disciplinary capacity or to its larger definition as a rationalist mode of explanation.

20. Strangely, though, Plato's sense of deferral—namely, the fact that the Ideas can never be fulfilled on earth but only serve as celestial guides of infinite ascent—is viewed by deconstruction as a violent, idealist metaphysics that privileges another world over this one, as it does infinitude over finitude. Jacques Derrida's deferral, while sharing a similarly idealist structure of futurity, is said to overcome Plato's by evoking a quasi idealism that translates infinite deferral into an immanent historical horizon. It could be argued, however, that this translation does not avoid, but may even commit, a violence potentially worse than the one Plato is accused of: the violence of believing that the chasm that separates imperfect life from the ideal or the "impossible" (the latter is a favorite topos of deconstruction) can be surmounted, at least through multiple theorizations if not in actuality.

21. See again Nancy, *The Inoperative Community*, particularly "Myth Interrupted," 43–70.

22. I am not referring to the field of classics, where scholarly interest in tragedy hardly needs legitimation, but to works in continental philosophy and critical theory, which continue to address the notions of tragedy and the tragic long after these fields

have theorized tragedy's end. The bibliography is extensive, but some sample titles from the side of continental philosophy include: David Farrell Krell's *The Tragic Absolute: German Idealism and the Languishing of God*, Dennis Schmidt's *Germans and Other Greeks: Tragedy and Ethical Life*, Véronique Fóti's *Epochal Discordance: Hölderlin's Philosophy of Tragedy*, Miguel de Beistegui and Simon Sparks's edited volume *Philosophy and Tragedy*, and Philippe Lacoue-Labarthe's interpretation of the Holocaust as historical rupture through Hölderlin's tragic caesura in *Heidegger, Art, and Politics: The Fiction of the Political*. As these titles indicate, however, their interest is chiefly in tragedy's modern translation from German idealism onward because, the argument goes, Greek tragedy can never be approached in itself—that is, outside its philosophical historicity and beyond its service to the modern search for absolute rifts. More culturally and politically inflected examples could be Judith Butler's *Antigone's Claim: Kinship between Life and Death*, with which I take issue in chapter 6, and Terry Eagleton's *Sweet Violence: The Idea of the Tragic*.

23. See, for instance, Derrida's work on democracy in *The Politics of Friendship* (44) and Nancy's in *The Truth of Democracy*. Both are attempts to configure the shape of a community within a democratic matrix, even though such a shape may indeed not be reducible to an already existing political system. Hence, Derrida emphasizes democracy's futurity, and Nancy asserts that democracy must be thought not simply as one among different kinds of polity but as the most impossible yet necessary dream of being human. Even the more pragmatic democratic theories, such as multiculturalism and its politics of identity as performance, assume this futural thrust of an ever-expanding inclusion of alterities (this is Butler's politics in *Antigone's Claim*). No matter how vehemently contemporary thought disavows the notions of perfectibility and ideality that inhere in such theories, it does not substantively avoid them. A more classical political vocabulary would call all such gestures "utopian." However poststructuralism may wish to evade these classical categories, it often does little more than repeat them in different words.

24. My understanding of democracy, contra Nancy, remains within the realm he considers theoretically problematic: I understand it as one political system among others—albeit a more humane or preferable one to some of us. To turn democracy into *the* way of being singular-plural in the world is to offer an undemocratic conception of it. To extend democracy beyond the limits of the civic sphere, rendering it a descriptor of one's intimate sense of humanity, is to politicize everything—a dangerous totalitarianism that should not have escaped Nancy.

25. On Nietzsche's emphasis on philosophy as contestation, see Acampora, "'The Contest between Nietzsche and Homer.'" For Acampora, Nietzsche's idea that contestation fostered a spirit of excellence among the Greeks was extended into a performative element of Nietzsche's own thought insofar as he sought out worthy rivals with whom to battle in the history of philosophy: "It is clear that Nietzsche views his own writing as playing a role in creating a contentious arena for the pursuit of new standards of literary and philosophical excellence" (102).

26. For such a comprehensive survey of the history of tragedy's reception from romanticism to Heidegger's philosophy, I direct the reader to Lambropoulos, *The Tragic Idea*. While my project also begins with romanticism, it extends to tragedy's recent reception in the work of Butler, Foucault, Nancy, and Andrzej Warminski, among others. Additionally, my interest is topical rather than historical. I focus in more detail on certain questions that tragedy has raised rather than on a systematic survey of all the thinkers who contributed to its reception.

27. Language denotes negatively and relationally—that is also to say, *relatively* (e.g., a cat is not a bat, is not a mat, and is not a hat). Language as a differential system cannot speak the affirmative oneness of essence. Most telling in this context is the manner in which Roland Barthes, the great (post)structuralist, would finish his career searching for the referent—that thing-in-itself, the essence we irrevocably lost in our Kantian modernity. In *Camera Lucida*, attempting to find this truth in the field of intimacy through a particular photograph of his mother, Barthes complains that all her other photographs showed her "differentially, not essentially" (66): they confirmed who *she is not* but failed to reveal who *she is*. For Barthes, too, difference does not bring forth essence.

28. The relation of the *Apology* to tragic drama has already been highlighted by various scholars through different angles. For particular citations, see chapter 4. My reading will involve specifically the relation it draws between tragedy and the parrhesiastic demeanor.

29. This is why plot (*muthos*) is more important to Aristotle than character (*ethos*) (*Poetics* 1450a37–38). This point is also emphasized in Herbert Muller (8), Laura Jepsen (3), and T. R. Henn (17–18), among others.

1. ORIENT/OCCIDENT, ANCIENTS/MODERNS

From the sixth ode of Τὸ Ἄξιον Ἐστί, 66. Asterisks punctuate typographically the metric caesura within each line of the couplets and are used by the poet as well as the translators Jeffrey Carson and Nikos Sarris (*The Axion Esti* 155). The modern Greek poet, who acknowledged Hölderlin as a great influence, speaks here of the liminal geographical and historical destiny of Hellenism.

1. "To Casimir Urlich Böhlendorff, No. 236." This, the first of two letters to Böhlendorff in which Hölderlin elaborates on ancients and moderns, is the one from which I will be exclusively quoting in this chapter. The English translations of this letter, the remarks on Sophocles, and the essay on antiquity all refer to Thomas Pfau's edited volume *Essays and Letters on Theory*. The English translations of the poetic works refer to the bilingual edited volumes *Friedrich Hölderlin: Poems and Fragments*; *Hymns and Fragments*; *Hyperion and Selected Poems*; and *Odes and Elegies*. All citations from *Antigone* refer to the David Grene translation of the Chicago edition.

2. On this aspect of Hölderlin's reception, see Warminski, "Hölderlin in France," 30.

3. And a response to a nature that has nothing in common with ours: "Nicht mehr Natur, sondern Antwort auf eine Natur, die nicht die unsere ist" (Szondi 98).

4. Warminski relays Gombrich's attempt to differentiate between an Egyptian artwork and its (mis)appropriation by the Greeks to show that Gombrich, despite his good intentions, falls into the hermeneutic trap: the difference he detects between the two is itself the result of applying the already Greek art-historical assumptions during his comparison (42–44).

5. Lacoue-Labarthe's essay begins by defining speculative thought as tragedy; hence, its Aristotelian imitative and cathartic presuppositions follow.

6. The notion of unworking (*désœuvrement*, or inoperativity) comes from George Bataille's antiutilitarian philosophy; but in its deconstructive usage, it is severed from the anthropological framework of Bataille's thought. With this severance contemporary theory hopes to, but cannot, efface the anthropologically and historically motivated ethics behind its own taboo on tragic death; for why would the unworking of death be so ethically central to deconstruction, had it not been for the senseless deaths Europe had to come to terms with in its postwar introspection? In other words, reaching for the rhetorical death (the empty death) as an antidote to the tragic death (the meaningful death that theory has proclaimed universally impossible after the camps) is itself the result of an anthropologically and historically interested ethics. Ironically, this motivation has to be repressed so that contemporary thought cannot be critiqued for having instrumentalized death yet again in its effort to achieve the contrary. As to the politics of transcendentalizing and universalizing this "empty" death on the basis of the modern European war experience, it is both historically and morally problematic, to say the least.

7. Nietzsche's Dionysus does not remain simply the dialectical opposite of Apollo that he seems to be in *The Birth of Tragedy* (1872). The Dionysian changes dynamically throughout Nietzsche's work; and in *The Twilight of the Idols* (1888), it stands for a balanced totality of form and passion in the example of Goethe. In paragraph 49 of the fragment "Expeditions of an Untimely Man," Nietzsche writes of Goethe, "What he aspired to was *totality*; he strove against the separation of reason, sensuality, feeling, will. . . . But such a faith is the highest of all possible faiths: I have baptised it with the name of *Dionysus*" (102–3). Still, paragraph 4 of the next fragment, "What I Owe to the Ancients," seems to contradict this: "We are affected quite differently when we probe the concept 'Greek' which Winckelmann and Goethe constructed for themselves and find it incompatible with that element out of which Dionysian art evolved—the orgy. I have, in fact, no doubt that Goethe would have utterly excluded anything of this kind from the possibilities of the Greek soul. *Consequently Goethe did not understand the Greeks*" (108–9). Of course, it could well be that Goethe's misreading of the Greeks does not affect his own stature as a Dionysian artist in Nietzsche's eyes.

8. See again Kitto's passage on the Greek middle, which I quote in my introduction. A likely reason for why the Greeks have persisted as a locus of philosophical inquiry is that they were neither completely reflexive nor completely naïve, neither completely mimetic nor completely abstract. They enjoyed the precarious but also felicitous position of knowing just enough yet not suffering from the anxiety of

influence. In them, one recognizes the beginnings of self-conscious thought, before it has come to paralyze the creative energies.

9. Reinhardt's distinction between the betrayed mortals of Sophocles and the divine certainty that supersedes all suffering in Aeschylus is largely convincing. But once particular tragedies are considered, this general comparison does not always hold. *Antigone* is a case in point: On the one hand, she is abandoned by the city and by her sister, betrayed by the divine justice she serves and that cannot spare her; she says that much in her lamentation. On the other, her blood tie is never to be questioned, her belonging is irrevocable, and she is absolutely certain of the welcome she will receive once she joins her dead. The riddle of Antigone may be exactly this: invented by a Sophoclean worldview of strife, she behaves with the certainty of an Aeschylean character. This is the reason Hölderlin read her as a "fallback" caesura to earlier Greek religiosity.

10. For a different perspective on whether *Antigone* or *Oedipus Tyrannus* is the most Greek of tragedies for Hölderlin, see Krell, "A Small Number of Houses in a Universe of Tragedy." Krell disagrees with both Lacoue-Labarthe and Dastur that *Antigone* is the more profoundly Greek tragedy, maintaining that they confuse the character of Antigone with the actual play. For Krell, Hölderlin understands the structure of *Oedipus Tyrannus* to be still the truly Greek tragedy. The deathless death belongs to *Oedipus at Colonus*, which is the Hesperian play, not *Oedipus Tyrannus*, where the word is still as murderously factual as it could be (Krell, "A Small Number of Houses," 116n11).

11. For the maternal aspects of Antigone's relation to Polyneices, see Jacobs, "Dusting Antigone."

12. This division is rearticulated in Hegel's aesthetics as the division between symbolic art and classical art. The former is the Oriental form of art par excellence, where the form—namely, the material sensuousness of the presentation—overwhelms the content of the work, while the latter achieves the ideal balance between form and content, which means that the form of the classical work is further spiritualized than it was in symbolic art.

13. This idea of the Greeks awaiting completion is resonant in Heidegger's "Hegel and the Greeks." Warminski also repeats it inasmuch as he reads the Greeks as incapable of reading themselves. For a more recent elaboration of it in relation to Hölderlin's translation of *Antigone*, see Augst, "Difference Becomes Antigone."

14. The figure of Oedipus is poignant because his search for his lost origin dramatizes the Hesperian (that is, Hölderlin's own) search for origin in the antique world.

15. Signs of this rupture were in place by the end of the seventeenth century, when the quarrel of ancients and moderns actually began. For a historical exposition of this quarrel, see DeJean, *Ancients against Moderns*.

16. David Irwin introduces his edition of Winckelmann's texts: "Winckelmann is also significant as a forerunner of modern art historians, recounting the art of a past

culture not merely as a chronological sequence of events, or of artists' lives, but in terms of evolving styles" (3).

17. Though this project involves the antitragic ethics of French thinkers such as Blanchot, Derrida, Levinas, and Nancy, the French reception of tragedy has been more productive in other quarters: Sartre, Barthes, and Simone Weil, among others, have offered more sympathetic readings of tragedy and understood its necessity for modern ethics.

18. This ineluctability of the Greeks is at the heart of the expression "the tyranny of Greece over Germany," which, ever since the 1935 publication of E. M. Butler's book by the same title, has become a staple in discussions of Germany's reception of the Greeks, and of the political dangers to which this distorted identification has led in the twentieth century.

19. That we may have entered modernity through an inaugural translation of Judaic (personal) morality and a simultaneous repression of Hellenic (political) aestheticism is an argument compellingly made by Vassilis Lambropoulos in *The Rise of Eurocentrism*. Lambropoulos's work is interested in restoring the sociopolitical dimension of interpretive practice, which he understands to have suffered from the modern insistence on individual autonomy—the sense, that is, that one reads and interprets a text all alone. In Lambropoulos's genealogical study, the rise of autonomy resulted from the Protestant Reformation's preference for individual interpretation of scripture that reflects a personal relation to God and that was itself a translation of a Judaic hermeneutic practice. Even though my current project defends a certain understanding of individual freedom, I am not opposed to Lambropoulos's critique of individualism as a political hindrance. To the contrary, my defense of autonomy specifically within a tragic context is predicated on the radical political potential that such a notion of autonomy entails: the exceptional tragic individual is also an example of political anticonformism. I am thus largely sympathetic to his genealogy also for the following reason: in exchanging Greek aestheticism for the morality of a personal relation with God, the moderns have also forgotten an important political dimension that underlined the sacredness of tragic theater specifically. Theater as ritual was experienced communally, thus also offering a model of political reading—albeit not a reading of scripture but of an event. Still, given recent European history and the more recent advent of identity politics, it is not surprising that Lambropoulos's observations met with pointed, if not dismissive, language in the work of Jonathan Boyarin. Boyarin's critique, which makes it sound as if Lambropoulos is hallucinating the profound (and for that reason also invisible) forgetting of Hellenism in modern thought, is quite problematic: because Boyarin's education taught him "to believe that European universalism was indeed Greek in inspiration and Christian in effect," he rejects the idea that "such figures as Auerbach, Horkheimer and Adorno, and Derrida operate on a more elite level of cultural criticism and therefore represent vestiges of a more profound and powerful regime of knowledge" that is anti-Hellenic (138). The appeal to the general educational culture as a proof of the continuing

importance of the Greeks, however, does not engage Lambropoulos's genealogical point that reveals in this Greco-Judaic translation a process through which modernity has come to articulate *philosophically* an entirely new set of universal values. This philosophical translation, whether it concerns Adorno and Horkheimer's *Dialectic of Enlightenment* or Derrida's critique of the violence of Greek metaphysics, does indeed involve hostile positions against the notions of mimeticism, mythology, self-sameness, and so on—in short, "Hellenic" notions. This hostility is not merely occasional, as Boyarin suggests. It is not a matter of a thinker's cultural slip that can be corrected with a lesson on multicultural diversity. The hostility is and must remain *necessarily* systemic if it hopes to yield a legible philosophical translation or revaluation from one system to the other. For example, Boyarin accuses Lambropoulos of capitalizing on one unfortunate quote where Derrida sweepingly identifies the Greek metaphysics of the "Same" as the "origin or alibi of all oppression in the world" (Derrida qtd. in Lambropoulos 229–30). One quote, Boyarin contends, cannot be representative of how Derrida views the Greeks (Boyarin 133). This certainly sounds reasonable. However, while it is true that Derrida does not mention the Greeks by name every time he calls for a deconstruction of a classical concept, it is in fact the Greek philosophical edifice and its founding assumptions *as a whole* that he must destabilize if his deconstruction is to have any systemic efficacy. And while I do understand the objection that Derrida is neutral because he does not ultimately demand the eradication of the deconstructed categories, I also understand that this neutrality is not always so effective, nor even a desideratum in all cases. In my own educational counterexample to Boyarin's, I do not see at all that the terms "presence" and "self" are being as neutrally received by the current academic establishment as the terms "absence" and "alterity." Had this been the case, I would not have engaged with this project. In fact, Lambropoulos is not unique in noting this Protestant philosophical translation and sublation of Hellenism into Judaism. Before him, George Santayana had argued that the providential element of German idealism "is a revealed philosophy. It is the heir of Judaism. It could never have been formed by free observation of life and nature, like the philosophy of Greece or of the Renaissance. It is Protestant theology rationalized" (11). Santayana added, "In this [German idealist] philosophy imagination that is sustained is called knowledge, illusion that is coherent is called truth, and will that is systematic is called virtue" (19). It seems to me that Boyarin's critical stance against Lambropoulos responds *mostly* in an identitarian fashion to a genealogy of modernity, which he either unwittingly or programmatically reads as itself being motivated *only* by identitarian concerns: in other words, he reduces Lambropoulos's insight to a "thinking in Greek"—a Greek complaint, that is, and a rather unfounded one at that.

20. See "Brod und Wein" ("Bread and Wine," in *Hyperion and Selected Poems*, 178–89) and "Der Einzige" ("The Only One," in *Hymns and Fragments*, 82–87), in which Dionysus and Christ are both spoken of as gods of appearance and disappearance.

21. The disincarnate Hebrew god is most often contrasted to the Christian incarnation. However, it is important to note that the Judeo-Greek contrast with respect to personhood and embodiment stems from the times preceding Christianity, since Greek art (particularly in the form of tragedy) and philosophy (in the person of Socrates) insisted as much on the sensuous as on the spiritual. On the currently much contested issue of cultural continuity in Greece, Apostolos Apostolopoulos offers an erudite study, in which the ancient Greek insistence on embodiment forms a subtle but continuous undercurrent of the Greek experience from antiquity to the present. Apostolopoulos writes of a particular form of "incarnation," as he calls it—the tragic-Socratic incarnation—which recurs as a model of conduct in various seminal figures of modern Greek literature and politics. His book marks an untimely intervention within contemporary Greek criticism, since the latter—in its neophyte practice of multiculturalism—reduces a bit too hastily any claim of ancient influences, even by some of the most renowned and mindful modern Greek writers, to knee-jerk nationalism. While I share the worry about nationalism, I think that this kind of negativity, so typical of the work of criticism, misses the force of the creative endeavor that is by nature overarching, connective, and affirmative.

22. Though the victory of monotheism supports claims of cultural and philosophical continuity between ancient Hebrew and modern Jew, just as it immediately disables any similar modern Greek claim to the past on the basis of the conversion (see my note 27 in this chapter, on Fallmerayer's added racialized support of this cultural claim against the modern Greeks), it is fruitful to keep in mind that such division should not be historically hypostatized on either side. The literature on the mutually exclusive worldviews of Hellenism and Judaism competing for the parentage of the West is vast, while the old debate of "Athens versus Jerusalem" is still alive. As a representative, but by no means exhaustive, sample of works on this topic, see Matthew Arnold's "Hebraism and Hellenism," in *Culture and Anarchy*; Eric Auerbach's "Odysseus' Scar," in *Mimesis*, which proposes modern European literature as an heir of two opposing ancient models of writing—the Greek (open, all-disclosive) and the biblical (terse, mysterious); Lionel Gossman's "Philhellenism and Antisemitism," which claims European philhellenism to be predominantly a symptomatic byproduct of anti-Semitism—a claim itself corroborating Lambropoulos's observations of "mis-Hellenism" that Boyarin deems unfounded; finally, the distinction between Athens and Jerusalem (between reason and revealed religion) pervades Leo Strauss's work, but the secondary sources on this topic are too many to include here. In literature, the most enduring translation of Greek into Jew, effecting a parallel shift from ancient epic to modern novel, remains James Joyce's *Ulysses*.

23. Of course, the Greeks were not monotheistic, but the holy pathos Hölderlin ascribes to them allegorizes Oriental/Semitic piety as Greek nature. Warminski writes, "And if we understand Greek *nature* ('the fire from heaven,' 'holy pathos') as 'Oriental' or 'Egyptian'—as other Hölderlin texts would authorize us to do—such translation means transforming the Orient (the Egyptians)—that which is radically

foreign for us because it is not our foreignness—into Greece—that which is natural, national, proper, our own, and so forth" (35–36). In other words, by making the Greeks (who are our own foreigners) Orientals, we bring the Orientals (our irreducible foreigners) closer.

24. Again, I do not mean to suggest that poststructuralism is a unified discourse. I use this term somewhat synecdochically and thus with a permanent sense of unease, pressed by the lack of a better word, and for concision's sake. What it designates loosely is some of the dominant strains of postwar French thought and their literary-critical reception. Deconstruction and its ethicotheological offshoots, as well as several branches of critical theory, all privilege Judaic, or at least monotheistic, ethics and view history in terms of a futural, messianic temporality. For an analysis of the implications of Greek thought for poststructuralism's rethinking of the political, see Leonard, *Athens in Paris*.

25. On the notion of self-determination as violence, see de Vries and Weber, *Violence, Identity, and Self-Determination*. This is not the proper venue to go into specific arguments as to exactly when, for whom, and for what conscious and unconscious reasons Western theory has decided that political self-determination is a thing of the past, but this does not mean that such conclusion should pass by unsuspected. Suffice it to say this is another instance of the subordination of politics to ethics that has resulted, in part, from the idealist translation of tragedy into the tragic.

26. Such acts, whose sacrificial logic remains scandalously outdated for the modern mind, may range from the period of the Ottoman Empire, where insurrections had not simply a national but also a class character, to the German occupation and, more recently, to the struggle to overthrow the junta (1967–74).

27. One can only speculate in this vein about the racializing project of someone like Jakob Philipp Fallmerayer (1790–1861), whose "scientific" aim was to prove the "genetic" discontinuity between ancient and modern Greeks: "The race of the Hellenes has been wiped out in Europe. Physical beauty, intellectual brilliance, innate harmony and simplicity, art, competition, city, village, the splendor of column and temple—indeed, even the name has disappeared from the surface of the Greek continent.... Not the slightest drop of undiluted Hellenic blood flows in the veins of the Christian population of present-day Greece" (qtd. in Leeb 55).

28. His work is not available in English, but he is considered the founder of modern Greek historiography, having written a monumental, six-volume survey of Greek history from the ancient times to his present, arguing for cultural continuity.

29. See, for instance, the essays anthologized in Stephanos Pesmazoglou's Μύθοι και ιδεολογήματα στη σύγχρονη Ελλάδα, available only in Greek.

30. Given the timing of my book, many Germans would openly beg to differ with Pesmazoglou on this point, and Germany's official economic disenfranchisement of their European Union partner these days is one of the many expressions of how Europe has for a long time now felt no such resemblance with its former parent and current poor relative. Needless to say, the contemporary Turk, the *Gastarbeiter*, who by

implication also looks more like a Western European than like Genghis Khan according to Pesmazoglou, is not necessarily accepted as such by German society at large.

31. See, for instance, Gyömörey's *Ἡ δύση τῆς Δύσης* and Apostolopoulos's *Η Δύση των φαντασμάτων και η μέσα Ελλάδα* for this side of the debate. Gyömörey wrote his book originally in German and then translated it into Greek, while the other text is not available to non-Greek speakers. It is imperative to note that the treatment of continuity in both texts is by no means biological or deterministic. Rather, it is philosophical, literary, and cultural, focusing on the vicissitudes of the notions of freedom and justice from the time they structured the ancient world and its tragic predilections to the more recent history. Gyömörey offers a convincing link between the historical absence of a consolidated, rigid class structure in Greece from ancient times through Byzantium to modernity, and the related persistent attitude toward freedom in Greece's thinking and revolutionary past. On Apostolopoulos, see note 21 of this chapter. I wish to emphasize that what draws me to this notion of freedom is not its ethnically Greek provenance but the fact that it offers a practical expression of a nonabsolutist version of the individual, which is urgently needed in the wasteland of globalization. Equally, what is compelling about it is not its Greek continuity but rather its anachronistic insistence that today the individual may not (yet) be completely liquidated, its freedom not completely usurped, and that, symmetrically, the free individual does not have to signal automatically the bourgeois, atomistic specter so feared by poststructuralist theory.

32. The poetry of C. P. Cavafy, Andreas Kalvos, Angelos Sikelianos, George Seferis, and Odysseus Elytis is explicitly concerned with this relation to the ancient tradition and is available in English. I would also quote the renowned British classicist Bernard Knox, who wrote of the longevity of Greek language in a chapter aptly titled "The Continuity of Greek Culture": "The language inscribed on the fire-baked clay tablets found at Pylos, on the mainland, and at Knossos, on Crete, dating from about 1600 BC, is recognizably a primitive form of the language in which the newspapers of Athens are written today" (108). This chapter (107–30) also provides a rich historical and bibliographical discussion of the debates surrounding Greek continuity.

33. Gyömörey offers an interesting reading of the coalescence of Hellenism and Christianity around the common axis of antiauthoritarianism: viewing Jesus's teachings as a return to the earlier Hebrew prophetic tradition, which advocated divine authority against the official status quo of religion and against every archetype of domination, Gyömörey argues that Hellenism was indispensable in translating this antiauthoritarian thrust that was lost to the Jews in their postprophetic tradition (238–40).

34. Granted, Lacoue-Labarthe's Greece is simply an ideational construction—the Greece evoked by Hölderlin's text, in fact—but part of what interests me in this project is the not-so-innocent subtext of these inhuman historiographies.

35. The rise of postcolonial discourse has precipitated discussions of European territorialization in various areas of the world, but the complex mechanics of this

philosophical appropriation of Greece at the very historical moment that the modern Greeks were seeking to establish their national identity has received little to no attention in the English-speaking world. A notable exception is Stathis Gourgouris's *Dream Nation*, addressing the ambivalent, multilayered, and reciprocal relation between Enlightenment Europe and the nascent Greek state.

36. A good example of the hypostatization of necessity (or the Other) in continental philosophy is Emmanuel Levinas's *Existence and Existents*, in which being under the sway of the Other becomes the exclusive relation to Being—a condition that renders all resistance and all sense of subjective freedom impossible. This absolutization of the Other has become the dominant philosophical response to the Holocaust, with Maurice Blanchot, Jacques Derrida, Emmanuel Levinas, Jean-Luc Nancy, and Giorgio Agamben as some of its most eminent proponents. See also Simon Critchley's Levinasian reading of Racine's *Phèdre*, where he sums up Levinas's view of tragedy as follows: "Existence is not the experience of freedom profiled in rapture, ecstasy, or affirmation, but rather it is that which we seek to evade in a movement of flight that simply reveals—paradoxically—how deeply riveted we are to the fact of existence" ("I Want to Die" 170). This may be correct for the majority of human beings but absolutely not for the tragic hero or heroine; it is exactly the experience of freedom as affirmation to the point of hubris that firmly separates tragic existence from all others. For a critical gaze at Levinas's ethics, see Alford, "Emmanuel Levinas and Iris Murdoch."

37. This, Judith Butler's claim, I address in chapter 6.

38. Simon Goldhill's essay "Generalizing about Tragedy" presents a cultural history of the contestation of the term "tragic" as a potentially misleading philosophical generalization.

39. See Benardete, *Sacred Transgressions*, 3.

40. Another poststructuralist reception of Nietzsche is developed by Foucault, whose tragic understanding of genealogical practice I address in chapter 3.

41. Goldhill's prominent examples of the political appropriation of the tragic juxtapose nineteenth-century nationalism's claim to "suffering peoples" with the victimhood of identity politics. As particular examples of the latter sort, he cites rather jarringly the tragedy of the rape victim, of illness, and of the Palestinian people (46). This is not the place to venture into such a fraught political question, but I must admit that in the vast literature on the tragic in postwar scholarship, these are not the most visible cases that theorists attempt to appropriate, or even address. If anything, it has been the plight of the Jews that has become emblematic of a suffering so absolute in the "hierarchizing of tragic experience" (46) that it has necessitated a thinking beyond the tragic—a gesture that in Goldhill's own acerbic vocabulary (reserved in his essay for others) would be a claim to "unimpeachable status" (46).

42. As Charles Kahn explains, Heraclitus's charge against Homer mirrors the one against Hesiod. While Homer is wrong in wishing to end the strife between gods and men, because strife is necessary for the existence of the world, Hesiod misses the

principle of unity according to which night is the same as day. "Homer and Hesiod, the pre-eminent wise men and teachers of the Greeks, represent the general folly of mankind in failing to perceive the 'unapparent *harmonie*' in which the tension between opposing powers is as indispensable as their reconciliation within a larger unity" (Kahn 204).

43. In *Introduction to Metaphysics*, Heidegger distinguishes the early philosophical logos of the Greeks as not yet scientific but poetizing. Poetizing thinking, which still prioritizes thinking over its poetic dimension, enters into an intimate relation with thinking poetry, which prioritizes the poetic over thought. Heidegger identifies thinking poetry with tragedy, particularly of the Sophoclean kind: "The thinking of Parmenides and Heraclitus is still poetic, and here this means philosophical, not scientific.... In order to clarify this poetic thinking sufficiently in terms of its proper counterpart, we will now interrogate a thinking poetry of the Greeks. This poetry is tragedy—the poetry in which Greek Being and Dasein [a Dasein belonging to Being] were authentically founded" (154).

44. That this internal division of the Greeks is of structuring importance to any discussion of ancients and moderns is shown again in Heidegger's assessment of the split between early and classical Greek philosophy, where he aligns the former with the dawn of the thinking of Being and the latter with the forgetting of Being.

45. Whereas the bourgeois character of modern existence has obliged even the poets to succumb to its mechanistic outlook, trying to copy mechanically the rules of ancient prosody in their own practice, Hölderlin searches for a "lawful calculation": a form that befits the "living meaning" of the poem's content (*Essays and Letters* 101). Essentially, Hölderlin criticizes modern poetry for being a perfunctory calculation, thus lacking true measure and skill. For the Greeks, skill qua techne was a mode of disclosure, which means that craftsmanship itself partook in poesis. For the moderns, skill is simply a mechanical application, a series of dead rules superimposed on the work.

46. In his remarks on Sophocles's translations, Hölderlin discusses immeasurable measure in relation to time, hence, to fate and fatality. The formal expression of this measure in the plays is the caesura, or catastrophe, which Hölderlin identifies with the appearance of Teiresias. On immeasurable measure in Hölderlin, see Heidegger, "... Poetically Man Dwells ...," 220–21. For a discussion of the ethical implications of measure since Hölderlin, see Kleinberg-Levin, *Gestures of Ethical Life*.

47. The relevant passage on "second sailing" comes from *Phaedo* 99d, where Socrates explains the turn away from the natural world to the study of the human soul. This passage and the method it sets forth for philosophical inquiry are intricately rich and have generated extensive commentary. The most notable treatment of the second sailing occurs in the work of Seth Benardete, who views it as the most essential performative turn that all Platonic dialogues take—a turn we should not miss if we are to access the most profound aspects of the dialogue.

48. Plato's attack against the tragic poets is launched mostly through his critique of Homer, whose *Iliad* Plato interprets as the first tragic work. Relevant passages abound particularly in books 2 and 3: 2.379d–e (against Homer's portrayal of the arbitrariness of Zeus's divine justice); 2.381d–e and 2.383a–c (against Homer's and Aeschylus's claim that the gods are wizards and shape-shifters who deceive the mortals through dreams and misleading omens); and 3.386a–393e (against the *Iliad* and, to a lesser degree, the *Odyssey*, for their negative depiction of death, which undercuts the heroic ideal, as well as for their representation of lamentation, to which even a hero like Achilles succumbs).

49. While the category of the impossible enjoys otherwise a privileged position in contemporary ethical thought (for instance, that ethical decisions are required precisely at moments that render such decisions impossible constitutes a topos in Derridean and Levinasian ethics), the impossible in the case of our relation to antiquity is to be understood only in its prohibitive dimension: it currently sounds preposterous to evoke antiquity in any other terms than simply to disown it. Even to long for what one knows to be impossible—and we hardly long for possible things—is often dismissed as sentimentality, as if this longing were not itself a mode of an ethical relation to the past.

50. For one such commentary that reads this pious infidelity as our "patriotic turn"—that is, as the turn toward our proper method of presentation of the sacred—see Blanchot's concluding chapter in *The Space of Literature*, entitled "Hölderlin's Itinerary."

51. I am referencing here Heidegger's famous quote in an interview with *Der Spiegel*—"only a god can save us"; see Heidegger, "'Only a God Can Save Us,'" 107.

2. AN OLD QUARREL

1. For a rhetorical analysis of the topos of the end of art as rumor in modern aesthetics, see Eva Geulen's seminal study *The End of Art: Readings in a Rumor after Hegel*. I was fortunate to encounter her thoughts on this topic in her seminars, as she was preparing the manuscript. For reasons pertaining to the larger stakes of this book, my path has taken me in a different direction, but the intellectual force this topic still exerts on me today has its sources in the passion and brilliance of my teacher.

2. "παλαιὰ μέν τις διαφορὰ φιλοσοφίᾳ τε καὶ ποιητικῇ" (*Republic* 10.607b5–6). For the Greek original of the Platonic dialogues, I use the Loeb edition. For the English translations of the *Ion* (by Lane Cooper), of the *Republic* (by Paul Shorey), and of the *Laws* (by A. E. Taylor), I refer to *Plato: The Collected Dialogues*, edited by Edith Hamilton and Huntington Cairns.

3. First of all, that rhetoric is not the opposite of mimesis, but perhaps its worst example, is made amply clear in Plato's critique of the Sophists as persons who mimic rather than seek the truth. Secondly, assuming this Platonic critique of rhetoric to be unfair, it is still hard to see how rhetoric's ultradiscursive nature would be capable of piercing through the armor of representation and of aesthetic discourse, when aesthetics is already a metadiscourse on art rather than the creative experience itself.

On the contrary, cathartic mimeticism, which Warminski critiques in an unspoken—if also superficial—convergence with Plato, is a far more likely alternative. Coming to us from the nonrepresentational world of tragedy and acting as a kind of mental and physical contagion, catharsis cannot refer to reflexive (representational) structures.

4. I owe my familiarity with Wind's work on Plato to James Porter, who provided me with the reference. Wind's interest in the continuing influence of the ancients on the moderns—the field the Germans identify as *Das Nachleben der Antike*—guided his study on the importance of pagan myth for Renaissance art. In terms of his intellectual affiliations, he was a student of Ernst Cassirer and Erwin Panofsky, a friend of Aby Warburg, and a distinguished associate of the Warburg Institute in London.

5. Wind offers Lessing's and Schiller's aesthetics and Kant's critical philosophy as varying examples of modernity's delimitation of the human faculties to relatively independent domains (9–13). Wilde's, Baudelaire's, and Proust's decadence and *l'art pour l'art* doctrine further exemplify the modern penchant for division (16–19). In contradistinction, for Plato, the good soul, which was also the happy soul, was based on the harmony and mutual cooperation of its faculties: when one part exceeded the rest, it had to be brought back to equilibrium.

6. See his chapter entitled "Mimesis and the Best Life: Plato's Repudiation of the Tragic," 98–117.

7. The most notable examples in the *Republic* come from book 3, where Plato explicitly links lamentation with women and chastises Homer for feminizing the heroes, and even Zeus, each time he portrays them in grief (388a–d). As such, Achilles should not mourn Patroclus, nor should Priam supplicate for the return of Hector's body, nor should Zeus grieve the death of his son Sarpedon (388b–c).

8. For a defense of the complexity of the concept of mimesis in Plato's and Aristotle's texts among others, see again Halliwell, who argues convincingly that the ancient notion of mimesis was far more dynamic than its modern reduction to imitation.

9. Unless otherwise noted, all parenthetical citations of Agamben in this chapter refer to *The Man without Content*.

10. Wind understands Plato's prohibition unambiguously but not independently of Plato's complicated relationship to art: "The more certain we are that Plato's conceptual thinking was preceded by, and consummated, an impulse towards the dramatic and mimetic representation, the more clearly we recognize from his own writings how difficult he found it to adopt such a verdict, how greatly he valued Homer's poetry before resolving to resist its spell; and the more strongly we sense in the style of his early and middle dialogues the power of that plasticity whose dangers he so vividly portrays, the more extraordinary it seems to us that this man, who evinced such great artistic gifts would have turned against art" (1).

11. This becomes clearer in chapter 5 with my analysis of *The Bacchae*, where Dionysus punishes the ones who succumbed to his possession.

12. The English translation of Agamben has a typo: "fillets of wood" instead of Plato's "fillets of wool" (ἐρίῳ στέψαντες).

13. Plato makes this exception in *Republic* 10.607a4. *Laws* 7.801e1–4 allows for hymns to the gods and encomia to the good men, while 802a1–3 specifies that encomia should never be written about living men. It is also important to recall here that for Plato, the worst kind of imitative poetry is the theater, since it requires an immediate identification of the actor with the fictional character. Plato prefers narrative poetry for the distance it keeps between character and narrator.

14. See Hölderlin, "Remarks on 'Antigone,'" in *Essays and Letters on Theory*, 111. I discuss this in chapter 1.

15. See Agamben, *Homo Sacer*.

16. Agamben's slippage lies in collapsing the category of living being (ζῶον) into that of the animal as beast, when the latter is only a subset of the former. This, coupled with his Heideggerian distaste for everything pertaining to life, yields the following reading of Aristotle:

> As we shall see, central to praxis was the idea of the will that finds its immediate expression in an act, while, by contrast, central to poiesis was the experience of pro-duction into presence, the fact that something passed from nonbeing to being, from concealment into the full light of the work. The essential character of poiesis was not its aspect as a practical and voluntary process but its being a mode of truth understood as unveiling, ἀ-λήθεια. And it was precisely because of this essential proximity to truth that Aristotle, who repeatedly theorizes this distinction within man's "doing," tended to assign a higher position to poiesis than to praxis. According to Aristotle, the roots of praxis lay in the very condition of man as an *animal*, a living being: these roots were constituted by the very principle of motion (will, understood as the basic unit of craving, desire, and volition) that characterizes life. (68–69)

The problem is not with the distinctions Agamben finds; the problem is that he hypostatizes them as irreconcilable, even when they are complementary, capitalizing on the violent logic that stark oppositions generate. Aristotle's view of praxis is more expansive than Agamben allows. For instance, in the *Poetics*, Aristotle defines the tragic characters as beings in action (πράττοντας) (3.1448a22), showing that poetry is wedded to praxis. Indeed, one of Aristotle's translators, James Hutton, clarifies in an explanatory note that, insofar as Aristotle defines poetry as a mimetic art, the imitation of human action is of primary importance, and for this reason, Aristotle "dismisses the lyric parts of tragedy from the art of poetry, placing them with Music" (81n1). It is the sense of action that makes plot so vital to the *Poetics*. But more importantly, the objection again in this passage, as in *Homo Sacer*, should be to Agamben's implicit but categorical separation of zoe and bios (where zoe is misread as exclusively animalistic and bios as exclusively human), when in fact such distinctions overlap in Aristotle. I take this opportunity to note that my earlier uncritical view of Agamben with respect to these distinctions, which is evident in previous publications, has since changed.

17. Obviously, the Greek distinction between poesis and techne is not translatable in the English term "art." When necessary, I foreground this Greek distinction, but I retain overall the term "art" to designate this other way of knowing, which philosophy has contested as illegitimate.

18. See note 16 of this chapter. It is at this point that Agamben cites Aristotle's distinction between poesis and praxis as an example of a thinking that did not limit all human activity to praxis. Again, insofar as Agamben identifies praxis with the modern obsession to produce commodities and that alone, he has a point in wishing to find an alternative mode of thinking. However, the problem is that praxis in Aristotle does not describe exclusively instrumental kinds of production. Instead of rereading ancient texts with modern meanings, it might be fruitful to enrich our impoverished concepts with the more expansive resonance of the ancient terms, at least when these ancient terms seem to offer wiser alternatives.

19. Interestingly, as poststructuralism launches its critique against the abstraction of metaphysics, it champions mostly abstract art—art without content and without any specificity except that of the medium.

20. The first chapter, entitled "The Most Uncanny Thing," discusses the uncanniness inherent in Kantian disinterest: because the artist is, above all others, interested in the work, he or she is also deemed to be art's most inappropriate beholder.

21. For the notion of inspiration as both a threat to the work and the only guarantee for a great work, see Blanchot, "Orpheus's Gaze."

22. Again, I am referring to the modern term "art," which designates any creative activity at large but which for the Greeks meant techne.

23. The prefatory note by Edith Hamilton and Huntington Cairns to their translation of this dialogue observes that up until the time of Socrates, "in all the arts in Athens the emotions and intellect had worked together. There was a balance of power. That is the uniqueness of Greek art; it is an intellectual art. In the *Ion* Socrates disputes the possibility of such a balance" (Hamilton and Cairns 215). To say that Greek art is an intellectual art may be an overstatement. Instead, the sense of this fragile balance between intellect and emotion, exteriority and interiority, has been often celebrated in later theorizations of Greek art in the West. Either way, however, the interesting point Socrates introduces in this dialogue is the very difference between cognition and affect. Whether art was more or less intellectual or emotional before did not matter much, because the difference between emotion and intellection as such was not yet in place.

24. Although this issue falls beyond the scope of the present inquiry, I wish to stress that the problematic of imitation becomes even more complex once we consider Plato's definition of education in terms of imitating role models. If art is deceptive because of its imitative quality and if education—the very process of instilling ethical and political principles in the future citizen—is itself based on imitation, then any simple equation of imitation and deception is immediately foreclosed, or Plato would run the risk of undermining entirely his own ethicopolitical stakes in education.

25. The passage concerns the *Theogony*'s tale of Uranus's violence against his children and his eventual castration by his son Cronus.

26. Agamben borrows this distinction from Jean Paulhan.

27. See Heidegger's epilogue in "The Origin of the Work of Art."

28. In relation to this, see chapter 3, where I discuss Heidegger's desubjectivized understanding of truth as something that aligns him with scientific objectivism, despite his own critique of science's propositional mode of thinking.

29. The argument would go that Hegel is inevitable because he does not simply speculate about the end of art. He actually points to what was already the modern historical reality. It was not Hegel who made the artist a critic; it was the romantic poets who were doing that already, turning art into pure reflection. Hegel himself even bemoans the submission of the creative force to the critical faculty and certainly disapproves of the self-conscious romantic irony. This is all very true; but insofar as this Western narrative of metaphysical nihilism assumes the Greeks at the origin of its line of thinking, the scheme becomes highly debatable. Even Plato, who often serves as the straw man of Western metaphysics, did not theorize art in a logical, metaphysical manner.

30. I am indebted to a long and inspiring e-mail correspondence with my friend and colleague Robert Scott Hubbard regarding the linearity of modern Hegelian temporality versus the nonlinear, noncausal thinking of Greek recurrence. I quote here from personal correspondence:

> Hegel's dialectic does work in a spiral.... Inspired I am sure by Dante as he was in many ways, [Hegel] creates his system in a series of *cercles dantesques* so to speak. ... I do not believe the Greeks saw history in this way; it was not that predictable to them, even after the fact. If X happens, then Y follows, but who is to say when or if X ever happens? It is certainly not pre-destined to happen, so history or time is not cyclical in its adherence to any law; just that human nature being what it is, these things are bound to happen, and when they do, Nemesis will strike.

In other words, human nature, despite whatever radical changes modern philosophy has seen in it, partakes in a fundamental continuity, a kind of cyclical repetition in the following sense: should circumstances arise that are similar to past events, human nature inclines to reproduce similar responses. Recurrence is not caused by outside causal forces; rather, human proclivity ensures the repeatability of an event. To quote Hubbard again: "[The Greeks] saw time as a recurrence. Now my understanding of this is not like watching the same movie over and over and over; of course, it does not exactly repeat itself. But there is a tendency for human actions (choice) to tend to the same ends (fate) for similar or the same kinds of actions." That our logic of improvement does not allow for recurrence does not mean that the Greek conception of history is any less realistic. After Hegel, we still keep speaking about history repeating itself, and we still find ourselves incapable of preventing its crimes. This remains the longest-standing wisdom of Greek realism, of which tragedy has proved the most enduring form.

31. I mean this both in the sense of the Hegelian spiral progress and even more strongly in its common political connotations.

32. It is Kant, not Hegel, who preserves art's nonconceptual supersensuousness in modernity. Kant's third critique defines the judgment of the beautiful as intelligible but nonconceptual (44).

3. HABEAS CORPUS

1. All citations from Foucault in this chapter are from *Fearless Speech*.

2. This is Ian Johnston's punchier rendition of Kaufmann and Hollingdale's "we are not 'men of knowledge' with respect to ourselves" from Nietzsche's *Genealogy of Morals* (15). Johnston's rendition is available online.

3. My references to Pryor's work on parrhesia come from a paper he delivered at a conference on *Normalization, Exclusion, Excess*, at California State University, Stanislaus, October 8, 2005.

4. For an overview of Foucault's career and its defining turns, see Eric Paras's intellectual biography *Foucault 2.0: Beyond Power and Knowledge*. As Sam Rocha writes in a review of the book, Paras "reveals that Foucault ended his life recovering the free subject he so famously (or infamously) put to rest," adding that, when it comes to Foucault's thought, "images of a seamless, anti-subject-power/knowledge-systematist, who began his journey with one project in mind and saw it through to the end, are ... the ones that we should consider suspect."

5. Kant's critical philosophy of transcendental subjectivity left us with this legacy. Heidegger's language of Being came to transcend that of the subject, but in historicizing Being, Heidegger radicalized instead of remedied modern relativism, which began with the discourse of the subject. A further parenthesis: I am aware that to read Foucault's outside with any hint of nonimmanence will be characterized as unorthodox by many. Foucault's undermining of ontological hierarchies and theoretical transcendentals has led most of his current readers to assign him to a place of pure immanence. I insist, at the risk of being called a "fool," on not reading him as statically: "Today new fools, or even the same ones reincarnated, are astonished because the Foucault who had spoken of the death of man took part in political struggle," wrote Deleuze in his *Foucault* (75), deriding those who could resolve this incongruity only by returning to the purportedly false notions of eternity and transcendence over Foucault's immanent practice. Perhaps I will be mistaken for such a fool; though, to begin with, I am not at all astonished that these two positions could be held by the same person. I am not astonished not only because I think that other visionary minds had already turned to immanence precisely in order to offer a glimpse of another—dare we say—better world (is not Marx's thinking this prototype?) but because I think that the most interesting thinkers change radically and unpredictably, and Foucault is famous for such turns. Regarding particularly his work on parrhesia,

it is true that Foucault speaks of *truth-telling* and not simply of truth, which means that truth is for him first and foremost an *effect* of a *practice*. However, if this equation between practice and idea, or even the outright priority of practice over idea, bespeaks his faith in immanence alone, we are still left to consider two important questions: (1) Why begin the history of this practice with Socratic parrhesia, which is, above all, a practice of ascent, a vertical, transcendental practice? and (2) Why commend it as obviously as he often does? I would respond that with Foucault we do not engage in a simple binary of immanence/transcendence any more than we do with the Greeks themselves (despite, of course, modern distortions that advocate the contrary). Rather, what takes place is some kind of immanent transcendence. Put bluntly, after a history of bad transcendence, immanence furnishes a way, a practice, for this other vision of the world that pierces through the very structures of this world that conceal it from view.

6. Schematically, there are two major competing interpretations: those who read Nietzsche as simply a natural philosopher who replaces morality with natural empiricism (naturalists or antirealists, especially in the Anglophone tradition) and those who read him as a moral philosopher interested in questions of truth and knowledge (the antinaturalists, who are largely identified with the continental tradition). Brian Leiter's entry on Nietzsche ("Nietzsche's Moral and Political Philosophy") in the *Stanford Encyclopedia of Philosophy* offers a succinct exposition of the relevant arguments associated with each interpretation. He himself is a strong representative of the naturalists, as his work criticizes what he sees as the moralization of Nietzsche. The antinaturalist interpretation includes a number of luminaries of the continental tradition from Heidegger and Derrida to Nietzsche's English translator Walter Kaufmann, among many others. A recent intervention that opposes both the strictly naturalist readings as well as the moral-relativist arguments of poststructuralism is Michael Steven Green's *Nietzsche and the Transcendental Tradition*. By looking at Nietzsche's influences from his own contemporaries, Green identifies the Kantian strands in Nietzsche's epistemology.

7. I thank again Scott Hubbard for all the conversations on the absolute as the notion that most absolutely divides ancients from moderns. My views have greatly benefited from his keen insights on both the Greek tragedians and modern thought.

8. See Gutting, "Michel Foucault."

9. I do not contest the fact that we have undergone such shifts, nor do I underestimate the fragmentation of the modern subject, which has been so pervasive as to call for the erasure of subjectivity from contemporary philosophical discourse. Rather, I am resisting the fundamentally salutary character with which such shifts have been announced, the eagerness—that deeply optimistic state of mind—with which every classical notion was subjected to a productive problematization. Such problematizations are often all but productive, especially when it is decided a priori that they will be productive simply by virtue of being problematizations.

10. Foucault's radicalism lies in the clarity with which he traces the usurpation of once-spontaneous practices by the processes of institutionalization and normalization.

11. Foucault's wording on the techne of rhetoric is noteworthy in light of his larger project of reconfiguring truth-telling as a technique of the self for modernity. If techne forms the exact opposite of immediacy, frankness, and directness that distinguish parrhesia, how are we to reconcile his interest in parrhesia as a *technique* of the self? The best answer comes out of Plato's *Apology*, where Socrates suggests that moral education is neither quite a techne nor really a matter of innate disposition. I discuss this in the next chapter, proposing that parrhesiastic conduct is something of a nontechnical techne.

12. Heidegger's thinking of aletheia changes throughout his work, though his refusal to align truth with a subject persists. Since it is the relation of truth to a subject in Greek antiquity that concerns me in this chapter, I limit my comments to this specific essay and to his general disinterest in the truth-speaker.

13. See, for instance, the preface to *The Case of Wagner*, 155, where Nietzsche speaks of the philosopher's need of self-discipline (*askesis*) in order to overcome decadence. As Nietzsche's heir, Foucault understands the practice of truth-telling in terms of an exercise (*Fearless Speech* 144). For a critical view of Foucault's emphasis on the ascetic in Greek antiquity, see Porter, "Foucault's Ascetic Ancients."

14. By this I do not mean that the Greeks believed philosophy can be applied to life or become the organon of political programs. Plato's *Republic* shows amply the theoretical nature of Greek philosophy: it contemplates a city of the mind; it does not intend to be a political manifesto. However, the Greeks are preoccupied with the way in which philosophy can furnish the guiding questions to the pursuit of the good life, which for them was also the happy life. In thus having actual ethical stakes outside its practice as a formal, systematic exercise, Greek thinking is practical. Gutting writes that Foucault's late philosophy on the Greeks thinks of them as not looking for theoretical truth. This may well be the case for Foucault, but it does not exhaust the Greek notion of truth. However, I do agree again with Foucault that there is a practical aspect to Greek philosophy, which is a direct effect of its ideality: only because it aspires to something better than what is at hand can it actually matter for the real world.

15. This conforms to Hegel's understanding of the precarious balance the Greeks had reached between interiority and exteriority, human and divine, will and fate, form and content. It is the reason why Hegel identified the height of Greek antiquity with the harmonious principles of classical art rather than with religion (divine exteriority) or thought (subjective interiority). The structure is similar here: neither is the teller owned by truth, nor does he own the truth. This means that if we contest the anthropocentrism of classical humanism, we should be equally wary of the potential despotism of philosophical or theological inversions, in which the human being is irrevocably determined by outside forces with no possibility of resistance whatsoever. Heraclitus's maxim that fate is character offers the most succinct answer

to either extreme: fate (the outside) shows itself in the path chosen by the individual character. For the Greeks, both aspects wholly conform to each other such that no priority is ultimately of any significance.

16. I am aware of the immediate objection that Plato was a critic of appearance and, as such, not a suitable example for the artistic predilection of the Greeks. Chapter 2 counters such a straightforward understanding of Plato as an anti-artist. It is actually my contention that Socrates becomes for Plato the singular instantiation and embodiment of the Idea.

17. Foucault thinks of Apollo as "the prophetic god whose duty it is to speak the truth to mortals" (51), but this is a paradoxical statement: strictly speaking, a god does not have duties toward mortals; and assuming that he does, it is the god's prerogative to forsake them. For an exposition of some reasons why Foucault might think of Apollo as a parrhesiastes, see Nikolopoulou, "Parrhesia as Tragic Structure in Euripides' *Bacchae*," 251–52.

4. PLATO'S COURTS

1. I use the Loeb for the original Greek of both the *Phaedrus* and the *Apology*; the translations are by Benjamin Jowett unless otherwise noted. The reference to *The Bacchae* is from the David Kovacs translation of the Loeb edition.

2. Both Seth Benardete (*The Rhetoric of Morality and Philosophy: Plato's Gorgias and Phaedrus*) and G. R. F. Ferrari (*Listening to the Cicadas: A Study of Plato's Phaedrus*) understand the speech/writing binary through this contrast and, in light of it, the structure of the *Phaedrus*. I concur as I am also indebted to both readings, at least insofar as this convergence allows them to be comparable.

3. The epigraph for this section is Keats's self-composed epitaph. Though these words are in fact written on a gravestone, intended to impress forever the poet's anger at the critical neglect his work suffered, they begin to echo differently when read through Plato and Socrates. Who says that oblivion may not be a better fate for one's words than violation and misappropriation?

4. On the disagreements as to the subject matter of the dialogue in the exegetical tradition, see Hackforth, Introduction, 8–9. Heidegger also observes this in his *Nietzsche*, referring to the various subtitles the dialogue has been given ("Περὶ Καλοῦ," or "On the Beautiful," and "Περὶ Ψυχῆς," or "On the Soul," are two others). Heidegger adds the topics of techne, logos, speech, language, truth, madness, the Ideas, and Being, maintaining each of these could also serve as a subtitle (191).

5. Ferrari gives two instances of Plato's critique of such scholarly pretense: Socrates's disinterest in the demythologization of the myth of Boreas, which would debunk it on the basis of a historical examination of its sources even though the point of the story remains valid (210), and his reproach of Phaedrus for discarding the story of Theuth based on its debatable origin rather than on its meaning. In our academic world, the penchant for intellectual pedigree is amusingly shown by questions such as: "Is this the book that 'everyone' is reading?" (217).

6. The claim that a dialogue on rhetoric demands to be read rhetorically is only half the story, since the *Phaedrus* submits rhetoric to the larger context of philosophy as love, as Hackforth also concedes (9–10). George Kennedy confirms that the Neoplatonic commentary of Hermeias, "the only one on the *Phaedrus* to survive from antiquity" (129), considered it a work as much about love as about rhetoric (127–29).

7. For a systematic historical and textual defense of the importance of the Sophists for Greek thought, see de Romilly, *The Great Sophists in Periclean Athens*.

8. On the question of breath as inspiration and the importance of nature in the *Phaedrus*, see Baracchi, "'Words of Air.'" Baracchi shows that philosophy as inspired discourse (and not simply as *écriture*) must take into account its sources in the elemental convergence of natural air and the divine spirit that inundates Socrates. See also Alejandro Vallega's reading of Plato, where he argues similarly that the philosophical logos arises out of phusis (72–74). In agreeing with them on this, I also differ from Ferrari, whose reading I find otherwise convincing. Ferrari views the natural backdrop as a perfect metaphor for the empty prettiness of rhetoric Phaedrus is enamored with, whereas he maintains that Socrates brings the city to the countryside (228). While it is true that Socrates turns from the knowledge of nature to that of the soul and that he jokes about learning nothing from trees but only from men (230d5–7), this landscape, as Baracchi shows, is much more than a foil to Socratic truth.

9. I borrow again Ferrari's term (211, 221). Ferrari describes aptly the authoritative or didactic properties of the letter as fetishistic and talismanic (209–11).

10. Richard Marback's *Plato's Dream of Sophistry* proves interesting on this point, since it proceeds from Plato's legendary deathbed dream, in which the philosopher foresaw anxiously that futurity will misread his dialogues as Sophistic texts. Marback challenges the opposition between Platonism and Sophism from Neoplatonism onward, arguing that the appropriations of Plato in the history of thought are more important than the actual dialogues. Thus, not only would Derrida's reading be more significant than the *Phaedrus* itself, but my own characterization of this reading as Sophistic would render Derrida the ideal and just reader of Plato—the reader who, like Marback, pays Plato his due by materializing Plato's worst nightmare. For the purposes of my own critical distinction between Plato and Sophistic rhetoric in this chapter (a distinction rendered necessary by the very topic of parrhesia), I stress this yet again: although Plato does not denounce all rhetoric, admitting even to its fruitful use in philosophical thinking, rhetoric's attested institutional practice remains largely repugnant to him—namely, the practice in which the Sophist targets the minds of others from a safe distance, scoring points rather than communicating. Certainly, Plato's reservations about Sophism do not prove that he is not indebted to it. On the other hand, downplaying them and extending Plato's longevity by proving his terrible dream right has its own costs. Ultimately, the evidence of the history of philosophy as a sophistic appropriation of Plato that Marback cites does not address the reason behind Plato's agony, an agony out of which philosophy was born: the crisis of figure and ground, representation and truth. If Plato is a Sophist, he is in an aberrant sense

of the term, signaling the crisis of Sophism; and it is for this peculiarity rather than for his conformance that he became such a point of return and reappropriation in the history of thought.

11. For an elaboration on this, see Woodruff, "Socrates and the Irrational."

12. A brief contextualization of my critical treatment of Derrida's *Phaedrus*: While his reading discloses some important aspects, it has also generated—perhaps unwittingly—a legacy of demonizing Plato as the origin of all that has gone awry with the West. Insofar as Derrida's project may be defended as a critique of certain conservative Platonisms more than of Plato himself, I think it is equally just to hold Derrida responsible for the Derridianisms he has produced. After all, if Platonism can occasion a legitimate critique of Plato, then Derridianism cannot be independent of its originator or be excused for being a misled and misleading byproduct of followers who do not grasp the master's deeper meanings. Were this the case, the democratic Derrida would end up looking ironically like Leo Strauss's esoteric Plato.

13. Socrates recognizes rhetoric's potential when put in the service of truth—hence, his comparison of the art of rhetoric to the art of healing (270b1–10). On the reform of rhetoric, see Hackforth, Introduction, 9.

14. To make his point, Plato constructs Lysias's speech in a caricaturish way (Hackforth 17).

15. Hamlet's letter to Ophelia addresses her as "the most beautified Ophelia," and Polonius is correct to read the epithet as "vile" (act 2, scene 2, lines 109–11). Hamlet later confronts Ophelia: "Ay, truly, for the power of beauty will soon transform honesty from what it is to a bawd than the force of honesty can translate beauty into his likeness" (act 3, scene 2, lines 111–13). Dishonest beauty is beautification.

16. A further twist of this cloak involves the gendering of the interlocutors: while the mantle in ancient Greece was aligned with effeminacy and lack of authority, ideal masculinity was represented as nude. The feminized Socrates tells of the effeminate boy a cunning old lover seeks, reversing in reality the terms of his speech: it is the elderly lover who has been feminized, yet it is also his logos that is meant to exert higher authority. For a discussion of the mantle in relation to femininity and feminization, see Michelakis, *Achilles in Greek Tragedy*, 37.

17. See, for instance, Aeschylus's Cassandra in *Agamemnon*: "Oh, flame and pain that sweeps me once again!" (line 1256). The gift of prophecy comes to her as fire, assaulting her body. Nicole Loraux reminds us that "at Delphi, according to cultic tradition, the Pythia is one of Cassandra's sisters" and that the Pythia also prophesied by being stricken, thus needing a "college of male interpreters [who] endeavored to translate [her visions] into a language that remained veiled, but was at least articulated" (76).

18. That a story about the origin of writing would be presented as a Semitic one is not surprising, and it dovetails with Derrida's own privileging of writing over speech. Claiming to be not a normative discourse, deconstruction would prefer us to accept this privileging of the letter as philosophically neutral. Still, deconstruction's valorization of the letter suggests its inflection by the Hebrew religion, which posits

the absent God of the Book as the truth that awaits beyond pagan myth, beyond meaning, and beyond the Greek valorization of presence over nonbeing.

19. This is the most important difference Derrida's reading introduces, and I believe wrongly, in Platonic scholarship—namely, that whatever the textual gaps, they are unintentional failures on Plato's part, not even ironically intended as some commentators have insisted. Benardete reads Plato always metaphilosophically through the second sailing (see my chapter 1, note 47), and Ferrari defends this story as thoroughly consistent with Plato's avowed intents, thus vindicating him not only against Derrida but also against ironic readings such as Ronna Burger's (Ferrari 213–15).

20. Ferrari rightly understands the idealization of this past not as a naïve story about good old times but as Socrates's self-reflexive gesture concerning his own belatedness (218–20).

21. A radical reading of Plato would not try to vindicate writing—which Derrida and even most of his critics are doing—but would try to show how writing may have signaled for Plato the decline of the ancient Greek world: note, for instance, how his critiques against the conceit of the poets point largely to the moment of Homer's written codification, after which rhapsodes engage in rote recitation and poor exegesis. Note also his admiration for the Spartan legislator Lycurgus, whose divine *rhetra* forbade the writing of the law. Plato was not a decadent as Nietzsche thought. Rather, much like his archenemy Nietzsche, Plato is the diagnostician of decline, and the role of writing in this decline may have yet to be seriously thought.

22. See Heidegger, "The Question Concerning Technology."

23. In his controversial *Preface to Plato*, Eric Havelock has written on the ways in which literacy changed the face of Greek culture, a theory that later influenced Walter Ong's *Orality and Literacy: The Technologizing of the Word*. Instead of espousing the clear-cut distinction Havelock draws between the literate Plato and the oral Socrates (303), however, I suggest that Plato used his own writing to articulate subtly the problematic of the newly popularized writing technology.

24. James Colaiaco's study maps a Hegelian understanding of tragedy onto the *Apology*, in which two equally legitimate claims collide: civic duty versus personal ethics, the collision of *Antigone*. Though I find the comparison to Antigone on target, I do not think that tragedies obey this perfect balance. The heightened tragic mode of *Antigone* and of the *Apology* issues from the voluntary sacrifice of personages who have not fallen from high to low as the classical Aristotelian definition of the tragic hero demands. For the structural connections between the *Apology* and tragedy, and its link to *Oedipus Tyrannus*, see Howland, "Plato's *Apology* as Tragedy."

25. It is puzzling why the age that has most staunchly criticized subjectivity for its solipsism has displaced this solipsism into language. While this move decenters the atomistic subject, it continues to privilege infinite solipsism once it is removed from the human being.

26. For Socrates, both democracies and tyrannies respond callously to the call of thinking. Democracy, however, runs more frequently the risk of haste, because

it empowers large numbers. Yet neither monarchy nor oligarchy is the remedy. His response, oddly egalitarian, echoes the Dionysian democracy of leveling. Not equal empowerment but equal disempowerment of everyone in front of thought: "I make myself available for questioning to anyone, rich or poor" (33b2–3).

27. For a study of the prototypical function of Socrates in the history of philosophy, see Nehamas, *The Art of Living*. For the notion of philosophy as a way of life, see also Hadot, *Philosophy as a Way of Life*. My thanks to Rodolphe Gasché for directing me to Hadot's work.

28. See Colaiaco, *Socrates against Athens*, 189.

29. See Sophocles, *Oedipus at Colonus* (lines 1410–13); for all references to this play, I have consulted the Chicago edition, translated by David Grene. See also Nietzsche's recounting of the myth of Midas and the divine Silenus in *The Birth of Tragedy*, 42.

30. That Socrates approves of Achilles's parrhesia remains largely unnoticed in scholarship, most probably because it contradicts the critical stance Socrates takes against him in the *Republic*—notably in his discussion of the guardians, for whom Achilles is an example to be avoided precisely on account of his independent thinking, as Mary P. Nichols argues (70–72).

31. See Colaiaco, *Socrates against Athens*, 184. Plato scholars detect in this comparison Socrates's reappropriation of the heroic ideal, but they do not focus on the fact that it is the moral principle of parrhesia that grants honor to Achilles: both of their tragic fates result from acting according to a self-issued morality.

32. On the redefinition of piety as "supportive service," see Christian Wildberg: "Intriguing evidence suggests that at the end of the fifth century a probably small group of intellectuals in Athens (to which not only Euripides, but also Socrates and perhaps Sophocles belonged) revised the traditional notion of piety by defining it in terms of 'supportive service' (ὑπηρεσία) and in consequence elevating the intrinsic moral and ontological status of mortals vis-à-vis the immortal gods" ("Piety as Service" 235).

33. The most illustrious modern advocate of a rhetorical Socrates is the young Kierkegaard, whose doctoral dissertation presented Socrates exclusively as an ironist. "On the whole, the entire *Apology* is splendidly suited for attaining a clear concept of Socrates' ironic activity," writes Kierkegaard, continuing in the footnote, "The whole *Apology* in its totality is an ironic work, inasmuch as most of the accusations boil down to a nothing—not to a nothing in the usual sense of the word, but to a nothing that Socrates simply passes off as the content of his life, which again is irony, and likewise his proposal about being entertained in the prytaneum or being fined a sum of money, and mainly the fact that it really does not contain any defense at all but is in part a leg-pulling of his accusers and in part a genial chat with his judges" (37). Nehamas's Socrates draws on Kierkegaardian irony so as to counterbalance the "overwhelmingly sincere, uncompromisingly honest" Socrates of Gregory Vlastos (Nehamas 52).

34. Agamben interprets the emptiness of Kant's formal law as the universal application of a principle without content—the "law in force without significance," as he refers to it throughout *Homo Sacer*.

35. His is the only other reading of the counterproposal as a serious rather than superfluous proposition that I have come across. Rojcewicz himself stresses that in the vast literature on the *Apology*, including the work of Kierkegaard, I. F. Stone, and more recently John Sallis, the nature of the counterproposal has not received sustained attention but only passing comments.

36. I opted for Fowler's rendering in the Loeb edition.

37. The contrast of Palamedes to Odysseus occurs also in the *Phaedrus*, where Socrates accuses Phaedrus for being schooled in the rhetoric of Odysseus and Nestor (cunning, self-interested rhetoric) rather than of Palamedes, who was a true man of virtue (261b9–c2).

38. Nicole Loraux has also argued that tragedy is antipolitical, like the Socratic form of parrhesia, but clarifies that the antipolitical is not apolitical. Rather, it proposes a politics outside the traditional contours of this term. See *The Mourning Voice*, especially the chapter "Tragedy and the Antipolitical."

5. EURIPIDES'S VERDICT

1. Nietzsche accuses Euripides of Socratism. In "Socrates and Euripides," Christian Wildberg shows that the connection between philosopher and playwright is not just speculative on Nietzsche's part but that historical evidence corroborates encounters between the two. For instance, although Sophocles was also a contemporary of Socrates, Socrates had not initiated a conversation with him but was keenly interested in Euripides's work (25).

2. I use the Loeb edition both for the original Greek and for the translation by David Kovacs. Therefore, all line numbers from *The Bacchae* in this chapter reflect the original Greek, since the Kovacs translation appears on the facing page from the original and does not provide line numbers.

3. For the notion of this play as metatragedy, see also Segal, *Dionysiac Poetics and Euripides' Bacchae*, especially chapters 7 and 9. Segal underlines its Heraclitian poetics of strife: "In the *Bacchae* this essential and paradoxical quality of tragedy, its counterpoise between the creative and destructive energies of life, emerges with a unique clarity and self-consciousness" (340).

4. The opening scene establishes Dionysus as the god of epiphany, the god who appears. On the symbolism of his theophany, see Walter Otto's magisterial *Dionysus: Myth and Cult*.

5. See Otto, *Dionysus*, for more on Zagreus as chthonic Dionysus (191) and on the Agrionia cult (103–5, 118–19). For a study of the Titans' sacrifice of the infant Dionysus, see Detienne, *Dionysos Slain*.

6. Zeitlin's work on Thebes as the "other scene" of Athens, or the "anti-Athens," as she calls it, proves crucial (144–45). Athenian society displaces its civic problems in

this aesthetic other scene of tragedy, whose other scene is another city-state. Thus, if Athens with Ion completes the transition, Thebes with Pentheus thwarts it.

7. Teiresias (line 367) and Dionysus (line 508) allude to the meaning of Pentheus's name. Pentheus speaks of "πέπονθα δεινά" (horrible sufferings), punning unwittingly on his name (line 643).

8. That Dionysus and Pentheus are mirroring doubles is suggested at various moments in the text: the former a son of heaven (Zeus), the latter of earth (Echion); the former enters the stage from exotic lands, the latter from outside the city (ἔκδημος) (line 215); both are disguised as revelers, though for different reasons; they support antithetical positions, yet both use cunning.

9. See Otto, *Dionysus*, 86–91.

10. Otto juxtaposes the ritual during which Dionysus enters the house of the king and takes the queen against similar rituals in Babylon: whereas in Babylon the time of the god's arrival is known so that the queen-priestess prepares for him in the temple, in Greece Dionysus appears suddenly in the palace, claiming her then and there. For Otto, this bespeaks the terrible immediacy of Dionysus, his incarnate and immediate existence among mortals (83–85).

11. There is disagreement among editors as to the speaker of this line because the preceding lines are missing from the ancient source. Loeb (Kovacs), Oxford (Diggle), and Chicago (Grene and Lattimore) propose Cadmus, and I have adopted this choice. The annotated Cambridge Greek edition by Sandys proposes Agave.

12. At the point where Dionysus, no longer in mortal disguise, pronounces the characters' fates, the text has a lacuna. So, it is possible that he had already spoken of the chorus in the missing lines, delivering the women as he had earlier miraculously unchained their shackled feet. Still, however, given the effusiveness with which they sing of the god as their liberator, it is curious that no mention of their own future and no victorious cries are to be heard in their closing words.

13. In his introduction to *The Bacchae*, Kovacs observes that Euripides uses this exodos also for his *Alcestis, Andromache*, and *Helen* (6). Kovacs omits another Euripidean tragedy that bears this identical ending and that shares with *The Bacchae* the terrible moment of infanticide: *Medea*. The only difference appears in the first lines of the chorus. In *Medea* the chorus speaks initially of Zeus as having many things in store: "πολλῶν ταμίας Ζεὺς ἐν Ὀλύμπῳ" (line 1415); in *The Bacchae* it is all the heavenly powers that assume many forms and surprise us: "πολλαὶ μορφαὶ τῶν δαιμονίων" (line 1388).

14. For a cursory history of the controversial reception of Euripides as either an atheist social critic or a deathbed convert, see again Kovacs's introduction to *The Bacchae*. Kovacs correctly remarks that "it is, however, no longer a universally accepted belief that Euripides was a skeptic, and we need not try so hard to construe the play as the work of one" (7).

15. In this conclusion, I have moved from *The Bacchae* to referencing *Antigone*. This is in part because, as I explained, Pentheus's parrhesia is compromised and cannot

stand as an unproblematic parallel to the Socratic parrhesia with which Foucault is also concerned. More importantly, however, my citation of *Antigone* is necessitated by my engagement with Hegel, who discussed the play as a dialectical conflict of equivalent claims: in contrast, I insist on an anti-Hegelian understanding of tragedy that welcomes the moral valuation of tragic choice.

6. Ῥίζα Αἱματόεσσα

The Greek title of this chapter is from Aeschylus's *Seven against Thebes* (line 755), where, as Gerald Else points out, we are given the genealogy of the atē (fate) that has struck the house of Labdacus and to which Antigone refers in the opening lines of Sophocles's play: Laios transgressed Apollo's warning and begat Oedipus, the parricide, and "'he dared in sowing (dared to sow) the holy plowland of his mother, where he was nurtured: a bloody root (ῥίζαν αἱματόεσσαν).' Out of this root, the womb of Iokaste which bore the blood-shedding brothers, has grown Sophokles' strange and poignant figure of 'the last root in Oidipus's house,' Antigone" (Else 17). All quotes and references from *Antigone* in this chapter are parenthetically cited with line numbers that reflect the original Greek and its English translation; in all cases, the first numbers correspond to the Loeb edition of the Greek original, and the second refer to David Grene's translation of the Chicago edition.

1. Butler admits that she is not interested in Antigone as a classicist but as a humanist (2). In other words, her reading of the play does not conform to the specialized philological demands of a classically trained scholar. It pertains to the larger philosophical questions that the play rehearses and that make it equally a classic for the more general humanities as for the particular discipline of classics.

2. It is not coincidental that Nietzsche, a philosopher of nature, was also a proponent of tragedy.

3. See "Letter on Humanism," written in 1947, in which Heidegger points to a peculiar reversal of priority committed by philosophy and theology: both have privileged the human being over Being, whereas Heidegger insists that it is Being from where every entity, including the human being, proceeds.

4. See section 3 of the preface to *The Gay Science*. Here Nietzsche speaks of the pain endured by the philosopher, but his remarks apply equally to the tragic hero, since the Nietzschean philosopher is modeled after the tragic hero: "I doubt that such pain makes us 'better'; but I know that it makes us more *profound*" (36).

5. The question of the relation between reader and spectator (lest we forget that *Antigone* is a visual act) is as suggestive as it is paramount and cannot be undertaken here in full length. It does not involve simply a terminological distinction but a philosophical investigation of the current privileging of reading as an interior act, which is at odds with the Greeks, whose fundamentally agonistic nature involved exposure, exteriority, and actualization.

6. It is not an overstatement to say that the first deconstruction of the tragic death happened not in a modern theoretical text but in another Greek literary text: the *Iliad*,

which, incidentally, Plato considered a prototragedy. In book 9, as Achilles tries to choose between a banal and a tragic-heroic death, he offers a powerful critique of the latter, having already suffered from his commander's corruption of the heroic values.

7. Recall Warminski's arguments about the empty death of inscription discussed in chapter 1.

8. This is similar to the distinction Hölderlin makes when he speaks of the Greek bodily death versus the Hesperian spiritual death in his translations of Sophocles.

9. I largely agree with Butler's critique of the law as representation. However, appropriating Antigone for explicit contemporary problems does not really differ from earlier readings.

10. In this sense, contemporary theory suffers from Platonism all the more as it vilifies Platonic idealism. Plato's pessimism concerning the human capacity for the good, however, is far more realistic than theory's projective, messianic awaitings.

11. The chorus calls her "αὐτόνομος" (autonomous; Grene translates this as "your own choice") (line 821/882).

12. Recall the discussion in chapter 4 of the story of Theuth, where Socrates critiques the invention of writing as a mnemonic device for increasingly complex societies.

13. While there is much to think about the multifaceted and constitutive relation of comedy to tragedy, it is important to be mindful of easy dialectical reversals. Butler wishes for a happy ending that gives Isaac back to his father, so to speak. She envisions a paradisial utopia of inclusion, though admittedly secular and not theological. In an even less generous assessment, one could argue that Butler's reading specifications for *Antigone* unwittingly effect a sanitization of tragedy reminiscent of some Christian editions of Shakespeare that rewrite the bloody endings, since their soteriology could not allow for tragedy.

14. Hegel's main problem is that he instrumentalizes the play to fit his historical vision of the evolution of civic organization from early, family-based societies to full-fledged nation-states. To do so, he omits or ignores nuances of the play that do not fit his scheme. Seth Benardete's *Sacred Transgressions* is written as a line-by-line analysis of *Antigone* in response to Hegel, showing all these details the philosopher glosses over.

15. The location of *Antigone* in the *Phenomenology of Spirit* functions as a passage from what Hegel viewed as the unreflexive moments of (Greek) ethical life to the reflexive, modern political organization of the state.

16. Whereas Loraux could make this argument on the basis of Antigone as a female mourner, the same way she establishes this with respect to *The Trojan Women* and *Electra*, I would add to Antigone's mourning her sense of defiance. This defiance may later be politicized, but it does not stem initially from political motives: she simply wants to bury her brother. This is not a political act, at least not for the Greek world where public duties were clearly demarcated from familial ones, and perhaps for a good reason: even though this public/private distinction attested to a profound gender problematic in the Greek world, the hasty gesture by which contemporary theory

politicizes the family as a site of power relations is not much better. To politicize the bedroom runs the risk of totalitarianism.

17. The word "exemplary" needs to be qualified to fit its ancient contexts: though the exemplary involves a didactic dimension in that everyone should try to model the heroic example, this is hardly the understanding of heroism in the ancient Greek world. Heroes, even down to the age of tragedy, were extraordinary and inimitable figures, not our neighbor whose courage surprises us in a difficult circumstance. If Greek heroes taught in their exemplarity, they did so primarily in showing how different they were from ordinary human beings, all the while propelling these ordinary persons to go beyond their limits.

18. In "Sophocles' *Oedipus Tyrannus*," Benardete reads Oedipal incest as the reinscription of the godly/bestial character of primeval incest in human relations.

19. The Loeb translation also starts in the same manner.

20. See, for instance, Gasché, "Kafka's Law." Gasché reads Benjamin's reading of Kafka, which in turn was influenced by Johann Jakob Bachofen's theory of cultural evolution. Gasché's article considers Judaic law as a punitive response to the sins of a prehistoric, natural world order (the mythic world order) that Bachofen had identified as the "hetaeric" or "tellurian" age. The law of this mythic world was unwritten and lacked delineation to the point of being licentious, or "promiscuous," as Gasché calls it (979). Written Judaic law came as punishment and redemption at the same time for this primordial sin. At this point, it is important to note that Antigone's insistence on law's primordial and unwritten nature is absolutely not of the order of this promiscuity. On the contrary, if ritual burial is one of the earliest (unwritten) laws, through which the human being showed its difference from the state of nature, then it is Antigone (the proponent of primordial, mythic, unwritten law) who stands for delineation from nature, not Creon (the civic, "historical" leader) who relegates another human being to the mouths of beasts. The primordial for Antigone is not the promiscuous but the just and most humanly self-evident duty that has been forgotten in the advent of the historical state and its conventions. Put differently, the ahistoric (which is also notably different from the prehistoric) is not the promiscuous but the morally absolute, while the historical is not the just but the contingent.

21. The standard translations "Ismene, my dear sister" (David Grene of the Chicago edition) or "My own sister Ismene, linked to myself" (Hugh Lloyd-Jones of the Loeb edition) do not adequately communicate the original's strange citation of the sisterly head that is in common.

22. Whether Antigone changes her mind about this when she tries to spare Ismene from the death penalty is another of these difficult Sophoclean turns that baffles the interpreters. It could be argued that Antigone wishes to protect her on account of Ismene being her sister and the last survivor of the Oedipal family (this would still be a decision based on self-sameness). In a more extrapolated speculation, Antigone may have forgiven Ismene her weakness because she came to accept that for the most part human nature is limited and self-interested. But we could also take Antigone

simply at her words: Ismene should not be punished for something she did not do. This fits the compassionate hypothesis but remains in concordance with Antigone's previous attitude that Ismene does not deserve the same, glorious fate as she who actually dared the deed.

23. Butler is indebted to Foucault's genealogy. Thus, in light of my earlier link between tragedy and genealogy, my critical stance toward Butler needs further clarification. The genealogical method aims at exposing the contingent in what appears necessary, and Butler exposes the tragic notion of fate to be a false necessity. Despite her potentially legitimate application of this formal principle, I am struck by the different outcomes Butler's genealogy yields than Nietzsche's, or even Foucault's. Whereas the latter thinkers tend toward pessimism, or at least ambivalence, hers is a clearly optimistic story. Nietzsche writes the decline of morals and of tragedy, and Foucault traces the degradation of truth-telling; Butler tells us how to protect the nonnormative family. I would ask, however, an even more fundamental question about the distinction between the contingent and the necessary: Why does our age *construct* the lack of necessity as the only necessity? How, in other words, do we know so certainly that constructedness is not itself a false necessity?

24. For an anthropological account of these early beginnings of human culture, linking the taboos of death and sexuality (and thus burial and incest), see Bataille, *Lascaux or the Birth of Art*, 31–33.

25. All subsequent citations of Benardete in this chapter refer to *Sacred Transgressions*.

26. In "The Sovereign," Bataille offers a model of sovereignty that rejects the customary understanding of this term within the realm of politics. Traditional political and juridical notions of sovereignty assume the sovereign's interest in consolidating power and accruing benefits to guarantee the continuation of his rule and the future preservation of his subjects. Bataille's sovereign, however, has nothing to do with this utilitarian picture. His violence does not aim at gaining control or securing power but at risking his own existence: "every man is sovereign if he puts his life in the hands of his caprice" (188). Despite its seeming arbitrariness, caprice means something very important: the liberation from utilitarianism and survivalism. This kind of transgression belongs to what Bataille calls "the sacred" in his *Theory of Religion* (53). Antigone's autonomy exhibits this structure of sacred violence, and she even describes herself as a religious criminal (ὅσια πανουργήσασα) (line 74/85).

27. The myth is clear that Polyneices invaded because of Eteocles's betrayal of the terms of their agreement, according to which he should have ceded the throne to Polyneices after a year, so that the two of them could reign alternately. Antigone remains enigmatically silent about this, as she neither tries to exonerate Polyneices nor condemn Eteocles. The point, however, remains the same: this is not the moment to publicize her politics concerning the oath of office. Confronted with the death of both her brothers, she is not willing to condemn the one who received the rites or to restore *legally* the reputation of the one who is denied them. Her familial duty is simply to bury the one unburied and let the honored man go undisturbed. As she

says to Creon of her capacity as a sister, "οὔτοι συνέχθειν, ἀλλὰ συμφιλεῖν ἔφυν" (My nature is to join in love, not hate) (line 523/575).

28. For an elaboration of *Antigone* in relation to the rise of civil law and for the importance of tragedy as a civic genre in ancient Athens, see Copjec, "The Tomb of Perseverance." Beginning her essay, Copjec remarks, "*Greek tragedy* is the term we commonly use to refer to it, but it would be more accurate to say *Attic* or *Athenian tragedy*; since it was *only* in the city-state of Athens that this aesthetic form was nourished and thrived" (233). Not only was tragedy born in Athens, where it also died, but in its rehearsal of legal, political, and ethical issues, tragic drama "also reached out a hand to help invent the very city that invented it" (233).

29. No endnote can do justice to this issue, but I am compelled at least to point at the fundamental differences of the notions of blood and earth in the play and the sinister tradition of blood and soil on which the modern nation-state has been built. Firstly, unlike soil, which refers to the land and is thus always reducible to a country, the chthonic refers to the earth below, transcending geopolitical specificity. Secondly, in *Antigone*, blood functions as a figure of mortality, attesting to interrelatedness rather than exclusion. Haemon, whose name means blood and who sheds his blood by Antigone's corpse, is exemplary of this interrelatedness: despite the irresolvable demands made on him, he manages to come off as a model citizen, a respectful son, and a devoted lover. For Haemon, listening to the legitimate complaints of other citizens and mediating the public's discontents to his father so as to counsel the latter against his tyrannical fantasies and rescue his beloved from death are all intertwined duties, not mutually exclusive positions as Creon considers them to be.

30. One could read *Oedipus at Colonus* as an elaboration of this principle. The exiled scapegoat arrives at a foreign land, seeking asylum and a restful place to die. The initial hostility of the chorus against him is corrected by their enlightened king, Theseus, who was once himself an exile and who identifies with the stranger's ordeal on the basis that any mortal being can share in such misfortune (lines 639–47). Later on, the chorus apostrophizes Cerberus as the guardian of the gate that receives many strangers, alluding to the fact that Hades is equally hospitable to everyone (lines 1786–91).

31. I borrow this notion of the transfigured figure from Claudia Baracchi's reading of the sun as the figure of the good in Plato's *Republic*. Even though Plato dislikes figures and metaphors, he uses them amply. The easy way to explain this contradiction is to say that he caves in to the figurative nature of language while critiquing rhetoric in bad faith or even that he is ironic, contradicting himself self-reflexively, as if he were a postmodern thinker. In "Beyond the Comedy and Tragedy of Authority: The Invisible Father in Plato's *Republic*," Baracchi offers a third, more productive possibility that is also more generous to Plato's thinking. She does so by transforming the representational function of the figure into a presentational one: wishing to designate the highest and most abstract of the Ideas—the good—Plato is in dire need of a suitable figure. He employs the sun because its sublime brightness evokes the qualities proceeding from the good. However, through this power of evocation, the sun itself

is transformed from functioning as a figure of the good to being the good itself. The sun, as a material object in the sky, which was meant simply to point to an ideality, sheds its materiality through the process of figuration and shines as that ideality; it goes, as Baracchi writes, "beyond the order of the figure" (170).

32. See the *Iliad* 5.339–42:

> and blood immortal flowed from the goddess,
> ichor, that which runs in the veins of the blessed divinities;
> since these eat no food, nor do they drink of the shining
> wine, and therefore they have no blood and are called immortal.

33. In other words, I agree with Bataille that humans first differentiate themselves from animals — and thus display their freedom — precisely in setting limits on themselves. As he succinctly puts it, "human life stripped of prohibitions is unthinkable" (*Lascaux or the Birth of Art* 31).

34. Butler writes variously of this overdetermination: "Antigone says 'brother,' but does she mean 'father'? . . . Considering how many are dead in her family, is it possible that mother and father and repudiated sister and other brother are condensed there at the site of the irreproducible brother?" (67); "When she claims that she acts according to law that gives her most precious brother precedence, and she appears to mean 'Polyneices' by that description, she means more than she intends, for that brother could be Oedipus and it could be Eteocles" (77); "The 'brother' is no singular place for her, though it may well be that all her brothers (Oedipus, Polyneices, Eteocles) are condensed at the exposed body of Polyneices, an exposure she seeks to cover, a nakedness she would rather not see or have seen" (79).

35. I am inserting extratextual information from the later play *Oedipus at Colonus* in response to Butler's citation of the curse of Oedipus, which is also extraneous to *Antigone*.

36. See Jacobs, "Dusting Antigone," 909–10. Reading the notorious monologue where Antigone explains why she buried her brother but would not risk her life to do the same for a husband or children, Jacobs concludes that it is because Polyneices stands for that which is irreproducible: with her parents dead, Antigone can have no more brothers.

37. Oedipus is summoned to depart from this earth by the gods themselves, in a scene shrouded in holy mystery, suggesting his transfiguration or apotheosis rather than an ordinary death.

38. In section 7 of *The Birth of Tragedy*, Nietzsche maintains that the origins of tragedy lie in the tragic chorus, rejecting the dominant sociopolitical, democratic conception of tragedy as the conflict between the sovereign and his people: "This [sociopolitical] theory may be ever so forcibly suggested by one of Aristotle's observations; still, it has no influence on the original formation of tragedy, inasmuch as the whole opposition of prince and people — indeed the whole politico-social sphere — was excluded from the purely religious origins of tragedy" (56).

7. ANTIGONE'S CHILDREN

The epigraph comes from the third psalm of Odysseus Elytis's Τὸ Ἄξιον Ἐστί, 42, and is translated in the Johns Hopkins edition of *The Axion Esti*, 143, by Jeffrey Carson and Nikos Sarris.

1. I will be referring primarily to the second of two versions of this poem. The first version does not include the story of Xanthos, which is of particular interest for me in this chapter. For the German, I have consulted the Stuttgart edition of the *Sämtliche Werke*. I refer to Michael Hamburger's translation of the second version in *Friedrich Hölderlin: Poems and Fragments*. For an alternate translation of the second version and for a translation of the final stanzas of the first (the only significant point of difference), I consult *Odes and Elegies*, edited and translated by Nick Hoff. For the reader's benefit of further comparison, I include both versions of the poem in German with the above-mentioned English translations in an appendix.

2. Hoff's rendering is more literal than Hamburger's on this point of equating the two voices. Hoff translates this: "You were the voice of God, thus I thought once / In holy youth; and still I say so!" The subjunctive form "seiest" intimates the distance between the younger and the more mature Hölderlin, even though the poet hastens to add that despite this distance and the intervening events that may have disenchanted his vision, he still stands by his earlier belief. The expression *vox populi, vox dei* translates rather remarkably in the modern Greek vernacular as "φωνή λαοῦ, ὀργή Θεοῦ" (voice of the people, wrath of God), and I believe this rendering can serve as a guidepost for our understanding of the modern Greek insurrectionary events I will be describing later on in this chapter. This adage does not simply equate the two paratactic parts of the Latin phrase through the repetition of the common term "voice," but makes explicit the *manner* of this equation: the *voice* of the people echoes the *wrath* of God. In other words, the voice of the people, which is considered a dissenting voice, a call of resistance against injustice, expresses God's wrath, which is also directed against injustice.

3. Hölderlin's apprehension about the destructive dimension of the voice of the people might well be read as a reflection on the French Revolution and the ensuing Reign of Terror. While I am not interested in developing here this particular tenet of his work, it should be noted that the poet has been claimed, celebrated, and demonized as a Jacobin supporter by a host of critics. For those interested in the debate, see Pierre Bertaux's contested *Hölderlin und die Französische Revolution*, which argues that the poet was not simply a Jacobin sympathizer but an activist and a conspirator in an assassination plot against the monarch. P. H. Gaskill's "Hölderlin and Revolution" engages critically Bertaux's thesis.

4. See Adorno, "Parataxis."

5. Hölderlin warns us of the excesses of those willing to die for their ideals, but he keeps silent about the perils involved in the alternative choice: slavery, humiliation, subjugation.

6. Adrian Del Caro writes of the simultaneous spiritual and political demands that were exerted on Hölderlin's work: "Certainly the society desired by Hölderlin was one different than his own, but a society that has room for its gods and lives harmoniously with nature is not necessarily the society of political reorganization, at least, not in the modern sense of *polis*" (53).

7. Herodotus's description can be found in *The Landmark Herodotus: The Histories* 1.176:

> When Harpagos led his army onto the plain of Xanthos, the Lycians attacked him suddenly and fought, a few against many, and with great valor. They were defeated, however, and forced to retire inside their walls. Once trapped in their city, they gathered together their women, children, possessions, and servants on the acropolis and set fire to it, burning up everything. Then, having sworn powerful oaths, the men of Xanthos went forth again to do battle against Harpagos. They all died fighting. And so, the present-day Lycians who claim to be Xanthians are mostly immigrants, with the exception of eighty families, whose ancestors at the time of the battle happened to be abroad and thus survived. That is how Harpagos took Xanthos. (96)

8. *Der Tod des Empedokles* (*The Death of Empedocles*) was written between 1798 and 1800.

9. Henry Smith Williams writes, "Tradition has it that he threw himself into the crater of a volcano that his otherwise unexplained disappearance might lead his disciples to believe that he had been miraculously translated; but tradition goes on to say that one of the brazen slippers of the philosopher was thrown up by the volcano, thus revealing his subterfuge" (78).

10. Hölderlin writes, "The tremendous element, the fire of the sky and the silence of the people, their life within nature, and their limitedness and satisfaction has continually affected me, and as it is said of the heroes, so I may say that Apollo has struck me" (*Essays and Letters on Theory* 152).

11. This painful exposure to the absence of God becomes in modernity the new form of heroism. For this Hölderlinian notion of the poet, see also his poem "Dichterberuf" ("The Task of the Poet") in *Hyperion and Selected Poems*, 152–57.

12. My thanks to Edward Batchelder, who pointed out this alternative translation to me and who discussed this poem with me at length. Christine Irizarry's translation comments were also invaluable. Whatever mistakes or omissions, they are my own.

13. In the Böhlendorff letters (printed in *Essays and Letters on Theory*), holy fire is associated with the Orient. Fittingly, the poem tells us that this saga reaches us from the East: "die wunderbare / Sage von Osten zu uns gelanget."

14. Note in this context the stanza about the eagle (the father-god) who throws his egrets out of the nest, provoking them with a fitting prong to take flight, so that they do not remain idle for too long. This image too is double-edged: not every fledgling

is meant for the long flight. The provocation applies differently to each, and some might be destined to return all too quickly.

15. The image of the terrestrial as a maternal counterpoint to the paternal fire of Aether is more explicit in the penultimate stanza of the first version. There the poet speaks of the value of hesitation as opposed to that of immediacy, judging that hesitation might be more certain and safer (sichrer) and of greater (größer) value to anyone worthy of being born, of having a mother (der Mutter wert). I translate "der Mutter wert" idiomatically, which changes the meaning of the stanza Hoff gives in his translation. It is not that hesitation is of more value to mothers; rather, hesitation should be the essence of all mortal beings, all beings worthy of a mother. Meanwhile, the image of the mother is described as she "who is all to all" (Die allen alles ist) — a possible reference to Gaia.

16. See Homer, *Odyssey* 11.482–91. Of course, retrospection from the grave is impossible; and as much as this passage shows mortal remorse at its limit, it also shows that the course one has taken might, after all, be the only appropriate course. Still, the chiasmatic wishes expressed by the two heroes suggest that human beings often cannot accept the fittingness of their fate: Odysseus, the earthly man, praises glory, while Achilles, the man of glory, wishes for earthly pleasures.

17. I refer here to a quote from Derrida's *Politics of Friendship* in which he disparages those participants in democracy who are unable to handle "contradiction" and "measurelessness," which he further frames as "the practice of putting 'truth' in quotation marks" (44). This position, I find, can easily devolve into relativism. While I am aware that many defenders of deconstruction will not agree with my alignment of deconstruction and cultural relativism, this quote says nothing less than that truth is relative, in itself a truism that repeats Hegel, Nietzsche, and Heidegger.

18. This account by Plutarch is from the chapter on "Brutus," §§30–31.

19. To be precise, Hölderlin does not use the conventional terms of a simile: "like" or "as." Instead, he uses the conjunctive *und* (and) to link the force that draws the rivers to the force that draws a people toward death:

Es ziehet . . .

. . .

Das wunderbare Sehnen dem Abgrund zu;
Das Ungebundne reizet *und* Völker auch.
(my emphasis)

Note the use of "reizen" in this context, where it again refers to the provocation of the unbound, the abyss — namely, something natural and inhuman.

20. As Hecuba states in *The Trojan Women*:

And yet had not the very hand
of God gripped and crushed this city deep in the ground,

we should have disappeared in darkness, and not given
a theme for music, and the songs of men to come.
(Lines 1242–45)

21. This is how "vorbereitet" must be understood in the sixteenth stanza: the Xanthians' second response was prepared in the sense that it was their fate—the human tendency toward historical repetition—but not that alone. They themselves were prepared to face this particular situation with this particular choice much more than Hölderlin allows for. This must be so, because human fate is never predestination but a fitting convergence of chance and character. The accident was prepared: this is tragic logic.

22. For Plutarch's Greek text, I consulted the Loeb bilingual edition. For the English translation, I chose Ian-Scott Kilvert's, because it is more colloquial than the standard one by Bernadotte Perrin and because some of its renderings stress more clearly the tragic dimension of this event.

23. The different conclusions themselves reflect the problematic that the insertion of the specific example of Xanthos entails in the second version. The first version presents the two paths—fiery or earthly—as an abstract dilemma, which can even be limited to refer to aesthetic orientations. By appending a historical example, the second poem gives a different urgency to the topic. The general theoretical preference for earthly quietude in the first version might not apply so neatly to the actual earthly problem of oppression in the second.

24. Heidegger elaborates on "das Ungeheuere" ("the homeless" or "the ex-centric") in his *Hölderlin's Hymn "The Ister,"* initially delivered as a lecture in 1942. David Nichols comments on the shift in Heidegger's thinking of tragedy away from the Nietzschean sense of strife and the will to power toward the "more tranquil possibilities within Hölderlin's poetry": "Instead of characterizing Antigone as a rebellious voice postured against the polis, as he had done in the 1935 *Introduction to Metaphysics* lectures, Heidegger now associates the heroine with a particular sort of dwelling." Nichols adds, "Heidegger chooses to ignore the oppositional strife that was a permanent fixture in Hölderlin's thought about Greek tragedy. The poet understood the importance of a heroic confrontation with beings in order for another beginning to take root." According to Nichols, Hölderlin retains the Greek sense of strife between human groundedness and the ecstatic aspect of humanity that never finds home on this earth. In contrast, the later Heidegger sees as the poet's task to try to make a dwelling for humans out of this strangeness. Obviously, this is a fine line to walk: I too think that, for the most part, Hölderlin is divided between these two poles, but I also think that this poem in particular opts clearly for the road of tranquility. Furthermore, as I have variously repeated throughout this book, what appears as abyssal tension to the moderns may not always be so for the Greeks: Antigone's ex-centric decision is possible only because she is unquestionably rooted.

25. I agree with Jacqueline de Romilly that the chorus by definition cannot intervene in the action (*Pourquoi la Grèce?* 226–27), but my point here addresses not this structural inability of the tragic genre but the language with which sentiments of compassion or judgment are expressed by various choruses.

26. Sameness, continuity, and respect for tradition are largely Eastern ideals, as the story of Xanthos is an Eastern story; indeed, Hölderlin thinks of the Greeks as Orientals. As I pointed out in the first chapter, however, such enormously generic geocultural categories are the unfortunate symptoms of philosophical abstraction and of German idealism's particular mode of return to the Greeks. I need only point to the depiction of the Egyptian pharaohs, which over the span of a millennium—from Menkaure to Ramses II, with the sole exception of the brief Amarna period—remained virtually identical in style. Compare this to the evolution of the Greek kouros from its first, Egyptian-like posture in the archaic period in the seventh century BC to the appearance of the *Kritios Boy* circa 480 BC, where within a couple of centuries the artistic conventions relating to the representation of the human body have been completely transformed, as have the philosophical assumptions of what it means to be human. Nevertheless, beside the fact that this very need to overthrow tradition is itself inaugural of the Greek tradition (and as such, the notion of progress could offer the sole justification for why the West traces its origins back to the Greeks), the point I am trying to make here about the importance of sameness refers to the specific political problematic raised by Hölderlin's poem. This is not just any sameness: the same political desire through which people resist oppression is concomitant with, not antithetical to, their existential desire to live in whatever ways make them different from others and even from themselves. Put simply, one cannot pursue aesthetically and culturally the "free use of the national" when one is not politically free to do so.

27. I am not suggesting that there was not any resistance against Hitler in Germany. Various groups had, at times, opposed the regime, such as the Social Democrats, Communists, students and industrial workers, and several clergy, among others. Yet as Klemens von Klemperer observes, the totalitarian nature of the regime could hardly be resisted in any other way than from within its own institutions: "The convergence of resistance and compliance was almost imperative. In many instances continued service to the Nazi state seemed to be justified by the calculation that it might be effective in causing obstruction and averting the worst excesses of the regime" (3). In other words, the nature of the regime produced a conspiratorial, dispersed, almost quietist form of opposition that never achieved the force of a mass movement. Klemperer quotes Hans Mommsen, saying that in Germany resistance was "resistance without the 'people'" (3).

28. I do not deny that collective desire, even in its most revolutionary potential, can be appropriated by nationalist agendas. The events I am about to describe during the Greek Revolution have also been mostly thought of as building blocks toward the grand edifice of the Greek nation-state. So was Hölderlin's and Nietzsche's thought appropriated, for that matter; but no serious thinker—and certainly not a committed

poststructuralist—would accuse them of being responsible for their misappropriation. If the threat of appropriation becomes such an obstruction to thinking, censorship is lurking around the corner.

29. My summary of Nancy's argument draws from the first two chapters of *The Inoperative Community*, 1–70.

30. For a critique of the alleged fascism underpinning Bataille's thought, see Winfree, "The Contestation of Community," particularly 36–38.

31. See particularly his section entitled "Kirilov," in *The Space of Literature*, 96–100.

32. Translation by David Grene in the Chicago edition.

33. For Levinas's treatment of death in relation to the Other, see *Time and the Other*, 68–79.

34. For the symbolism of virgin death by hanging, see Johnston, "Antigone's Other Choice."

35. I mean "right" not only in the juridical sense but in its strictly moral sense as well: it is not right to invest oneself with the moral authority of an underworld judge.

36. For a political defense of the existential freedom to die, see the discussion of an incident of anticolonial violence in Sartre, *Search for a Method*, 109. I wish to thank Jim Holstun for pointing out this passage to me.

37. De Romilly makes the point that the first tragedies were about recent political events, such as Phrynichus's *The Siege of Miletus* (not extant) and Aeschylus's *Persians*. It was only later that the poets resorted to the language of myth (de Romilly, *Pourquoi la Grèce?* 189). Nicole Loraux observes that the change in subject matter was necessitated by the overwhelming emotions that the enactment of real events produced in the audience, whereas the enactment through myth allowed some distance (89).

38. The ethnic origin of the Souliots has been disputed, though most agree that the first settlers were of Greek and Arvanite descent. The Arvanites were Albanian settlers to Greece from the medieval times, most of whom resisted Islamicization, kept their Christian Orthodox faith, and integrated themselves or were assimilated in Greece. During the 1821 Revolution, they identified ethnically and politically with Greece, providing some of its most distinguished national heroes. To this day, when minority issues arise—admittedly, still hot-button issues for the Greek state and the Greek national consciousness—the Greek Arvanite community refuses to claim minority status, considering itself integrated. Umut Özkirimli and Spyros Sofos, on the other hand, find this claim of integration to be complicit in a process of assimilation that was imposed to secure national identity formation. They criticize the national history of Constantine Paparrigopoulos, who—intent on rebutting Fallmerayer's thesis of the eradication of Hellenism in modern Greece by Slavic and Albanian migrations—represented the encounter between Greeks and Orthodox Albanians seamlessly, as one of mutual benefit and cross-fertilization. While Paparrigopoulos saw Souli as one such great moment of syncretism between the two cultures, Özkirimli and Sofos focus on the nationalist reasons for downplaying hybridization in favor of assimilation (Özkirimli and Sofos 47–48). The folklorist Kostas Biris, in turn, argues

that the ethnic origin of the first Souliots is to be found farther north in Albania, while André Gerolymatos describes them as "Orthodox Albanians" (149) and attributes the reputation of Albanians as military innovators chiefly to the "Orthodox Christian Souliot tribe of Epirus" (120). Still, regardless of ethnic roots, the Souliot identification with Greece earned them the title of "Greeks" by their Ottoman and Muslim Albanian enemies alike: Ali Pasha's secretary Athanasios Psalidas identifies the Souliots as Greeks fighting against the Albanians (Psalidas 62). It is evident from this long but hardly exhaustive note on the topic that the complicated tensions of a group's ethnic origin versus its self-identification and the tacit appropriations resulting from such identity conflicts are all the more exacerbated when the construction of nation-states is at stake, as was the case with Greece in the nineteenth century and Albania in the twentieth. However, what remains of interest to me in the resistance of Souli is not its national(ist) significance, which one cannot nonetheless deny either for the official Greek narrative of independence or for recent Albanian ethnocentrist claims to the Souliot legacy. What I find ethically compelling is this moment of holy madness, which the Souliots—particularly the women of Zalongos—repeated two millennia after ancient Xanthos, thus interrupting the modern world of historical reflection and linear progress by renewing the cycle of tragic repetition.

39. Instead of the term "Muslim Albanians," nationalist Greek histories use the more known, but pejorative, term "Turkalbanians."

40. Stamelos reinforces comparisons between Souli and ancient Greek communities based on honor, whether Homeric or Spartan; citing the Italian philhellene Giuseppe Pecchio, Stamelos writes that the Souliots preferred the ancient form of warfare in which the body was covered by a shield (Stamelos 29). Not only was the male Souliot destined to become a courageous warrior and attain glory, but his success in war was equated with his success in romantic love. Honor (the Homeric τιμή) connected both systems: honor in war and honor in love (30–32). Concerning judicial matters, Stamelos quotes the historian Christophoros Perraivos that there was no written law among the Souliots but only an unwritten code of honor. When a problem arose, the Council of Elders would consider it and then announce its verdict orally. It was expected that the condemned would obey with no appeals; and if not, the decision would be implemented coercively (Stamelos 62). Stamelos relates that Perraivos compared the Souliot austerity to the ancient Spartans (Stamelos 63). And like the ancient Spartan women, who were reputed to be as brave as the men, the Souliot women are also assigned exceptional courage. Tsolis, on the other hand, focuses on aspects of Souliot governance that he interprets to be democratic: he views as genuinely democratic the fact that the leaders were the first to sacrifice themselves (13, 14), rather than displace this responsibility onto others. This, however, is not necessarily a democratic trait but could be an instance of the code of honor, which required the leader to lead also in battle. Tsolis thinks of Souli as an immediate democracy (33); but in fact, it was a mixed system: only the leading families were represented in the Council of Elders, but the General Council included the leaders

of each family as well as anyone who had defended Souli in war, whether a family leader or not (34). Eventually, what Tsolis reads as democratic is the basic idea that the majority decided (34).

41. Souli and Souliot bravery became a favored subject of romantic painting. See, for instance, Eugène Delacroix's sketch *Souliots in Traditional Costume* (1824–25), Ary Scheffer's depiction of the suicide of the women of Zalongos entitled *The Souliot Women* (1827), Joseph Stieler's portrait of Souliot fighter Markos Botsaris's daughter entitled *Katharina Botsaris* (1841), and Edward Lear's landscape drawing *Rocks of Suli* (1849). For a comprehensive study of the influence of the Greek Revolution in French painting, see Athanassoglou-Kallmyer, *French Images from the Greek War of Independence, 1821–1830*.

42. I consulted the sequence of the wars Tsolis provides (51–54), which is generally in agreement with other standard historical sources.

43. For instance, after his visit to the pasha's court in 1809, Lord Byron writes admiringly of the cultural renaissance Ali brought about in the city of Ioannina but adds that he was "a remorseless tyrant, guilty of the most horrible cruelties," such as "roasting rebels" (27).

44. Though the outcome was victorious for the Souliots, Ali Pasha captured Fotos Tzavelas, the son of famed Souliot fighters Lambros and Moscho Tzavelas. Tsolis quotes from a letter from Lambros Tzavelas to Ali, who was threatening his son: "Some Turks like yourself want to say that I am a pitiless father, who will sacrifice his son for his own freedom. I respond that, if you take the mountain, you will kill my son, the rest of my family, and my compatriots. Then I will not be able to avenge his death; but if we win, I can have other children; my wife is young. If my son, young as he is, is not content to sacrifice himself for his country, then he does not deserve to live and be recognized as my son" (Tzavelas qtd. in Tsolis 71). Regardless of how severe and idealistic this stance appears, it is realistic as well. This pasha was notorious for his deceptive tactics, and no one could guarantee that he would honor his promise to release Fotos upon the Souliot surrender. Thus, Lambros's evocation of the mountain is not just romantic rhetoric but a statement of responsibility for the future: a victory over those mountains could enhance Ali's sense of triumph so that he would kill his hostages as well as the other rebels, and could put an end to the Souliot community. Considered in its idealist sense, this letter echoes the strange logic by which Antigone justified her act as being intended only for her brother. Like Antigone, who said that she could have another husband and other children but could never have another brother from the same parents who were now dead, Tzavelas reminds Ali that he can have another son if this one is killed but that what remains irreproducible once lost (for Lambros, his captured son, and the other Souliots) is freedom itself—the freedom that makes family, childbearing, and community possible.

45. On the significance of the actual facts versus the legendary aspect this suicide took on in its historical transmission, see Politis, "Ο 'χορός του Ζαλόγγου.'" Politis is interested in demythologizing the event and thus attempts to find all the competing

accounts, to expose the differences in the details, and to illustrate how the event became constitutive for nationalist agendas. However, aside from discrepancies concerning the number of women in several reports and Christophoros Perraivos's belated but influential insertion of the element of the dance (the ideological motives for which Politis sets out to disrupt), Politis does not deny that the suicide itself is a historical fact and not a legend. It is the account of J. L. S. Bartholdy, a Prussian traveler and diplomat friendly to the Ottoman court and not particularly sympathetic to the Souliots, that convinces Politis (Politis 267–68). Apparently, even Bartholdy was moved by the plight of the Souliots. While I remain sympathetic to the project of challenging the nationalist fervor with which such events are invested, I am not always convinced by the particulars of Politis's logic. Nor am I swayed by the sardonic tone with which he dismisses important European intellectuals as well as seminal modern Greek poets for their gullible philhellenism, to the point of calling poetry the space par excellence of mythmaking (*mythoplasia*)—where mythmaking is for him a derogatory term, the fabrication of lies (283). Politis begins his essay on Zalongos by questioning the lack of any Ottoman perspective in the description of these events, adding that the only person writing about the siege from the Ottoman point of view was the court poet, who did not refer at all to the events at Zalongos (267). But why would the court poet of Ali document the suicide of some Souliot women, either as an act of heroism or even as a desperate response to coercion? Unless he could subsume the incident within a general story of Ottoman triumph, any particular reference to such gruesome details as women killing their infants to avoid slavery would have cast the pasha in terrible light and likely would have cost the poet his head. Furthermore, since Politis regards poetry as lies anyway, why should we put any more faith in the Ottoman poet's version of the events? At any rate, as Politis himself soon admits, Bartholdy's account is close to an Ottoman-friendly account, and it seems to corroborate the fact of the suicide, albeit without the emotional element of the dance. Ultimately, Politis is more interested in discharging the emotional rhetoric connected to the transmission of the Zalongos suicide in philhellenic circles and the nascent Greek state than in doubting its occurrence.

46. With respect to the issue of madness and deliberation, it is instructive to mention the letter of Greek diasporic Enlightenment thinker Adamantios Koraes, dated April 22, 1803, in which he calls the Souliots the pride of the Greeks, notes how Europe recounts and admires their heroic deeds, and warns them to be wary of the cunning nature of Ali Pasha. Markedly, he adds that, although bravery is a heavenly gift, it must be accompanied by *phronesis* (temperance) (Koraes qtd. in Stamelos 10).

47. Tsolis refers to a text by Kitsos Tzavelas to the Third National Council of the Greeks, dated March 24, 1827, where Tzavelas underlines the Souliot sacrifice for a *koine patrida* (a common fatherland). Through this text, Tsolis presents the Souliots as bearers of a panhellenic vision and not as mere provincialists (15). In this context, it should be understood that even though fatherland and nation-state have for a long

time been conflated, *patrida*—like Hölderlin's *Vaterland*, which also suffered from its Nazi appropriation—is not reducible to a nation-state.

48. Arkadi is often compared to Koungi and to the explosion at Messolonghi, which happened after a failed attempt at a sortie by the besieged in April 1826. Karellis maintains the comparison to both (16). Greek military leader Panos Koronaios was reported to have greeted the determination of the Cretan rebels by saying, "Souli lives again at Arkadi" (Bledsoe 19). The exodus of Messolonghi lies chronologically between Souli and Arkadi; but I have not included it here, in large part because it remains more familiar in the West because of Lord Byron's death there. The profound impact that the siege of Messolonghi has had on European romanticism is also visible in Delacroix's renowned painting *Greece Expiring on the Ruins of Messolonghi*.

49. I am indebted to Giorgis Manousakis's succinct description of these events, from which I have largely sketched this historical summary. I have also cross-referenced the events with Vasileios Psilakis's history and the more recent study by Manolis Karellis.

50. Although religious affiliation has been a privileged marker of identification among the Greeks in their opposition to occupation, the Orthodox Church—despite its insistence to the contrary—unfortunately shares not only in the history of resistance but also in that of complicity and collaboration with some of the most repressive measures of the empire. A noteworthy example in the case of Crete was Metropolitan Dionysios Charitonides, described by the Greek consul at Chania, Nikolaos Sakopoulos, as "one of the most loyal servants of the Sublime Porte" (Karellis 31, my translation). The consul's report of November 28, 1866, relates that the metropolitan was invited by Mustafa Pasha to discuss how to contain the negative effects worldwide that the news of Arkadi's destruction would have on the empire (Karellis 31–32). Ioannis Barouxakis, vice-consul to Heraklion, reports on November 21, 1866, that the same metropolitan embarked on the Ottoman boat that brought the news of Arkadi "in order to communicate his respects to the Ottomans, and to express his reverence and congratulations to Mustafa Pasha for his victory" (Karellis 33, my translation). Interestingly, as Karellis notes (32), this report by Barouxakis is omitted from the comprehensive two-volume edition on the 1866–69 revolution published by the Academy of Athens on the centennial of the Arkadi holocaust, an edition that contains consular and other official documents pertaining to that period.

51. My source for Sakopoulos's numbers is Karellis, who extensively quotes relevant passages from the consular reports on Arkadi initially published by the Academy of Athens.

52. Karellis's recent study inclines toward Skoulas, whose name appears as the exploder on the omitted report by Barouxakis. Karellis's sensitive treatment of the discrepancy between tradition and new evidence is in sharp contrast to Politis's eagerness to reduce events to myths when their various accounts are divergent. Karellis writes, "Kostis Giampoudakis and Emmanuel Skoulas are not competing against each other as some incorrectly believe, or as others terribly imply for their own, ostensibly petty, reasons. To the contrary, they both participated in the desperate

but good struggle" (14, my translation). The point is that empirical accuracy, while contributing to truth, does not exhaust truth—namely, it does not exhaust the larger significance of the event. At any rate, we should not forget that during those times, the processes of information dissemination were not as technologically advanced as they are now: waiting for a boat to come one or two days after an event to give a summary is not the same as having photojournalists on site, and thus rumors were likely to grow. Even though this can compromise a certain degree of accuracy, it does not undermine the entirety of the event. Additionally, our ability to detect ideological motives behind certain modes of transmission in the past does not mean that the present critics and historiographers are innocent of their own ideological motives.

53. For the press reaction to Arkadi in Greece, Europe, and America, see Zambettakis, "Influence de l'holocauste d'Arkadi sur l' opinion mondiale." Throughout the Cretan struggle, Russia was the only power to advocate union with Greece. Its position is clearly stated in an indignant article of the newspaper *Moscow* concerning Arkadi's destruction, which accuses the Western powers for making a mistake in omitting Crete from the London Protocol (Zambettakis 417). Indeed, Arkadi produced the very same response in the British public, with both the *London Times* and London's *Daily Herald* advocating against their government's policy of neutrality (Zambettakis 421). Several important international figures in the world of politics and letters were deeply moved by the Cretan reaction. The most notable would be Italy's great revolutionary Giuseppe Garibaldi (Zambettakis 422–23) and the French romantic Victor Hugo (Zambettakis 423–24).

54. In the parallel plane of tragic theater, I am thus largely in agreement with Loraux's remark that the audience of tragedy is not a national or political audience but an "apolitical body known as the human race, or, to give it its tragic name, the 'race of mortals'" (89). However, as tragedy is never just one thing, I need to qualify her universalist conclusion by saying that this "race of mortals" has been and will most likely always remain divided, bound as it is to its specific identifications at various times (national, religious, socioeconomic, and so on). This is, in large part, what makes humans political in that very sense Loraux seeks to avoid, but this is also why they are mortal—namely, flawed and tormented—in the first place. Tragedy, despite its universality, is tragedy precisely because it knows that mortals will never recognize its universality. Thus, even though it addresses all human beings, it addresses them in their inability to learn who they are. In other words, for the antipolitical threnody to be heard, the political plot has to first unravel.

55. From London's *Daily Herald*, reprinted in *Le Siècle d'Athènes* and *Le Jour* (qtd. in Zambettakis 421).

56. For the Greek original, see Kalvos, Ὠδαί (1–20), 173–81. For a less literal and more colloquial rendering, see George Dandoulakis's translation, 79–82.

57. For the Greek original, see Kalvos, Ὠδαί (1–20), 193–99; and for Dandoulakis's translation, see 88–90.

Works Cited

Acampora, Christa Davis. "'The Contest between Nietzsche and Homer': Revaluing the Homeric Question." *Nietzsche and the German Tradition*. Ed. Nicholas Martin. Oxford: Peter Lang, 2003. 83–109.

Adorno, Theodor W. "Parataxis: On Hölderlin's Late Poetry." *Notes to Literature*. Trans. Shierry Weber Nicholsen. Ed. Rolf Tiedemann. Vol. 2. New York: Columbia University Press, 1992. 109–49.

Aeschylus. *Agamemnon*. Trans. Richmond Lattimore. *Agamemnon, Prometheus Bound, Oedipus the King, Antigone, Hippolytus*. 2nd ed. Chicago: University of Chicago Press, 1991. 1–60. Vol. 1 of *Greek Tragedies*. Ed. David Grene and Richmond Lattimore. 3 vols.

———. *Seven against Thebes*. Trans. Herbert Weir Smyth. *Suppliant Maidens, Persians, Prometheus, Seven against Thebes*. Cambridge: Loeb-Harvard University Press, 1963. 319–419. Vol. 1 of *Aeschylus*. 2 vols.

Agamben, Giorgio. *Homo Sacer: On Sovereignty and Bare Life*. Trans. Daniel Heller-Roazen. Stanford: Stanford University Press, 1998.

———. *The Man without Content*. Trans. Georgia Albert. Stanford: Stanford University Press, 1999.

Alford, C. Fred. "Emmanuel Levinas and Iris Murdoch: Ethics as Exit?" *Philosophy and Literature* 26.1 (April 2002): 24–42.

Apostolopoulos, Apostolos. *Η Δύση των φαντασμάτων και η μέσα Ελλάδα* [*The West of the Specters and Deepest Greece*]. Athens, Greece: Indiktos, 1998.

Aristotle. *Poetics*. Trans. and with an introduction and notes by James Hutton. New York: Norton, 1982.

———. *Poetics*. Trans. Stephen Halliwell. Cambridge: Loeb-Harvard University Press, 1995.

Arnold, Matthew. "Hebraism and Hellenism." *Culture and Anarchy*. New York: Oxford University Press, 2009. 95–105.

Athanassoglou-Kallmyer, Nina. *French Images from the Greek War of Independence, 1821–1830: Art and Politics under the Restoration*. New Haven CT: Yale University Press, 1989.

Auerbach, Erich. "Odysseus's Scar." *Mimesis: The Representation of Reality in Western Literature*. Trans. Willard Trask. Princeton: Princeton University Press, 1953. 1–20.

Augst, Therese Ahern. "Difference Becomes Antigone: Hölderlin and the Ethics of Translation." *Seminar* 38.2 (2002): 95–115.

Baracchi, Claudia. "Beyond the Comedy and Tragedy of Authority: The Invisible Father in Plato's *Republic*." *Philosophy and Rhetoric* 34.2 (2001): 151–76.

———. "'Words of Air': On Breath and Inspiration." *Epoché* 11.1 (2006): 27–49.

Barthes, Roland. *Camera Lucida: Reflections on Photography*. Trans. Richard Howard. New York: Hill and Wang, 1981.

Bataille, Georges. *Lascaux or the Birth of Art*. New York: Skira, 1955.

———. "The Sovereign." Trans. Michelle Kendall and Stuart Kendall. *The Unfinished System of Nonknowledge*. Ed. Stuart Kendall. Minneapolis: University of Minnesota Press, 2001. 185–95.

———. *Theory of Religion*. Trans. Robert Hurley. New York: Zone Books, 1992.

Benardete, Seth. *The Rhetoric of Morality and Philosophy: Plato's* Gorgias *and* Phaedrus. Chicago: University of Chicago Press, 1991.

———. *Sacred Transgressions: A Reading of Sophocles'* Antigone. South Bend IN: St. Augustine's Press, 1999.

———. "Sophocles' *Oedipus Tyrannus*." *The Argument of the Action: Essays on Greek Poetry and Philosophy*. Ed. Ronna Burger and Michael Davis. Chicago: University of Chicago Press, 2000. 71–83.

Benjamin, Walter. "The Work of Art in the Age of Mechanical Reproduction." *Illuminations*. Trans. Harry Zohn. Ed. Hannah Arendt. New York: Schocken, 1969. 217–52.

Bertaux, Pierre. *Hölderlin und die Französische Revolution*. Frankfurt: Suhrkamp, 1969.

Biris, Kostas. Αρβανίτες: οι Δωριείς του νεότερου Ελληνισμού [*Arvanites: The Dorians of Modern Greece*]. 3rd ed. Athens, Greece: Melissa, 1997.

Blanchot, Maurice. "Orpheus's Gaze." *The Siren's Song: Selected Essays by Maurice Blanchot*. Trans. Sacha Rabinovitch. Ed. Gabriel Josipovici. Sussex, England: Harvester Press, 1982. 171–76.

———. *The Space of Literature*. Trans. Ann Smock. Lincoln: University of Nebraska Press, 1982.

Bledsoe, Thomas. *The Story of Two Heroic Monasteries: Arkadi and Preveli, Crete*. Athens, Greece: House of the Double Axe, 1966.

Blundell, Mary Whitlock. *Helping Friends and Harming Enemies*. Cambridge: Cambridge University Press, 1989.

Boyarin, Jonathan. *Thinking in Jewish*. Chicago: University of Chicago Press, 1996.

Browning, Elizabeth Barrett. "The Dead Pan." *The Poems of Elizabeth Barrett Browning*. New York: James Miller, 1874. 279–88. Vol. 1 of 4 vols.

Butler, Eliza Marian. *The Tyranny of Greece over Germany: A Study of the Influence Exercised by Greek Art and Poetry over the Great German Writers of the Eighteenth, Nineteenth, and Twentieth Centuries*. New York: Macmillan, 1935.

Butler, Judith. *Antigone's Claim: Kinship between Life and Death*. New York: Columbia University Press, 2000.

Byron, George Gordon. *Lord Byron: Selected Letters and Journals*. Ed. Leslie A. Marchand. Cambridge: Belknap-Harvard University Press, 1984.

Cactus Philological Collective [Φιλολογική Ομάδα Κάκτου]. Εισαγωγή [Introduction]. Πλάτων: Φαῖδρος [*Plato: Phaedrus*]. Athens, Greece: Cactus, 1993. 17–24.

Colaiaco, James A. *Socrates against Athens: Philosophy on Trial*. New York: Routledge, 2001.

Copjec, Joan. "The Tomb of Perseverance: On *Antigone*." *Giving Ground: The Politics of Propinquity*. Ed. Joan Copjec and Michael Sorkin. London: Verso, 1999. 233–66.

Critchley, Simon. "*Il y a*: Holding Levinas's Hand to Blanchot's Fire." *Maurice Blanchot: The Demand of Writing*. Ed. Carolyn Bailey Gill. London: Routledge, 1996. 108–22.

———. "'I Want to Die, I Hate My Life——Phaedra's Malaise." *Rethinking Tragedy*. Ed. Rita Felski. Baltimore: Johns Hopkins University Press, 2008. 170–97.

Dastur, Françoise. "Hölderlin and the Orientalisation of Greece." *Pli* 10 (2000): 156–73.

De Beistegui, Miguel, and Simon Sparks, eds. *Philosophy and Tragedy*. London: Routledge, 2000.

De Duve, Thierry. "Five Remarks on Aesthetic Judgment." *Umbra* 1 (1999): 13–32.

DeJean, Joan. *Ancients against Moderns: Culture Wars and the Making of a Fin de Siècle*. Chicago: University of Chicago Press, 1997.

Del Caro, Adrian. *Hölderlin: The Poetics of Being*. Detroit: Wayne State University Press, 1991.

Deleuze, Gilles. *Foucault*. Trans. Seán Hand. Minneapolis: University of Minnesota Press, 1988.

De Romilly, Jacqueline. *The Great Sophists of Periclean Athens*. Trans. Janet Lloyd. New York: Oxford University Press, 1992.

———. *Pourquoi la Grèce?* Paris: Editions Fallois, 1992.

Derrida, Jacques. "Plato's Pharmacy." *Disseminations*. Trans. Barbara Johnson. Chicago: University of Chicago Press, 1983. 61–172.

———. *Politics of Friendship*. Trans. George Collins. New York: Verso, 2006.

Detienne, Marcel. *Dionysos Slain*. Trans. Mireille Muellner and Leonard Muellner. Baltimore: Johns Hopkins University Press, 1979.

De Vries, Hent, and Samuel Weber, eds. *Violence, Identity, and Self-Determination*. Stanford: Stanford University Press, 1997.

Eagleton, Terry. *Sweet Violence: The Idea of the Tragic*. Oxford: Blackwell, 2003.

Else, Gerald F. *The Madness of Antigone*. Heidelberg: Carl Winter Universitätsverlag, 1976.

Elytis, Odysseus. Τὸ Ἄξιον Ἐστὶ [*The Axion Esti*]. In Greek with a translation by Edmund Keeley and George Savidis. Pittsburgh: University of Pittsburgh Press, 1974.

———. *The Axion Esti. Collected Poems of Odysseus Elytis.* Trans. Jeffrey Carson and Nikos Sarris. Revised and expanded edition. Baltimore: Johns Hopkins University Press, 2004. 119–90.

Euripides. *The Bacchae of Euripides.* Ed. John Edwin Sandys. Cambridge, England: University Press, 1880.

———. *The Bacchae.* Trans. William Arrowsmith. *The Eumenides, Philoctetes, Oedipus at Colonus, The Bacchae, Alcestis.* 2nd ed. Chicago: University of Chicago Press, 1991. 191–262. Vol. 3 of *Greek Tragedies.* Ed. David Grene and Richmond Lattimore. 3 vols.

———. *Bacchae. Helena, Phoenissae, Orestes, Bacchae, Iphigenia Aulidensis, Rhesus.* Ed. J. Diggle. 2nd ed. Oxford: Oxford University Press, 1994. 289–356. Vol. 3 of *Evripidis Fabvlae.* 3 vols.

———. *Bacchae.* Ed. and trans. David Kovacs. *Bacchae, Iphigenia at Aulis, Rhesus.* Cambridge: Loeb-Harvard University Press, 2002. 11–153. Vol. 6 of *Euripides.* 6 vols.

———. *Medea.* Ed. and trans. David Kovacs. *Cyclops, Alcestis, Medea.* Cambridge: Loeb-Harvard University Press, 1994. 293–427. Vol. 1 of *Euripides.* 6 vols.

———. *The Trojan Women.* Trans. Richmond Lattimore. *The Libation Bearers, Electra, Iphigenia in Tauris, Electra, The Trojan Women.* Chicago: University of Chicago Press, 1960. 243–95. Vol. 2 of *Greek Tragedies.* Ed. David Grene and Richmond Lattimore. 3 vols.

———. *The Trojan Women.* The Trojan Women *and* Hippolytus. Trans. Edward P. Coleridge. Ed. Drew Silver. Mineola NY: Dover, 2002. 2–27.

Ferrari, G. R. F. *Listening to the Cicadas: A Study of Plato's Phaedrus.* Cambridge: Cambridge University Press, 1990.

Finlayson, James Gordon. "'Bare Life' and Politics in Agamben's Reading of Aristotle." *The Review of Politics* 72 (2010): 97–126.

Fóti, Véronique. *Epochal Discordance: Hölderlin's Philosophy of Tragedy.* Albany: State University of New York Press, 2007.

Foucault, Michel. *The Care of the Self.* Trans. Robert Hurley. New York: Vintage, 1988. Vol. 3 of *The History of Sexuality.* 3 vols.

———. *Fearless Speech.* Ed. Joseph Pearson. Los Angeles: Semiotext(e), 2001.

———. *The Use of Pleasure.* Trans. Robert Hurley. New York: Vintage, 1990. Vol. 2 of *The History of Sexuality.* 3 vols.

Gasché, Rodolphe. "Kafka's Law: In the Field of Forces between Judaism and Hellenism." *MLN* 117.5 (2002): 971–1002.

Gaskill, P. H. "Hölderlin and Revolution." *Forum for Modern Language Studies* 12.2 (1976): 118–36.

Gerolymatos, André. *The Balkan Wars: Conquest, Revolution, and Retribution from the Ottoman Era to the Twentieth Century and Beyond.* New York: Basic Books, 2002.

Geulen, Eva. *The End of Art: Readings in a Rumor after Hegel.* Trans. James McFarland. Stanford: Stanford University Press, 2006.

Goldhill, Simon. "Generalizing about Tragedy." *Rethinking Tragedy*. Ed. Rita Felski. Baltimore: Johns Hopkins University Press, 2008. 45–65.
Gossman, Lionel. "Philhellenism and Antisemitism: Matthew Arnold and His German Models." *Comparative Literature* 46.1 (1994): 1–39.
Gourgouris, Stathis. *Dream Nation: Enlightenment, Colonization and the Institution of Modern Greece*. Stanford: Stanford University Press, 1996.
Green, Michael Steven. *Nietzsche and the Transcendental Tradition*. Champaign: University of Illinois Press, 2002.
Gutting, Gary. "Michel Foucault." 2 Apr. 2003, substantive revision 17 Sept. 2008. *Stanford Encyclopedia of Philosophy*. Accessed 13 Nov. 2009. http://plato.stanford.edu/entries/foucault/.
Gyömörey, Lorenz. Ἡ δύση τῆς Δύσης: ἡ ἀπομυθοποίηση τῆς Εὐρώπης καὶ ὁ Ἑλληνισμὸς [*The Sunset/Decline of the West: Hellenism and the Demythologization of Europe*]. Athens, Greece: Papazisi Publications, 1995. Originally published as *Auf den Spuren der Mütter*. Vienna: Zsolnay-Verlag, 1977.
Hackforth, R. Introduction. *Plato's* Phaedrus. Trans. R. Hackforth. Cambridge: Cambridge University Press, 1952. 1–18.
Hadot, Pierre. *Philosophy as a Way of Life*. Trans. Michael Chase. Ed. Arnold I. Davidson. Oxford: Blackwell, 1995.
Halliwell, Stephen. *The Aesthetics of Mimesis: Ancient Texts and Modern Problems*. Princeton: Princeton University Press, 2002.
Hamilton, Edith, and Huntington Cairns, eds. *Plato: The Collected Dialogues*. Bollingen Series 61. New York: Pantheon, 1963.
Havelock, Eric A. *Preface to Plato*. Cambridge: Belknap-Harvard University Press, 1963.
Hegel, G. W. F. *Introductory Lectures on Aesthetics*. Trans. Bernard Bosanquet. New York: Penguin, 1993.
———. *Phenomenology of Spirit*. Trans. A. V. Miller. Oxford: Oxford University Press, 1977.
Heidegger, Martin. *Being and Time*. Trans. John Macquarrie and Edward Robinson. New York: Harper and Row, 1962.
———. "Hegel and the Greeks." Trans. Robert Metcalf. *Pathmarks*. Ed. William McNeill. Cambridge: Cambridge University Press, 1998. 323–36.
———. *Hölderlin's Hymn "The Ister."* Trans. William McNeill and Julia Davis. Bloomington: Indiana University Press, 1996.
———. *Introduction to Metaphysics*. Trans. Gregory Fried and Richard Polt. New Haven CT: Yale University Press, 2000.
———. "Letter on Humanism." Trans. Frank A. Capuzzi and J. Glenn Gray. *Basic Writings*. Ed. David Farrell Krell. Revised and expanded edition. New York: HarperCollins, 1993. 213–65.
———. *Nietzsche*. Trans. David Farrell Krell. New York: HarperCollins, 1991. 2 vols.
———. "'Only a God Can Save Us': *Der Spiegel*'s Interview with Martin Heidegger (1966)." Trans. Maria P. Alter and John D. Caputo. Reprinted in *The Heidegger Controversy: A Critical Reader*. Ed. Richard Wolin. Cambridge: MIT Press, 1992. 91–116.

———. "The Origin of the Work of Art." *Poetry, Language, Thought*. Trans. Albert Hofstadter. New York: Harper Collins, 2001. 15–79.

———. "... Poetically man dwells ..." *Poetry, Language, Thought*. Trans. Albert Hofstadter. New York: HarperCollins, 2001. 211–27.

———. "The Question Concerning Technology." *The Question Concerning Technology and Other Essays*. Trans. William Lovitt. New York: Harper and Row, 1977. 3–49.

Henn, T. R. *The Harvest of Tragedy*. London: Methuen, 1956.

Herodotus. *The Landmark Herodotus: The Histories*. Trans. Andrea L. Purvis. Ed. Robert B. Strassler. New York: Anchor Books, 2009.

Hölderlin, Friedrich. *The Death of Empedocles: A Mourning Play*. Trans. David Farrell Krell. Albany: State University of New York Press, 2008.

———. *Essays and Letters on Theory*. Ed. and trans. Thomas Pfau. Albany: State University of New York Press, 1988.

———. *Friedrich Hölderlin: Poems and Fragments*. Trans. Michael Hamburger. London: Anvil Press Poetry, 2004.

———. *Gedichte nach 1800*. Stuttgart: Kohlhammer Verlag, 1953. Vol. 2 of *Sämtliche Werke: Kleine Stuttgarter Ausgabe*. Ed. Friedrich Beißner. 6 vols.

———. *Hymns and Fragments*. Trans. Richard Sieburth. Princeton: Princeton University Press, 1984.

———. *Hyperion and Selected Poems*. Ed. Eric Santner. New York: Continuum, 1990.

———. *Odes and Elegies*. Trans. and ed. Nick Hoff. Middletown CT: Wesleyan University Press, 2008.

Homer. *The Iliad*. Trans. Richmond Lattimore. Chicago: University of Chicago Press, 1961.

———. *The Odyssey*. Trans. Richmond Lattimore. New York: HarperCollins, 1999.

Howland, Jacob. "Plato's *Apology* as Tragedy." *The Review of Politics* 70.4 (2008): 519–46.

Hubbard, Scott. "Re: Aeschylus manuscript." E-mail to the author. 15 Aug. 2009.

Irwin, David. Introduction. *Winckelmann: Writings on Art*. By Johann Joachim Winckelmann. Ed. David Irwin. London: Phaidon, 1972.

Jacobs, Carol. "Dusting Antigone." *MLN* 111.5 (1996): 890–917.

Jepsen, Laura. *Ethical Aspects of Tragedy: A Comparison of Certain Tragedies by Aeschylus, Sophocles, Euripides, Seneca and Shakespeare*. New York: AMS Press, 1971.

Johnston, Sarah Iles. "Antigone's Other Choice." *Helios* 33S (2006 Supplement): 179–86.

Kahn, Charles, ed. *The Art and Thought of Heraclitus: An Edition of the Fragments with Translation and Commentary*. Cambridge: Cambridge University Press, 1999.

Kalvos, Andreas. Ὠδαί (1–20) [*Odes (1–20)*]. Ed. M. G. Merakles. Athens, Greece: Estia Bookstore, I. D. Kollaros and Co. SA, n.d.

———. *Odes*. Trans. George Dandoulakis. Nottingham, England: Shoestring Press, 1998.

Kant, Immanuel. *The Critique of Judgment*. Trans. Werner S. Pluhar. Indianapolis: Hackett Publishing, 1987.

Karellis, Manolis. Ιστορικά σημειώματα για την Κρήτη: από την επανάσταση του 1866 ως την κατοχή [*Historical Notes on Crete: From the 1866 Revolution to the German Occupation*]. Heraklion, Greece: University of Crete Publications, 2005.

Kennedy, George A. *Greek Rhetoric under Christian Emperors*. Princeton: Princeton University Press, 1983.

Kierkegaard, Søren. *The Concept of Irony with Continual Reference to Socrates*. Ed. and trans. Howard V. Wong and Edna H. Hong. Princeton: Princeton University Press, 1989.

Kitto, H. D. F. *The Greeks*. Harmondsworth, England: Penguin, 1951.

Kleinberg-Levin, David Michael. *Gestures of Ethical Life: Reading Hölderlin's Question of Measure after Heidegger*. Stanford: Stanford University Press, 2005.

Knox, Bernard. "The Continuity of Greek Culture." *The Oldest Dead White European Males and Other Reflections on the Classics*. New York: Norton, 1994. 107–30.

Kovacs, David. Introduction to *Bacchae*. *Bacchae, Iphigenia at Aulis, Rhesus*. Cambridge: Loeb-Harvard University Press, 2002. 2–10. Vol. 6 of *Euripides*. 6 vols.

Krell, David Farrell. "A Small Number of Houses in a Universe of Tragedy: Notes on Aristotle's περὶ ποιητικῆς and Hölderlin's 'Anmerkungen.'" *Philosophy and Tragedy*. Ed. Miguel de Beistegui and Simon Sparks. London: Routledge, 2000. 88–116.

———. *The Tragic Absolute: German Idealism and the Languishing of God*. Bloomington: Indiana University Press, 2005.

Lacan, Jacques. "The Essence of Tragedy: A Commentary on Sophocles's *Antigone*." *Seminar VII: The Ethics of Psychoanalysis*. Trans. Dennis Porter. Ed. Jacques-Alain Miller. New York: Norton, 1992. 243–83.

Lacoue-Labarthe, Philippe. "Caesura of the Speculative." *Typography: Mimesis, Philosophy, Politics*. Trans. and ed. Christopher Fynsk. Cambridge: Harvard University Press, 1989, 208–35.

———. *Heidegger, Art, and Politics: The Fiction of the Political*. Trans. Chris Turner. Oxford: Blackwell, 1990.

Lambropoulos, Vassilis. "On the Notion of the Tragedy of Culture." *Agon, Logos, Polis: The Greek Achievement and Its Aftermath*. Ed. Johann P. Arnason and Peter Murphy. Stuttgart: Franz Steiner, 2001. 233–55.

———. *The Rise of Eurocentrism: Anatomy of Interpretation*. Princeton: Princeton University Press, 1993.

———. *The Tragic Idea*. London: Duckworth, 2006.

Leeb, Thomas. *Jakob Philipp Fallmerayer: Publizist und Politiker zwischen Revolution und Reaktion (1835–1861)*. Munich: C. H. Beck, 1996.

Leiter, Brian. "Nietzsche's Moral and Political Philosophy." 26 Aug. 2004, substantive revision 27 July 2007. *Stanford Encyclopedia of Philosophy*. Accessed 25 Aug. 2009. http://plato.stanford.edu/entries/nietzsche-moral-political/.

Leonard, Miriam. *Athens in Paris: Ancient Greece and the Political in Post-War French Thought*. Oxford: Oxford University Press, 2005.

Levinas, Emmanuel. *Existence and Existents*. Trans. Alphonso Lingis. Pittsburgh: Duquesne University Press, 2001.

———. *Time and the Other*. Trans. Richard A. Cohen. Pittsburgh: Duquesne University Press, 1987.

Loraux, Nicole. *The Mourning Voice: An Essay on Greek Tragedy*. Trans. Elizabeth Trapnell Rawlings. Ithaca NY: Cornell University Press, 2002.

Manousakis, Giorgis. *Κρητικές επαναστάσεις: 1821–1905* [*Cretan Revolutions: 1821–1905*]. Chania, Greece: National Research Institute "E. K. Venizelos," 2004.

Marback, Richard. *Plato's Dream of Sophistry*. Columbia: University of South Carolina Press, 1999.

Marx, Karl. "The Eighteenth Brumaire of Louis Bonaparte." *The Marx-Engels Reader*. Ed. Robert C. Tucker. 2nd ed. New York: Norton, 1978. 594–617.

McCollom, William G. *Tragedy*. New York: Macmillan, 1957.

Michelakis, Pantelis. *Achilles in Greek Tragedy*. Cambridge: Cambridge University Press, 2002.

Muller, Herbert J. *The Spirit of Tragedy*. New York: Knopf, 1956.

Nancy, Jean-Luc. *The Inoperative Community*. Trans. Peter Connor, Lisa Garbus, Michael Holland, and Simona Sawhney. Ed. Peter Connor. Minneapolis: University of Minnesota Press, 1991.

———. *The Truth of Democracy*. Trans. Michael Naas. Bronx NY: Fordham University Press, 2010.

Nehamas, Alexander. *The Art of Living: Socratic Reflections from Plato to Foucault*. Berkeley: University of California Press, 1998.

Nichols, David. "Antigone's Autochthonous Voice: Echoes in Sophocles, Hölderlin, and Heidegger." *IWM Junior Visiting Fellows' Conferences* 25 (2009). Institut für die Wissenschaften von Menschen. Accessed 30 Oct. 2010. http://www.iwm.at/index.php?option=com_content&task=view&id=120&Itemid=125.

Nichols, Mary P. *Socrates and the Political Community: An Ancient Debate*. Albany: State University of New York Press, 1987.

Nietzsche, Friedrich. *The Birth of Tragedy and The Case of Wagner*. Trans. Walter Kaufmann. New York: Vintage, 1967.

———. *The Gay Science: With a Prelude in Rhymes and an Appendix of Songs*. Trans. Walter Kaufmann. New York: Vintage, 1974.

———. *On the Genealogy of Morals*. Trans. Ian Johnston. Last revision Jan. 2009. johnstonia. Accessed 8 Nov. 2008. http://records.viu.ca/~Johnstoi/Nietzsche/genealogypreface.htm.

———. *On the Genealogy of Morals and Ecce Homo*. Trans. Walter Kaufman and R. J. Hollingdale. New York: Vintage, 1989.

———. "On the Uses and Disadvantages of History for Life." *Untimely Meditations*. Trans. R. J. Hollingdale. Cambridge: Cambridge University Press, 1983. 57–123.

———. *The Twilight of the Idols*. Trans. R. J. Hollingdale. Harmondsworth, England: Penguin, 1968.

Nikolopoulou, Kalliopi. "Elements of Experience: Bataille's Drama." *Obsessions of Georges Bataille: Community and Communication*. Ed. Andrew Mitchell and Jason Kemp Winfree. Albany: State University of New York Press, 2009.

———. "Parrhesia as Tragic Structure in Euripides' *Bacchae*." *Epoché* 15.2 (Spring 2011): 249–61.

Nussbaum, Martha. "Sophocles' *Antigone*: Conflict, Vision, and Simplification." *The Fragility of Goodness: Luck and Ethics in Greek Tragedy and Philosophy*. Cambridge: Cambridge University Press, 1986. 51–82.

Ong, Walter J. *Orality and Literacy: The Technologizing of the Word*. London: Routledge, 1988.

Orwell, George. *1984*. New York: Harcourt Brace Jovanovich, 1977.

Otto, Walter F. *Dionysus: Myth and Cult*. Trans. Robert B. Palmer. Bloomington: Indiana University Press, 1965.

Özkirimli, Umut, and Spyros Sofos. *Tormented by History: Nationalism in Greece and Turkey*. London: Hurst, 2008.

Paras, Eric. *Foucault 2.0: Beyond Power and Knowledge*. New York: Other Press, 2006.

Pesmazoglou, Stephanos. "Η μυθολογική θεμελίωση του νεο-ελληνικού κράτους" ["The Mythological Foundation of the Modern Greek State"]. *Μύθοι και ιδεολογήματα στη σύγχρονη Ελλάδα* [*Myths and Ideologemes in Contemporary Greece*]. Scientific Symposium (23–24 Nov. 2005). Athens, Greece: Research Institute for Modern Greek Culture and General Education, 2007. 19–41.

Plato. *Apology*. *Euthyphro, Apology, Crito, Phaedo, Phaedrus*. Trans. Harold North Fowler. Cambridge: Loeb-Harvard University Press, 1990. 68–145. Vol. 1 of *Plato*. 12 vols.

———. *Apology*. Trans. Benjamin Jowett. *Selected Dialogues of Plato*. Revised edition by Hayden Pelliccia. New York: Modern Library, 2001. 279–323.

———. *Ion*. Trans. W. R. M. Lamb. *The Statesman, Philebus, Ion*. Cambridge: Loeb-Harvard University Press, 1925. 406–47. Vol. 8 of *Plato*. 12 vols.

———. *Ion*. Trans. Lane Cooper. *Plato: The Collected Dialogues*. Ed. Edith Hamilton and Huntington Cairns. Bollingen Series LXXI. New York: Pantheon, 1961. 215–28.

———. *Laws*. Trans. A. E. Taylor. *Plato: The Collected Dialogues*. Ed. Edith Hamilton and Huntington Cairns. Bollingen Series LXXI. New York: Pantheon, 1961. 1225–1513.

———. *Phaedo*. Trans. Hugh Tredennick. *Plato: The Collected Dialogues*. Ed. Edith Hamilton and Huntington Cairns. Bollingen Series LXXI. New York: Pantheon, 1961. 40–98.

———. *Phaedrus*. *Euthyphro, Apology, Crito, Phaedo, Phaedrus*. Trans. Harold North Fowler. Cambridge: Loeb-Harvard University Press, 1990. 412–579. Vol. 1 of *Plato*. 12 vols.

———. *Phaedrus*. Trans. Benjamin Jowett. *Selected Dialogues of Plato*. Revised edition by Hayden Pelliccia. New York: Modern Library, 2001. 111–97.

———. *The Republic*. Trans. Paul Shorey. Cambridge: Loeb-Harvard University Press, 1930 and 1935. 2 vols.

———. *The Republic*. Trans. Paul Shorey. *Plato: The Collected Dialogues*. Ed. Edith Hamilton and Huntington Cairns. Bollingen Series LXXI. New York: Pantheon, 1961. 575–844.

———. *Symposium*. *Plato: The Collected Dialogues*. Ed. Edith Hamilton and Huntington Cairns. Bollingen Series LXXI. New York: Pantheon, 1961. 526–74.

Plutarch. *Lives, VI: Dion and Brutus, Timoleon and Aemilius Paulus*. Trans. Bernadotte Perrin. Cambridge: Loeb-Harvard University Press, 1918. 11 vols.

———. *Makers of Rome, Nine Lives: Coriolanus, Fabius Maximus, Marcellus, Cato the Elder, Tiberius Gracchus, Gaius Gracchus, Sertorius, Brutus, Mark Antony*. Trans. Ian Scott-Kilvert. London: Penguin, 1965.

Politis, Alexis. "Ο 'χορός του Ζαλόγγου': Πληροφοριακοί πομποί, πομποί αναμετάδοσης, δέκτες πρόσληψης" ["The 'Dance of Zalongos': Information Emission, Transmission, Reception"]. *Μύθοι και ιδεολογήματα στη σύγχρονη Ελλάδα* [*Myths and Ideologemes in Contemporary Greece*]. Scientific Symposium (23–24 Nov. 2005). Athens, Greece: Research Institute for Modern Greek Culture and General Education, 2007. 267–98.

Porter, James I. "Foucault's Ascetic Ancients." *Phoenix* 1–2 (Spring–Summer 2005): 121–32.

———. *Nietzsche and the Philology of the Future*. Stanford: Stanford University Press, 2002.

Pryor, Benjamin. Paper presentation on Foucault and parrhesia. Conf. on Normalization, Exclusion, Excess. California State University, Stanislaus, 8 Oct. 2005.

Psalidas, Athanasios. "Περιγραφὴ Γεωγραφικὴ Ἠπείρου καὶ Ἀλβανίας" ["Geographical Description of Epirus and Albania"]. *Γεωγραφία Ἀλβανίας καὶ Ἠπείρου* [*Geography of Albania and Epirus*]. Edited with notes and introduction by Athanasios Papacharisis. Ioannina, Greece: Editions of the Society of Epirotic Studies, 1964. 47–66.

Psilakis, Vasileios. *Ἱστορία τῆς Κρήτης ἀπὸ τῆς ἀπωτάτης ἀρχαιότητος μέχρι τῶν καθ' ἡμᾶς χρόνων* [*History of Crete from Early Antiquity to the Present*]. Vol. 4. Athens, Greece: Arkadi Publications, 1970.

Reinhardt, Karl. *Sophocles*. Trans. Hazel Harvey and David Harvey. New York: Barnes and Noble, 1979.

Rocha, Sam. Rev. of *Foucault 2.0: Beyond Power and Knowledge*, by Eric Paras. *Education Review* 27 July 2008. Accessed 23 Dec. 2008. http://edrev.asu.edu/reviews/rev680.htm.

Rojcewicz, Stephen. "The Feasts of the Gods in Homeric Epic and Socrates' *Apology*." *Collection du Cirp* 1 (2007): 180–97. Accessed 25 July 2009. http://www.cirp.uqam.ca/documents%20pdf/Collection%20vol.%201/10.S.Rojcewicz.pdf.

Santayana, George. *Egotism in German Philosophy*. New York: Charles Scriber's and Sons, 1940.

Sartre, Jean-Paul. *Search for a Method*. Trans. Hazel E. Barnes. New York: Vintage, 1968.

Schmidt, Dennis J. *On Germans and Other Greeks: Tragedy and Ethical Life*. Bloomington: Indiana University Press, 2001.

Segal, Charles. *Dionysiac Poetics and Euripides' Bacchae*. Princeton: Princeton University Press, 1982.

Shakespeare, William. *Hamlet*. Ed. Cyrus Hoy. Second Norton Critical Edition. New York: Norton, 1992.

Sophocles. *Antigone*. Trans. David Grene. *Agamemnon, Prometheus Bound, Oedipus the King, Antigone, Hippolytus*. 2nd ed. Chicago: University of Chicago Press, 1991.

177–232. Vol. 1 of *Greek Tragedies*. Ed. David Grene and Richmond Lattimore. 3 vols.

———. *Antigone. Antigone, The Women of Trachis, Philoctetes, Oedipus at Colonus*. Ed. and trans. Hugh Lloyd-Jones. Cambridge: Loeb-Harvard University Press, 1994. 1–127. Vol. 2 of *Sophocles*. 3 vols.

———. *Oedipus at Colonus*. Trans. David Grene. *The Eumenides, Philoctetes, Oedipus at Colonus, The Bacchae, Alcestis*. 2nd ed. Chicago: University of Chicago Press, 1991. 107–190. Vol. 3 of *Greek Tragedies*. Ed. David Grene and Richmond Lattimore. 3 vols.

Stamelos, Demetris. Λαογραφικά Σουλίου: Από το έτος της Σουλιώτικης παλικαριάς ως τον αιώνα μας [*Folkloric Traditions of Souli: From the Era of Souliot Bravery to Our Century*]. Athens, Greece: Pitsilos, 1988.

Steiner, George. *Antigones*. New Haven CT: Yale University Press, 1984.

Szondi, Peter. "Überwindung des Klassizismus." *Hölderlin-Studien*. Frankfurt am Main: Suhrkamp, 1970. 95–118.

Tsolis, Michalis. Σουλιωτών ολοκαύτωμα: Το Σούλι, ο φάρος της Ελλάδος [*The Holocaust of the Souliots: Souli, the Beacon of Greece*]. Athens, Greece: Noesis, 2003.

Vallega, Alejandro A. *Sense and Finitude: Encounters at the Limits of Language, Art, and the Political*. Albany: State University of New York Press, 2009.

Vernant, Jean-Pierre. *The Origins of Greek Thought*. Ithaca NY: Cornell University Press, 1982.

Von Klemperer, Klemens. *German Resistance against Hitler: The Search for Allies Abroad, 1938–1945*. Oxford: Clarendon, 1994.

Warminski, Andrzej. "Hölderlin in France." *Readings in Interpretation: Hölderlin, Hegel, Heidegger*. Minneapolis: University of Minnesota Press, 1987. 23–44.

Wildberg, Christian. "Piety as Service, Epiphany as Reciprocity: Two Observations on the Religious Meaning of the Gods in Euripides." *Illinois Classical Studies* 24–25 (1999–2000): 235–56.

———. "Socrates and Euripides." *A Companion to Socrates*. Ed. Sara Ahbel-Rappe and Rachana Kamtekar. Malden MA: Blackwell Publishing, 2006. 21–35.

Williams, Henry Smith. *A History of Science, Part 1*. Whitefish MT: Kessinger Publishing, 2004.

Winckelmann, Johann Joachim. "On the Imitation of the Painting and Sculpture of the Greeks." *Winckelmann: Writings on Art*. Ed. David Irwin. London: Phaidon, 1972.

Wind, Edgar. "Θεῖος Φόβος (*Laws*, II, 671D): On Plato's Philosophy of Art." *The Eloquence of Symbols: Studies in Humanist Art*. Ed. Jaynie Anderson. Oxford: Clarendon, 1983. 1–20.

Winfree, Jason Kemp. "The Contestation of Community." *The Obsessions of Georges Bataille: Community and Communication*. Ed. Andrew J. Mitchell and Jason Kemp Winfree. Albany: State University of New York Press, 2009. 31–46.

Woodruff, Paul. "Socrates and the Irrational." *Reason and Religion in Socratic Philosophy.* Ed. Nicholas D. Smith and Paul Woodruff. Oxford: Oxford University Press, 2000. 130–50.

Zambettakis, Emmanuel E. "Influence de l'holocauste d'Arkadi sur l'opinion mondiale." *Kritika Chronika* 8 (1954): 413–27.

Zeitlin, Froma I. "Thebes: Theater of Self and Society in Athenian Drama." *Nothing to Do with Dionysos? Athenian Drama in Its Social Context.* Ed. John J. Winkler and Froma I. Zeitlin. Princeton: Princeton University Press, 1990. 130–67.

Index

absence, xxxviii, 128, 138
Acampora, Christa Davis, 261n25
Achilles, 216, 288n6, 295n16; Socrates and, 147, 284n30
Adorno, Theodor W., 89, 266n16
Aeschylus, xxxii, 15–16, 45, 264n9; *Agamemnon*, 155, 244, 282n1; *Niobe*, 19; *Persians*, 298n37
The Aesthetics of Mimesis (Halliwell), 55, 56
afterlife, xxvii
Agamben, Giorgio, 71, 75, 257n4; on Aristotle, 71, 274n16; on art collecting, 83; on art's future, 87; on Kant, 85, 285n34; on modern art, 73, 75–76, 82, 83, 89; on Nietzsche, 84, 85; philosophical loyalties of, 70–71; on Plato, xxxiv, 62–66, 68, 71–72, 78–80, 88; on poetry, 53, 74, 275n18
Agamemnon (Aeschylus), 155, 244, 282n1
agency, xxvi, 38, 97, 107
Ajax, 155
alienation, xxxviii–xxxix, 85
Ali Pasha, 239, 300n44
allegory, 27, 52, 122
alterity, xxvi, xxxviii, 177, 187, 270n36;

and freedom, 17; Levinas on, 231–32, 270n36; and truth, 107
ancient-modern relation, xxi–xxii, xxxviii, 25, 35, 43, 56; discontinuity in, xxi, 28, 29; as radical rift, xxviii, xxxii, 45, 264n15
Antigone, 171–208; and autonomy, 186, 187, 290n26; and blood kinship, 187, 192, 200–201, 264n9; Butler on, xxxvii, 171–72, 174, 176–78, 186, 191–92, 196, 287n1; and choice, 187–89, 191, 289–90n22; Creon and, 168, 182–83, 190–91, 199; and death, 38, 175, 191, 192, 194, 195–96, 206, 211, 230; and fate, 14, 197; and harmony of words and deeds, xxxvii, 188; Hegel on, 178, 181, 287n15, 288nn14–15; Heidegger on, 193–94, 296n24; Hölderlin on, 12, 16, 17–19, 20; hubris of, 19–20, 190; as inspiration for philosophy, xxxvi–xxxvii; Ismene and, xxxix, 187–89, 289–90n22; and law, 119, 120, 137, 185, 198, 289n20; Loraux on, 178, 288n16; and nature, 39, 289n20; and Niobe myth, 17–18, 19; and Oedipus, 21; as parrhesiastic character, 110; and politics, 55, 176,

317

Antigone (*continued*)
177, 178, 179, 180–81, 226, 288n16; Polyneices and, 199, 290n27; and representation, 176–77, 178, 179–80; secrecy of, 207; and self, 186–87, 189–90; and strife, 225; and temporality, 14, 198, 201, 205; tragic nature of, xxxvi, 177–78; transparency of, xxxvii, 208; uncanniness of, 201, 225

Antigone's Claim (Butler), 176, 177

Antiope (Euripides), 44

Apollo, 13, 263n7; Foucault on, 115, 280n17; Socrates and, 117, 142, 144

Apology (Plato), 117, 119, 139–56, 190, 279n11; as tragedy, xxxv, 283n24

Apostolopoulos, Apostolos, 267n21, 269n31

appearance, 109, 280n16

Aristotle, xxxii; Agamben on, 71, 274n16; *Poetics*, 45, 274n16; on praxis, 275n18; on tragedy, 14

Arkadi, 240–45, 302–3nn48–53

art: abstract, 275n19; collecting, 82–83; contemporary view of, 54–55, 57, 71, 73, 75, 82–83; divine origin of, 63–64, 72, 80; and freedom, xxxiv, 56, 65, 83; future of, 87–88; Greek, 8, 15, 21, 24–25, 53, 57, 87, 263n4, 275n23, 279n15; Hegel on, xxxiii, xxxiv, 22, 53, 55, 58–62, 67, 69, 70, 87–89, 264n12, 276n29; and imitation, 6, 7, 66, 67, 72, 73, 79, 81, 275n24; Kant and, 58, 82, 84; and metaphysics, 87, 276n29; modern, xxxiv, 73, 75–76, 81–82, 84, 85, 89; and nature, 6, 13, 57, 58–59, 74, 81; Nietzsche on, 49; origin and originality in, 76–77, 79; and philosophy, xxxiii, 55, 57, 70, 72; Plato on, xxxiii, 53–58, 61, 62–69, 71–74, 77–81, 88–89, 90; and poetry, 8, 52, 63, 77–78, 80, 89; and politics, 72, 73, 75, 82, 87; sensuous aspects of, 61, 89; spectators of, 84, 85; state and, 54, 61; and truth, 56–57, 67, 72, 74, 75, 76, 81, 88–89, 90

Athenian society, 110, 180, 285–86n6, 291n28

Auerbach, Eric, 267n22

authenticity, xxxviii, 73, 216

autonomy, xxiv, 185, 265n19; Antigone and, 186, 187, 290n26; of art, xxxiv, 60

Babylon, 286n10

The Bacchae (Euripides), xxv, xxxvi, 115, 157–68, 227, 285n3; Dionysus in, 157–58, 161, 162, 163–64, 166, 167, 286nn8–10, 286n12; duplicity in, 161, 162–63; parrhesia in, 112, 113, 161; summary of, 157–58; as tragedy, 158, 164–65, 285n3

Bachofen, Johann Jakob, 289n20

Baracchi, Claudia, 138, 281n8, 291n31

Barouxakis, Ioannis, 302n50

Barthes, Roland, 262n27, 265n17

Bartholdy, J. L. S., 300–301n45

Bataille, Georges, 257n4, 263n6, 292n33; on community, 228–29; on sovereignty and politics, 290n26

Baudelaire, Charles, 273n5

beauty, 131, 229, 282n15; Hegel on, 59, 67; Plato on, 59–60, 67, 134, 137; and rhetoric, 131; and truth, 67

Being and Time (Heidegger), 230

Bekir Pasha, 239

belief, 102, 104, 163

Benardete, Seth, xxxvi, 135, 271n47, 283n19, 289n18; on Antigone, 194, 199, 201, 288n14; on *Phaedrus*, 127, 137; *Sacred Transgressions*, 288n14

Benjamin, Walter, 257n4

Bertaux, Pierre, 293n3

Biris, Kostas, 298–99n38

The Birth of Tragedy (Nietzsche), 263n7, 292n38

Blanchot, Maurice, xxxvii, 39, 230, 231, 234
blood, 193, 195, 202; figurality of, 202–3, 291n29, 292n32; and soil, 199, 291n29
blood kinship, 195, 198–99, 203–4; Antigone and, 187, 192, 200–201, 264n9; ethical centrality of, 200; and family, 199–200; and law, 181–83
Blundell, Mary Whitlock, 196
Boyarin, Jonathan, 265n19, 266n16
breath, 124, 281n8
Browning, Elizabeth Barrett, 35
Brutus, 218–20, 222
Butler, E. M., 265n18
Butler, Judith, xxxvii, 171–72, 174, 176, 186, 196, 287n1; on Antigone's death, 191–92; on incest taboo, 201–2, 203–5, 292n34; on representation and politics, 176–78
Byron, Lord, 300n43, 302n48

Cactus Philological Collective, 126
caesura, xxi, xxiii, xxiv, 8, 14, 15
"Caesura of the Speculative" (Lacoue-Labarthe), 8, 263n5
Cairns, Huntington, 275n23
Camera Lucida (Barthes), 262n27
Cartesianism, 106, 108
Cassandra, xv–xvi, xvii, xviii–xix, 212, 282n17
catharsis, xxii, 44, 67, 71–72, 273n3
Cavafy, C. P., 269n32
censorship, 84
certainty, 11, 264n9; contemporary theory and, xxx, 50; of uncertainty, 217
Charitonides, Dionyslos, 302n50
choice, xl, 97; Antigone and, 187–89, 191, 289–90n22; fate and, 196; tragedy and, xxix, xl, 167, 211, 232
Christianity, 29, 36, 267n21, 269n33
classicism, xxiv, xxv, 6, 7, 21, 260n16; imitation of Greeks by, 57–58
Colaiaco, James, 283n24
comedy, xx, xxix, 288n13
community, xxviii–xxix, 228–29; and myth, 257n4
complementarity, xxxii, 16, 223
The Concept of Irony with Continual Reference to Socrates (Kierkegaard), 156
conscience, 137, 183; law as voice of, 184, 190–91
Copjec, Joan, 291n28
Creon, 14–15, 200, 206, 225–26; and Antigone, 168, 182–83, 190–91, 199
Crete, 241–43, 302n50, 303n53
Critchley, Simon, 231, 232, 270n36
critical theory, xxiii, xxiv, 260n22, 268n24
The Critique of Judgment (Kant), 58
cultural criticism, xxiv, 265n19
cultural relativism, 295n17

Dastur, Françoise, 12–13, 17
David, Jacques-Louis, 22
death, xvii, 10, 17, 230–32, 234, 244; Antigone and, 38, 175, 191, 192, 194, 195–96, 206, 211, 230; banality of, 175; God and, 232; Greek view of, 288n8; Heidegger on, 230; human longing for, 210, 218; and human will, xxxvii; Levinas on, 230, 231, 232; and meaningfulness, 12, 229; poststructuralism on, xxxvii, 9, 230; Socrates on, 146–47, 148, 153–55; and suicide, 223–24, 230; tragic, xvii, xxxvii, 9, 229, 235, 263n6, 287–88n6
deception, 78, 80–81, 114, 275n24
deconstruction, 123, 156, 263n6, 282–83n18; and cultural relativism, 295n17; and parrhesia, xxiv; on Plato, 125, 260n20; poststructuralism and, xxiii, 268n24; on presence, 37, 137; of speech, 95

319

de Duve, Thierry, 75, 82, 83
deferral, xxiv, 260n20
Deleuze, Gilles, 277n5
Del Caro, Adrian, 294n6
Delphic oracle, 117, 142, 144
Delphic Sibyl, 82
democracy, xxviii, 160, 261nn23–24; Athenian, 146; as crisis of parrhesia, 106; Socrates on, 283–84n26; and truth, 123, 159
de Romilly, Jacqueline, 44, 297n25, 298n37
Derrida, Jacques, xxxvi, 39, 127, 260n20, 295n17; on democracy, 261n23; on Greek metaphysics, 266n16; on Plato, xxxvi, 121, 122–23, 281n10, 282n12, 283n19, 283n21; on speech, 95, 156, 282n18
Dionysus, 13, 29, 76, 144, 263n7; in *The Bacchae*, 157–58, 161, 162, 163–64, 166, 167, 286nn8–10, 286n12
divine, 16, 65, 66, 115; and art, 63–64, 72, 77, 80; duplicity, 158–59; and fear, 64, 71–72; and law, 183–84, 185; and love, 215; and poetry, 66, 78, 79, 89, 214; Socrates on, 132, 133, 142, 148, 151; truth, 159
divine (holy) madness, 21, 212, 214; and art, 63–64, 72, 79, 81; Hölderlin on, 19, 216; poetic nature of, 225; Socrates defense of, 132, 133
Dost Bey, 238
Duchamp, Marcel, 82

Eagleton, Terry, xix, 258n7
education, 141–42, 275n24, 279n11
Egypt, ancient, 135, 263n4, 297n26
Electra (Euripides), 113–15
Else, Gerald, 174, 195, 208
Elytis, Odysseus, 269n32
Empedocles, 12–13, 213, 294n9
Enlightenment, 22, 85, 236

ethics, 16–17, 137, 163, 263n6; and ontology, 43; and politics, xxv, xxxviii, 268n25; and presence, 137–38; and self, xxv, xl
Euripides: controversial reception of, 166, 286n14; Foucault on, xxxvi, 104, 110, 112–18, 120, 158; modernity of, xxiv–xxv; Nietzsche on, 45, 157, 166, 285n1; parrhesia in, 112–18; self-reflexivity of, 45; as tragic poet, 45, 160, 164, 166–67; works: *Antiope*, 44; *The Bacchae*, xxv, xxxvi, 112, 113, 115, 157–68, 227, 285n3; *Electra*, 113–15; *Hippolytus*, 114; *Ion*, 112, 113, 115, 117, 158; *Medea*, 286n13; *Orestes*, 112, 117–18; *The Phoenician Women*, 112–14; *The Trojan Women*, xv–xvi, xviii–xix, 222, 257n2
exemplarity, 83, 180, 289n17
Existence and Existents (Levinas), 270n36

Fallmerayer, Jakob Philipp, 268n27
family, 172, 178, 189, 199–200. *See also* blood kinship
fascism, 257n4
fate, xix, 211, 244, 271n46; Antigone and, 14, 197; and choice, 196; Heraclitus on, 279–80n15; historical, 220, 221; tragedy and, 187, 196, 198; and will, xxvi, 193
Fauriel, Claude, 238
Fearless Speech (Foucault), 93, 98
Ferrari, Giovanni R. F., xxxvi, 138, 283nn19–20; on *Phaedrus*, 122, 124, 136, 260n17, 280n5, 281n8
Finlayson, James Gordon, 71
fire, 213–14, 228, 294n10, 294n13
Foucault (Deleuze), 277n5
Foucault, Michel, 104, 277n4, 277n5, 279n10; on Apollo, 115, 280n17; on Euripides, xxxvi, 104, 110, 112–18, 120,

158; *Fearless Speech*, 93, 98; genealogical project of, xxxiv, 101, 102, 103, 112; on history of thought, 102–3; on parrhesia, xxiv, 93, 94, 96, 98, 103–8, 112, 121, 155–56, 277–78n5, 279n11, 279n13; on philosophy and tragedy, 93, 97, 168; on self, 94, 107, 279n11; on Socrates, xxxv, 104, 168; on truth, 98, 105, 112, 139, 277–78n5

freedom, 11, 16, 28, 30, 31, 270n36; alterity and, 17; art and, xxxiv, 56, 65, 83; contemporary Greek world and, 32, 35, 269n31; Hegel on, 61; nature and, 4–5; and necessity, xxix, 37, 38, 39; Nietzsche on, 26, 39; and responsibility, 33, 118, 137, 191; Socrates on, 142; tragedy and, xxxix, xl, 28, 40; truth and, 111

French Revolution, 214, 293n3

Gasché, Rodolphe, 289n20
gendering, 117, 282n16
genealogy, xxxiv, 98, 101–4, 112; of tragedy, xxxii, 101, 104
George, Stefan, 4
German idealism, xxiii, xxiv, 32, 87, 266n19; on Greeks and Hellenism, xxi, xxxiii, xxxiv, 25, 33, 34, 297n26; and Sophocles, 15–16; and tragedy, 37, 38, 56
Gerolymatos, André, 298–99n38
Geulen, Eva, 272n1
Giampoudakis, Kostis, 242
Goethe, Johann Wolfgang von, 22, 263n7
Goldhill, Simon, 40, 270n41
Gombrich, E. H., 8, 263n4
Gossman, Lionel, 267n22
Greece, ancient: accessibility and inaccessibility of, 10–11, 30; as allegorical, 8; archeological method of viewing, 260n16; Athenian society in, 110, 146, 180, 285–86n6, 291n28; continuity and discontinuity with, xxxiii, 28, 29, 32–33, 34, 36, 37, 71, 267n21, 268n27; early-classical split in, 41; equilibrium and balance of, xli, 14, 15, 263–64n8, 279n15; gendering in, 282n16; German idealism and, xxi, xxxiii, xxxiv, 25, 33, 34, 297n26; Germany's reception of, 29, 30, 265n18; Heidegger on, xxxi, 264n13; heroism in, 289n17; and Hesperia, xx–xxi, 7, 8, 10, 29; Hölderlin on, 4, 14, 15, 17, 20, 23–24, 27, 30, 47, 51; imitation of, xxi, 6, 22, 23–24, 57–58; and law, 134–35, 137; modern Greek view of, 36, 268n27; modernity and, xxi, 30, 65, 266n16; and nature, 5, 6, 13; Nietzsche on, xxxi–xxxii, 226, 229, 259nn12–14; Occidental-Oriental debate on, xxxiii, 36, 161; orientalization of, 4, 12–15, 17, 20, 27, 30, 267–68n23, 297n26; pathos of, 25, 47–48; philosophy of, 41, 108, 267n21, 271n44, 279n14; philosophy of life of, 108, 279n14; poetry of, 12, 21, 58, 135; poststructuralism on, xxi, xxiii, 21; and reason, xxx, 21–22; and reflexivity, 44; religiosity of, 139; seduction as crime for, 116; thought for, 107–8; and tragedy, 55, 109, 110, 160–61, 173, 180, 207, 291n28; view of history in, 36, 276n30; Xanthos heroism in, xxxvi, 213–28, 234–36, 294n7

Greece, modern, xxxvi, xxxvii, 34, 270n30; Arkadi heroism in, 240–45, 302–3nn48–53; current economic crisis in, 268n30; erasure of, 31, 32; Europeanization of, 33; Souliot heroism in, 237–40, 298–301nn38–47; and struggle for freedom, 32, 35, 268n26; view of ancient Greeks by, 36, 268n27

Greek art, 8, 20, 21, 22, 53, 57, 263n4; harmony and serenity in, 15, 21–22, 279n15; intellect and emotion in, 267n21, 275n23; and metaphysics, 87, 266n16, 266n19; passionate aspects of, 24–25

Greek language, 35–36, 269n32

Green, Michael Steven, 278n6

grief, 61, 273n7

Gutting, Gary, 101

Gyömörey, Lorenz, 32–33, 269n31, 269n33

Hackforth, R., 281n6

Hadjidakis, Josef, 242

Hadzi Achmet Pasha, 238

Halliwell, Stephen, xxxiv, 55, 56

Hamburger, Michael, 215

Hamilton, Edith, 275n23

Hamlet, 131, 282n15

Havelock, Eric, 283n23

Hecuba, xvii–xviii, xix, 227

Hegel, Georg Wilhelm Friedrich, xx, xxxix, 76, 168, 279n15; on Antigone, 178, 181, 287n15, 288nn-15; on art, xxxiii, xxxiv, 22, 53, 55, 58–62, 67, 69, 70, 87–89, 264n12, 276n29; dialectic of, 60–61, 276n30; on the Idea, 59, 62, 88, 89; and Plato, 58, 60, 69; on state, 32, 61, 178

Heidegger, Martin, 4, 7, 37, 75, 277n5, 280n4; on Antigone, 193–94, 296n24; as critic of humanism, 173, 287n3; on death, 230; on Greeks, xxxi, 264n13; on Nietzsche, 39; on poetry, 41, 271n43, 296n24; poststructuralism and, 106; on truth and truth-telling, 106–9, 279n12; works: *Being and Time*, 230; "Hegel and the Greeks," 264n13; *Hölderlin's Hymn "The Ister,"* 296n24; *Introduction to Metaphysics*, 193–94, 271n43; *Nietzsche*, 280n4

Hellenism, 259n15; and Christianity, 269n33; European reception of, 33–34; and Judaism, 29, 266n19, 267n22. *See also* Greece, ancient

Henn, T. R., xix

Heraclitus, xxxii, 40–41, 43, 270–71n42; on fate, 279–80n15

Herodotus, 135, 213, 294n7

heroism, xvii, 232; in ancient Greece, 289n17; in contemporary thought, xxvi, 294n11; and myth, 228, 229, 230, 238; Socrates on, 147, 153, 284n31

Hesiod, 40–41, 80, 81

Hippolytus (Euripides), 114

history, 27, 28, 89, 227, 243; Greek view of, 36, 276n30; Nietzsche on, xxi, 259n12; poetry and, 225, 227; and repetition, 196, 223, 276–77n30; and tragedy, xx, 225, 258n10; and truth, 224

Hitler, Adolf, 228, 297n27

Hoff, Nick, 215

Hölderlin, Friedrich, xxi, xxxvi, 3–26, 209–37, 271nn45–46; anticlassicism of, 21, 259n11; on Antigone, 12, 16, 17–19, 20; and caesura, xxi, 8, 14; on death, 210, 288n8; on divine madness, 19, 216; fire as sacred for, 213–14, 294n10; on Greeks' nature, 47; on Greeks' orientalism, 4, 14, 15, 17, 20, 27, 30; on imitation of Greeks, 23–24; on modernity, xxv, 3–4, 21, 41, 58; on Orient-Occident relation, 5, 11, 12, 13; on poetic voice and language, 36, 210, 227; political views of, 11, 31, 294n6; on reflexivity, 21, 46, 51, 224; on Sophocles, xxxiii, 26–27, 28, 40; on tragedy, xxvi, xxxiii, 12–26, 40; on vox populi, 209–10, 213, 293nn2–3; works: "Bread and Wine," 36; *Hyperion*, 31; "Letters to Böhlendorff," xxxiii; "The Perspec-

tive from Which We Have to Look at Antiquity," 23–24; "Remarks on 'Oedipus,'" 42; "Stimme des Volks," xxxvi, 209–16, 220–28, 233–34, 247–56, 293nn2–3, 296n23
holy madness. *See* divine (holy) madness
Homer, xxvi, 214; Heraclitus on, 40–41, 270–71n42; *The Iliad*, 19, 147, 213, 272n48, 287–88n6; Plato on, 80, 81, 273n7, 288n6; Socrates and, 55, 78
Homo Sacer (Agamben), 257n4, 274n15, 285n34
Horkheimer, Max, 266n16
Hubbard, Robert Scott, 276n30
hubris, 17, 20, 185, 270n36; of Antigone, 19–20, 190
human beings: as defined by language, 96; and dignity, xviii, xx, xxvii; freedom and necessity for, xxix, 17, 37, 38, 39; and gods, 135; and perdition, 193–94, 195; self-limitation of, 203, 292n33; and terrestrial life, 216, 295n15; tragic nature of, xxix; will of, xxv, 193. *See also* fate
humanism, 173, 233, 287n3
human nature, 5, 276n30
Hutton, James, 274n16

Idea: Hegel on, 59, 62, 88, 89; Platonic, 146; Socrates on, 146
ideality, xvi, 108, 261n23, 279n14
identity politics, 261n23, 265n19, 270n41
The Iliad (Homer), 19, 147, 213; as first tragic work, 272n48, 287–88n6
"Ily y a" (Critchley), 231
imitation, xxiv, 57–58; art and, 6, 7, 66, 67, 72, 73, 79, 81, 275n24; of Greeks, xxi, 6, 22, 23–24, 57–58; of nature, 6, 22–23, 81; Plato on, 66, 72, 79, 80–81, 274n13, 275n24; poetry and, 66, 80, 274n13. *See also* mimesis

impossible, 47, 272n49
incest taboo: Butler on, 201–2, 203–5, 292n34; Oedipus and, 191, 204, 289n18
The Inoperative Community (Nancy), 257n4
Introduction to Metaphysics (Heidegger), 193–94, 271n43
Introductory Lectures on Aesthetics (Hegel), xxxiii
Ion (Euripides), 112, 113, 115, 117, 158
irrationality, xxvii, 63, 69, 212
Irwin, David, 264–65n16
Ismene, xxxix, 187–89, 289–90n22

Jacobs, Carol, 205, 292n36
Jews, 30, 31, 32, 270n41
Jowett, Benjamin, 143
Judaism, 265n19, 267n21; Hellenism and, 29, 266n19, 267n22; valorization of writing in, 282–83n18

Kahn, Charles, 270–71n42
Kalvos, Andreas, 244–45, 269n32
Kant, Immanuel, 5, 10–11, 259n11, 285n34; and art, 58, 82, 84; Nietzsche on, 84–85; and tragedy, xx, 38; on transcendental, 84–85, 277n5
Karellis, Manolis, 243, 302n48, 302n52
Keats, John, 280n3
Kennedy, George, 281n6
Kierkegaard, Søren, 156, 284n33
kinship. *See* blood kinship
Kitto, H. D. F., xli, 263n8
Klemperer, Klemens von, 297n27
Klossowski, Pierre, 257n4
Knox, Bernard, 269n32
Koraes, Adamantios, 301n46
Koronaios, Panos, 302n48
Kovacs, David, 286nn13–14
Krell, David Farrell, 264n10
Kurt Pasha, 239

Lacan, Jacques, 174, 191–92
Lacoue-Labarthe, Philippe, 8, 27, 36, 263n5, 269n34
Lambropoulos, Vassilis, 260n18, 265n19, 266n16
language, 9, 96, 224, 262n27, 283n25; Greek, 35–36, 269n32; and obfuscation, xxx, xxxv, 95; Plato on, xxxv; Socrates and, 141, 149; of tragedy and of politics, 197; translation and, 121. *See also* rhetoric
law, 180; Antigone and, 119, 120, 137, 185, 198, 289n20; as dead letter, 150, 285n34; divine, 183–84, 185; Greeks and, 134–35, 137; Judaic, 289n20; and kinship, 181–83; and love, 119, 125, 133; Plato on, 119, 132, 134–35; and representation, 176, 185–86, 288n19; Socrates on, 119–20, 186; as voice of conscience, 184, 190–91; written and unwritten, 134–35, 137, 183–85, 186
Leiter, Brian, 278n6
Lessing, Gotthold Ephraim, 22, 259n11
Levinas, Emmanuel, xxxvii, 39; on death and alterity, 230, 231–32, 270n36
logos and bios, 109, 114, 165, 167
Loraux, Nicole, 28, 185, 257n2, 282n17, 298n37; on Antigone, 178, 288n16; on tragedy, xviii, xxvi, 197, 258n5, 303n54
love, xxxvi, 124, 215, 281n6; and law, 119, 125, 133; Plato on, xxxv, 119, 126, 131; Socrates on, 127, 148; and speech, 125; and truth, 124, 125–26, 148
Lycurgus, 283n21

madness. *See* divine (holy) madness
The Madness of Antigone (Else), 174
Manes, 12–13
Manousakis, Giorgis, 242
The Man without Content (Agamben), 62–63, 71, 78–79, 83, 84
Marback, Richard, 281n10

Marx, Karl, xx, 225, 258n10
Marxism, xix–xx, 258nn7–8
Maxut Aga, 238
McCollom, William, xl
measure, 21–22, 48; poetry and, 41–42, 271n46; tragedy and, 49
Medea (Euripides), 286n13
melancholy, xxii, 39
memory, xxi, 95; writing and, 136, 137
metaphysics, xxiii, 39, 87, 275n19; and art, 87, 276n29; Greek, 87, 266n16, 266n19; Plato and, 260n20, 276n29; and presence, 37, 137, 138
mimesis, 29, 54; cathartic, 68, 273n3; Plato's theory of, 62; and rhetoric, 52, 272–73n3. *See also* imitation
modern art, xxxiv, 73, 81–82, 85, 89, 275n19; limitlessness of, 75–76; spectators of, 84, 85
modernity, xxi, xxv, xxxi, 21, 27, 29, 85, 221, 294n11; ancients and, xxi, xxvii, xxxi, 41, 43–44; Greeks and, xxi, 30, 65, 266n16; and Jews, 30, 31; and rationalism, xxiii, xxxi, xxxiii, 24, 101, 192; self-reflexiveness of, 40, 46, 48, 82; and tragedy, xxii, xxv, xxviii, xxx–xxxi, 11, 49, 172; and truth, 98, 105, 106, 108, 163, 279n11
monotheism, 31, 35, 267nn22–23
morality: art and, 60; Nietzsche on, 98–100, 102, 278n6
mortality, 175, 191, 198, 230; blood and, 203, 291n29
mourning, xvii, xxvi, 28, 68
multiculturalism, 261n23, 267n21
Mustafa Kokka, 239
Mustafa Pasha, 238, 241, 302n50
myth, 235, 260n17; and community, 257n4; and heroism, 228, 229, 230, 238; and poetry, 298n37, 300–301n45; and tragedy, xxii–xxiii; and truth, 122, 235, 245

Naas, Michael, xxvi
Nancy, Jean-Luc, 228–29, 257n4, 261n23
nationalism, xxx, 267n21, 270n41; dangers of, 35, 228, 297–98n28
nature, 12, 48, 138, 173, 281n8; art and, 6, 13, 57, 58–59, 74, 81; freedom and, 4–5; Greeks and, 5, 6, 13; imitation of, 6, 22–23, 81; spontaneity and, 5, 65, 74
necessity, 90, 270n36; freedom and, xxix, 37, 38, 39; poststructuralism on, 39–40
neoclassicism, 259n11
Nietzsche, Friedrich, xxv, xxix, xxxi, 50, 96, 101; on Dionysus and Apollo, 13, 22, 263n7; on Euripides, 45, 157, 166, 285n1; on freedom, 26, 39; on genealogy, xxxiv, 102; on Greeks, xxxi–xxxii, 226, 229, 259nn12–14; on history, xxi, 259n12; on Kant, 84–85; on morality, 98–100, 102, 278n6; on pain and suffering, 99, 173, 287n4; on philosophy, 102, 230, 261n25, 279n13; and Plato, 99, 283n21; poststructuralism and, 259–60n16; on Socrates, xxii, xxxi–xxxii, 46, 49, 148, 259n14; on tragedy, xxii, xxiii, 25–26, 39, 45, 207, 258n7, 287n2, 292n38; works: "Attempt at Self-Criticism," 259n14; *The Birth of Tragedy*, 263n7, 292n38; *The Case of Wagner*, 279n13; *Genealogy of Morals*, 98; "The Hammer Speaks," 26; "On the Uses and Disadvantages of History for Life," 259n12; *The Twilight of the Idols*, 26, 263n7; *Untimely Meditations*, xxi; "What I Owe to the Ancients," 25
nihilism, xxix, 39, 234
Niobe, 17–20
nostalgia, xxii, 22, 27, 39
Nussbaum, Martha, 192, 200

objectivity, 86–87, 99–102, 134; ancient commitment to, 98, 99, 101; scientific, 106; subjectivity and, 98, 100, 102. *See also* truth
Odysseus, 155, 216, 285n37, 295n16
Oedipus, 20–21, 49–50, 110, 208, 264n14; Dastur on, 12, 13, 17; and holy madness, 21, 213; and incest taboo, 191, 204, 289n18
Oedipus at Colonus (Sophocles), 226, 264n10, 291n30
Oedipus Tyrannus (Sophocles), xxxi, 14, 16, 115, 264n10
omens, 131–32
oratory, 127, 128, 145–46. *See also* rhetoric; speech
Orestes (Euripides), 112, 117–18
orientalization: Greece and, 4, 12–15, 17, 20, 27, 30, 267–68n23, 297n26; and Occidental-Oriental debate, xxxiii, 36, 161
originality, xxiv, xxv, 11, 27, 76; art and, 76–77
Orpheus, 76, 78
Orwell, George, 206
Otto, Walter, 163, 165, 286n10
Özkirimli, Umut, 298–99n38

paganism, 29, 36
Palamedes, 155, 285n35
Paparrigopoulos, Constantine, 33, 268n28
parataxis, 210
parrhesia, 93, 110, 116, 118, 163; in *The Bacchae*, 112, 113, 158, 159, 161, 163, 165; and citizenship, 112–13; democracy as crisis for, 106; distortions in, 113–15; etymology of, 94; in Euripides, 112–18; Foucault on, xxiv, 93, 94, 96, 98, 103–8, 112, 121, 155–56, 277–78n5, 279n11, 279n13; as heroism, 147, 284n31; in *Phaedrus*, 125; philosophy

parrhesia (*continued*)
and, 96, 120, 144; power of, 96–97, 111; and presence, 96; and rhetoric, 104–5, 121, 141–42; Socrates and, 94, 139–40, 145, 147, 153, 284n31; and speech, 94, 95, 97, 109, 111, 155–56; as technique of the self, 93, 107, 141, 279n11; and tragedy, 104, 110, 163, 165, 167; and truth, 105, 106, 107, 109, 111, 144, 277–78n5, 279n15
passion, 14, 48, 60, 122–23
passivity, xxvi–xxvii, 17, 29, 97, 233
Pecchio, Giuseppe, 299–300n40
Peloponnesian War, xvi
Pentheus, 157–66, 286n8
performance, 67–68
Perraivos, Christophoros, 299–300n40, 300–301n45
Pesmazoglou, Stephanos, 34, 268–69n30
Phaedrus (Plato), 63, 121–39, 285n37; on beauty, 59–60; Derrida on, xxxvi, 122–23; on law, xxxvi, 119, 134; on love, xxxv, xxxvi, 119, 131; Lysias speech in, 127–29; rhetorical dimension of, 122, 281n6; Socrates in, 128, 130, 138, 156, 185; as tragic work, xxxv–xxxvi; on writing, xxxvi, 134–36, 185
Phenomenology of Spirit (Hegel), 178, 288nn14–15
philosophy, 41, 57, 102, 281n8; Antigone as inspiration for, xxxvi–xxxvii; and art, xxxiii, 55, 57, 70, 72; Foucault on, 93, 97; Greek, 41, 108, 267n21, 271n44, 279n14; of life, 108, 279n14; metaphysical, xxvi, 127; Nietzsche on, 102, 230, 261n25, 279n13; and parrhesia, 96, 144; Plato on, xxxiii, 68, 69–70, 130, 134; and poetry, xxxiii, 40, 42, 43, 57, 64–65, 69–70, 86–87, 130; and rhetoric, 104, 130; Socrates on, 117, 142, 148; and tragedy, xxvii, xxxiii, 43, 49, 56, 97; and truth, xxxv, 93, 104, 120, 133, 143
The Phoenician Women (Euripides), 112–14
Phrynichus: *The Siege of Miletus*, 298n37
piety, 47–48, 142, 284n32
Plato, xxxii, 52–57; on absence and presence, 128; Agamben on, xxxiv, 62–64, 65–66, 68, 71–72, 78–80, 88; ambivalence about art, 56, 63, 65, 69, 88; on art and imitation, 66, 72, 274n13; on art and society, 54, 65; on art and truth, 57, 74, 88; on art's divine inspiration, 72, 77–78, 81; banishing of artists and poets by, xxxiii–xxxiv, 56–57, 61, 65, 66, 67, 68, 72, 73, 80, 83; on beauty, 59–60, 67, 134, 137; and censorship, 58, 84; contemporary theory on, 125, 260n20, 288n10; critique of tragic poets by, 80, 272n48; Derrida on, xxxvi, 121, 122–23, 281n10, 282n12, 283n19, 283n21; on equilibrium in art, 54, 273n5; on good and bad poets, 60, 66, 79, 80; Hegel and, 58, 60, 69; on Homer, 80, 81, 273n7, 288n6; on imitation, 66, 72, 79, 80–81, 274n13, 275n24; on language, xxxv; on law, 119, 132, 134–35; on love, xxxv, 119, 126, 131; and metaphysics, 260n20, 276n29; on morality, 54, 99; Nietzsche and, 99, 283n21; on philosophy, xxxiii, 68, 69–70, 130, 134; on philosophy-poetry relation, xxxiii, 69–70; on poetry as politically unreliable, 62, 79; on recognition and recollection, 143; on rhetoric, 105, 128, 129, 130, 134, 281n10, 291–92n31; sense of deferral of, 260n20; on sensuousness, 89, 90; and Sophism, 281–82n10; suspicion

of art by, xxxiv, 53–54, 67; theory of mimesis, 62; on tragedy, xxxiv, 43, 55–56, 272n48; as tragic philosopher, xxxiv, xxxvi, 55–56; on truth, xxiv, xxxv, 47, 67, 74, 99, 105, 122, 124–25, 134; works: *Apology*, xxxv, 117, 119, 139–56, 190, 279n11, 283n24; *Gorgias*, 44; *Ion*, 77–78, 81, 89; *Laws*, 274n13; *Phaedrus*, xxxv–xxxvi, 59–60, 63, 119, 121–39, 156, 185, 281n6, 285n37; *The Republic*, xxxiii, 42, 43, 55, 60, 66, 69–70, 77, 78–81, 272n48, 273n7, 279n14; *Symposium*, xxix, 74; and writing, 124–25, 132, 135–36, 137, 138–39, 283n21, 283n23

Plato's Dream of Sophistry (Marback), 281n10

"Plato's Pharmacy" (Derrida), xxxvi, 121

Plutarch, 117–18, 213; on Xanthians, 218–20, 222–23, 225

Poetics (Aristotle), 45, 274n16

poetry: Agamben on, 53, 74, 275n18; and art, 8, 52, 63, 77–78, 80, 89; divine lot of, 66, 78, 79, 89, 214; Greek, 12, 21, 58, 135; Heidegger on, 41, 271n43, 296n24; and history, 225, 227; and imitation, 66, 80, 274n13; and measure, 41–42, 271n46; modern, 227, 271n45; and myth, 298n37, 300–301n45; and philosophy, xxxiii, 40, 42, 43, 57, 64–65, 69–70, 86–87, 130; Plato on, xxxiii–xxxiv, 53, 60, 62, 66, 67, 69–70, 79, 80, 274n13; poststructuralist view of, 226–27; and praxis, 74, 274n16, 275n18; Socrates on, 42–43, 55, 77–78, 89, 143

politics, xxvi, 10, 177, 290n26; Antigone and, 176, 177, 178, 179, 180–81, 226, 288n16; and art, 55, 72, 73, 75, 82, 87; and ethics, xxv, xxxviii, 268n25; identity, 261n23, 265n19, 270n41; Socrates and, 179; and tragedy, 197

The Politics of Friendship (Derrida), 261n23, 295n17

Politis, Alexis, 239–40, 300–301n45

Polyneices, 199, 204–6, 290n27, 292n34, 292n36

Porter, James I., 259–60n16

postcolonial discourse, 269–70n35

poststructuralism, xxvii, 37, 38, 98, 226–27, 261n23; about, xxiii, 268n24; abstract art championed by, 275n19; antimimeticism of, 8–9; on death, xxxvii, 9, 230; devaluing of sensuousness by, 8–9, 89; on Greeks and antiquity, xxi, xxiii, 21; and Heidegger, 106; logic of finitude by, 175; messianism and, 30, 258n7; on necessity, 39–40; Nietzsche's appeal to, 259–60n16; and Plato, 125; and rationalism, xxix–xxx, xxxi; on tragedy, xxix, xxxii, 258n8

praxis, 74, 177, 274n16, 275n18

presence, xxxviii, 94, 96, 127; as contested notion, xxxiv, 95; deconstruction and, 37, 137; as embodied appearance, 137–38; Heidegger on, 106–7; and metaphysics, 37, 137, 138; Plato on, 128; and speech, xxxix, 95, 104

progress, xx, 11, 27, 69, 87, 227

Prometheus, 111

prophecy, 131–33, 145, 191, 282n17

Protestant Reformation, 265n19

Proust, Marcel, 273n5

Pryor, Benjamin, 96, 97

Psalidas, Athanasios, 298–99n38

Psilakis, Vasileios, 242

rationalism, xxx, xxxvi, 22, 46, 192, 193; modernity and, xxiii, xxxi, xxxiii, 24, 101, 192; in opposition to reason, xxix–xxx

reflection, xxx, 7, 56, 224, 235; and tragedy, 25, 48–49

reflexivity, 44, 48, 108; Hölderlin on, 46, 51; self-, xxx, 40, 167; tragedy and, 45–46, 49, 223
Reinhardt, Karl, 15–16, 264n9
relativism, 100, 101, 277n5; cultural, 295n17
religion, 139, 143, 144
repetition, xl, xlii, xliii, 24, 57; history and, 196, 223, 276–77n30
representation, 20; Antigone and, 176–77, 178, 179–80; Hegel on, 65; and law, 176, 185–86, 288n19; Plato on, 57; and presentation, 202, 291–92n31
The Republic (Plato), 273n7, 279n14, 284n30, 291–92n31; aesthetic didacticism of, 60; on art, 78–81; on expulsion of poets and artists, 55, 66; on philosophy and poetry, xxxiii, 69–70; on tragedy, 43, 272n48
responsibility, xl; freedom and, 33, 118, 137, 191
rhetoric, 10, 27; and beauty, 131; and mimesis, 52, 272–73n3; and parrhesia, 104–5, 121, 141–42; and philosophy, 104, 130; Plato on, 128, 129, 130, 134, 281n10, 291–92n31; Socrates and, 125, 129, 130, 131, 140, 148–49, 152–53, 284n33; Sophists and, 114, 123, 126, 134; and truth, 105
The Rise of Eurocentrism (Lambropoulos), 265n19
Rocha, Sam, 277n4
Rojcewicz, Stephen, 150–51, 285n35
romanticism, xxi, xxiv, xxv, 22, 258n11

Sakopoulos, Nikolaos, 242
Santayana, George, 266n16
Sartre, Jean-Paul, 28, 257n2, 265n17
Schmidt, Dennis, 11, 38
science, xxii, 106
secrets, 207

seduction, 116, 126–27
Seferis, George, 269n32
Segal, Charles, 285n3
self and selfhood, xl, 30, 94, 151–52, 190, 232; Antigone and, 186–87, 189–90; division within, xxxviii–xxxix; and ethics, xxv, xl; and Other, xxxix, 187; parrhesia and, 93, 97, 107, 141, 279n11; self-pity, xvii, xix; self-relation, xxxiv, 97, 189, 230–31
self-determination, 31, 40, 188, 222, 268n25
sensuousness, 20, 61, 62, 71, 89, 264n12
Sikelianos, Angelos, 269n32
Sisyphus, 155
Skoulas, Emmanuel, 242, 302n52
social construction theory, xxiii, xxiv, xxxvii, 172, 173
Socrates, 260n17, 281n8, 282n16, 285n1; and Achilles, 147, 284n30; and Apollo, 117, 142, 144; on death, 146–47, 148, 153–55; and Delphic oracle, 117, 142, 144; on democracy, 283–84n26; on divine madness, 132, 133; and divine mission, 142, 151; on double beginning, 42, 271n47; and education, 141–42, 279n11; Foucault on, xxxv, 104, 168; on freedom, 142; on heroism, 147, 153, 284n31; and Homer, 55, 78; and knowledge, 144; and language, 141, 149; on law, 119–20, 186; on love, 127, 148; Nietzsche on, xxii, xxxi–xxxii, 46, 49, 148, 259n14; on oratory, 145–46; and parrhesia, 94, 139–40, 145, 147, 153, 284n31; in *Phaedrus*, 128, 130, 138, 156, 185; on philosophy, 117, 142, 148; on poets and poetry, 42–43, 55, 77–78, 89, 143; political resistance by, xxxiv, 150; on politics, 179; and prophecy, 145; and rhetoric, 125, 129, 130, 131, 140, 148–49, 152–53, 284n33;

328

on righteous speech, 140–41; and Sophists, 94, 123, 143; and tragedy, xxii, xxix, 156, 167, 168, 259n14; trial of, 120, 140, 149–52, 167–68, 190–91, 285n35; and truth, xxxiv, xxxv, 94, 96, 120, 125–26, 147, 148, 152; and writing, 109–10, 132, 185

Sofos, Spyros, 298–99n38

Sophism, 105; Plato and, 281–82n10; and rhetoric, 114, 123, 126, 134; Socrates and, 94, 123, 143

Sophocles, xxi, xxxvii, 16, 19, 38, 171–208, 264n9, 285n1; German idealism and, 15–16; Hölderlin on, xxxi, 26–27, 28, 40; literary propensities of, 12, 13–14; tragic outlook of, 225; works: *Antigone*, xxxi, xxxvi, xxxix, 14–15, 16, 119, 137, 171–208, 225–26, 287n15, 289–90n22, 296n24; *Oedipus at Colonus*, 226, 264n10, 291n30; *Oedipus Tyrannus*, xxxi, 14, 16, 115, 264n10

Souli, 237–40, 298–302nn38–47; mass suicide in, 239, 300–301n45; world impact of, 300n41, 301n46

sovereignty, 290n26

speech, 104, 188–89; Derrida on, 95, 156, 282n18; and love, 125; and parrhesia, 94, 95, 96, 97, 109, 111, 155–56; and presence, xxxix, 95, 104; Socrates on, 140–41; spontaneity of, 104, 110; and truth, 95, 104, 108; and writing, xxxiii, 110, 122, 127, 131, 138

spontaneity, 11, 42, 215–16, 221, 224; and nature, 5, 65, 74; and speech, 104, 110

Stamelos, Demetris, 237, 299–300n40

state, 189, 243; and art, 54, 61; Hegel on, 32, 61, 178

Steiner, George, 174

"Stimme des Volks" (Hölderlin), xxxvi, 209–16, 220–28, 233–34, 247–56, 293nn2–3, 296n23

Strauss, Leo, 267n22

subjectivity, xl, 82, 83, 95, 99; criticisms of, 278n9, 283n25; Levinas on, 231, 232; and objectivity, 98, 100, 102; transcendental, 84–85, 229, 277n5; and truth, 96, 105

suffering, 28, 99, 185, 264n9; tragedy and, xix, 173

suicide, 230, 232, 233; Arkadi mass suicide, 242; Souliot mass suicide, 239, 300–301n45; Xanthian mass suicide, xxxvi, 213, 222, 234–35

Symposium (Plato), xxix, 74

Szondi, Peter, 4, 6–7, 11

techne, 114, 144, 193, 194, 279n11; art and poetry as, 72, 77

technology, 75, 136–37

Teiresias, xxi, xxii, 14

temporality, xxv, 88, 98, 129, 138, 148, 276n30; Antigone and, 14, 198, 201, 205; divine, 183, 184, 185; in Greek thinking, 13, 87; tragic, 223

theater, xxxiv, 55–56, 265n19, 274n13

theory, xxiii, 50, 260n19; and praxis, 177

Theuth parable, 133, 136

thought, 264n8; art and, 62; Foucault on history of, 102–3; and truth, 108, 109

tragedy: and actuality, 224, 227; and agency, xxvi, 97, 195; *Antigone* as, xxxvi, 177–78; Aristotle definition of, 14; audience of, 298n37, 303n54; *The Bacchae* as, 158, 164–65, 285n3; character and circumstance in, 211–12; and choice, xxix, xl, 167, 211, 232; and comedy, xx, xxix, 288n13; community and, xxviii–xxix; contemporary interest in, xxvii, xxviii, 44, 260–61n22; contemporary theory's antipathy to, xix, xxiii–xxiv, xxviii; as contestation, xxvi, xxvii, xli, 37, 49,

tragedy (*continued*)
55, 166, 270n38; and death, xvii, xxxvii, 9, 229, 235, 263n6, 287–88n6; end of, xxiii, xxvii, xxix, xxxiii, 37, 46, 49, 258n7; ethical debates in, xxv, xxxix; Euripides and, 45, 160, 166–67; and farce, xx, xl, 46, 225, 243, 258n10; and fate, 187, 196, 198; Foucault on, 93, 97, 168; and freedom, xxxix, xl, 28, 40; and genealogy, xxxii, 101, 104; German idealism and, 37, 38, 56; as Greek genre, 55, 110, 160–61, 173, 180, 207, 291n28; Heidegger on, 296n24; and heroism, xxvi, 147, 235, 289n17; history and, xx, 225, 258n10; Hölderlin on, xxvi, xxxiii, 12–26, 40; and holy madness, 64, 212, 214–15; human action and, xvi, xvii, xix, 16, 28, 173, 235, 244; and human law, 206; and inevitability, xlii, 196; Kant and, xx, 38; Levinas on, 270n36; Loraux on, xviii, xxvi, 197, 258n5, 303n54; and measure, 49; modernity and, xxii, xxv, xxviii, xxx–xxxi, 11, 49, 172; and myth, xxii–xxiii; Nancy on, 229, 230; necessity in, xxxix, 90; Nietzsche on, xxii, xxiii, 25–26, 39, 45, 207, 258n7, 287n2, 292n38; parrhesia and, 104, 110, 163, 165, 167; *Phaedrus* as work of, xxxv–xxxvi; and philosophy, xxvii, xxxiii, 43, 49, 56, 97; Plato on, xxxiv, 43, 55–56, 272n48; Plato's *Apology* as, xxxv, 283n24; and politics, 197; poststructuralism and, xxix, xxxii, 258n8; progressives and conservatives on, xix, 258n7; public dimension of, xxxviii; and rationality, xix, 192, 258n5; realism of, xvi, xx; and reflection, 25, 48–49; reflexivity and, 45–46, 49, 223; sacrifice in, 38, 180; sanitization of, 288n13; scholarly bibliography on, xxxii, 262n26; Socrates and, xxii, xxix, 156, 167, 168, 259n14; and sublime, 38; and suffering, xix, 173; and theater, 55–56; and "the tragic," xxiii–xxiv, xxv–xxviii, 25, 40, 455–56; and truth, xxiv, xxxv, 93, 162; Xanthian story as, 234

translation, 29, 97, 266n16; of Greek tragedy, 28; language's dependence on, 121

The Trojan Women (Euripides), xv–xvi, xviii–xix, 222, 257n2

Troy, 222, 295–96n20

truth: and alterity, 107; ancient commitment to, 99, 101; art and, 56–57, 67, 72, 74, 75, 76, 81, 88–89, 90; *The Bacchae* on, xxxvi, 161–62; degradation of, 114, 133; democracy and, 123, 159; Dionysian, 165; divine, 159; figurality and, 134; Foucault on, 98, 105, 112, 139, 277–78n5; and freedom, 111; Heidegger on, 106–9, 279n12; historicist view of, xxxv, 12, 122; and history, 224; and love, 124, 125–26, 148; modernity and, 98, 105, 106, 108, 163, 279n11; and myth, 122, 235, 245; and parrhesia, 105, 106, 107, 109, 111, 144, 277–78n5, 279n15; and passion, 122; path to, 122, 125, 126; *Phaedrus* on, xxxv–xxxvi, 119; philosophy and, xxxv, 93, 104, 120, 133, 143; Plato on, xxiv, xxxv, 47, 67, 74, 99, 105, 122, 124–25, 134; as relative, xxxv, 216, 295n17; and rhetoric, 105; Socrates and, xxxiv, 94, 96, 120, 125–26, 147, 148, 152; Sophists and, xxxvi, 94, 123; and speech, 95, 104, 108; and subjectivity, 96, 105; and thought, 108, 109; tragedy and, xxiv, xxxv, 93, 162; writing and, 124

The Truth of Democracy (Nancy), 261n23

truth-telling. *See* parrhesia

Tsaparis, Suleiman, 238–39
Tsolis, Michalis, 237, 238, 240, 299–300n40, 300n44
The Twilight of the Idols (Nietzsche), 26, 263n7
Tzavelas, Fotos, 300n44
Tzavelas, Kitsos, 301n47
Tzavelas, Lambros, 300n44

"Überwindung des Klassizismus" (Szondi), 4
Ulysses (Joyce), 267n22
uncertainty, xxx, 216–17
Untimely Meditations (Nietzsche), xxi
unworking, 9, 263n6

Vallega, Alejandro, 281n8
Vernant, Jean-Pierre, 41
"Voice of the People." *See* "Stimme des Volks"
vox populi, 209–10, 213, 226

Warminski, Andrzej, 52, 65, 263n4, 264n13, 267n23; reading of Hölderlin by, 5–10, 27

Weil, Simone, 265n17
Wildberg, Christian, 284n32, 285n1
Wilde, Oscar, 273n5
Williams, Henry Smith, 294n9
Winckelmann, Johann Joachim, xxi, 27, 57, 258–59n11; as forerunner of modern art historians, 264–65n16; on Greek art, 21–22, 24–25; on imitation, 22, 23, 24
Wind, Edgar, 53–54, 63–64, 273n5
Wolff, Christian, 57
words and deeds, 146, 147; Antigone's harmony of, xxxvii, 188
writing: fetishization of, xxxiii, 124; and memory, 136, 137; Plato and, 124–25, 132, 135–36, 137, 138–39, 283n21, 283n23; Socrates and, 109–10, 132, 185; and speech, xxxviii, 110, 122, 127, 131, 138; and truth, 124

Xanthos, 213–28, 234–36, 294n7; mass suicide in, xxxvi, 213, 222, 234–35

Zeitlin, Froma, 157, 285n6

IN THE SYMPLOKĒ STUDIES IN
CONTEMPORARY THEORY SERIES

*Tragically Speaking: On the
Use and Abuse of Theory for Life*
Kalliopi Nikolopoulou

To order or obtain more information on
these or other University of Nebraska Press
titles, visit www.nebraskapress.unl.edu.

www.ingramcontent.com/pod-product-compliance
Lightning Source LLC
Chambersburg PA
CBHW021338300426
44114CB00012B/996